Gender and Sexuality in African Literature and Film

GENDER
AND
SEXUALITY
in African Literature and Film

Edited and Introduced by
Ada Uzoamaka Azodo and Maureen Ngozi Eke

Africa World Press, Inc.

P.O. Box 1892
Trenton, NJ 08607

P.O. Box 48
Asmara, ERITREA

Africa World Press, Inc.

P.O. Box 1892
Trenton, NJ 08607

P.O. Box 48
Asmara, ERITREA

Book design: Saverance Publishing Services
Cover design: Ryan Shelton

Library of Congress Cataloging-in-Publication Data

Gender and sexuality in African literature and film / edited and Introduced by Ada Uzoamaka Azodo and Maureen Ngozi Eke.
    p. cm.
Includes bibliographical references and index.
ISBN 1-59221-468-1 (alk. paper) -- ISBN 1-59221-469-X (pbk. : alk. paper)
1. African literature--20th century--History and criticism. 2. Sex in literature. 3. Sex role in literature. 4. Motion pictures--Africa. 5. Sex in motion pictures. 6. Sex role in motion pictures. I. Azodo, Ada Uzoamaka, 1947- II. Eke, Maureen N.

PN849.A35G46 2006
809'.933538--dc22
                          2006036110

Table of Contents

AFRICAN LITERATURE
Survey of the Historical and Geographical Scope of Gender and Sexuality in
African Literature
-17-

Acknowledgements

Our profound gratitude goes to all our contributors for their collegiality, patience, and understanding through the many years it has taken this volume to see the light of day.

We thank very much Ryan Shelton, studio artist, graphic designer, and marketing and communications specialist at Indiana University Northwest at Gary for the eloquent book cover design.

We are grateful to Luc Devroye, School of Computer Science, McGill University, Montreal, Canada (www.jeff.cs.mcgill.ca/luc/index.html), for his *Sekushii* (Japanese for 'sexy') font symbols, part of the larger body of *Sugaku* (Japanese for 'mathematics') series, which in various combinations can represent all imaginable human gender types; some of these symbols we have employed in this volume:

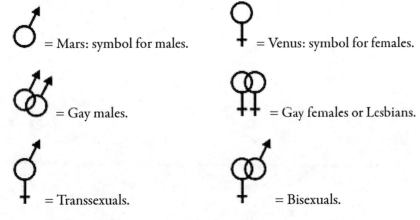

= Mars: symbol for males.   = Venus: symbol for females.

= Gay males.   = Gay females or Lesbians.

= Transsexuals.   = Bisexuals.

We thank Africa World Press in-house editor, Angela Ajayi, for her professionalism, and work of detail; any flaws that remain are entirely ours.

Lastly, but not the least, we appreciate immensely our indefatigable publisher, Kassahun Checole, for his unending and persistent encouragement of African scholarship and production of knowledge through publishing.

Preface: Genesis

Ada Uzoamaka Azodo and *Maureen Ngozi Eke*

If an answer does not give rise
To a new question from
Itself, it falls out of dialogue.
-Mikhail Bakhtin

The title of this preface, "Genesis," is doubly important; it signifies how our collaboration as co-editors for this scholarly anthology began, and expresses our hope for a disengagement of gender and sex in African creative arts, and in all contemporary society, so that issues of difference may be more properly viewed. In our persuasion, this is one cardinal way of redressing social injustices and abuse of human rights in Africa and its diaspora and, by extension, all over the world.

Whereas some critics think that self and social identities are dependent on a culture's view of gender, others, more conciliatory, believe that gender should not limit individual capacity, being an arbitrary notion. Still, a third skeptical group thinks that gender is complex, intricate, and contradictory, at once everything that affects and impacts our lives or nothing at all. In view of such divergent viewpoints, gender and the attendant human sexuality, may at times appear simple and easy to define, but their peculiar nature belie any simplicity. Although frequently evoked in, and underpin, all human acts, activities, and relationships, it is necessary to bring into focus in the contexts of African literature and film in this volume the notions of gender and sexuality, in order that we may understand more appropriately how African creative artists and their reading public view the two phenomena.

African societies, like all world contemporary societies, is evolving. Interpretations of gender and sexuality are shifting too, calling into question age-old assumptions of binary sexual orientations, gendered roles, relationships, and identities. As current debates on gay rights and same-sex marriages rage at all levels of many contemporary societies, discourse on the diversity of gender and sexual identities can no longer remain a tabooed topic in African creative arts. To the question to adherents (practitioners) and non-adherents (non-practitioners) alike, on whether homosexuality is a choice the individual makes, responses often attest to the difficulty of defining homosexuality, and spell the importance of the study of gender, sexuality and sexual orientation for the acceptance, equality, and humanity of all, not the least of whom are male homosexuals, female homosexuals or lesbians, and other subordinated gender and sexual groups. Witness as well the ill effects of the capitalist economy and virulent politics that are manifestly destroying the foundations of human life and rights, cultures and civilizations, and consequently alienating people from one another, their families, and society. Consequently, gender and sexuality become subjects that need urgent address.

The idea of this anthology dates back to the annual conference of the Modern Language Association of America (MLA) held in Washington, D.C, in December 2001. The occasion was a late afternoon screening and discussion of the film on homosexuality in the Ivory Coast, *Woubi chéri*, presented by the African Literature Division (ALD) of the MLA, as part of their annual activities at the conference. Maureen Ngozi Eke, ALD member, had supplied the film, courtesy of California Newsreel, and had also earlier in the day presented an enlightening paper on it. Ada Uzoamaka Azodo, also ALD member and incoming president of the executive committee, led the discussion that followed the screening of the film, as holders of two opposing viewpoints debated the meaning of *Woubi chéri*. Carole Boyce Davies, member of the ALD, and past president of the executive committee, saved the day, by calling the question, and suggesting that the ALD explore gender and sexuality in African literature the following year in Richmond, Virginia, as part of the annual paper presentation sessions at the African Literature Association (ALA).

At the center of the controversy in Washington D. C. had been homosexuality in postcolonial Africa. The question was not whether it existed, but rather whether homosexuality was a lifestyle brought on by social and political conditions in urban areas, thanks to colonization; whether homosexuality was a psychiatric condition that was amenable to cure; whether homosexuality was a psychological disorder, and whether homosexuality was inherited. A minority opinion held that it was a recent lifestyle brought about by neocolonial social, economic, and political conditions in African urban areas, which mimic conditions in big cities in the West, where capitalism has pushed human sexual desire into the domain of choice, has separated sexuality from procreation through empowering individuals, materially, to exist comfortably outside of the traditional family space, thanks to their salaried work, and has thus eroded traditional values and support systems for the needy who would ordinarily remain in the family hold and, if not able to do anything else, at least reproduce the next generation of citizens. They blamed capitalism with its cutthroat competition for sidelining the disadvantaged and less aggressive, not to mention the attendant alienation of individuals from traditional family structures, due to exodus from the rural areas to the urban areas and modern cities in search of paid jobs.

The opposing viewpoint was in accord with what seemed to be the filmmaker's intention, namely, that homosexuality was not a matter of choice the individual made, but rather a disposition by biological determinism coupled with early socialization in dominant male surroundings in childhood, and the natural or imposed evolution of historical, political, economic, and social circumstances in the life of an individual. The make-up of this majority group included a number of persons of the medical profession, self-declared scholars of gender and sexuality, and some gays and lesbians. They railed against any new suggestion that homosexuality was a result of psychiatric conditions and thus amenable to cure, and rejected the notion that homosexuality was a medically treatable psychological disorder that could even be inherited.

What remained difficult to determine at the end of the debate was the nature of homosexuality in Africa, the identity of the homosexual in Africa, and the correlation of that identity with aspects of African culture, including sex roles, sexual division of labor, and political organization at the family and community levels.

The following year 2002, Azodo organized and chaired a panel on "Gender and Sexuality in African Literatures" in Richmond, Virginia. The charge to a panel of three participants--Ada Azodo, Maureen Eke, and Naana Horne--was "to examine a text or texts by an African woman author that employs women's histories, locations, and spaces to interpret self and notions of difference in African literature, showing shifting and interlocking views of the contemporary woman that tend to (re) define gender and sexuality." For obvious reasons, Carole Davies was unanimously chosen as discussant for the panel presentations.

In her opening remarks, Azodo recalled the genesis of the topic in Washington, D. C. the year before, restating the two opposing viewpoints. She brought uproarious laughter to the room-packed audience when she stated that the mere idea of the panel topic appeared funny, since human beings in the larger society were busy exploiting their gender and sexuality, according to their will and fantasy, and completely oblivious of what rhetoric on gender and sexuality in African literatures a group of academics had gathered that morning to debate. Then, Azodo placed four specific notions in focus before the audience: (i) gender and sexuality is not yet a topical issue in African literature today; (ii) the two opposing viewpoints about gender and sexuality are part and parcel of our democracy and forty-three chromosomes from our mothers and fathers; (iii) the human male-female duality at birth resolves itself at adolescence, but nonetheless lingers to a lesser or higher degree throughout the days of our lives, (iv) dialogue is imperative, especially in the wake of protestations, contestations, and representations by subordinated and minority groups. The panel's expectations at the end of the session, she added, was not to have solved the gender and sexuality questions once and for all, and this simply because they are evolving issues, and like all evolving issues are open-ended and without closure. On the contrary, panelists and audience were to have dialogued to such an extent that each person went away a little wiser than she or he had come. Employing John Stuart Millin's succinct and insightful article, "Why Consider Opposing Viewpoints?" as a clincher, Azodo concluded:

The only way in which a human being can make some approach to knowing the whole of a subject is, by hearing what can be said about it, and studying all works in which it can be looked at by every character of mind. No wise man [or woman, *her addition*] ever acquired wisdom in any mode but this.[1]

Viewed in light of the right of expressive freedom, Millin upholds the imperative of exercising one's human right to freedom of expression, rather than merely enshrining it in the constitution.

Curiously, none of the panel presentations in Richmond focused on homosexuality, but rather on broader issues of gender, with sparse allusions to sexuality, an initial sign that significant literary themes on sexuality were lacking in African literature. The panel was, however, a resounding success for the presentations elicited several questions and answers.

As we reveled in our success in the corridors of the conference room, Eke suggested that we co-edit a scholarly and critical anthology on "Gender and Sexuality in African Literature," using our own panel presentations as seed contributions. On Azodo's suggestion later on, when work actually began on the anthology, the scope of the study was expanded, first to bring in films where homosexuality has had more consistent and fuller examination by filmmakers, and second the African diaspora so as to reflect social, economic, and political situations there, a strategy that would bring in factors of race, ethnicity, and class in the discourse on gender and sexuality.

Given the long time it has taken to complete the editing of a volume of this magnitude, the said seed contributions have found their ways into other edited volumes. Horne's article, "Sexual Impotence: Metonymy for Political Failure in Ama Ata Aidoo's *Anowa*" will appear in an anthology on Notions of Manhood in African Literatures and Film, co-edited by Helen Mugambi and Tuzyline Jita Allan. Eke's "Casting Gender and Sexuality in Tess Onwueme's *Shakara Dance-Hall Queen*" will be published in a critical anthology on the Nigerian playwright, to be edited by Eke. A version of Azodo's paper, "Gender and Sexuality in Feminist Discourse: Dislocation, Disorientation, Madness, and Death in Ken Bugul's Fiction," has appeared as "Ken Bugul's *Le Baobab fou*: A Female Story about a Female Body," in a volume entitled *New Women's Writing in Africa Literature* in the Cambridge journal, *African Literature Today*, Volume 24, 2004, 77-90.

Interestingly, many of the chapters of this book on gender and sexuality writ large confirm the quasi-absence of thematic concern for homosexuality as a literary subject in Africa, and consequently the dire need for writings and critical studies on homosexuality in African creative arts. This perceived lacuna certainly does not impute the insignificance of sexual minorities as a thematic subject, but rather spells the difficulty, mysteriousness, and complexity of the subject, which need to be addressed.

A volume such as ours, we reiterate, attests to the disquiet that African writers and filmmakers still feel in broaching a topic such as homosexuality, because it runs against the perceived norm. Traditionally, however, minority sexualities within African cultures are viewed as expressions of human sexual desire that are difficult to acknowledge, least of all respond to in oneself. For that reason, writers and filmmakers still find them to be difficult subjects to address in modern times, because African cultures do not yet readily and openly address these issues. Whereas earlier traditional African fiction examined masculinity and femininity, patriarchy and sexual division of labor along the lines of gender and sex roles, later postcolonial and postmodernist writers go a little further by centering the marginal characters enough to (re) examine their complexity and contradictions. These writers are also associated with fragmentation, rupture, and globalization, and are less aligned with moralism, synthesis, and Africanism.

Reading, as a critical activity, is all about reflecting on and imagining the contents of the texts, not to find in them absolute solutions, analyses or interpretations; after all, the role of the reader is to co-write a work of fiction as a product of its author's imagination through a peculiar response. And, the writers themselves have quite a few problems. First, there is the writer's inadequacy to give expression to individual and collective feelings and thoughts, due to insufficient language at his disposal, especially foreign language. Second, happiness eludes those among them who are adherents of particular ideologies, and this shows in a particular work of fiction. Third, there is the ever-present failure of society to protect individual freedom from oppression and subjugation, resulting in writers being exiled from their father- or motherlands, or books banned from circulation when they are not burned.

Gender and sexuality are grave issues of our time that must be addressed by literature and film industries desirous of staying healthy. With society increasingly maturing, seen in the breaking of the silence about sexuality, African literature and cinema have come of age. They must now faithfully and accurately reflect society and the times by openly, frankly, and honestly discussing gender and sexuality.

As editors, we call on critics to continue to shake up and unsettle society, in order to subtly change values and reorient convention. We also urge upcoming African writers and cineastes to take the risk of embracing difficult subject themes from which earlier African literatures and cinema have shied away, to give increased attention to sexual marginality, given that African creative art should not be static, if it intends to move society further than where it stands at the present moment.

Note
1.   Mary E. Williams. Ed. *Homosexuality*. San Diego: Greenhaven Press, Inc. 1999: 9.

Introduction

Shifting Meanings, Erotic Choices

Absence of evidence can never be assumed to be evidence of absence.
—Stephen O. Murray and Will Roscoe. *Boy Wives and Female Husbands: Studies in African Homosexualities* (1998: 261)

Gender and Sexuality in African Literature and Film is designed with one goal in mind: to draw attention to the paucity of current state of knowledge of homoeroticism as an integral part of gender studies in African literature and African cinema. We believe that the field of the Humanities could be rendered more complete with the addition of Africa's complex understanding of the wide and expansive range of human gender and sexuality.

Consequently, this book is organized around two key aspects of human creative and artistic activities in Africa, namely, literature and film. From that angle of vision, this anthology becomes compellingly a rare alchemical object matter that will help debates on sexuality and human rights on the African continent and in its diaspora. At the end of the anthology, we provide an index to key terms and personalities highlighted throughout the book, in order to reinforce the assertions we make hereunder and the necessity to disentangle sex from gender as essential aspects of human life, because they do not necessarily cause the other nor is one dependent on the other. Thus, this study affords us the opportunity to investigate the correlation between gender and sex as categories of human identities, on the one hand, and on the other hand, the correlation between gender and creative artistic practices. As critics, we will be able to look at characterization, textual structure and plot, not in terms of biology, but, rather, in terms of identification. Nothing compels any character to identify with traditional norms in sex and gender roles.

The essays in this anthology have been carefully selected with a mind to respond to some cardinal questions of our time. How do African literature and film see and grapple with the issue of gender and sexuality? Are the prevailing views biologist, essentialist, non-essentialist, or constructionist? If they do exist, what kinds of evolutions have gender and sexuality undergone throughout African history and society, from pre-colonial to postmodernist times? Consequently, what differences between men and women do African literature and film see, and how do they mirror them? Have African writers and filmmakers challenged or reinforced these differences? Do African female creative artists view gender differently from their male counterparts? Does the genre employed by the artist affect the depiction of gender and sexuality? Indeed, how has sexuality affected the depiction of gender? And, lastly, how have race, ethnicity, nationality, and class affected representations of gender and sexuality in African literature and film? These are obviously a lot of questions to which answers will be found only by critically thinking about and analyzing how African literature and film interact with social and political life in Africa and the diaspora, and then challenging what cultural biases that may be unearthed about so-called epistemologies based on accepted assumptions, inherited ways of understanding the world, and viewing literary and filmic practices in Africa. In this study, we shall explore the depiction of gender and sexuality in their varied facets, so as to question the obvious and engage fundamental issues of belief, and social, economic, and political activities (see Zinn, Hondagneu-Sotelo, and Messner: 2005).

One would have thought that a call for scholarly articles on gender and sexuality for a volume like this at the beginning of the twenty-first century would inundate the editors with papers on sexuality and gender being as they essentially are aspects of human life and human experience. Not so in the contexts of African literature and film, as the process of article selection for this study has revealed. We ask rhetorically, does the homosexuality question make waves yet as a hot and prevailing literary topic in Africa? In the film industry, does it form part of grand discourses on engendering human rights? The fact that only cursory mention of homosexuality exists in African literature, and that only a few have been recorded to date on homosexuality in African film, do say that a lot of work still needs to be done. It nonetheless signifies an assumption that not just male homosexuality, lesbianism, and bi-sexuality, but also all the other shades of in-between genders and sexualities in general, are subjects that demand critical scrutiny and waiting to be apprized. These are some of the issues that inform the kinds of essays we have retained for this volume, not to mention the way we present them in this volume.[1]

We do not expect that our readers would follow our thinking without some rumination. Thus, we will hereunder guide thinking on the functions of African literature and film in the forging of individual and group identities, especially identities founded on sex and gender, through the definition of sex and gender in the African context. The next important question is why gender and sex in Africa are such important literary and filmic subjects for exploration. The response to this cardinal question allows us to link African feminism and "minority" studies to our study of gender and sexuality in this volume, for gender encompasses also notions of sex, sexual orientation, reproduction, class, and power. Traditionally, biological sex is designated by the male or female genitalia, and their owners respectively are deemed to be masculine or feminine. This is by no means a new fact that has just emerged.

In Africa, however, the traditional scenario runs something like this: a male will one day become a father and will carry arms to defend the community after the ceremonies of puberty and circumcision that socialize the individual. He might become a leader or an elder, if he proves himself either in war, hunting, farming as a head of family, and a community notable figure. He can then hope to become an ancestor upon his death. The female, for her part, after corresponding puberty and circumcision rites, can hope to become a mother some day, bear and rear children, even nurture other children in the community that are not necessarily her biological children. She can enter the class of leaders /elders of the community by her sheer age and achievements, although this is rare. According to this African traditional way of thinking, fostered by rituals and initiatory rites of adolescence and puberty, normal girls are feminine and normal boys masculine. Any deviation from these norms are frowned upon and ridiculed. However, when individuals prove impossible to redirect they are condoned as aberrations.

The fact that African literature at the present time deals enormously with problems of gender stereotyping, which divides human beings rigidly into two genders, male and female, with no allowance for alternative identities, demonstrates that gender in itself is a great human problem; it controls all issues of human life in Africa as elsewhere. Based on biological (natural) determinism, which puts the burden of reproduction on women in a pronatal culture, African traditional society has regulated the structure of society along reproduction lines. Different roles and responsibilities are assigned to men and women, following the general argument, as indicated above, that one's gender is the same as one's sex. More forward-looking awareness has since debunked this line of thinking as obsolete and many African writers continue to grapple with this problem in their search for solutions for the grave social problems on the land.

Modern African writers see motherhood at once as reason for joy and woes for women. They see women's place to be in the home space, where they are confined to domestic chores, bearing and rearing of children, a practice that has to do with the prevalent traditional perception of the ideology of gender and power. Whereas the man roams the wild looking for adventure in work and war, the woman remains sheltered, protected, and powerless. Her pseudo-independence is debunked and proven to be a mere sham as soon as she is in the presence of her man, be he her father, brother, uncle, or husband. Ama Ata Aidoo, Mariama Bâ, Flora Nwapa, Buchi Emecheta, and others, all pioneering and major women writers of African first wave feminism, have written extensively on this absence, and traditionally instituted silencing, of women.

Clearly, sexual division of labor in the private space is at the root of patriarchy, where the male is at the center, is supreme and the norm, and the female is in the periphery, is subordinate and different. Women are controlled by being told to behave like women, cry like women, walk like women, sit like women, and that means do things differently from a man, less conspicuously or spontaneously. Then again, patriarchy also demands masculinity, sometimes, extreme masculinity, from all men in the community. Because, not all men are given to, nor want to be, aggressive, domineering, and lack the abilities for nurturing. this study will uphold the view that patriarchy is a social system inimical to both males and females in the community. For the common good, therefore, we will emphasize the unequal aspects of gender considerations in traditional African settings.

Beyond tradition, as African societies moved into the colonial era, and into independence, post-independence (modern) and now postmodern times, a new class issue has arisen, still based on the assumption that biological sex is the same as gender. Society has become divided into the rural and the urban, the elite and the plebeians. The terms are no longer equal for the master and his slave, where the latter might be a gardener, steward, or cook. And the difference is not always limited to class, for race comes into the equation with attempts at decolonization, neocolonization, and postcolonial writing. For example, white males are categorized as naturally given to homosexuality, as seen in Maryse Condé's *Heremakhonon*, about the narrator's experiences in an imaginary West African nation of the twentieth century. In Buchi Emecheta's novel with an ironic title, *The Joys of Motherhood*, an African man works as cook, washer man, "small-boy" (gofer), etc., and is "feminized" by the whites for whom he generally works. His wife is ashamed of him and would rather not talk about her husband's job with friends, and in bed, she feels that she is sleeping with a woman, at best a non-male, who is overweight, "soft" and is not as "strong," that is virile, as a normal "wiry" African man should be.

It will therefore be necessary to emphasize multiple differences in the considerations of gender and sexuality in this anthology, especially to see different representations of gender in relation to issues of class and race. Some women of the dominant and advantaged race or class may have more privileges and power than the men and women of the dominated and marginalized race or class. In the end, it will be pertinent to recognize that a nation state might be multicultural in intent, yet in practice oppressive to racial and sexual minorities.

Indeed, very often gender studies grapple with the meaning of sex (culture, social construction) and the origin of sex differences (nurture, essentialism), given the ever-expanding interrelationship between sexuality, ethnicity, and race. According to essentialists, men and women are sexually different, thanks to biological determinism. The differences are natural, and are not socially constructed. Essentialists do not, however, go as far as to condone social injustices based on sex, like reserving part-time jobs or none at all for women. Anti-essentialists or social constructionists, on the other hand, argue that differences between men and women are cultural, not natural, and so are socially constructed. Even the visible, obvious, physical differences are held to be virtual differences until actualized and only then do they take on their meaning from their social interpretation. The argument here is in the explanation of sex differences, their understanding--not their existence--only because there are a lot of social and political implications for both parties and their adherents.

First, if one goes by the essentialist (traditional, natural) view of gender, then African society has no hope for change as far as racism, violence, and other aggressive behaviors against sexual and racial minorities are concerned. However, if one goes with the social constructionist view (contemporary, cultural), then one might hope to change the status quo through arguments, reconstructions, and reforms of the social and political structure and so forth. This latter, political and social vision of relations between men and women, is certainly more positive than the former, biological view of sex and gender. We shall argue that gender, sexual, racial, and other social and political categories are created and sustained by historical determinisms, and therefore must be taken into account in considering the formation of individual and collective identities.

And this brings us full circle to the definition of gender as an arbitrary notion that does not seem to predict human actions in Africa, yet is ubiquitous and controls human activities, like sexualities, as well as authorial or filmmaker's language, selections, and choices. Readers will rely on this view of gender to comprehend contributors' articles in this anthology. Because the social constructionist views of gender are more akin to the postmodernist mode of thinking today, it opens up several possibilities for the benefit of African literature and film. There is a relationship between the text and its author in new, complex, and complicated ways, now beginning with the premise that sex is not equal to gender. Hence an African woman writer can write a "masculine" text and a man writer a "feminine" text. Second, certain characters may not identify with their biological sex or might even cross-identify with the opposite gender, or crisscross between masculine and feminine genders and sexualities. Third, sexuality is reviewed in terms of its naturalness or lack of it. If we learn nothing from the effacement of boundaries between sexual and gender identities, it is, first, that a person's gender identity may differ from her or his sexual activities, and second, that there are the possibilities of endless sexual expressions to which one individual being is prone. For example, even within a heterosexual relationship, a situation of inverse fellatio and anal coitus could arise. The same goes for adherents of homosexuality, who often find themselves in heterosexual or bisexual relationships. In the end, readers will be called upon to think critically about sex and gender in the African and African diaspora contexts, the belief systems, their impact on society, the understanding of social, economic, and political issues governed by them, and how sex and gender relate to issues of ethnicity, race, class and categories of difference, *ad infinitum*.

From this angle of vision, then, writing a scholarly and critical volume of essays in postmodernist and postcolonial times on gender and sexuality on the large fields of African literature and film and the diaspora appears frustrating, given that the bulk of writings are in the broad realm of gender and sexuality, and in literature, as such. What is more, Africans have myriad manifestations of sexuality, which make the mere discussion of it daunting. And, furthermore, gender and sexuality were not problematic issues of discussion in traditional Africa, thanks to its fluidity, as Ruth Morgan and Saskia Wieringa have amply demonstrated in their recent book, *Tommy Boys, Lesbian Men and Ancestral Wives: Female Same-sex Practices in Africa* (2005). It is only recently that a problem has arisen, due to the association of gender and sexuality with racism, sexism, class, and ethnicity.

In the pages that follow, we shall analyze and interpret the much broader (than Morgan-Wieringa's effort), groundbreaking, and recent discussions on African homosexualities collected and edited by Stephen O. Murray and Will Roscoe in *Boy-Wives and Female Husbands: Studies of African Homosexualities* (1998). We will conclude with the presentation of each chapter contribution and what it brings to the grand discussion of gender and sexuality in this volume.

THEORETICAL EXPLORATION OF HOMOSEXUALITIES IN AFRICA

Stephen O. Murray and Will Roscoe in their equally recent, extensive, and groundbreaking research in some fifty African societies have encoded the theoretical and analytical exploration of African homosexualities. To date, their book, *Boy-Wives and Female Husbands: Studies in African Homosexualities* (1998) is the most comprehensive theoretical and empirical study yet in understanding the phenomena of gender and sexuality in Africa.

Murray and Roscoe begin with the premise that just because anthropologists and other observers, including literary writers, linguists, and sociologists, have never really paid serious attention to homosexuality in Africa does not mean that homosexuality did not and does not exist. Murray and Roscoe disabuse the reader's mind of a unitary and homogenous Africa with one homosexuality. They assert that the claim of the absence of sexuality in Africa was a European myth, carefully crafted, like so many other "inventions" and "Orientalisms" (Edward Saïd) of Africa as a foil to the so-called European civilization, progress, adulthood and deviancy, often juxtaposed to the so-called "naturalness,"(read primitivism, childhood, and normalcy) of the "Other." Since then, European scholarship has attributed exceptions to their invention of sexuality in Africa to Arabic, European or other influences.

Murray and Roscoe respond, saying that according to their empirical research, pockets of African culture have condoned in the past an age-stratified homosexuality, activated especially during war times, when warriors "married" boys to do errands for them in the day, and then doubled as their "wives" at night. Sometimes, it was a situational or opportunistic adolescent phase that passed. Then, there were other cases linked purely to homoeroticism, where certain individuals found pleasure in the company of others of the same sex. The authors contend, therefore, that African homosexuality is neither incidental nor random, but rather "is a consistent and logical feature of African societies and belief systems." Therefore, it is not a phenomenon that is unitary, nor predominantly sexual, with fixed internal psychological motivation as in the West.

Postcolonial African studies, in a reverse colonial discourse, seeks to replace Western "genuinely perverse" with an African "genuinely normal," and blames the West for the importation into Africa of colonial practices and institutions that work against African perceived hyper sexuality. In the African diaspora, the same criticism of the West holds sway, as Randy Conner demonstrates in his *Blossom of Bone: Reclaiming the Connections between Homoeroticus and the Sacred*. Quoting Public Enemy, a rap group, he writes:

> There is not a word in any African language, which describes homosexual. If you want to take me up on that, then you find me, in the original languages of Africa, a word for homosexual, lesbian or prostitute. There are no such words. They didn't exist (San Francisco: Harper San Francisco, 1993: 37).

Well, Murray and Roscoe would refute this assertion, given their findings on African homosexualities, if Public Enemy is understood as *not* saying that in traditional Africa gender and sexuality were not fixed constructs and defined an individual permanently. They would also refute the claim by filmmaker Sissoko's *Woubi chéri* that words for homosexuality did not exist in traditional Africa. Murray and Roscoe attest from their empirical study of fifty traditional African societies that Africans always had homosexual patterns and words to describe those who desired their own sex.

African postcolonial studies also disclaim European inventions and constructions of African customs that no longer exist, but also blame colonialism for the so-called contemporary "immoralities" in Africa, including homosexuality. On the contrary, assert Murray and Roscoe, it is European myth that condones its view of an Africa full of super-virile men and lascivious women, myths borne out by such lopsided media reports on the prevalence of AIDS in Africa today beyond what other races are experiencing. The two illustrious researchers reiterate the imperative of abandoning myths about African sexuality, myths about Western beliefs and values of love, sexuality, and personal relationships as monogamous, voluntary, and marriage as a relationship of mutual choice and sexual attraction, in order to properly understand African homosexualities.

Western feminism promotes equality and so tends to disapprove of all relationships of unequal status, be they male-male, female-female, or male-female. In Africa, on the contrary, assert Murray and Roscoe, all levels of arrangements abound, to the extent that boy-wives can accept to be given to older men in a kind of slavery, or deep bond of love. Others in rebellion can seek these liaisons to protest or resist their social situation as passive victims. It is possible to de-emphasize gender, but emphasize status in traditional African societies. In such circumstances, age, lineage, and seniority take precedence over junior status. African marriages can happen between individuals in male and female roles, not necessarily between biological males and females. One question that has arisen is whether social males are a neuter or third gender, and this question will recur as a leitmotif as we continue the exploration of Murray and Roscoe's ideas.

Murray and Roscoe's groundbreaking and empirical book, *Boy-Wives and Female Husbands: Studies in African Homosexualities*, has sought to understand African homosexualities in all is complexities, and is divided into four broad geographical regions—*Sub-Saharan Africa*: The Horn of Africa, the Sudan, and East Africa; *West Africa*: including the West and the interior of the Sudan region; *Central Africa*: from the tropical rainforests to the equatorial region, the Congo basin, and East to Tanzania; *Southern Africa*: from Mozambique and Zambia to South Africa and Namibia. The authors explain that their research is uneven for some areas are more or better studied than others, an observation that merely reflects the early stages of homosexuality studies in Africa, which in the year 2004 is only a decade and a half old. Female-female sex patterns are very poorly studied yet, due to lack of adequate information on them. Nonetheless, these studies contribute to the social construction of gender and sexuality in Africa in particular, and in general, the world, given the roles that feminist scholars and other scholars of gender studies, history, and anthropology have played and are playing.

Despite the divergence between Western and non-Western patterns, still some patterns recur across historical periods and cultures. The question that anthropological research asks is what factors affect the occurrence and regularity of patterns within a given pattern? Murray and Roscoe contend that evidence about African homosexualities from across the continent, languages, families, social and kinship organizations and subsistence patterns refute the claim that Africa had no homosexual patterns and no words to describe those who engaged in same-sex desire. Homosexuality is traditional and indigenous to Africa, the Western researchers assert, although cross-racial and cross-cultural patterns may have influenced groups of Africans and non-Africans. The authors submit that throughout Africa, age and gender are generally the key bases for social organization. African homosexualities, however, have three most common patterns: gender-differentiated roles, age-differentiated roles, and egalitarian or mutual relations, which could occur more or less in either male-male or female-female, relationships.

First, gender-differentiated social status exist for males or females who engage in cross- or mixed gender behaviors, men or women who deviate from strictly masculine or feminine ways of doing things—for example a male who likes to cook, sew, or do his hair like women. Whereas it is difficult to observe as well their sexual conduct in the bedroom, it must be assumed that "lack of evidence is not evidence of absence,"—the eponymous epigraph is poignant—as Murray and Roscoe have stated, adding that such male-females cannot be expected not to perform the female role on the bed. It is such females that have often been noted to be spirit mediums and shamans in possession religions. The pertinent question raised by this is what number of genders exists? Is one either male or non-male? Indeed, does a third gender exist, where one is male, female, both or none of the above? As Murray and Roscoe note, the local definitions of 'non-male' category may include females, that is, boys seen as unfledged males, eunuchs, men whose genitalia is partially or totally excised, and uninitiated and/or unmarried and/or childless adults, seen as failed males, even though they have sex exclusively with women, for after all, they may have fully developed male genitalia.

Second, age-differentiated homosexual pattern is the most common, found in instances where women are absent or forbidden (courts, war camps, mining compounds, and trading parties), and range from institutionalized practices (among the Mossi and Azande ethnic groups) to non-formalized and sanctioned patterns. Murray and Roscoe find that the older male generally penetrates the younger one, although in certain cases the penetration happens mutually, hence asymmetry is not always the case, but includes reciprocity. In more complex situations, the older males pay "bride wealth" to the family of the younger partners, thus turning them into "boy-wives" in war times; they perform the feminine roles of wives in the day and receptive sexual roles at night. Murray and Roscoe conclude that with such practices as these "idioms of age and gender overlap." This alternative identity can last a lifetime, but also only until the younger, penetrated, or receptive one attains adult status. In that case, his role is merely social and sexual, not social and political (outlaw status) as in Western societies. Cross and mixed gendered behavior is the most common, again raising the question of whether there is a third gender, neutral, non-male, or non-female, and other. Age-stratified same-sex pattern ranges from institutionalized relations to others that lack any formal organization or sanction in societies where they occur. Another pertinent observation is the difficulty in distinguishing between spontaneous, incidental behavior as happens between peers in boarding high schools where the relationship is given all kinds of special names, from the more formal and institutionalized practice as seen in mining compounds and war camps.

Third, egalitarian homosexuality is seen more with those societies that rely on animal husbandry. It is more amorphous, for it is sometimes a spontaneous desire between two male adolescents, and sometimes in institutionalized settings as in boarding schools. In colonial times, it existed between men and lower status males, usually master and his servant. There were also cases of "special friendships" between married adult males who engaged in reciprocal sex away from women during fishing or trading expeditions, observe Murray and Roscoe. In general, female same-sex patterns follow patrilineal systems of inheritance: women with higher income bracket seem to welcome female same-sex pattern.

Murray and Roscoe also furnish a detailed deduction of beliefs, attitudes toward, and judgments of homosexual behavior in Africa. Some males, South African miners who go for long months without their wives in the mining city, have reportedly found homosexuality fulfilling, even "beautiful." Sometimes, they have preferred their boy-wives to their wives when they did not just like / love them as much as their wives. Except for or where there is the presence of Islam and Christianity, Murray and Roscoe found that traditional African belief did not see homosexuality as sinful or as evidence of mental illness or disease. However, the Pangwe of the Cameroon, a group that holds similar worldview as the West, without any known intercultural influence, sees all sexual relations as sinful, including heterosexuality; they would, however, exonerate children, since they are held to be incapable of sin. The Pangwe do believe that a man can transmit the power to acquire wealth and other missing qualities to another through sexual intercourse, and would punish all cases of illicit affairs, be they heterosexual or homosexual.

Murray and Roscoe have attempted to grapple with African traditional explanations of homosexuality by noting esoteric and down-to-earth views from different groups in their book. Some groups like the Fanti of Ghana explain away homosexuality in terms of light and heavy souls, irrespective of the individual's biological sex. Women with heavy souls desire same-sex erotic desire, and men with light souls also crave same-sex relationships, where heavy soul is native to male as light soul is to female (Christensen 1954: 92-43). The Bantu of North Kavirondo are not less judgmental; they see *luswa*, the impurity of homosexual desire, as existing in the blood of an individual who desires another of the same sex (Wagner 108-109). Quoting an Nginé soldier, punished for attempting to engage in homosexual act, in "Same-Sex Life among a Few Negro Tribes of Angola," Falk furnishes one of the numerous statements from the indigenous peoples of Angola about "the naturalness, normality, and even banality of same-sex relations: "Doesn't the Sergeant know that there are men who from their youth on desire women, and others, who are attracted only to men? Why then should he be punished now? After all, he knows not why God created him like this—that he can only love men!" (Murray and Roscoe 1998: 271).

Homosexuality in Africa also raises the issue of identity and the roles played by individuals. Murray and Roscoe compare Western and African homo-sexualities, concluding that individuals exploit their named identities to define and understand themselves, and participate occasionally in sexual subcultures that are essentially drawn from African gender-defined and age-based patterns, which are dissimilar from Western ones. In the case of the South African mine workers, already cited above, the only recorded Western influence would be in the fact that white colonial economy imposed the estrangement of men from the women.

The question of duality of gender, with the possibility of a third gender, is an issue that arises from the study of African homosexuality, as we have noted repeatedly above. First of all, African homosexuality refutes the notion that social identities are uniquely produced by social, historical, and economic factors.[1] Second, gay and homosexual identities exist cross-culturally. Hence in the West where homosexuality defines an individual's lifestyle and identity as homosexual, such an identity does not arise uniquely from historical and social factors specific to Western societies alone. On the contrary, in Africa the issue is different, for men indulge in homosexual acts even when they are married and have children. In other words, even if an alternative gender status lasts a lifetime, the role played in age-related homosexual relationship is temporary. In Africa, gender roles are constantly shifting, although men and women are expected to pay their dues to society by procreating, because Africa is pronatal and the production of eligible heirs is of paramount importance.

Therefore, sometimes older, more affluent, women may choose to become female husbands and assume husband rights over other younger, poorer women, for several reasons, not the least of which is a childless marriage or a marriage that has not produced a son. Hence, what is important is not the femininity or masculinity of the individual, nor is it her or his desire of a partner of the same sex, as much as it is to maintain a semblance of "a conventional image of married life." Murray and Roscoe conclude that Africans, unlike Westerners, are not compelled to either repress their same-sex urges or become enemies of society. On the other hand, African culture inhibits formation of subcultures of homosexuality, stigmatization, and identity construction as homosexual, simply because such identities could lead to different kinds of illicit sexuality, including prostitution and commercial and non-commercial homosexuality (Murray 1995a: 33-70; 1977c: 14-21).

Murray and Roscoe also sought a correlation between the pattern of same-sex desire and the organizational structure of the group, in order to establish a pattern of some sort. They found that whereas they studied mainly agrarian societies, yet those individuals engaging in egalitarian relationship appear to come mostly from cultures that engaged in animal husbandry. The matrilineal kinship patterns also tend to promote age-related and gender-differentiated patterns of same-sex relationships. Third, female same-sex patterns predominate where women contribute significantly to subsistence. The suggestion is that societies that produce higher status women tend to condone female same-sex patterns of the egalitarian or age-related kinds. Curiously, in pockets of culture, where boys are encouraged to be free in relationships with girls, they are also relatively free to engage in sexual relations with each other. Murray and Roscoe conclude that it is a bizarre practice and doubt if indeed homosexuality is caused and promoted by lack or absence of women.

With regard to urbanization and gender-based same-sex patterns, Murray and Roscoe find that in class-based African societies the norm is egalitarian or age-based patterns, concluding that the organization of homosexuality go hand in hand with the increasing complexity of society. This implies that individuals develop alternative gender statuses, which involve distinctive and lasting identities, along with manners of dress, work roles, social statuses, religious functions, etc. These distinctions are evidently more complex than the roles individuals play in often short-term, age-differentiated or egalitarian relationships.

Will Roscoe has suggested in earlier works that the diversification of gender roles tends to follow growth in social specializations. He nonetheless did not observe many instances of alternative gender statuses in religious and civic roles, what he has termed "a state third gender," where, for example, such an individual is consulted by leaders of the community. However, eunuchs, court pages, and religious leader roles often signal the combining of alternative gender statuses and state functions.

Another pertinent question that arises generally from any discussions about homosexuality and that arise from the Murray-Roscoe study is what causes homosexuality. Is same-sex relations produced and sustained by a particular type of division of labor? For example, do situations where women are the primary sustainers of existence promote lesbianism? Does their status as primary producers of subsistence prevent the occurrence of same-sex desire among these women? Murray and Roscoe wonder if this is all due to economics or to fulfill sexual desire, to be able to form a socially accepted relationship with a member of the same sex or engage in sexual acts not possible with the opposite sex? They observe that in cultures with belief systems that recognize only two genders, the gender of individuals in roles for nonmasculine men and nonfeminine women are adjusted to match their sexual preference, as seen for example in the men-women (see *les homme-femmes* in Senegal) who participate in and sing praises of women in women's festivities. Throughout Africa, note Murray and Roscoe, gender roles shift, and men and women, temporarily or permanently, exceed normal bounds in various ways, but almost no one is exempt from the requirement to procreate.

Suffice it to say, in regard to female homosexuality, the most recorded findings in the African past are about egalitarian relationships, where one woman, usually the older and more affluent, claims some of a man's prerogatives and acts towards the other as a husband would. This prevalent egalitarian relationship lends credence to the notion that gender is the major idiom of homosexuality for men and women in Africa. Nonetheless, instances of age-differentiated relationships tend to suggest the contrary. For example, in the case of female husbands the female of higher status playing the role of husband is almost always older than the "wife." More often than not, female husbands do engage in heterosexual marriage themselves, only becoming female husbands later in their lives (1998: 264).

Despite colonial and neocolonial upheavals, and vicissitudes of recent history in Africa, assert Murray and Roscoe, the West is not responsible for homosexuality in Africa, for same-sex activities appear indigenous and natural to Africa, despite the lack of subcultures, public identities, roles, and social acceptance that could compare to Western gay and lesbian lives. South Africa, however, has taken the lead in Africa in merging sexual rights with human rights, going as far as protecting gay rights with a constitutional amendment, and becoming the first country in the world to do so. Kevan Botha and Edwin Cameron explain South Africa's constitutional protection of gays in an article entitled "South Africa," in *Sociological Control of Homosexuality: A Multi-National Comparison* (1997: 37):

> [This] is no doubt the product of our peculiar history, where institutionalized discrimination against people on the ground of race was perfected through the legal system. The racial legacy has given the majority of South Africans repugnance for the use of legal processes for irrational discrimination. Gays and lesbians have been among the direct beneficiaries. For all South Africans, however, as with racial

issues, the problem now is to reconcile constitutional promises with daily practices (qtd. in Murray and Roscoe 1998: 278).

Evidently, the roles that race has played and continues to play in institutionalized discrimination against sections of humanity makes it a paramount facet of studies of any minority groups. Roscoe and Murray conclude: "the future of African homosexualities is certainly one of greater visibility, greater dialogue—and greater risks" (ibid.). *Boy Wives and Female Husbands: Studies of African Homosexualities* throws a lot of light on the ethnocentrism of gender and sexuality question in Africa. It widens the scope of studies in homosexuality that is still at the early stage when it even exists in African literature and film.

STRUCTURE OF THE ANTHOLOGY

We have structured this anthology around two major fields: AFRICAN LITERATURE and AFRICAN FILM. These two broad rubrics together enclose five thematic subsections or parts made up of seventeen chapters. This strategy, we believe, should facilitate the use of the anthology as a secondary source for research and for classroom instruction on gender and sexuality in particular, and African and African Diaspora literature in general.

Part One: Social and Historical Transformations of Gender and Sexuality explores gender and sex in the political economy of postcolonial discourse. All four chapters in this section are on fictional texts, and treat African works of literature on misogyny, maleness, femaleness, femininity, masculinity, and homosexuality. Erica Hoagland's "What kind of Woman Are You, A'isha? Misogyny and Islam in Ibrahim Tahir's *The Last Imam*," demonstrates convincingly how Islamic orthodoxy, misogyny, and hypocrisy converge in the objectification of wives in the Harem. Pinkie Mekgwe, in "Constructing Postcolonial Maleness in Ayi Kwei Armah's *Fragments*," explores the intricate ways in which the relationship between gender construction, decolonization, and nation building are symbolically represented in sexual forms: the colonized man is seen as female and never attains true freedom, that is, his ideal existence. Chukwuma Okoye's "Posting the Agenda in African Women's Writing: the Postcolonial Condition in Promise Okekwe's Novels," treats the complications and implications of a postcolonial perspective of gender and sexuality, stressing the need for the reading of new African women's writing for what they unearth about and contribute to gender and sexuality in Africa, including discussions on homosexuality. To close this first part is Najat Rahman's "The Fragmented Heritage in the Reconstruction of Home: Assia Djebar's *L'amour, la fantasia*." Thanks to the tool of writing and language passed on by a father to his daughter, author Djebar in exile is able to recapture her fragmented autobiography and history of her nation, Algeria, while in search of home, love, heritage, and a remedy to silence violence against women.

Part Two: Rumbles of Race in Gender and Sexuality Matters explores the African diaspora factors of race and racism in gender and sexuality questions, and what they have to do with the level of social and sexual injustices in society. It is a new look at the benefits of individual and collective revolutions in curbing social and historical injustices. The three essays in this section deal in turn with deconstructions and subversions of male/female, and black/white binaries, first in the multicultural space of Montreal in Canada, then in the African immigrant community of Belleville in Paris, and finally in the Caribbean. In "The Issue Is Race: Gender and Sexuality in Dany Laferrière's North-American Autobiography," Ada Uzoamaka Azodo explores the four-part fictional autobiography by the Haitian Dany Laferrière on the sexual and racial oppression of immigrants of African descent in Montreal. Adapting Judith Butler's theory on sexual minorities to racial minorities, the chapter explores Laferrière's strategic use of textual and racial politics to resist the feminization of the black race. In Stacy Fifer's "Building Alternative Communities: Race and Female Sexual Agency in Calixthe Beyala's *Amours sauvages*," Belleville, a Parisian Harlem, provides a subversive space for the exploration of gender and sexual activities as women, ordinarily treated as second-hand citizens, assume their personal and collective sovereignties, become heads of family, and fight patriarchy. Lastly, in "Feminine Transgression and Crossing Over: Maryse Condé's *I, Tituba, Black Witch of Salem*, Amy Lee redefines and reconstructs black female identity often cast negatively in reference to that of the male in the Caribbean, due to racism resulting from the past of slavery.

Part Three: Contestations, Protestations, and Representations has three contributions as well that explore performance, corporeal practices, and individual lifestyles, including woman-woman marriage, excision, and incest in father-daughter relationships. Egodi Uchendu's "Woman-Woman Marriage in Igboland," sees largely gender-based female same-sex relationship as part of the fabric of African tradition and culture, and as a pragmatic and practical arrangement for solving many types of social problems, including infertility, adoption, need for a male child, and domestic services, among so many others. Jill Eagling's "Uncovering Incest in Father/Daughter Relationships: Displacement and Distancing Strategies in Buchi Emecheta's *The Family*" and Evelyne Mpoudi Ngolle's *Sous la cendre le feu*, is one of the earliest studies on record of father-daughter relationships in African literature, where incest mirrors gender and sexual oppression of the female by the dominant male. Bernadette K. Kassi's « Représenation(s) de l'excision dans le roman ivoirien: des *Soleils des indépendances* (1968) d'Ahmadou Kourouma à *Rebelles* (1998) de Fatou Kéita », recapitulated in English by Ada Uzoamaka Azodo as "Representation(s) of Excision in the Ivorian Novel: From Ahmadou Kourouma's *The Suns of Independence* (1968) to Fatou Kéita's *Rebellious Women* (1998) by Bernadette K. Kassi," for the benefit of non-French readers, explores the issue of excision from two divergent, masculine and feminine, viewpoints that have to do respectively with the sex and gender of the novelists. This chapter underlines the importance of gender and sexuality as primary conditions for understanding how a writer, and by extension, an individual, looks at reality and society.

Part Four: Social Constructions of Homosexual, Lesbian, Bisexual, and Transvestite Identities treats gay male and female bodies and the politics of gender and sexual identity and representation. There are also three chapters in this section, the first two being studies of literary works, whereas the third is the study of a film. M. Catherine Jonet, in "She Doesn't Know the Truth about Me: [T]he Shaping Presence of the Closet in Amma Darko's *Beyond the Horizon*," explores the silencing of sexual minorities, which carries over into the silencing and sexual exploitation of women in a rare Occident-Africa conspiracy. In the exploration of sexual alternatives in the presence of the evolution of history, economy, and culture, individuals engage in new sexual acts, all along latent in them, which surface as they search for their identities in the obsessive and harsh present. As fragmented selves betray multiple sexual identities, presences fall out of closets, dangerous encounters happen, sometimes beyond ethnic communities, and expanding on to regional and global scales, concludes Jonet. Miriam Gyimah's "Dangerous Encounters with the West: Gender, Sexuality, and Power in Ama Ata Aidoo's *Our Sister Killjoy*" explores lesbianism between a German, white, woman and a Ghanaian, black one, seeing sexual exploitation, commodification, and objectification of the African female body by a white. Lastly, Maureen N. Eke's "*Woubi chéri*: Negotiating Subjectivity, Gender, and Power" studies the first filmic acknowledgement of a new vocabulary to describe homosexual identities in Abidjan, Ivory Coast. In this film, the directors see an inherent problematic acceptance of homosexuality as an alternative and valid way of life in contemporary African societies, suggesting that gendered identities are performed.

Part Five: Social Constructions of Masculine and Feminine Identities has four articles on film that explore masculinity, femininity, and power, as well as eroticism and constructions of gender. Keith M. Harris' "Stand up, boy!' Sidney Poitier, 'boy', and Filmic Black Masculinity" observes the effect of racial slurs on the black race, as well as how the subversion by the so re-invented, through resisting the name-calling, results in the creation of black masculinity. In a provocative title, Anastasia Valassopoulos asks: "Does the *Season of Men* Require the Harvest of Women? A Tunisian Filmmaker's Vision." This essay explores gender and sexual conflicts that arise when migrant male workers return home, assert their maleness at the expense of their women, and the latter who, having assumed personal agency in their husband's absence, resist gender oppression, but are nonetheless compelled to submit to the men by sheer weight of tradition. Christiane P. Makward's "The Sex Appeal of Idrissa Ouedraogo's films: *Yaaba* (1989), *Tila* (1990), *Samba Traoré* (1993), *Le cri du coeur* (1994), *La colère des dieux* (2002) is a gynocentric study of five films in which eroticism and conflicts between African traditional unwritten laws about nudity and the universal taste for representation of sex on the screen run galore. Victoria Pasley, in "Representations of Gender in Three West African Films: *Finzan, Touki Bouki* and *Hyenas*," studies Cheikh Oumar Sissoko and Djibril Diop Mambety's strategies as filmmakers in depicting and reevaluating constructions of masculinity and power, strategies needed by all persons interested in inserting women's voices in the power sharing process with men.

CONCLUSION

One cannot but look ahead towards more profound work on gender and sexuality, both by creative artists, including, but not limited to, African writers and filmmakers. Anthropologists, linguists, critics, and all who engage in the study of human society, all note the linkages between the political economy, race, sex, and gender, which are evident in the objectification of women and the subjugation of racial and sexual minorities, not to mention how capitalism with its emphasis on productivity, product manufacturing, and the attendant "enslavement" of individuals in their work places, over long periods of time, may support new and alternative conceptions of sexuality and erotic desires and relationships in African urban societies. Such conditions, consequently, may privilege homosexuality over heterosexuality. Somewhat cheekily, contentiously, we ask: Does the twenty-first century signal the coming death of heterosexuality? Put differently, will homosexuality overtake heterosexuality, even replacing it, as the norm in the future? We leave open-ended the discourse on gender and sexuality in Africa, inviting our readers to consider and imagine their attendant impact on individuals, societies, cultures, and histories, in the future.

Note

1.　See Jacques Corraze. *L'Homosexualité. Que sais-je?* Paris: Presses Universitaires de France (5e Édition), 1982. Chapter 2. "L'homosexualité dans la perspective psychanalytique," 34-41.

AFRICAN LITERATURE

Survey of the Historical and Geographical Scope of Gender and Sexuality in African Literature

In this critical anthology, we are called upon to investigate the representations of gender and sexuality in selected literary works and films of Africa and its diaspora as part of a research process on the understanding of both phenomena, from the earliest times to the present, and to make projections for the future. The shifting environment of the postmodern/postcolonial times makes this study all the more important, imposing a number of imperatives. We ask: Does homosexuality exist in Africa? If so, is its practice pervasive? How do Africans view same-sex desire? To what measure do African writers blur gender and sexual identities, which blurring makes it impossible to accept same-sex desire as part of the complicated, complex, and contradictory nature of human chromosomal make-up?

Clearly, in African traditional worldview, gender is a fluid notion; males and females are merely biological bodies that exist, getting actualized into what they become at a given time. In fact, women can "marry" other women for various reasons, including a woman's need to play the male role by another woman, infertility, cultural boy-child preference, need for domestic help, and inability of a wife to perform her conjugal duties by her man. When there is a dearth of males or sons, women can function as men or sons, thanks to the gender roles they play. Boys can also become wives, when female company is needed, but is absent. Husbands can become females as well, when the wife is not able to fulfill domestic chores, which are seen traditionally as the woman's domain. Even when a husband is deemed not to be performing at the level expected of a male, thanks to economic, cultural, and political expectations in the community, he can be regarded essentially as a female too. An often-quoted example is Chinua Achebe's *Things Fall Apart*, where the garrulous hero Okonkwo calls another man less successful, less masculine, and less aggressive than himself an *agbala*. Ordinarily; it is an Igbo term that means simply "woman," but which can be derogatory when used to designate a man. Another popular example is the phenomenon of *Homme-femme* (man-woman) in Senegalese culture, where some men by nature attune more to women and women's activities than to men and their culturally designated activities. Aminata Sow Fall demonstrates in the first of her eight novels to date, *Le Revenant*, that men-women follow women around, and function as leaders or facilitators at women's gatherings without any abashment. They are very much accepted by the women as what they are, men-women.

Indeed, in the African past, no rubber stamp was put on an individual beyond biological sex. One was either male or female, because genders changed as sex roles changed. A husband can be a female of a feminine sex or male of a masculine sex. By the same token, a daughter can be a male, depending on the peculiar social gender she performs. To quote a famous example, the Egyptian Hepshepsut, female by her sex, yet male in her role as Pharaoh, was represented publicly as male in male garb. Other lesser known cases have been treated collectively by Ifi Amadiume in her famous essay, "Male Daughters and Female Husbands," to signify that it is common for women and men in traditional Africa to switch roles and genders according to their social and political circumstances (Amadiume 19).[1]

Historical and sociological changes have modified life and living in Africa over the centuries. Traditionally as shown above, gender and sexuality had a history and cultural motivation of their own, having nothing to do with nature or nurture. People rose to a given occasion, engaged temporarily or permanently in actions or roles as a matter of expediency; they were not necessarily defined by such actions or roles. The roles were dropped, changed, or modified for other roles or acts, on demand. In other words, gender and sexuality were part and parcel of social and cultural processes of the community. They were touchable phenomena, and pervious to human agency. One could surmise by borrowing a leaf from Simone de Beauvoir, who once stated during the European feminist second-wave era that one was not born male or female, one became man or woman, depending on the role called upon to play, and the gender that went with such a role or act.

Modernity and postmodernity have changed conditions in Africa, due to society's cultural, economic, and political evolutions. In this study, there are at least two types of representations: historical shifts and shifts in popular culture.

In history, there are shifts from the Amazons, Queens, and Pharaohs, to the educated women of contemporary times, liberated, and economically powerful, who exploit their sexuality with freedom. The shifts in popular culture go from polygamy, or more specifically polygyny, where family was seen as a self-contained business, to today where individuals exploit their sexuality to have a good time, pure and simple. Sexuality is fast becoming divorced from procreation and the need to grow the numbers of the group. The five historical stages of African literature that affect gender and sexuality in Africa roll one into the other, and comprise the following: tradition; colonization since the 1940s; political independence since the 1960s; neocolonial/post-independence/modern era since the 1970s and including the 1980s, and the postmodern/global era of the 1990s to the present.

Traditionally, gender was a fluid construct in Africa, a changing phenomenon that allowed individuals to play different roles assigned to them or that they took on by themselves. We will not belabor this point any longer.

With the colonization of the continent since the 1940s things changed, starting with the objectification of men and women by white colonial personnel to fulfill their sexual desires. As recounted by Ferdinand Oyono in *Houseboy*, white masters slept with their African maids as part of the unwritten contract of service. And the girls, like slaves, were constrained to answer the master's call or lose their jobs. Sometimes, maids still lost their jobs after the masters had their liberties with them. Even boy servants were not spared, for their masters used them to satisfy their sexual urges at night when they doubled as "wives," as Maryse Condé notes in *Heremakhonon*, a novel about the author-narrator's personal experiences in an imaginary West African country. In East Africa, as Kenyan writer Ngugi wa Thiong'o notes, white wives had to endure, just like white wives of slave masters in the Americas, the agony of knowing that their husbands slept with native women, sometimes their own maids, as part of their privileges in Africa. Mineworkers, particularly in South Africa, regularly went without the company of their wives for long periods under colonization, since they were allowed home only one month in the year. This phenomenon has given rise to one category of polyandry in Africa, where women have a "home" husband and an "away" husband at the same time. The home husband gives space to the away husband on leave to enjoy the company of the shared wife. In such circumstances in modern Africa, it is no longer important who the father of the child is. In the cities, like Johannesburg, where the men work, men satisfy their sexual urges with a growing class of prostitutes. As a cumulative result, sexuality has become liberated of traditional mores. There is lack of education for women and men about sexual diseases, and the objectification of women by men as tools for their sexual satisfaction is rampant.

With political independence since the 1960s, and thanks to 1975, the first year of the decade for women's liberation, new, albeit few, writings by women counter phallocentrism in male written texts as women gain awareness of their double colonization, first by black men under patriarchal traditions and structures and then by the white men, who governed by Capitalist interests, privileging black men over black women as productive force for raw materials for overseas industries. Subsequently, women were seen as mere helpers to men and were often confined to the domestic space. As often as possible, women writers of the first wave of African feminism urged women to get education, gain a certain measure of economic freedom, no matter how small, for their self-confidence and self-sovereignty. Nigerian Flora Nwapa, for example, urged women to subvert prostitution, if it is the last option left for them, to gain equality with men, who must be persuaded to give up some of their economic power and influence. Nwapa meant that women should no longer merely serve as objects of pleasure for men or their economic appendages, but should ask for as much pay as possible for the sale of their bodies, and invest their earnings for their future and that of their offspring. Such savings could be used to pay for houses, clothing, and cars for themselves and their children, and for their children's school fees [*Never Again* (1975) and *Women Are Different* (1986)]. Many feminist critics dubbed Flora Nwapa a man-hater for insisting that prostitution was employment in the secondary sector of the national economy and therefore was a worthy occupation. Yet, for Nwapa, all women do is merely play the male game, turning patriarchy on its head by calling the terms of their servitude to men. The "cash Madams" or "thick Madams" in post civil war Nigeria were very influential and rich women who controlled businesses and markets with such astuteness as was not often seen with most women. And Nwapa sovereignly approved of them, although some moralists abhor her stance.

That such strong, traditional African women were not represented as the heroines of the first wave of women's writing in Africa has prompted Obioma Nnaemeka to wonder aloud why; she accuses the writers, accommodationists, as Charles Nnolim dubs them, of being incapable of breaking with the past, and supporting men's representation of women as weak, ineffective individuals. Nnaemeka sees the writers as still living in fear of their male counterparts whom they do not want to provoke. By their manner of characterization, they suggest that women cannot totally succeed without men. This first feminist era also brought forward a belief according to which every African woman is a prostitute, married or not, thanks to the unequal terms of association inherent in the part-romantic and part-economic/business marriage relationships. The more affluent a man is the more beautiful his wife, and the more wives, mistresses, or concubines that he can acquire.

During the post-independence era, also known as neo-colonialist era, the 1970s and including the 1980s, despite political independence, Africans had no economic independence and so still depended heavily on the ex-colonial mother country. Africans often went abroad to study, in order to profit from their continued association with the former European masters. To their shock, the Africans found themselves in strange environments, for in a given neighborhood, they would be the only blacks around. They were "exotic" objects for Western and European gazes, when they were not treated as exotic fruits for consumption as well. Ken Bugul, Ama Ata Aidoo, Buchi Emecheta, and Dany Laferrière, among many others, have individually dealt with these issues of reinvention of African and African diaspora identities in their writings. Evidently, this phenomenon of name-calling transforms the individual's identity and notion of self, not to mention gender and sexuality. Historical, economic, and cultural developments do indeed affect and transform individual genders and sexualities. Excessive masculinity already evident in traditional Africa got out of hand as African elite men sought to surpass the past white masters in violence and masculinity. They kept strings of mistresses paid for with embezzled public funds, as seen for example in *Xala*, a novel by Sembène Ousmane. Polygyny, already part of African culture, ran galore. And women, particularly professional women, accepted to be "kept" by powerful and influential men in society often called "Big Men" for the advantages they got from the association: personal freedom to engage in chosen enterprises and professions. Even today, the practice continues. How else can one explain that today in Senegal, despite the woes of women in polygynist homes, polygyny has about doubled in frequency rather than declined?[2] In fact, polygynist males and their concubines seem to be quite lucid about what they do. In the diaspora, Laferrière of Haitian origin has explored how racism has feminized African and diaspora men, for sometimes they do not mind being "kept" like mistresses by Western women, thanks to the economic and sexual advantages they reap from such relationships.

Finally, in postmodern and global times, from the 1990s to the present, Africa is opening up to gender and sexuality studies. Women's Studies programs admit women and men alike. Male nurses are no longer an aberration, after all the medicine men of yesteryears were almost always male. Literary writers like Tess Onwueme in *The Headless Body*, and *Tell It To Women: An Epic Drama for Women*, Ken Bugul in *The Abandoned Baobab*, prolific Promise Okekwe in her numerous novels, and other second-wave women creative writers are exploring alternative sexualities and writing about them, even lesbianism and homosexuality, in long and short fiction. Furthermore, filmmakers are beginning to address homosexuality in Africa. Critics are even questioning heterosexuality as the norm, given the rereading of scholars like Sigmund Freud who held that all human beings are inherently homoerotic, and that conditions of economy, history and culture promote the tendencies of homosexuality, and actualize them into reality (Azodo 2004). Other theorists, who happen not to have been documented as big philosophers, also posit that gender and sexuality are inherently fluid and shifting constructs, for nothing is proper or the norm about them. For instance, in some cultures in the world cold hemispheres, a man could offer his wife to a houseguest on a visit, in recognition of their closeness and friendship. By the same token, among the Igbo of Nigeria and some cultures in Southern Africa, a host could kill his dearest friend for going to bed with his wife in similar circumstances. What is more, the notion of family is being redefined, as groups of people form new alliances based on business, religion, and other interests. Indeed, colonial ideas of eroticism are changing and women gaze at men as much as men gaze at women. The myth of the super libido of the black male is also being challenged.

Indeed, there is a certain intersection of race, sex, gender, and power that this anthology intends to explore.

Notes

1. Amadiume states in *African Matriarchal Traditions: The Case of Igbo Societies*, 1995 (1987: 29):

    > Two examples of situations in which women played roles ideally or normally occupied by men, that is, what I have called male roles, in indigenous Nnobi society, for example, were "male daughters," daughters who have been accorded the status of sons to enable them to continue their father's line of descent, and "female husbands," women who married other women. In either role, women acted as family heads. The Igbo word for family head is the genderless expression *di-bu-uno*. The genderless *di* is a prefix word, which means specialist in or expert at or master of something. Therefore, *dibuno* means one in a master relationship to a household and those who live in the house. As this word is genderless, a woman in this position is referred to as *dibuno* in the same term as a man in this position would be called. A husband was simply *di*, that is, one in a master relationship to others, whereas in English, because of rigid gender construction, a female head would be referred to as mistress and a male head as a master. In indigenous Nnobi society and culture, there was one head or master of a household at a time, and "male daughters" and "female husbands" were called by the same term, whose English translation would be master. Some women were therefore masters to other people, who included men and women.

2. Ada Uzoamaka Azodo. "Interview with Aminata Sow Fall." March 14, 2005. In: Critical Essays on Aminata Sow Fall. Unpublished Scholarly Anthology. Trenton, N. J.: Africa World Press (forthcoming 2007).

Works Cited

Achebe, Chinua. *Things Fall Apart*. London: Heinemann, 1958.

Aidoo, Ama Ata. *Our Sister Killjoy*. London: Longman, 1977.

—. *An Angry Letter in January*. London: Coventry /Sydney / Aarhus: Dangaroo Press, 1992.

Amadiume, Ifi. *Male Daughters and Female Husbands: Gender and Sex in an African Society*. London: Zed Press, 1987.

Azodo, Ada Uzoamaka. "Ken Bugul's *Le Baobab fou*: A Female Story about a Female Body." In: *New Writing in African Literature. African Literature* Today, Vol. 24, 2004: 77-90.

Bâ, Mariama. *So Long a Letter*. (Trans. Modupé Bodé-Thomas). Ibadan and London: Heinemann, 1980.

Bugul, Ken. *Le Baobab fou*. Dakar: Les Nouvelles Éditions Africaines, 1983.

—. *The Abandoned Baobab* (Translated by Marjorie de Jager): Chicago: Lawrence Hill Books, 1991.

Emecheta, Buchi. *Kehinde*. London: Heinemann, 1994.

Mikell, Gwendolyn. *African Feminism: The Politics of Survival in Sub-Saharan Africa*. Philadelphia: University of Pennsylvania, 1997.

Nnolim, Charles. "A House Divided: Feminism in African Literature." In: *Feminism in African Literature: Essays on Criticism*. Ed. Helen Chukwuma. Port Harcourt: Pearl Publishers, 2003: 252-263.

Nwapa, Flora. *Never Again*. Enugu: Nwamife Publishers, 1975: rpt. Trenton: N.J: Africa World Press, 1992.

—. *One is Enough*. *Enugu*: Tana Press, 1981; rpt. Trenton: N.J: Africa World Press, 1992.

—. *Women Are Different*. *Enugu*: Tana Press, 1981; rpt. Trenton: N.J: Africa World Press, 1992.

Onwueme, Osonye Tess. *Tell It To Women: An Epic Drama for Women*. Detroit: Wayne State University Press, 1997.

—. *The Missing Face* (revised edition). New York: African Heritage Press, Ltd. in affiliation with the African Books Collective, Oxford, United Kingdom, 2002.

Sembène Ousmane. *Xala*. (Translated by Clive Wake). Westport, CT.: Lawrence Hill and Co., 1983.

Sow Fall, Aminata. *Le Revenant*. Dakar: Les Nouvelles Éditions Africaines, 1976.

PART ONE

SOCIAL AND HISTORICAL TRANSFORMATIONS OF GENDER AND SEXUALITY

Gender and Sex in the Political Economy of Postcolonial Discourse

Chapter 1

"What Kind of Woman Are You, A'isha?" Misogyny and Islam in Ibrahim Tahir's *The Last Imam*

Erica Hoagland

The opposition between self and community/society is, I would suggest, a western construction, but one which we often use in orientalist ways, assuming that white western women are individuals with personalities and a sense of their rights, while third world women abroad or at home, are members of the community, connected to society through roles and responsibilities, lacking 'desire'. . .

—Chilla Bulbeck, *Re-Orienting Western Feminisms: Women's Diversity in a Postcolonial World,* 58)

The Koran, and not the wisdom of men, is presented in this novel as the final arbiter. One can thus understand the power that those who have mastered its interpretation wield in Ibrahim Tahir's text.

—Ahmed Bangura, *Islam and the West African Novel: The Politics of Representation,* 124-125

In 1984, Nigerian writer Ibrahim Tahir published his novel *The Last Imam,* which tells the tale of a flawed village Imam at the turn of the nineteenth century. Four years later, Salman Rushdie's much bally-hoed novel *The Satanic Verses* began its polarizing journey, a journey it continues to this day, though without, perhaps, the same level of intensity that accompanied it when the Ayatollah Khomeini announced his *fatwa* against Rushdie on Valentine's Day, 1989. Though Tahir's writing does not engage in the linguistic gymnastics characteristic of Rushdie's writing, his first (and so far, only) novel is a complex and rich look at Islamic fundamentalism, accommodation, village life and village politics, and the sexual politics of a polygamous household.

Unfortunately, Tahir's novel has received scant attention from literary critics, particularly in the West, which has made an Islamic avatar out of Rushdie, to the detriment of talented Islamic writers like Tahir. *The Last Imam* is perhaps "doomed," if not to simple obscurity in the West, then to be seen as little more than a "village novel." Its "local" rather than global and cosmopolitan viewpoint, and Tahir's commitment to Islamic thought, may alienate Western readers, the very audience Tahir's novel most needs to reach. Still, how might a Western audience or critic be able to successfully navigate a text imbued with a pervasive

"Islamic ethos"(Bangura 186) without some familiarity with the Islamic faith and Islam's history? In other words, can a Western audience understand Tahir's text and the faith traditions of which it is largely comprised, without relegating the text to a mere fundamentalist and, therefore, backward rant? I would argue that a Western audience could; Tahir's extensive use of Koranic injunctions is not only "reverential," as Bangura notes, but also structured in such a way that a Western audience may access the idea/ideology, which permeates *The Last Imam*. Nonetheless, why write to a Western audience? Tahir's novel is not solely intended for a Western audience, but rather forms part of not only a reformist project that seeks to (re) institute Islamic orthodoxy in West Africa. It is a novel that in its examination of orthodoxy as located in the figure of Imam Alhaji Usman addresses the hypocrisy of orthodox Islam's central proponent in the text, the Imam himself, calling into question strict adherence to dogma. Where Rushdie's *The Satanic Verses* is considered by some as controversial and by others as not only controversial but blasphemous into the bargain, because Rushdie challenges the authority of the Koran as the literal and unadulterated word of God, Tahir's *The Last Imam*, on the other hand, is not seen as controversial, despite its own challenges. Instead, it is dismissed by critics as fundamentalist and totalitarian. Viewed within a monolithic context, *The Last Imam* is stripped of its potency.

Part of the analysis of Tahir's text must address the tension between authority and the word, and authority from the Word. For Ahmed Sheikh Bangura, the Koran " . . . is the final arbiter" in Tahir's text; those " . . . who have mastered its interpretation" wield the power, and while this refers most directly to the Imam and his manipulation of the Koran, Bangura's own privileging of his position as an "insider," particularly as he critiques "outsiders" (Westerners) and their interpretations and usage of Koranic verse, rather emphatically cancels out the majority of the West and its critics (125). Nonetheless, " . . . disentitling white women (or white men) from speaking about the other is likely to produce a discourse from below which is just as exclusivist, provincial, and discriminatory in its suppressions and repressions as the master discourses of colonialism and elitism" (Alcoff qtd. in Bulbeck 208).

Although I will respond to Ahmed Bangura's reading of *The Last Imam* and the suppositions that have shaped that reading, I will focus on the potential misogyny of the text and where or to whom this misogyny may be traced. In addition, this chapter focuses on the other "domestic saga" of Tahir's novel – the Imam's relationship with his wives, with a particular focus on the character of A'isha, the Imam's first wife – and a re-reading of the Imam's character taking into account the embedded conflict between his faith and his family.

WOMEN, ISLAM, AND NIGERIA

The Quran treats a woman's identity from the point of view of a jealous husband. She cannot appear attractive outside the home, she

cannot have friends beyond the family circle, and she cannot have a
life free from the supervision of her husband.

—Barbara Callaway & Lucy Creevey, *The Heritage of Islam:
Women, Religion, & Politics in West Africa*, 30

According to Barbara Callaway and Lucy Creevey, "Islam was . . . spread not
only as a religion but . . . as a civilization" in Africa, and while "[m]any features
of pre-Islamic customs would survive . . . there were major changes in peoples'
lives and expectations" (9). Not surprisingly, the lives of African women changed
significantly as Islam created a space for itself in Africa, and this is especially true
of the women in northern Nigeria. The Hausa people first experienced Islam
through Muslim traders who began arriving in northern Nigeria in the twelfth
century. Even after Islam began to spread there, women of the ruling classes continued to enjoy considerable autonomy and influence. However, "[b] y the six-
teenth century, the erosion of the standing, influence, and authority of women
titleholders coincided with the growing influence of Islam" (12). Two centuries
later, *Mallams* (Muslim teachers) ". . . began to voice their disapproval of that
part of the surrounding Hausa culture that was not purely Islamic, particularly
the practice of Bori [a state religion led by ruling class women], the 'nakedness
of women,' and the mixing of the sexes in public in defiance of Islamic law"
(Bivar and Hiskett in Callaway and Creevey 12).

By the early nineteenth century, Nigeria experienced the profound *jihad* led
by Fulani Islamic reformer Shehu Usman dan Fodio. The *jihad* was a response to
growing unrest with the incompatibility of Muslim practice with Hausa tradition. Dan Fodio's *jihad*, which lasted from 1804 until 1812, had a profound
impact on Hausa women. The reformer ". . . saw the authority royal women held
over other women as one of the fundamental manifestations of the un-Islamic
nature of Hausa society" (Hiskett, 67; Callaway and Creevey, 13). Thus, while
ruling-class women suffered the loss of status and title, common Hausa women
were encouraged to learn Arabic in order to read the Koran and understand
the rights afforded them in Islam. By the early twentieth century, the "Indirect
Rule" policy of imperialist Britain served to consolidate and strengthen Islam's
position in northern Nigeria by assuring local/traditional authority, which in
turned assured Islamic law in the Hausa states, as did the policy's cutting off
of Christian missionaries from the area. This allowed, "Islam [to become] ever
more deeply entrenched, and Usman dan Fodio's legacy of ideas remain[s] part
of the ethos of the area to the present time" (Callaway and Creevey, 14). This
"ethos," as we shall see, pervades Tahir's text and his novel's "hero" (and descen-
dant of dan Fodio), Alhaji Usman.

Before turning my attention to Tahir's text, I would like to briefly examine
how Islam affects the lives of its women followers in Nigeria. It is not my intention, however, to enter into the complex and formidable debate about women's
rights in Islam here; rather, I offer a cross-section of interpretations and view-

points intended to put into context my own study of Tahir's text, and in particular, the women of his story.

Barbara Callaway and Lucy Creevey, in their study of Islam in West Africa, separate conservative northern Nigeria from the more liberal Senegal. While seclusion is more common in northern Nigeria, modest behavior and dress are considered appropriate in Senegal. Callaway and Creevey are quick to point out, however, that ". . . Islam, through its teachings and the cultural norms imported from North Africa and the Middle East, reinforced the patriarchal elements already present in society" (188). Thus the more conservative nature of Hausa culture is at least partly responsible for the considerable limits it imposes upon the autonomy of its women. Pre-Islamic society in Nigeria also did little to protect ". . . those rights women did possess": "Thus, men that had sufficient resources could marry as many women as they liked, and nothing except the power of an earlier wife's family could force the husband to treat her as well as he treated more recent wives" (33). Essentially, women were at the mercy of men, a contention that has been transferred to Islamic practice in Western thought. Arguing against the supposition that Islamic women in Nigeria are powerless, Callaway and Creevey note that it was Islam that ". . . provide[d] a bill of rights" for women, giving them the right to their dowry or bride price, inheritance rights, and the right to the money they had earned (33). "Islam also gave women family rights they had not had, limiting the number of wives a man might take, giving a mother rights to her children, and obligating the father to maintain them even if under the mother's care" (33).

Barbara Cooper notes that "[b] y the time of the British conquest of the caliphate territories in the first decade of the twentieth century, to be a proper Muslim woman meant ideally to be secluded and veiled, although such was not possible for all women, and was certainly not possible for the slave population" (21). The ". . . highly tolerant and syncretic variety of Islam [that] had prevailed throughout the Hausa kingdoms" fell under the force of dan Fodio's *jihad*, which made way for a more orthodox vision of Islam in Nigeria. Like Callaway and Cooper, Cooper also finds that ". . . that war against many of the practices that the jihadists found most objectionable was fought on the domestic front, for women were in a sense the guardians of the syncretic practices through which the urban Islam of the court could be reconciled with the pre-Islamic beliefs of the farmers of the region" (26).

Like other Muslim women who are secluded, Hausa women ". . . live in a world of women" (Callaway & Creevey 35), and their most intimate relationships tend to be with friends, family members, and, in cases of plural marriage, other wives (37). Their lives are defined by their family and their service to their family, and any education a Muslim woman receives focuses largely, if not completely, on the Quran, which, along with the *hadith*, or sayings, attributed to the prophet Mohammed, outlines the expected behavior for women (and men). "In theory, women in seclusion are wholly dependent on their husbands for food, shelter, and support, but, in fact, they are very active economically" (Callaway

& Creevey 96). Secluded women do engage in economic activities they may pursue within the home, such as preparing foodstuffs, but most Hausa women do not participate in the public wage sector. Callaway and Creevey conclude that the deeply entrenched position of Islam and patriarchy amongst the Hausa is largely the result of *when* northern Nigeria began to convert to Islam. Further, "[i]n societies that converted later and were located where contact with the West was greater," such as Senegal, ". . . the degree of domination and distortion of preexisting traditions is less than it is in Hausaland" (188).

While Islam has assured women certain rights, ". . . the fact remains," note Callaway and Creevey, "that Muslim law, based on the *Sharia*, does discriminate against women more than do current Western codes" (183). In Tahir's novel, these rights, or what may be perceived as a lack thereof, as well as the conflict between African tradition and Islamic practice, provide a subtle subtext in the case of the former, and, in the case of the latter, comprise a significant portion of the text's thematic tension. I now turn my attention to the novel itself.

A'ISHA AND THE IMAM

Ahmed Sheikh Bangura argues that Ibrahim Tahir's novel *The Last Imam* takes as its central theme "the confrontation between Islam and local custom," in which "the intractable conflict between Islam and the pre-Islamic Fulani-Hausa cultures of Muslim Northern Nigeria" is played out against the familial and religious struggles of Alhaji Usman, the Imam of Bauchi (107, 108). This focus on orthodoxy in Tahir's novel and Ahmadou Kourouma's novel *Les Soleils des Independances*, notes Bangura, works against Lemuel Johnson's contention that "the Afro-Islamic context is primarily accommodationist" (108). Though Bangura acknowledges Alhaji Usman's weaknesses and hypocrisy, the last Imam is nonetheless a "warrior of Islam," bent on eradicating the heathen traditions of Hausa-Fulani culture in order to establish a utopia based on/in puritanical Islam (180, 176). Bangura's "orthodox" reading of Tahir's novel, however, cancels out any possibility of reading the text outside the context of Islamic fundamentalism; his brief acknowledgements of the Imam's hypocrisy are little more than excuses for deeply flawed behavior and reflects Bangura's erasure of the other "domestic saga" in Tahir's text: the Imam's relationship with his wives. Bangura reads Tahir's text as a lament for Islamic orthodoxy, which must bow under the pressures of pragmatism and accommodation. Bangura's refusal to read the Imam's orthodoxy (and his flawed interpretation of Islamic practice) as responsible for the Imam's troubled family life and religious conflict reduces Tahir's novel to the level of a flat sermon, in which conflict is not so much a catalyst for meaningful revelation than a simple annoyance, a hindrance, in the quest for dogma.

Bangura's misreading of Tahir's novel is largely based on his misreading of the Imam. His acknowledgement of the Imam's flaws is shallow; the Imam is an arrogant, unbending man, who cannot be commended for facing his flaws, because he does so only superficially, canceling out the viewpoints of others.

The Imam is so caught up in being the Imam and having the last word that the man cannot see where, and more importantly, why, he has erred. For a quarter of a century, Alhaji Usman has served as the Imam of the Bauchi Empire, a position held by his family for generations. Usman is the last "true" Imam of the Empire, a "marked man of Allah" (16) whom "Allah had seized [. . .] and afflicted [. . .] with unshakeable devotion and an insatiable desire to serve his fellow men" (2). Noted in his youth for his piety, Usman, the favorite son of his father the Imam, wishes only to serve Allah, a desire that ultimately conflicts with the socio-political realities of a figure such as the Imam. Having decided to remain celibate, so that he may devote himself fully to his religious studies and his faith, Usman soon comes into conflict with his father, who would have him married. By Usman's seventeenth birthday, his father has accepted for his son the alms marriage offered by a local trader, Alhaji Bukar, to his daughter A'isha. When Usman voices his concerns that marriage will interfere with his studies, the Imam tells him that,

> . . . Women are no trouble at all. Be a good provider, a good guide, a good brother, father, everything that any human being would want to have. It isn't difficult, once that has been achieved, to get them to obey you as a husband and give you full control over your household and the freedom you need for your work. And besides, think of all the laws about the relationship between men and their wives. They are easy enough to obey, even the one about being equal in your love to all of them. (18)

It is here that Tahir introduces a central theme to his work, one that Bangura glosses over: the treatment of wives. It will be Usman's inability to adhere judiciously to the Qu'ranic injunction, that a man married to more than one wife distributes his affections equally, that will lead to discord in his household. However, Usman's failure runs deeper than that; his insistence on an orthodox lifestyle and the impossibility of that lifestyle amidst the changing colonial climate in nineteenth century Africa, coupled with his disdain for cultural traditions and superstitions, not only alienate him from the people he so wants to serve, but insure his downfall.

Usman has difficulty accepting his father's viewpoint; his father notes that it would be scandalous for the Imam's son to reject an alms marriage, reminding his son that an alms bride ". . . is the bride of Prophet Mohammad, the charity done to him" (19). His father further points out that Usman would be considered an unbeliever, if he abstained from marriage. Only after his father has cited Mohammed as an example does Usman bend, though grudgingly. He goes through with the marriage, but chooses to remain celibate within the marriage. Once again, his father confronts Usman, who tells his father that he cannot consummate the marriage in the "traditional way," a "distasteful practice" in which while the "husband was taking [the wife] . . . the girl screamed and howled and announced her pain and her entry into womanhood for all to hear" (23). What Bangura calls a "domestic saga" between Usman and his father culminates in

Usman doing as his father wishes, but not first before passing judgment on the Imam: Usman "would much prefer [his father] as the unbending man of God, who gave not an inch away to the demands of questionable loyalties. This he felt, was one occasion when his father should not have yielded an ounce of his convictions" (23). Here Tahir provides the first of many instances of the conflict between accommodation and orthodoxy. Usman cannot forgive his father accommodating a "common Hausa heathen custom," but his father does not sway; Usman thus charges off to fulfill his father's wish and prove his manhood (24).

Usman rushes into his wife's room, and A'isha, stunned at the sudden and violent appearance of her husband, backs herself into a corner, terrified. Without a word, Usman proceeds to take his wife:

> She was under him, struggling, legs beating about, arms flailing, striking his face and chest. He was hard as stone and heavy as lead. She let out a stifled scream. She bit his fingers and scratched his chest. The pain was a spur and his urge now a cascading torrent bore him on. Clothes torn into shreds and her naked body against his, soft, slender and warm, still struggling, still screaming, making him stronger. Her soft tender centre burning his loins like a block of ice, forcing him into her like a horse nervous at the brink with a burning spear thrust at its tail. She was young, raw and hard, but that one angry destructive push, a short sharp yelp of pain, and his vengeance and misdirected passion and fervour found their course. (25)

This disturbing scene, so completely overlooked by Bangura, deserves special attention, given that the relationship between Usman and A'isha is in some ways more profound than his relationship with the slave Hasana. There are several ways to read this scene. The first and most obvious reading is that of marital rape. The next morning, Usman's father confronts his son about his actions the night before: "Last night was ugly. Did you go mad?" (25). Usman, already slightly disgusted with self, nonetheless arrogantly replies to his father that he intended his actions to be "ugly," if only to prove his father's error in accommodating the heathen custom at the expense of Usman's faith. His father points out that A'isha's cries were not ordinary and tells his son that he must have injured her. Indeed, Usman's attack left A'isha "stuck to the palm leaf mat, caught there by the dry cake of her own blood" (28). Usman "could see now that her struggles and her cries the night before were not the same as the ritual cries of the typical Hausa bride obeying the conventions of her own people" (28). A'isha leaves for a seven-day convalescence during which Usman is wracked with regret. A'isha's excessive bleeding and painful cries suggest that she may have undergone infibulations, known to exist in Northern Nigeria (Lightfoot-Kramer 31).

Tahir introduces information that leads to yet another reading of Usman's attack on A'isha, one in which Usman is held with respect and admiration for his "manliness": "It was with some relief [. . . that] he discovered that the new status he had acquired had some undisclosed value, which conferred on him even greater uniqueness and esteem in the eyes of the townspeople. When the old men looked at him at school the whites of their eyes smiled at him, a mock indulgent smile in which he could detect their appreciation, envy and some sort of undeserved respect, the type which people usually thought they should hide" (28-29). This rather misogynistic response to Usman's violent attack on his own wife may perhaps be interpreted as a cultural one (and a cultural response not, it must be stressed, endemic to African or Islamic cultures alone) in which violence upon women is accepted as patriarchal right. Yet another reading extends the conflict between African traditions and Islamic doctrine; not only does Usman's disagreement with his father's accommodation reflect this conflict, but so too does the acceptance of Usman's actions by a supposedly Muslim community. If this reading is appropriate, then it may be assumed that Tahir is, as Bangura rightly notes, highly condemnatory of African traditions. This condemnation serves to support Islamic correctness, but Tahir makes this problematic through the figure of the hypocritical Usman and his own revered father, whom Usman will learn later, has committed the same kind of "sins."

Perhaps, even more difficult to address are the explicit scenes Tahir incorporates into his text. Driven by lust and pity in his relationship with A'isha, which is largely sexual and not also a spiritual one, Usman's couplings with his first wife are detailed and disturbing for what they suggest of the Imam's unconscious misogyny. If we are to read Tahir at all in the figure of the Imam, such a reading becomes quite problematic in its implications. One can read Tahir as commenting against the hypocrisy of the Imam, and more specifically, against unbending orthodoxy, even in the face of his support of it. However, if the Imam at all embodies Tahir's own ideologies, then it would seem that Tahir approves of the Imam's treatment of his wives. This, in turn, would suggest perverse authorial intentions on the part of Tahir, a reading, which one does not wholly endorse, yet cannot completely deny. Furthermore, what is the purpose of the inclusion of such descriptions? Are we to infer, for example, that the Imam is obsessed with sex and takes more delight in such acts than a pious man should? Or are these descriptions evidence of a latent misogyny in the text itself in which A'isha, in particular, is the fulcrum for all of the Imam's troubles, including his lust, but, more importantly, his continual crisis of faith?

In order to address these questions, it is necessary to consider the Imam's relationship with A'isha, but also his other marriages, as well as his relationship with Hasana, the mother of his favorite son, Kasim. With A'isha's return, Usman indulges in his sexual relationship with his forgiving first wife, and,

> [i]n this eager state he acquired after a year, a second wife and a third and fourth. The last two brought with them two concubines, one each from the descendants of the slaves of their families. He lived with them all but kept his distance in the daytime, enjoying his power over them. Deep inside he was still worried about his loss of passion in his faith. To allay the suspicions of his father and other men he felt compelled to make vigorous demonstrations of

his enthusiasm in prayer at the mosque and in the lessons at school. The ploy worked and by the time he was thirty-five and the father of twelve children no one in Bauchi doubted him and his authority as a great man of learning and devotion in Islam. (30)

Here Tahir obviously questions Usman's behavior, calling his actions a "ploy" and noting, rather sardonically, Usman's "vigorous demonstrations" of faith. Tahir's emphasis on Usman's religious behavior makes it easy to overlook the connection he implicitly draws between Usman's loss of faith and his relationship with his wives. Usman enjoys his power over his wives and concubines; he flirts in and out of their lives at nighttime, when he takes his pleasure with them. The crisis of faith, first precipitated in his rape of A'isha, then extended in his multiple marriages and taking of concubines, is then further heightened by his obsession with the slave girl Hasana, who occupies his thoughts even during his hajj with his father.

Usman's relationship with Hasana is as dominant in the text as his relationship with A'isha, and, for that matter, his son with Hasana, Kasim. The "love triangle" that exists, first between Usman, Hasana, and Kasim, and then later, when Usman tries to resuscitate that triangle with A'isha in the place of Hasana, is set up by Tahir in direct opposition to the orthodoxy, which both he and Usman champion. Where Usman tries again and again to reconcile the two, Tahir realizes that the two are not commensurate, at least not in the unbending way that Usman would have it. While Tahir's text may not argue for accommodation, it is not as monolithic as Ahmed Bangura argues. The reform project into which Bangura places Tahir's text seems largely ignorant of colonial, postcolonial, and global realities.

Hasana presents an even more formidable threat to the Imam's faith than A'isha or any of his other wives and concubines. Where he is pulled to A'isha by pity, he is pulled to Hasana by love. As with his description of A'isha, Tahir objectifies Hasana: "Eyes as beautiful as the eyes of the Sahara gazelle, their whites like the milk moon in the blue Sahara sky. Her limbs, long, lissome, chocolate-brown" (31). Usman equates his love for Hasana with his rekindled religious passion (brought about by his trip to Mecca). Hasana and his faith become "inseparable" (31). It may be argued that Usman did not fulfill his pilgrimage, because " . . . her image [. . .] pursue[d] him and [. . .] he found himself wishing the work of the *hajj* would be over quickly, so he could go home to her. He saw her in his mind through all the acts of the pilgrimage" (31-32). Upon returning from Mecca, Usman resolves to make Hasana his concubine. He sends her gifts reflecting his intent and then two weeks after his return " . . . he said a prayer to consecrate their union, not because it was necessary but because it made it much more glorified . . . she resisted and he was afraid to do her harm, but the fear incinerated his desire. Tenderly he took her and she screamed" (34). Once again, Usman is guilty of rape, yet there is no guilt that accompanies this particular rape as it did with his attack on A'isha. Instead, Hasana is ". . . the Fatima to his Mohammed and the gates of Heaven were open to receive them"

(35). He feels that Hasana " . . . should have happened to him before A'isha and the others. What he took in A'isha had given him doubts, had robbed him, even though for only a time. In her it increased it. In her he found Allah and his work and in all he did from that night on he excelled himself" (35). It should be noted that it is while on pilgrimage that Usman's father dies, and Usman, already deeply conflicted, becomes the next Imam. He revels in his new authority and power and he extends this power to his own household, enforcing strict purdah upon his wives and ever watchful of his reputation amongst the Muslim community. The Imam is not only blinded by love and lust for Hasana, but blinded by power and status. Nonetheless, it is upon the shoulders of Usman's wives and concubines that the blame for his fall will be placed. And though the Imam appears to acknowledge this conflict, he does not see that the inherent conflict is in himself, not in the temptations offered in the "nubile" body of Hasana or his other women.

For thirteen years, the Imam enjoys "his Paradise on Earth" until Hasana dies (35). The Imam is inconsolable, promising his beloved that he will look after and protect their son. In his grief, A'isha takes care of him, reminding him of his place as the Imam. The Imam's indulgence in his relationship with Hasana is neither lost on his other wives and concubines, nor on the community. A'isha points out to Usman that "[w]hen Allah took [Hasana] away, it was being said in the town, [that] he did so only to save the Alhaji from himself, from straying too far from the right path" (38). Connecting once more the Imam's dereliction of his religious duties to his personal life, and particularly to his relationship with his women, Tahir continues to create a problematic interpretive space in which the Imam's culpability in his own downfall is underscored by Tahir's rather antagonistic rendering of the women and their influence on Usman. Still, Tahir does not let the reader escape so easily, because Tahir as both a harpy and a pitiable creature draws A'isha, who bears the brunt of the Imam's hostility. A'isha is self-serving like the Imam, but she is also practical, a characteristic almost wholly alien to the Imam. Her pragmatic approach conflicts with the Imam's orthodoxy and it is to his own detriment later in the story that he chooses to ignore her warnings about his unbending will.

A quarter of the way through the text, A'isha steps forward as a major player in Tahir's story. After A'isha convinces him to move on, the Imam once more throws himself into his religious duties, lavishing affection on Kasim, but continues to indulge in his grief. The Imam is only titular head of the household; A'isha "arranged the purchase of the food, sending alms to the poor, sending representatives to the funerals in the town and when the time came she even paid the annual cattle tax" (38). Usman makes A'isha the stepmother of his son, but this arrangement fails; Kasim greatly dislikes A'isha; in fact, "she and that horrible feeling of the presence of something deadly which her company had always given him" serve to further intensify his hostility toward her while at the same time calling into question whether A'isha is at all a likeable character (65). Indeed, Tahir devotes a considerable portion of his text to the animosity between the two. A'isha's disappointment and anger at being refused by Kasim as his step-mother leads to a war of the wills in which Kasim is often the loser; his misbehavior and disrespect towards A'isha and the other women earn him daily beatings from his father. In fact, the beatings become so regular and fathers in the town begin to use Kasim as a warning to their children to mind their own behavior. The hostilities reach a breaking-point when A'isha accuses Kasim of stealing the money for the corn grinder and Kasim, in turn, accuses A'isha of lying and throws a stone at her, striking her on the forehead. Rather than endure his father's anger and beating, Kasim runs away. This breaking from the father marks a similar, though more dramatic breaking between father and son first begun with Usman's breaking from his own father. Kasim's departure further exaggerates the Imam's crisis of faith, while also undermining his authority within the community that places the blame for Kasim's departure on the Imam, as well as on his wives.

It is at this point in the novel that Tahir takes an interesting turn, devoting an entire chapter to A'isha. Like ". . . most Hausa girls and youths of her background she was a Muslim without getting involved with that side of her faith which demanded the total submission of her person. She preferred, instead of the pious talk, to think of the person she would marry as someone she herself had chosen, someone who had spoken tender words in her ear, someone of whom she could sing unashamedly in the marketplace" (48). Yet A'isha is " . . . forever at [the Imam's] heels," suggesting that A'isha has, at the very least, submitted to (or rather, become obsessed with) her position as the Imam's first wife, demanding the attention and respect due to the first wife of such an individual, both by the Imam himself and by the other wives and concubines (52). Angered by her parents' decision to give her away in an alms marriage, A'isha is only assuaged by the revelation that she is marrying the Imam's son and not a beggar, a common match in an alms marriage. The parallel between Tahir's A'isha and the historical A'isha, who was given to the Prophet by her father in an alms marriage, is extended by Tahir's reconfiguring of the name of Abu Bakr (the historical A'isha's father) into Alhaji Bakur. Like the historical A'isha, Tahir's A'isha is childless; where the historical A'isha is cited for her interpretation and promulgation of hadith or sayings of the prophet, Tahir's A'isha guides the Imam through the tangles created by the conflict between the Islamic faith and African tradition. Unlike the historical A'isha, as we have seen, who is largely portrayed in a positive context, Tahir creates a more dynamic A'isha, whose flaws and desires make her a more realistic figure.

Recalling the night Alhaji "pounced on her (A'isha) like a wild animal" and her perception of her relationship with him (Alhaji), Tahir the author notes:

> That was a night of terror she could never forget; and also of pain,
> a kind of pain, which had stuck in her mind like a facet of her own
> nature, something from which, she could not escape, one which had
> made her incapable of thinking about herself without thinking of
> Alhaji Usman. She only had to hear his voice or the sound of his

slippers or for him to touch her and she would feel shock waves travelling through her entire body. Her loins would grow suddenly hot and restless and the cavity of her chest would become deep like a bottomless desert well into which her heart sank with the compulsive urge of a pebble dropping down a hillside. And after the pain there were the nights he lay with her and inserted himself into her, deep as the date palm root sinks in the earth and tight as the tooth fits into the gum, moving in and out, up and down, side up, side down, until she felt him sending her into such depths of ecstasy that the rest of her body disappeared and consciousness was one hold of tenderness between her legs where their lives touched. This she had always desired and wanted from him, and had subjected her to him until she grew to feel that she deserved him for herself alone. (50-51)

Tahir does several interesting things here. First, he continues to write A'isha as a sexual object, but in writing from A'isha's "perspective" he complicates such a one-sided reading by introducing what could be read as a codependent and even masochistic element to A'isha's relationship with the Imam. Unable to think of herself outside of her connection to her husband, A'isha would appear to be little more than a clingy and submissive wife. Alhaji would thus benefit from such a dynamic with A'isha and his other wives, and indeed, he "enjoy[s] his power over them" (30). However, the Imam's relationship with his wives, particularly when he begins his relationship with the slave-girl Hasana, is vexed at the very least, and becomes volatile when the Imam refuses to accept Hasana's death and continues to ignore his responsibilities to his wives and concubines. Returning to A'isha, Western readers in particular would read her as a tragic figure because she identifies and defines herself through her man and her ability to please him: " ... the first year of her marriage, the one year she regarded as the happiest if not the only happy one in her marriage [...] [s]he remembered the moments in that year when Alhaji Usman would stand by the door wanting something [...] and she had only to stretch her hand towards the banking in that room before the desired article was his. Then, she would watch his smile of satisfaction, and swell with pride..." (46). In that first year A'isha had Alhaji all to herself; shortly after that first year, Alhaji begins to collect more wives and concubines, forcing A'isha into the background. Rather than submit, A'isha, with some relish, demands the respect and deference expected by a first wife from the other wives. In return, the other wives and concubines treat A'isha with kid gloves, careful not to incur her wrath, but not so submissive that they do not, from time to time, challenge her authority, as is the case when A'isha is caught lying about Kasim and the money for the corn. The growing alienation in her relationship with Alhaji, particularly after he becomes the Imam and takes on added responsibilities, leads to A'isha's defensive posturing and jealousy. A'isha's codependency is also marked by masochism, which again renders her a sexual object. The violence of her first coupling with Alhaji creates a perverse association with her husband that extends to her relationship with him and the desire she feels for him. A'isha wishes to be "tamed" by the Imam, but with the addition of other women to the household, the Imam no longer has the time to devote to this task, and when Hasana enters his life he no longer has the interest. The theme of "taming A'isha" is an important one, particularly as the struggle for dominance is central to the Imam's relationship with his first wife.

A'isha's "suffering" and possessiveness, her command over the household and the other women, are highlighted by her failure as a woman: she has borne the Imam no children who have lived, unlike his other wives and concubines. It is possible to read A'isha's inability to have children who survive childbirth in two ways, both of which lay the blame not on A'isha, but the Imam. The physical brutality of A'isha's first sexual encounter with Alhaji may have damaged her reproductive system. The Imam's coldness to his first wife (and his other wives), and his veneration of his relationship with Hasana may also have contributed to A'isha's problem. A'isha is deeply scarred by her inability to bear healthy, live children; instead of blaming Alhaji or anyone (or anything) else, she blames herself: " . . . she had always feared that she was in some way responsible for their deaths; not that she could remember anything she had done which could have directly killed them, but that there was, perhaps, something bad about her body and her womb which denied her babies the life she believed all mothers should be capable of giving their young" (172).

Twice Tahir has hinted at "something bad" in A'isha. In the citation above, Kasim notes a "deadly presence" when A'isha is near. Her attempt to cast aspersions on Kasim's character in order to bring the Imam closer to her only succeeds in making the reader suspicious of her motivations. Her blasphemy as she wrestles with Hasana's hold over the Imam, coupled with the ambivalence of A'isha's "submission," casts doubt on her as a Muslim. Still, early in the story, Tahir tells the reader that A'isha " . . . like most Hausa girls and youths of her background [. . .] was a Muslim without getting involved with that side of her faith, which demanded the total submission of her person" (48). In other words, A'isha is not a "true Muslim." But she is like "most" Hausa, who practice accommodation of African tradition and culture within their faith.

Her submission comes at a time when the Imam is most inflexible; he refuses to "bend" regarding his sermon on marriage and illegitimacy (see below), and he also refuses to bring Kasim home, despite A'isha's pleadings and the grumblings of the village. Obsessed with discovering the ". . . secret of [Hasana's] hold on the Alhaji," A'isha "[i]n desperation" had "fallen back on Allah" (173). Upon receiving no response from Allah, A'isha calls upon "her inner resources" and she is determined to win the Imam back "with or without Allah" (174). The morning after she makes this determination, A'isha wakes up ". . . fully resolved and completely faith-free" (174). Twenty pages later, A'isha tells the Imam that she has "learned submission," but submission to what (193)? A'isha does not submit to the will of Allah, but rather to her situation. She realizes that she cannot have the Imam as she once did, nor can she compete with the memory of Hasana. She submits in order to save the Imam; rather than continue her struggle, she asks the

Imam to bring Kasim home, because the village people ". . . say Allah does not forgive any man for treating an orphan like him so badly and because of that Allah took away your head and made you say the things you said in your last sermon. The things which make the people hate you now" (193). The Imam then accuses A'isha of blasphemy. Islam views blasphemy as "contemptuous, irreverent speech or sacrilegious acts, not only about God, but also about the Prophet Muhammad and all other prophets, and the members of these prophets' households, as well as the holy scriptures, including the Qur'an, and other things that are of a similar religious nature (read sacred)" (Ali, http://muslim-canada.org/aposn06. htm). While A'isha is advising the Imam to lie about his recent behavior, which is sinful in itself, the nature of the lie suggests blasphemy. In essence, the lie suggests that Allah deliberately misled one of his servants. However, the Imam's status as a holy man entrusted with the spiritual well being and growth of his community, who leads the prayers and preaches sermons in the mosque, makes the lie even more blasphemous. Ostensibly, A'isha's resolution to win back the Imam with or without the help of Allah makes her an apostate, which Islam defines as one who has turned away from the faith after being a Muslim (Ali, http://muslim-canada. org/aposno4.htm). Ultimately, Tahir leaves the reader with only the judgment of the Imam, who views A'isha as a blasphemer, but the Imam's own flaws and weaknesses should, at the very least, render such a judgment suspect.

Tahir has posed quite a challenge to the reader in his construction of A'isha. It is difficult to determine whether Tahir feels sorry for the Imam's beleaguered first wife or whether he views her as a shrew. Certainly she differs significantly from other representations of her namesake, the historical A'isha, who ". . . serves as a role model for the modern Arab woman," and, it may be assumed, Muslim women throughout the world (Elsadda, 37). The beloved wife of the prophet, A'isha, was married to Mohammed for nine years. After his death, she became a respected transmitter of *hadith*, dying some forty-eight years after the death of the prophet, at the age of sixty-six (Elsadda, 42). Belonging to the ". . . 'ideal age' in Islamic consciousness" (43), and given her status as a role model, it would seem that representations of the historical A'isha would support the orthodox Islamic vision of the dutiful wife and mother. However, A'isha is written as an active political figure by Nabia Abbott according to Elsadda, and a ". . . tremendous influence on the intellectual and social life" of her time by Zahia Qadura (45). Elsadda notes that 'Abbas Mahmoud Al-'Aqad's biography of A'isha ". . . reads as a pretext for stating Al-'Aqad's views on current women's issues," which Elsadda views as certainly conservative and "almost misogynist" (47). In Al-'Aqad's biography A'isha is a coy, vain, and jealous creature, who, had she stayed in the home, would have been an "exemplary figure" (48). Thus "Al-'Aqad's biography of A'isha is less about the outstanding attributes of A'isha than about her historical mistake in crossing the boundaries that separate the private and the public spheres" (Elsadda, 50).

The biography of A'isha and Mohammed's other wives written by A'isha 'Abdel-Rahman provides an interesting parallel to Tahir's A'isha. 'Abdel-

Rahman, Elsadda notes, alludes to A'isha's ". . . 'overwhelming jealousy' and 'her irresistible desire to monopolize his affections'" (52). In effect, 'Abdel-Rahman "domesticates" A'isha by ". . . understat[ing] A'isha's role as jurist and interpreter of religious texts," (52) and thus "[h]er marginalization of the political and interpretive role of A'isha indirectly affirms the dominant ideas about women's traditional roles in Islamic societies" (53). Elsadda points out that Fatima Mernissi takes a feminist approach and ". . . emphasizes A'isha's political role and her distinguished status as a transmitter of Hadith" (54).

Elsadda points out that "[b]iographies of women have historically been used as prescriptive texts for determining the role women should play in a given society" (59), and certainly the examples she provides in her review article show how biographies of A'isha have both reinforced and challenged traditional Islamic viewpoints on women as Arab countries have attempted to address women's roles within shifting political and economic climates. But, what can one make of Tahir's A'isha? As already noted, she is given to the Imam in an alms marriage, as the historical A'isha was given to Mohammed. The fathers of both A'ishas share similar names: the historical A'isha's father was Abu Bakr, a close companion of the prophet; the father of Tahir's A'isha is named Alhaji Bukar. Like the historical A'isha, Tahir's A'isha is also childless. Unlike the historical A'isha, however, Tahir's A'isha is not, and never was, the beloved of her husband.

In an admittedly loose way, Tahir's A'isha also mirrors her historical name-sake insofar as she provides her own translation (or transmission) of the Imam's "sayings" or interpretations, which act as a practical counterpoint to the Imam's increasingly desperate attempts to wrest control over his household and his people through self-serving sermons and injunctions (see my more in depth discussion below). The Imam's ban on the *gwaro* ceremony and his sermon on bastardies and marriage elicit sharp criticism from the village as well as A'isha, who tells him to "think and bend" (192), in other words, to be more conscious of his people's needs. Earlier in the story, as the Imam moves about, inconsolable in his grief over the death of Hasana, it is A'isha that will compel the Imam to take up his religious tasks once more, pointing out that

> . . . if he could not accept that Allah could take away what He had given him in the first place what good would his leadership be to the people in Bauchi? What would it sound like if it was said that Alhaji Usman, the holy man, had lost his faith because Allah had taken away the woman he loved? How could he lose all the years of hard work he had spent before Hasana? When Allah took her away, it was being said in the town, he did so only to save the Alhaji from himself, from straying too far from the right path. (Tahir 37-38)

Certainly, this may be read as self-serving on A'isha's part, this making herself ". . . available to him night and day" (37) so that the Imam ". . . became more and more dependent on A'isha for everything and she spent more and more nights in his chamber than was her due" (38). Even at moments when A'isha could be read as relatively selfless and concerned with the well-being of her husband, Tahir casts doubt on her character and motivation and suggests that she is to blame for ". . . eroding the feeling he felt for the boy [Kasim, his son with Hasana] and a gulf was steadily pushing him further and further apart from him" (39). A'isha, the "gulf" between father and son twice over, first between the Imam and his late father, and then between the Imam and his son, seems to elicit little sympathy from her creator Tahir.

Then again, Tahir's position regarding A'isha is difficult to pinpoint. He appears to sympathize with A'isha's childless condition and the desperation it evokes: after becoming Kasim's official stepmother, A'isha is overwhelmed with feelings of tenderness for the boy and a desire to recreate the love triangle that exist with Kasim, the Imam, and Hasana with A'isha taking the place of the dead concubine. But "[w]hen Kasim rejected her it was as though somebody had cut her to the bone with a war dagger and proceeded to twist the blade and the point in the wound" (53). Kasim's rejection of A'isha leads her to accuse Kasim of stealing money and thus drives a wedge between the boy and his father. The pitiable A'isha becomes a scheming and vindictive shrew, causing the Imam to ask in frustration: "What kind of woman are you, A'isha" (75)?

What kind of woman, indeed. As noted above, Tahir casts A'isha as a sexual object and a highly sexed being. She uses her body to ensnare the Imam and their intense physical intimacy is played out against the general antagonism of their relationship. Her past submission in bed has since given way to the "tyranny" of her "physical manipulations" and ability to outlast the Imam sexually (84). Once more, Tahir describes A'isha as a horse, bucking and whining under the Imam, an "unbroken colt" with "an embrace as demanding as death" (84). The "artifice" of her sexual confidence only "plung[es]" A'isha "deeper and deeper into frustrating captivity while [the Imam's] resolve to treat her like everybody else remained untouched by her wiles. And he knew that, and enjoyed her artifice, and his willing collaboration the more" (85). Here is highlighted the Qu'ranic injunction that a man must treat all of his wives equally; A'isha is at fault for her refusal to accept this and the Imam's supposed adherence to this principle. However, the Imam's domestic history has clearly shown this not to be the case and so it is not surprising, given the Imam's previous behavior with Hasana, and A'isha's powerful desire to be first in his affections, that husband and wife share equal blame for the tense environment they have created, a kind of cat and mouse game in which it is unclear who is the cat and who is the mouse.

Later in the narrative, as tensions continue to swell between the Imam and his household, and particularly with A'isha, Tahir extends his animal metaphor literally when the Imam tames the wildest horse in the village. The violence of the stallion Akawal's taming, leaving the animal "a beaten messed up heap" (144), is not unlike the violence of the Imam's initial "taming" of A'isha. Both acts make the Imam proud and the men of the village once more look approvingly at their Imam for his strength. Indeed, the Imam takes to riding Akawal on a regular basis, equating his taming of the horse to his newfound confidence in his religious authority. In fact, the two appear to be almost one and the same. However, while the Imam is successful in taming the stallion, he is never entirely successful in taming A'isha, who continues to challenge his authority.

I have already elaborated at some length the violence associated with the Imam's sexual relationships, most especially his sexual relationship with A'isha but also to some degree with Hasana. Inflamed by the fear evident in both women the first time he has sex with them, and further aroused by their pain and struggling, which again suggests that the women may have undergone some form of female genital circumcision, the Imam's misogyny is also reflected in the rather perverse association he makes between pleasure and pain, his sexual objectification of women, and the gratification he derives from his authority over his wives and concubines, which is extended to the power he holds over the people of Bauchi. Hasana and A'isha are the most central women figures in the book and in the Imam's life. However, here are three things: a brief and closer examination of the Imam's perceptions of women and his relationship with all of his wives and concubines; how his attitude contributes to his infamous declaration against the *gwaro* ceremony, and his sermon about bastardies. Situated within the context of a return to orthodoxy, these declarations are more reflective of the Imam's increasingly desperate desire to regain control of his household than his piety and devotion. Tahir makes it difficult to separate the Imam's orthodoxy from his own desires, so that the "reformist project" into which the novel may be placed, is rendered problematic by the Imam's hypocrisy.

At the beginning of the novel, before household tensions become intense, the Imam feels ". . . he was a good husband" to all his wives, ". . . guid[ing] them in their acts of worship and whenever there was some trouble had only to sermonize to them about the duties of the wife to her husband, just like his father sermonized about everything" (30). In this, the Imam reflects the implicit arrogance of his father's advice regarding the treatment of wives. The Imam's attitude infantilizes his wives, lowering them to the status of subservient (and petty) children, who must be kept in line. In turn, the Imam casts himself as the exasperated husband, who must constantly contend with his wives' jealousy and scheming. For the women of the household, ". . . Alhaji Usman occupied a position not so different from that of a god. His authority, capricious and somewhat absolute, was one the women, or anybody else for that matter, dared not question" (45). This is a position the Imam enjoys; the arrogance of the Imam, both in public and in private, is symbolized in his "prating" confidently through the compound and through the streets of Bauchi in his slippers. Even as his authority begins to disintegrate within and without his household, the Imam continues to "prate," suggesting that he has yet to bend. The misogyny present in the text, evident in the Imam's relationships with his wives, comes not from Islam so much as it comes from the disappointment and anger the Imam feels when he is denied a life devoted only to serving God. The anger he feels is then played out in his relationship with A'isha in particular, and in his overall perception of his relationship with his wives.

One cannot, however, separate the teachings the Imam has received from his father from the actions of the Imam himself. In other words, the Imam's misogyny is, to a considerable degree, learned from his father and his father's rather flippant (and also loaded) remark that "women are no trouble at all." The response of the village men the night after the Imam's violent rape of A'isha suggests that the misogyny shown by the Imam is shared. The rape, a physical acting out of the tension between Islam and pre-Islamic African culture upon the body of a woman in turn situates women's bodies as the battleground from Islamic supremacy, a war played out most clearly in the household of the Imam. Furthermore, because the rape is at least partially a response to the Imam's distaste for "heathen" African customs, the response of the village men (who represent those very customs) situates the misogyny of the text within African culture or as a by-product of the conflict between Islam and African culture. Connecting African culture and misogyny also reflects Tahir's hostility to indigenous African culture, a hostility seen when the Imam, upon coming home shortly after Kasim has thrown a stone at A'isha for accusing him of stealing money, sees ". . . the grim circle of women sitting [. . .] like ritual carvings in a juju shrine" (59). Presumably this would position the women in a hostile space and the Imam the unfortunate sacrifice. The Imam responds with typical misogynistic arrogance: "They should have been loud and quarrelsome so he could shout them down and obtain their submission with the weight of his authority over them" (59). This authority comes not only from his position as husband, but his position as Imam and his mastery of words and the Koran, which is seen most tellingly when the Imam uses that mastery to outlaw *gwauro* and sermonizes about bastardies.

During Ramadan, the month long Islamic observance of fasting, the people of Bauchi, stressed by the demands of Ramadan, take their pleasure in an African custom called *gwauro*, a ceremony which ridicules and humiliates men who have divorced their wife/wives and found no replacement(s) before Ramadan. For the Imam, this becomes a time of great uncertainty. Privileging and loving his son above the rest of his family, the women of his household threaten to leave him on the eve of Ramadan, thus making the Imam of Bauchi a *gwauro*, vulnerable to the *gwauro* chief and public humiliation. At one of the *gwauro* ceremonies in the village, the Imam announces that the practice will cease. Using the power derived from his mastery of the Koran, the Imam

> ... spouted into their besotted brains verses from the Holy Koran, from the Hadith, the teachings of the Prophet Mohammed (Peace and blessings of God be upon Him) and even from Arab literature and history. Some of the quotations were ones they themselves had known; many they had only half-known and still more, they had *never even dreamt existed at all*. And yet he was making sense, *forcing* the least likely verses to fit into the subject of the *gwauro* ceremony. The most indefatigable perverts of doctrine could not have done better! (108; *my italics*)

The Imam's outlawing of *gwauro* is his first public action that actually serves a private purpose and fear. Ahmed Bangura overlooks this very powerful indictment of the Imam by Tahir in which the Imam is positioned alongside "indefatigable perverts of doctrine."

The Imam's "perversion" of the Koran to suit his own needs is even more explicit when the Imam delivers a sermon against divorce and bastardies after a painful confrontation with Malam Shu'aibu, a local Islamic teacher, who has taken in Kasim, and who, it is revealed, is the Imam's bastard brother. Malam Shu'aibu tells the Imam that their father raped the Malam's mother, a slave girl. He tells the Imam that while their father " . . . shunned women he was honest about his feelings toward them, quite unlike you in this respect" (159). "Shunned" suggests the late Imam may also have been misogynistic, or at the very least, shunned them in order to perform his religious duties. The late Imam's "feelings" toward women is more ambiguous; once again, it may suggest misogyny, or it may suggest the late Imam's honesty about his sexual desires. The Malam continues, telling the Imam that as he watched the Imam grow up he saw Alhaji " . . . become gradually worse, and very different from our father. I saw you become more and more dangerously omniscient in your lessons with the old men in the school and in your sermons in the mosque" (163). Once again, the Imam's perversion of doctrine is brought to the fore, and it is his bastard brother that draws the first explicit connection between the Imam's private life and his public persona and responsibilities.

The Malam's revelation stuns the Imam, whose violent disavowal of his ancestors is quickly retracted as he resolves to purify the Bauchi emirate by declaring that any child conceived out of turn (i.e., a man going to a wife when it is not her turn) is a bastard. The Imam's sermon is also fed by his own fear that Kasim may be a bastard as well. Shunning his other wives, the Imam devoted himself emotionally and sexually to Hasana. The Imam refuses to believe that he could be guilty of rape, choosing instead to once more project his private fears into the public arena. This decision will lead to the Imam's fall.

The Imam is guilty of refusing to submit to the will of God, or rather, seeing the will of God aligned with his own will. Thus, the decisions he makes regarding the *gwaro* ceremony and divorce and bastardies, which are clearly manifestations of his own fears of being divorced during Ramadan, as well as voiding his union with Hasana (and making him a rapist), he sees within the context of God's will, which calls for purification. While the Imam may earnestly wish for a pure Bauchi, he does not see that this desire stems from his own impurity; instead he projects his fear of impurity onto the people of Bauchi, blaming them in effect for his own sins. His wives as well receive blame, both by the Imam and the village; the disorder of the Imam's household infects the community, which eventually leads the Emir to "de-turban" the Imam in an effort to save his people from a flawed, rather than pure, Islam. The Imam views this decision as blasphemy, blind to the practicality of the Emir's choice. The conflict between accommodation and orthodoxy is not so much a matter of an unwilling and superstitious people refusing to submit to the will of God, but the inability of a religious leader to separate his private life and his public duties.

Hoda Elsadda notes that "[i]n Arab societies, women are assigned the role of custodians of tradition and 'authentic culture,' a situation similar to many other societies in the aftermath of colonialism" (37). It is reasonable to extend this contention to Muslim women as a whole, whose duties include the promulgation of the faith to their children. Writing from her perspective as a Muslim Arab woman, Elsadda, in her investigation of twentieth-century literary representations of Mohammed's beloved wife A'isha, takes as her central concern the perpetuation of common stereotypes of Arab women from two particular sources. First, Elsadda disputes the perpetuation of the stereotype of Muslim women as helpless and oppressed by "local" nationalist discourses and modern Islamic projects, both of which seek to ". . . maintain the status quo," particularly that of male privilege (39). The West also perpetuates this stereotype of oppressed Muslim women to ". . . justify acts of interference in the affairs of 'undemocratic' and 'sexist' Arab states" (39). Again, it is reasonable to extend Elsadda's argument here to Muslim women outside the Arab world. Western perceptions of oppressed and silent Muslim women heavily influence the ways in which Muslim women are read in the novels in which they appear. In other words, Western audiences no doubt *expect* to find Muslim women fitting the stereotypes perpetuated by "Orientalist" discourse. That was the assumption at the beginning of this study. The character of A'isha does make such a reading at once extremely difficult and too simplistic, because her desire to "serve her man" can neither be attributed to her faith nor to her culture. On the contrary, her desire is to be first in her husband's affection. While the choices she makes are always bound by the reality of the "adultery-proof, lechery proof purdah" in which she lives, A'isha is far from powerless. Her ability to disrupt the household in her quest for satisfaction is only eclipsed by the Imam's ability to facilitate such disorder through his self-centered actions.

While this reading of *The Last Imam* has focused on the complex figure of A'isha, the story is first and foremost the story of her husband. And his story follows a familiar pattern, perhaps, most reminiscent of Shakespeare's King Lear of the eponymous title. Like that Western tragic king, the Alhaji is also guilty of excessive pride and an unbending nature. As is so often the case, he who does not bend is bound to break. King Lear is humbled by insanity and the loss of his throne and power; likewise, the Imam is, supposedly, humbled when he is de-turbaned by the Emir and loses his own authority. But, does the Imam break? Is he truly humbled? Does Tahir leave the Imam repentant or does the Imam remain inflexible, certain in his authority over the word? While Tahir gives no easy answer to any of these questions, he does admire the Imam.

Evidently, the Imam is less generous than Tahir and certainly less generous than Ahmed Bangura, who sees him as "this last warrior of Islam" (Bangura 2000: 118). What is admirable in the Imam is his willingness to acknowledge his flaws, and, to a certain degree, address them. However, his implacable pride and self-righteousness complicate any claims one can make about the sincerity of his repentance, particularly given their self-serving and transitory nature.

Because the authorial intention is that the Imam reflects his household, Bauchi village, and its people, it is difficult to separate him from any reading of his wives, particularly A'isha. Tahir's positioning of the Imam as the primary entrance point into the text creates a complicated interpretive space, because of the Imam's flaws. Furthermore, it is difficult to discern where Tahir ends and his literary creation begins. This suggests that an analysis focusing more on Tahir's relationship to his text and to his protagonist would be especially interesting, as would an analysis examining the historical and political context in which Tahir wrote and set his work. Clearly, Tahir respects the Imam's orthodoxy, but condones neither his hypocrisy nor his treatment of his wives. Even the holiest of men is human. Tahir remains sympathetic with the Imam throughout the text, even when the Imam is at his worst. Obviously, A'isha is a pitiable character, but as in Tahir's case, our sympathies are mitigated, due to her flaws, especially given the role she plays in creating a contentious relationship with her husband and co-wives. She is not a victim of Islam, but she does bear the brunt of her husband's self-serving interpretations of the faith. Tahir imbues her with power, though often this is expressed through shrewish behavior. Both the Imam and A'isha appear humbled at the text's close. The reader is aware, however, that given their nature, their humility as expressed is problematic for the pride of the one and the pain of the other.

Works Cited

Alcoff, Linda. "The Problem of Speaking for Others." *Cultural Critique* 20 (winter 1991-1992): 5-32.

Bangura, Ahmed Sheik. *Islam and the West African Novel: The Politics of Representation.* Boulder: Lynne Rienner Publishers, 2000.

Bivar, A. D. H. and Mervyn Hiskett. "The Arabic Literature of Niger to 1804: A Provisional Account." *Bulletin: School of Oriental and African Studies* 25.1 (1962): 142-158.

Bulbeck, Chilla. *Re-orienting Western Feminisms: Women's Diversity in a Postcolonial World.* Cambridge: Cambridge University Press, 1998.

Callaway, Barbara and Lucy Creevey. *The Heritage of Islam: Women, Religion, and Politics in West Africa.* Boulder: Lynne Rienner Publishers, 1994.

Cooper, Barbara. "Gender and Religion in Hausaland: Variations in Islamic Practice in Niger and Nigeria." In: *Women in Muslim Societies: Diversity within Unity.* Ed. Herbert L. Bodman and Nayereh Tohidi. Boulder: Lynne Rienner Publishers, 1998. 21-37.

Elsadda, Hoda. "Discourses on Women's Biographies and Cultural Identity: Twentieth-Century Representations of the Life of 'A'isha Bint Abi Bakr." *Feminist Studies* 27.1: 37-64.

Hiskett, Mervyn. "Kitab al-Farq: A Work on the Habe Kingdoms Attributed to Uthman dan Fodio." *Bulletin: School of Oriental and African Studies* 23.3 (1960): 553-579.

Johnson, Lemuel. "Crescent and Consciousness: Islamic Orthodoxies and the West African Novel." In: *Faces of Islam in Sub-Saharan African Literature*. Ed. Kenneth Harrow. London, Portsmouth: Heinemann, 1991. 239-260.

Lightfoot-Kramer, Hanny. *Prisoners of Ritual: An Odyssey into Female Genital Circumcision in Africa*. New York: Harrington Park Press, 1989.

Tahir, Ibrahim. *The Last Imam*. London: KPI, 1984.

Chapter 2

Constructing Postcolonial Maleness in Ayi Kwei Armah's *Fragments*[1]

Pinkie Mekgwe

In *Fragments*, as in most of his novels, Ayi Kwei Armah is concerned with procreation and re-creation. The novel is, therefore, replete with scenes of sexual intimacy and language is often used in a sexually suggestive way. In its theme, this novel seems to follow an earlier one, *Why Are We So Blest?*,[2] in a linear manner. With no 'potent' male at the onset of independence, the new male is constructed from a hotchpotch of circumstances. The novel begins by capturing this male absence.

Baako has been away from home for many years, having gone to study abroad. His mother, Efua, pines for him. "I hope he comes, that's all" (35), Efua confides to Juana, a young Puerto-Rican doctor she meets on the beach. "He will come back a man. A big man" (ibid.). From the onset, the language is sexually suggestive. Coming is intricately linked with manhood.

The ability to come, in sexual terms, denotes that one has attained manhood and is active in procreation. Coming is also pleasurable. It is the peak of sexual activity. In the instance of those who come back from abroad, the coming of the returnee brings pleasure to their families and relatives. In the changing economy of post-independence Ghana, however, a man's coming attains complex dimensions that have implications for his relations with his female counterparts. For a man to be termed a man, he has to 'come properly' in economic terms.

Brempong is another Ghanaian man who has been abroad. When he comes, he is ceremoniously met at the airport by many of his people who are led by his sister. His arrival is captured in sexual innuendo. The sister receives him: "Ooooh my own brother!" she screamed, caught in an orgasmic shudder: "You have come, you have come again to me!"' (56). The sister's words capture the political climate of the era of independence where 'power' (that which is socially enabling) is returned to the hitherto dispossessed rightful owner. As Ghana is given back to Ghanaians to rule, so the brother returns from the West to his eagerly waiting family. The line between country/nation and the male breadwinner becomes blurred.

Baako returns home on the same plane as Brempong. Brempong is astoundingly materialistic and wise to Ghana's new ways in a way that Baako is not. Brempong talks obsessively about the goods he has brought from abroad: suits, two cars, a 'sharp eyes' lighter; tape recorders, a deep refrigeration plant for his mother. And still he keeps buying. He buys tax-free drinks and tobacco on the plane. "It's no use", Brempong said, "going back with nothing. You may not have the chance to travel again in a long time. It's a big opportunity, and those at home must benefit from it too'" (53). Brempong, whose coming brings orgasmic pleasure to his people, also points out to Baako that he ought to have secured a job before coming back to Ghana: '…if you come back prepared, there's nothing to worry about', he tells Baako (45).

Manhood in postcolonial Ghana then, becomes hinged on male productivity. The woman becomes the consumer. Brempong travels with his wife, Eugenia, who is presented as a walking advertisement for consumerism. Eugenia is introduced as 'a generous mass of a wig' (41) and before we are told her name, she is once again referred to as 'a dark head crowned with the mass of a wig' (48). Without uttering a word, Eugenia relays her demanding nature with her 'restless' behavior on the plane. The couple is the epitome of the new consumerist Ghana for which Baako is ill prepared.

Such producer/consumer gender construction renders the female a receptacle. It deprives her of agency and turns her into one who awaits the fruits of male agency. Efua is such a woman. She has long been awaiting the coming of her son, Baako. She says:

> All my hopes went with him, and he was going to leave me here, like an old woman on the shore, struggling to take my snuff in a hurricane (34).

When Baako finally arrives, Efua is very happy even though Baako 'came so suddenly' as to not allow his family to get ready for him. Baako's coming, it soon becomes clear, is not only abrupt; it is also incomplete. As they drive home in Baako's friend Fifi's car, Efua,

> …was smiling now, completely at ease in the enfolding luxury of the red leather upholstery. [...] In a moment she was leaning forward all the way to touch his left ear and cheek, and she was asking in a near-whisper filled with wonder and gladness, "When is yours coming, Baako?"
>
> "What?" he asked, surprised.
>
> "Yours, your car, so that my old bones can also rest" (71).

That Baako has no car, an insignia of masculine success in postcolonial Ghana, marks him out as a different returnee or 'been-to'. Success: 'making it', and its converse, have concomitant implications for gender relations. Young women, as Baako comes to learn, chase after any 'been-to' who has a car, irrespective of whether or not he is married. Christina is one such woman. She too wears a wig. Baako meets her in Fifi's office:

> The woman had an unmistakably seductive air about her. When she spoke, she drew the words out as if she herself were deep inside a

dream from which she was reluctant to emerge, so that every syllable fell from her lips with the softness of something lubricated with a sensuous and delicious fatigue. No movement of hers was quick. Even the closing and opening of her eyelids was done as if any normal speed would cancel the pleasure she got from them (67).

Christina has no qualms about having an extra-marital affair with the married Fifi. She even suggests that if Fifi cannot get away from his wife, he should instead send Baako, whom she hopes has brought his car.

Baako's 'been-to' power is once again put to the test when his sister, Araba, has to give birth in the hospital. Without a job, Baako's mode of coming is found wanting. His sister is denied entry into the good wing of the hospital where normally, a 'been-to's relative would have been welcome. Araba, nevertheless, is thankful to Baako when the baby is safely delivered. It is his coming, she insists, that has brought her the baby: '...it is such a good thing, your coming. Already you have brought me this, the baby' (85).

The incestuous nature of the sexual innuendo surrounding both the successful arrival of Brempong and the conception of Araba's baby; the reference to promiscuous and adulterous behavior in the persons of Fifi and Christina are pointers to the moral depravity of a consumerist culture that depends on the importation of finished goods as a mode of 'production'. Postcolonial Ghana as depicted in *Fragments* is a world that is reminiscent of that of Dambudzo Marechera's *The House of Hunger*. Writing about the complexities of postcolonial return, Marechera depicts home as a place of hunger. The hunger is an absence of moral nourishment. It is a presence of poverty and vice where prostitution, both literal and metaphorical, abounds, rendering the whole society soiled and debased.

In *Fragments*, prostitution of the male is commonplace. Brempong has prostituted his soul to Western consumerism. His vision is narrowed only to materialistic hoarding of exotic goods. Fifi Williams is 'a real man' because, as the taxi driver explains to Baako, Fifi is a 'Swinging nigger. That means a tough guy. Plenty of good time' (63). The head of Ghanavision, the corporation for which Baako works for a short while, is Asante-Smith. He is a young man reputed to have 'the sweetest tongue in all of Ghana for singing his master's praises. [...] And it doesn't matter to him even when the masters change. He can sing sweetly for anybody "who *dey for top*" (46). To 'make it', to be of their male worth within the present structure, the men thus prostitute themselves, albeit in different ways.

At Ghanavision, Baako is not allowed to create and produce anything worthwhile. Life at Ghanavision is microcosmic of the life of the society at large. It is one long ceremony that lacks substance. Everything is done for the show and not for what it is worth. When Baako writes a social documentary on the prevailing Ghanaian society, raising awareness to its flaws, his efforts are dismissed. It soon becomes clear to Baako that he is expected to do nothing but accept his pay check at the end of each month. His alliance with Ghanavision becomes another form of prostitution. Like paid-for sex, the work draws neither depth of feeling nor enjoyment. It is only about receiving money and in the process, compromises the receiver's sense of self-worth while highlighting the lewd nature of the payer.

The obsession with importing goods from abroad, which Baako refers to as 'cargo mentality', has become a definitive way of living in this society. A man is expected to provide material goods. It does not matter how he does it. Cargo mentality is characterized by exhibitionism. This kind of mentality, however, weighs the man down heavily as demonstrated in the third chapter.

The chapter is entitled "Edin," which translates, "What is your name?" In posing this question, the chapter speaks to the notion of identity. Here we are introduced to Juana, the young Puerto-Rican doctor who has been drawn to Ghana by a desire to find herself. The explorations of her mind are played out in a journey form. She drives around the country and, on the particular afternoon that she is to meet Efua for the first time, she comes across a strange scene. A sick dog is lying in the middle of the road. A group of men, wearing khaki shorts that mark them out as government employees, forms a circle around the dog and move in to catch it. A young boy pleads with the men to leave the dog alone as it is his, and though it is sick, he explains, it is harmless. Rather than listen to the boy's pleas, one of the men picks the helpless boy up and throws him to the ground. As the men close in on the dog, they show no visible hurry '...but the male desire to be the first made all those backs wet with sweat twitch now and then with their own impatient inward heat' (17). The men are many. They carry weapons. And yet 'a fear could be seen in them whose strength was strange, seeing that the source of it was such a powerless thing' (18).

Masculinity is on display. It is characterized by violence and irrationality. This kind of masculine display is borne out of malformed notions of manhood, and this is made manifest in the portrayal of one of the male characters:

> He was a short man, with something swollen and out of shape about his shortness, so that the eye on first seeing him searched unordered for some twisting cause, for something perhaps like a hump upon his back. But there was nothing there to explain the twistedness, until the baffled eye descended and was struck in the region of the sweating man's loins with the sight of a scrotal sac so swollen that within the tattered pants containing it had the look of a third and larger buttock winning a ruthless struggle to push the original two out of the way (18).

This man, we are told, has the maniacal desire to kill the defenseless dog that surpasses that of any of the other men in the group:

> ...the man with the swollen scrotum raised his weapon high toward the sun: it was a pickax with a handle made lean in the middle but thickening toward the ends to fit the hole in the metal head and the opening made by grasping human hands.

> The way in which the eager, fearful carefulness of the whole circle was broken by the descent of the last man's pickax was so swift and so sudden that even though the blow had been expected, it still surprised the watching eye, and the trueness of its aim was uncanny. For the point of the implement went in not far from the exact middle of the dog's head. In the first few moments nothing happened save for a twitching movement – it could have been of joy or of fear – that ran down the tight body of the man who had shattered the dog's life. That, and a whimper barely audible, a sound expressing not surpassed sadness but a final acceptance, and it came from the boy who had tried desperately to save his friend (19).

Soon man and animal become indistinguishable, one from the other:

> Then around the buried point of the weapon the dog's life began its final coming. It was white at first, the matter of the animal's brains, then blood mixed it with a tentative light brown that deepened into red with a stronger flow. [...] The last man with the swollen sac was twitching no longer. [...] The drip of life came down from the upturned end of the pickax. But from the man himself something else had commenced to drip: down along his right leg flowed a stream of something yellow like long-thickened urine mixed with streaks of clotted blood (19-20).

This scene is captured with a power and vividness that stays with the reader throughout the reading of *Fragments*. The effect this has is to highlight the presence of this sickness at all levels of society. Captured under the chapter on identity, the scene brings out the linkage between power and destruction, and how these shape male identity and gender relations. The dog is symbolic of the lowest strata of society. In its innocence and helplessness, it is directly linked to its friend, a small boy. He is unable to save it from the men who are in 'government uniform'. The men, in their uniform, are representative of nation guardianship. They are also, with their collective strength and weapons, evidently, the bearers of power.

The focus on male genitalia speaks directly to the notion of masculinity. Here we are confronted with a manhood whose location of sexual reproduction, the scrotum, is swollen and weighed down. Since the man brings the cargo, the weight on the male genitalia is a direct reference to the cargo mentality that has gripped the nation. It is revealed as a poison that interferes with healthy production in as much as it interferes with healthy reproduction. What could have been man's power to create is contaminated. Such contamination has implications on male-female relations, a point captured in the abnormality of male sexual pleasure as displayed in the scene of the dog killing.

In normal circumstances, a man attains orgasm in a healthy, consensual sexual encounter with a partner. However, orgasmic pleasure is here predicated upon the murder of the innocent:

The boy was still weeping, and the shout had turned his silent grief into a hysterical mixture of suffering for his lost dog and mockery of the killer. But for the killer himself, a wild feeling of relief seemed to have come in place of the first, short fear. Something that had stayed locked up and poisoned the masculinity of his days was now coming down, and in spite of all his shame he seemed seized by an uncontrollable happiness that made him walk with the high, proud, exaggerated steps of a puppet (20).

The cargo mentality upon which maleness is constructed manifests itself in exhibitionism. This exhibitionism in the scene above is revealed as sick and perverted. Exhibitionism becomes so central to the authentication of masculinity that even when it is destructive, it is still acceptable to the male. This is why, though the man in the scene above is ashamed of his disgusting come, which is the same color as the dog's 'last coming' and is all in the open for all to see, he is nevertheless happy and proud.

The scene focuses on the base: animals and the lowest members of the society, in order to bring out what is in essence the basic nature and, therefore, foundation of Armah's Ghanaian society. We see a similar trend of exhibitionism in the been-tos: Brempong's 'sharp' woolen suit, hardly suitable for the warm Ghanaian weather; the flashy 'German-made' cars; a commercial size refrigeration plant for domestic use. That the goods are unsuitable, even vulgar and wasteful is not the point. What matters to men like Brempong is the show and ceremony of it: "... the mere outward show of power and joy hiding impotence" (62).

Ultimately, the implications reach the national level. Nation building is not possible without productivity on the nation's part. Such productivity, it is clear, is not possible in the prevailing circumstances. There is rampant corruption; no work is done; the powerful hold those under their command in subservience. The end result is that it is the country and the nation with it that is being prostituted for the luxuries of a corrupt few.

Baako, who, as we have already noted, is different from the other masculine figures, becomes the seeker of alternative masculine construction. He wishes to create and contribute positively to nation building. He refuses to take advantage of his position at Ghanavision by turning down the perks: a bungalow and free televisions otherwise meant for the community. Instead, he resigns and goes on a countrywide journey with his lover, Juana.

Juana and Baako are drawn together by similar circumstances. Baako has anxiety problems for which he needs a prescription. Juana is the psychiatrist. A Puerto-Rican, she is working in Ghana, because she has come searching for peace and meaning to her life. As she explains to Baako, she too has been sick. Together they embark on a search for a new way of life. From the onset, attention is drawn to their sexual relations. How they relate to each other as man and woman becomes mirrored in their lovemaking. Their first sexual encounter is slow and exploratory. It is a warm, moonlit night. They lie by the seaside, feeling their way around each other's bodies. Baako undresses Juana:

> When he too was naked he lay beside her on the sand and she could see the night light sharp on his face. He continued caressing the inside of her thighs and brought her left hand up to touch his own nipple. When he felt her wetness and came into her, his movement was diffident... (119).

Sex brings together past and present. Baako keeps his weight off Juana, such that Juana is surprised at how light he is in comparison to her ex-lover and husband, Max. There is a suggestion here that a relationship with the considerate Baako will not weigh Juana down. Max is the source of the 'sickness' that has brought Juana to Ghana. Baako has met Juana in his search for healing. As they tentatively start on their new journey, their union holds promise:

> She watched him, a little amused to see how carefully he moved, as if he thought he could bruise her going in and out. She pushed her hips and felt him now deep against her. Now he was rubbing her, a bit too hard, so that she felt slightly sore. She reached for his hand, but before she could touch it all her control went out of her body, the salt taste of the air was deep in her throat, and she was saying words she'd thought she could never use again, and there was one moment when nothing that had happened to her made any difference, and all the steadying, controlling separatenesses *(sic)* between things did not matter at all to her. She could feel him come after her, and she held her body taut to keep him in longer, but after a while he got soft and she felt him wet against her hair before he turned and lay beside her also looking up into the sky, saying nothing (120).

They go on to have sex again, this time in the sea, where Baako brings Juana up to "a long coming so complete that she felt her head go beneath the water but did not care..." (125). For a change, 'coming' is a point of focus not for the male but for the female. This is an indicator that Baako and Juana's relationship is being built upon a different set of values. Here in the fluidity of the sea, the fragmented psychological and physical dimensions of the couple are brought back together. The sea is a site of initiation. Sex in the sea is symbolic of rebirth: "Here we're supposed to do it all when we're born, anyway. The first swim and the first fuck. There's a saying there's no way you can get out of your mother without" (125), Baako explains to Juana.

The significance of Baako and Juana's union is carried beyond the individual couple. Change, it seems, is slowly but surely taking place for others as well. This is attested to by the interesting spectacle the couple sees from the seaside. A group of fishermen is at work. The men are pulling a rope 'with hostility'; "their legs and thighs bulging with too much packed-in power, arms filled with rigid muscle, moving all at once in too many undecided directions" (127). Then a boy arrives. He beats out a drum and sings first for the fishermen, and then with the fishermen as they pick up his tune. The boy, as Baako points out, gives the men "something they didn't have. A softness of voice, piercing, melodious, *like a woman's*" (128-129; *my emphasis*]. A generational exchange takes place with the result that the men are able to pull the rope rhythmically and effectively. This scene speaks directly to the need for transformational masculinity. The suggestion is that male brute strength is not the answer. Instead, true and effective strength derives from closing the gap between 'powerful' men, and powerless women and children.

Even as Baako and Juana's union seemingly offers an ideal alternative to male-female relations in this community, problems remain. The cargo problem is nation-wide and enmeshed. On one of their journeys, Baako and Juana witness the drowning of a cargo-carrying driver, Skido. The couple helps to fish him out of the sea. The couple's love develops, as Baako observes, because of the 'emptiness' that surrounds them and pushes them closer. Baako is alienated from his society. Juana does not belong with the society either. We are reminded of this when she takes out leave and has to go back home to Puerto-Rico. While she is gone, Baako is haunted by the death of Skido, the nature of which is symbolic of the rot in which his society is drowning.

The privilege of an educational development that is accorded the male provider only and not his female counterpart finally becomes Baako's undoing. While the educated man might be viewed as privileged, for as long as his female counterpart lags behind, the apparent privilege manifests itself as a destructive force. The demands placed on the educated man by his women folk would be unnecessary if both male and female had the same earning power. Above all, the message that Armah's novel carries forth is that such disparity between the sexes in the post-colonial nation leads to a breakdown in communication and understanding across the gender line. With Juana away, this last point, particularly, becomes clear. Baako lacks a companion capable of fully understanding his psychological torment. In the end, Baako disintegrates and is certified mad.

The fragments of which maleness in the postcolonial nation of Armah's novel is constructed prove varied, complex and incompatible.

Notes
1. Armah's *Why Are We So Blest* is another novel in which sex is employed as a trope to explore colonial masculinity(ties).
2, Note how J. M. Coetzee also uses dogs as a marker of vulnerability in his novel *Disgrace,* London: Vintage, 2000.

Works Cited
Armah, A. K. *Fragments*. London: Heinemann, 1974.
---. *Why Are We So Blest*. London: Heinemann, 1974.
Fanon, Frantz. *The Wretched of the Earth*. London: Penguin, 1967.

Chapter 3
Posting the Agenda in African Women's Writing: Gender and the Postcolonial Condition in Promise Okekwe's Novels

Chukwuma Okoye

Many critiques of postcolonialism chafe at the perplexing inclusionary or totalizing discursive practice which presents the 'postcolonial' as a monolithic representation thereby robbing the discourse of concise location, a practice which, in its amorphousness, admits within its definitional umbrella almost every site of contestation between dominant and marginal discourses. This practice elides the social, historical, epistemological, economic, and geopolitical processes which construct(ed) distinct forms of discourse in every 'post-colony', the very "material conditions which give rise to post-colonial difference" (Mishra and Hodge 1994: 287).

In addition to this and other problematics Arjun Mukherjee identifies in postcolonial theory "an overriding concern with 'parody' of imperial 'textuality' which is distorting the field as it focuses on a very limited number of authors, the ones whose texts can give back what the theory is looking for" (1990: 7). Thus, the agenda of postcolonialism which, according to Franz Schulze-Engler, is "ultimately based on a politics of decolonization," "to dismantle those colonial-imperial discourses that still dominate the formerly colonized world" (1998: 31), is paradoxically defeatist. When presented as re-writing or interrogating imperial hegemony[1] postcolonialism does not only occlude the various peculiar narratives evolved in the ex-colonies, but "also actively re-invents and privileges its necessary antagonist, the empire, which it needs to validate its epistemological stance" (31). Thus its theoretical leverage is only measured from a hegemonic benchmark, a grand narrative within whose ambience postcolonialism is accommodated.

Also related to the 'writing-back' paradigm is the objectification of postcolonialism, a mercantilism which invents and celebrates the otherness of the ex-colonies, by complicit, largely diasporized postcolonial intellectuals for exchange in the Anglo-American marketplace. The politics of otherness as scripted by the West underscores the binary of dominant and subordinate structures. Where a dominant discourse is construed as independent and technologically advanced the subordinate other valorizes its condition of 'post-' or 'advanced' coloniality and underdevelopment. Where a dominant discourse claims marginalization, as in Western feminism, the other, such as its non-Western versions, narratively productifies its 'double' (or 'triple') jeopardy of marginalization. Thus postcolonial intellectuals subscribe to the trope of 'authenticity' and, under Western midwifery, studiously engender postcoloniality as differently or otherwisely constituted from a center that is the icon of Enlightenment, the West. To construct 'authenticity' and further the prospect of marketability of postcolonialism the aesthetes of otherness arduously engage in a constant avowal of difference. According to Minh-ha "Authenticity in such contexts turns out to be a product that one can buy, arrange to one's liking, and/or preserve" (267). Certainly, 'authenticity' becomes an artifact suitable for display on the shelves of modern Western architecture such as David Rockefeller's apartment (Appiah 1991: 337-338). This kind of difference is productified for the consumption of the West. This is the politics (and most importantly, the economics) of postcolonialism: "We no longer wish to erase your difference. We demand, on the contrary, that you remember and assert it" (Minh-ha, 268). And only on this condition, if I may add, would you be garlanded as a postcolonial import in the postcolonizing world.

Appiah observes that

> To sell oneself and one's products as art in the marketplace, one must, above all, clear a space in which one is distinguished from other producers and products—and one does this by the construction and the marking of differences. (1991: 342)

So 'marking' of identity in the Anglo-American marketplace becomes a spurious enterprise constituted by dubiously constructed differences modeled after the dominant script in the West on non-western cultures. Appiah further opines that

> Postcoloniality is the condition of what we might ungenerously call a *comprador* intelligentsia: a relatively small, Western-style, Western-trained group of writers and thinkers, who mediate the trade in cultural commodities of world Capitalism at the periphery .... (348)

Thus these African interpreters of Africa for the marketplace of Europe and America are the non-fictive prototypes of Yambo Ouloguem's Saif in *Bound to Violence:* the dubious fakers of authenticity; experts in "alterism," the construction, celebration and marketing of self as Other" (Appiah 1991: 354).

Francis N. Njubi, in "African Intellectuals in the Belly of the Beast," establishes three typologies of African intellectuals working in America: "the comprador intelligentsia, the postcolonial critics and the progressive exiles" (6). He defines the first as those used as agents for the promotion of neocolonialist policies in Africa (7); the second as those who take advantage of their color, nationality and location in the West to become expert interpreters of the African experience for Western audiences" (8); while the third and the last use their experience in exile to join the struggle for the liberation of their people from the pangs of neocolonialism and the social, political, economic and intellectual empowerment of Africa (10). What is interesting is that Kwame Anthony

Appiah himself is typified as a postcolonial critic, that genus of African intellectuals who interrogate the African experience along accommodationist lines, adopting Postmodernist/Eurocentric perspectives for their invention and construction of a 'new' Africa that is more palatable to the taste of the West. This is more like his mediating 'comprador intelligentsia' described above.

In all of these what is recommended is a circumscription of the boundaries of postcolonialism against other similarly engaging discourses; a literal clearing of the amorphous deck to fix the term within a precise historical, geopolitical and epistemic construct that is independent of the predatory magnanimity of postmodernism.

This conceptual disquiet also marks the terrain of feminism and gender representation. Some non-western 'feminists' feel silenced and colonized by the universalizing feminist agenda wherein Western feminists position themselves metonymically as champions of womanhood. Chandra Mohanty observes that mainstream feminism's

> (A)ssumption of women as an already constituted, coherent group with identical interests and desires, regardless of class, ethnic or racial location or contradictions, implies a notion of gender or sexual difference or even patriarchy ... which can be applied universally and cross-culturally. (261)

In "Feeling Foreign in Feminism" Maivan Clech Lam interrogates the universal relevance of feminist agendas articulated in the United States "where white "professional" or bourgeois feminists typically speak of, or for, the general experiences and needs of women" (1994: 866). She describes as "filmic" those itineraries articulated by white feminists and some "Western feminists of colour" that fail to represent other subjects and realities.

Secondly, even when non-Western identities and subjects are acknowledged they are often undifferentiated. Thus the 'postcolonial/Third World woman' is often generically represented as a single subject.

Paralleling the postcolonial parodic schema or writing-back model, gender discourse in Africa often takes imperial feminism as its signpost from which it proposes to disinter itself. This leads to the canonization of texts that legitimize imperial feminism by holding it up as the lodestone by which others are defined. Ironically, these texts present that construction of the oppressive patriarchal gender stratification in Africa already scripted in the West as barbaric and bestial. Iterating the politics of othering, Western feminists present themselves as sophisticated, independent and civilized, while the African or Third World woman is "ignorant, poor, uneducated, tradition-bound, domestic, family oriented, victimized, etc." (Mohanty 1995: 261). African feminist writers, such as Buchi Emecheta and Calixthe Beyala, perpetuate this rather de-historicized and mythic image of African masculinity which the West uses to legitimize 'postcolonialism' (in this context conceived as 'advanced-' or 'improved-' rather than 'after-' colonialism), to justify the oppressive imaging of the fate of the

'Third World Woman' which guarantees the canonization of such texts because they present the sort of portraiture which the West finds most consumable. In demonizing the postcolony these African feminists echo imperial feminism and present the West as the haven of sexist liberation.

As with postcolonial theorizing, which currency in the postcolonies is suspect, so it is with some African feminist perspectives on gender and patriarchy. Do postcolonial feminist writers and critics, mostly diasporized and reconditioned by the pervasive crisis of identity in alien (ating) geography, truly reflect gender structures in the postcolonies or do they construct discourses after Anglo-American matrixes? Does Buchi Emecheta, for instance, chronicle the truly oppressive postcolonial condition of today's woman in Nigeria, her native country, or does she simply perpetuate the already written image of patriarchy as the singular tyrannical African institution from which the female must be liberated by the Enlightened West? The answer(s) to these questions is/are rather obvious.

In an essay, "Fela and His Wives: The Import of a Postcolonial Masculinity," Derek Stanovsky (1992) identifies the conditions under which importation from the postcolonies into the West are encouraged: Firstly, such an import must perpetuate the image of the African male as misogynist, a Western profiling which invents the African patriarchal system as innately oppressive of women. Secondly, it must launder the self-image of the West as "the source of all enlightened and progressive politics, especially with regard to women" (4). Thus the West serves as the haven for oppressed African women.[2] What obtains is a situation where a small class of bourgeois, educated women who are often not even physically, socially, culturally and psychologically located in postcolonial geographies as to boast of any real first-hand experience, speak for the African woman and defend her against imagined patriarchal brutality. Little wonder then that the most celebrated of African female writers in the West are those who fodder this construction of the bestialization of the African female by the African male, a script which is great music to the self-righteous ears of the West and which propels it to arrogantly affirm, like the Biblical Pharisee: "God, I thank you that I am not like other men" (Luke 18: 11).

Chikwenye Okonjo Ogunyemi (1985) posits that the African woman faces greater complexities than can be ridiculously reduced to patriarchy and sexuality, and that she shares almost all of these problems with the African male. She observes that "The intelligent black woman writer ... empowers the black man ... hence her books end in integrative images of the male and female worlds" (68-69), while Buchi Emecheta, "deeply grounded in the British and Irish feminism in which she was nurtured ... tends to feminize the black male, making him weak, flabby, and unsuccessful" (66-67). Such an

> African feminist writer's position is complicated by the fact that her work sometimes lacks authenticity, since the traditional African woman she uses as protagonist is, in reality, beset with problems of survival and so is hardly aware of her sexist predicament. (67)

This 'deck-clearing' underscores the works of Promise Okekwe, one such 'intelligent black woman writer,' whose narratives are grounded in a post-independent (postcolonial?) African nation, whose concern is with the immediate, more contemporary—rather than the invented—social and political realities of her society, and who narrates the prevalent social and political inequities that beleaguer her people irrespective of their gender. Described by Femi Osofisan as "a tireless and amazing book-churning machine, with two collections of short stories, three books of drama, four collections of poetry, ten full-length novels, and twenty-seven children's books" (*The Guardian*, Feb. 22, 2003: 39), Okekwe is indeed a machine of sorts considering that, in addition to all the attendant hurdles on the track of the public and domestic terrain that married women must assail in a most disabling society such as hers, she is a banker by profession. Notably, she is not an academic like most writers in Africa. In spite of this she finds the narrative energy to minify the profiles of some of the most garlanded African writers with the sheer volume of her works. Hence Osofisan regrets that such a colossus is "still regularly confined to the margins of discourse" (39). The reasons for this are not far fetched, although many feminists would hastily confine this to her sex and conveniently overlook the fact that all is not well even in the institution of African women's literary criticism. Apart from her relative indifference to the fashionable postcolonial 'writing-back' schema which is based on the construction of otherness, an indifference which makes her not quite marketable in the Anglo-American literary marketplace, female critics have largely ignored her works, because her themes are more extensive than the restricted separatist and confrontational rhetoric of much of feminist creative and critical production.

Many critics have noted the exclusionary imperative of male-dominated critical practice wherein female writers are concertedly undersubscribed in the establishment of African literature. However, Carolyn Kumah observes that "female identified/authored criticisms are gradually subverting these exclusionary and marginalizing practices." She admits nonetheless that "the perspective from which many of these feminist critics are examining the works of African women is also problematic" (3). Notably, what has been actively criticized as the inequitable canonization of male-produced and male-oriented texts is paradoxically re-invoked in the creative and critical performance of female writers in Africa. No criticism of African women's writing, especially by women themselves, is complete without attention to the work(s) of any of Buchi Emecheta, Mariama Bâ, Ama Ata Aidoo, Calixthe Beyala, Bessie Head, and so on. So where are all the other female writers, some of whom have produced more works than the canons could ever produce in their lifetimes? Apart from the fact of geography, the reason for exclusion from the postcolonial gender canonic institute is, of course, more thematic than aesthetic. Their bane is probably the non- or under- problematization of patriarchy. By thematically representing the immediate realities of their societies' quotidian experiences these writers have produced materials that fail to subscribe to the Western script for texts by women from non-Western cultures. But not so for the canons, especially the rookies often admitted on the basis of one or two creative works, whose lodestar is simply to impugn the patriarchal institution as the fundamental bane of Everywoman in Africa. This is despite the significant submissions of such scholars as Ifi Amadi-ume (1987), Molara Ogundipe-Leslie (1994), and Oyeronke Oyewumi (1997), who have illustrated the absurdity in the practice of applying Western concepts of gender and sexuality to non-Western cultures. These and many more scholars have submitted that the inequitable gender structure in Africa is significantly a Western import.

In this essay I limit myself to Promise Okekwe's latest novels, a triptych collectively entitled *A Trilogy of Tomorrow's Yesterday*, containing the novels *Hall of Memories* (2001*), Zita-Zita* (2002), and *Fumes and Cymbals* (2002). These are really three volumes of an extended narrative, more like a serialized novel than the conventional trilogy which can be usually read independently. Oso-fisan suggests that "it is probably the problem of length that obliges the author to separate the story into three books" (39). I limit my interest to exploring some of the most trenchant themes in the novels and situating them within the postcolonial and gender discourses with a view to investigating how 'postcolonial' Okekwe is in her agenda, if indeed the term could be made meaningful at all, and how peculiarly 'Africanist womanist' she is in her narrative strategy.

A Trilogy of Tomorrow's Yesterday is essentially the story of three generations of Michael Igini's family. The narrative begins with Zita-Zita and her psychotic recollections of the events of her past. Her mother dies while she is very young and she has to live with her father and a wicked step-mother who, apparently out of jealousy and her own childlessness, tries to murder her. Failing to do this she crudely and viciously scarifies her with thirty-six facial marks. After losing her stepmother to madness and her father to death she winds up a domestic maid in President Michael Igini's residence. In this status she is wooed by the President himself and she eventually ends up with a pregnancy for him. Burdened with guilt and sorrow she turns down his impassioned marriage proposal and leaves for France where she bears her baby, Michael Igini Jnr. Michael Jnr. himself grows into a dashing, reckless and wayward young man and at the tender age of fourteen fathers Raphael Igini, a more admirable and thoughtful young man.

Okekwe's epic is not, however, essentially about these men but the women who influence and are influenced by them. First is Aku, the amiable, kind, progressive, articulate and assertive wife of Michael Igini. She is everything a mother could be to Zita-Zita. A good mother to her children, a good wife to her husband, a surrogate mother to the motherless and handicapped, a good minister to her people in general, Aku represents the ideal woman whose agency is by no means diminished by patriarchal imperatives, a woman who recognizes and acknowledges the powers and limitations of womanhood as well as that of manhood. She is at once ready to give in to a man when she feels it reasonable but ready to fight when she feels threatened or unjustly silenced. She is not confrontational in her 'womanist' agenda and is respected and loved by all. Even Michael Igini, the husband who divorces her because of her assertiveness and refusal to be domesticated like a pet, admires her greatly. Her identity exemplifies a resolution of all sorts of contestations. She is rich by virtue of her political status but carries the interest of the poor at heart. She is a woman but is apparently indifferent to gendered positionalities. She does not make friends or enemies on the basis of gender considerations. She is equally indifferent to the politics of race for she is married to a Caucasian in a union described as transcending "the boundaries of race, tongues, hearts and even souls" (*Zita-Zita*, 12).

Second is Afiadu, the one who marries Michael Igini after Aku leaves him. She is in several respects Aku's antithesis. She is extroverted, non-assertive, childless, unloved, domestically entrapped, wicked, selfish and docile. She fails to carve out for herself an independent identity safe her attachment to the position of First Lady. She is described as being nothing other than "fashionable, loud, very loud and flamboyant, displaying all the wealth of Nigeria on her rather dainty pigmentation" (*Hall of Memories,* 154).

These three women are the central characters in Okekwe's *Trilogy*. Through them Okekwe weaves her epic saga whose interest is not really in the construction of dramatic characters and elegant plots but the narration of the social and political disjuncture—undeniably fictive but often recognizably biographic—of a truly 'postcolonial' African state. Her agenda is not radically feminist, in the overt sense of valorizing womanhood and vilifying patriarchy, but is a passionate concern with the social, economic and political travails of her people. Her concern is with the masses, the victims of oppressive policies inhumanly instituted and pursued by those in positions of authority. She decries incidents of deprivation, "deaths, kidnaps, abuse of human rights and acts of felony," (*Hall of Memories*: 193); "selfish, greedy, dubious, fraudulent, bestial" leadership, (181) and wonders why "must it be the same old cats, the same blind bats, the same spiders and their webs, the same cunning, self-seeking criminals" (178). This condition prompts Raphael to agonize: "... Is this democracy? Senseless killings, lawlessness, anarchy, corruption. Are these components of democracy?" (*Fumes*: 80). These "self-seeking criminals" and their victims are not products of gender stratification but are men and women who are positioned differently along the stratum of power and weakness, hegemony and marginality. Okekwe does not also problematize neocolonialism by pervasively implicating imperialism in the various socio-political ills that embattle her society. Her narratives locate the fundamental sources of oppression and empowerment within her immediate social, political and geographical space. She creates weak and powerful men and women, admirable, villainous, corrupt and honest men and women; men and women who oppress and are oppressed. These characters are in no way directly under any form of imperial hegemony or colonial/neo-colonial aegis. As McClintock notes, "many contemporary African ... cultures, while profoundly affected by colonization are not necessarily *primarily* preoccupied with their erstwhile contact with Europe" (*Emphasis in the original*; 294). So, it is with Okekwe for although she does not implicate imperialism in her narratives, she is nonetheless aware of its deleterious presence among her people. The cantankerous Captain Black, in his bombastic crudity, launches at Frederick McDermott in condemnation of the action of the young Nigerian girls brutishly used as sex objects by white men in Nigeria:

> For her, at her age, 22, to be so asinine as to be conned by your people still, after their enslavement of us when we were nincompoops and sold our people to you to use as you pleased, after destroying our tradition and disrupting our otherwise smooth lives, after teaching us how to steal, cheat, gun down people, including our own brothers as they do over there in your wild cities. (*Fumes*, 233)

He also rages against their continued oppression of the people through their dubiously prosperous transnational businesses and immense political clouts procured through the complicity of prominent Nigerian politicians (*Fumes*: 242-243; 244 – 246). But it is in the story of the fearless journalist, J. K. Shakpa that Okekwe aptly narrates the postcoloniality in Nigeria and, by extension, the whole of Africa:

> Right from the time when Britain colonized Nigeria ... His ancestors dug up coal and oil and gave everything to ... the white man who slept in a hammock and introduced structures and organizations, which were good... After all, the so-called power he took from them, he handed over to them to do what they wished with. And what did they do, they killed one another, quarrelled among themselves and swore to keep everything to themselves.
>
> The white man ... stood and watched from a distance. He took what one brother offered him to keep. He kept and made something good out of it. The other brother also brought things for him to keep. He kept and kept all their secrets. ... And when one decided to kill the other and solicited for the stranger's assistance, he offered it in his magnanimity, supplying the arms and ammunition, the logic of hatred and death and the poisonous weapons of acrimony. (*Fumes*, 352)

Similarly, although Okekwe's narrative cannot be reduced to a gender disquisition, she is not oblivious of the feminist itinerary for she displays an acute familiarity with the trenchant issues in the feminist discourse. In her narratives, she interrogates these contentious issues not by baring their oddities but by presenting integrative and harmonious communion. However, she inevitably arrives at the condition which feminists agitate for but in an effortless, cordial, and non-confrontational fashion. The ultimate goal of feminism is the correction of the inequities of power among the sexes; a society without gender discrimination and conflict, where each gender is defined and accommodated but not stratified or hegemonized. This is exactly the society that Okekwe presents in her trilogy.

Elaine Showalter in *The Female Malady: Women, Madness and English Culture* (1985) observes the theme of madness which pervades most writing by women and associates it with the domestic entrapment and repression of individual expression—creative, social, sexual, public and private—which women experience in English culture. According to Goodman *et al*, this theme of "women and madness" is "recurrent in much literature by and about women" (1996: 109). They submit that the theme is innately gendered not only because the male do the naming but the male is also responsible for the repressive denial of self-expression which instigates the madness (10). In African literature by women this theme is also notably prevalent.[3] In Okekwe's trilogy it is rather ubiquitous. There are several stages and forms of madness brought upon by all sorts of conditions. The first is Ekenma's for which neither repression of sexuality nor domestic entrapment are implicated, as is indicated in English culture by Elaine Showalter. Rather Ekenma's madness is ascribable to unrestrained sexuality. Even with a good and loving husband she could not control her sexuality. She persists in an illicit extra-marital affair with a man whom she herself entrapped by diabolical means. Her madness is retribution for all her wicked ways, which include adultery, attempted murder and malicious scarification of an innocent girl. When the *Umuada,* "those great daughters empowered by tradition by the virtue of their position as daughters of the town" (*Hall of Memories:* 72), evict her from her husband's house, Onyeoma, her husband, is obviously not supportive of their action. He continues to visit her even on the streets where her madness takes her.

A more complicated psychotic malady is that of Zita-Zita, a condition for which some men and women are equally responsible. She is abused as a child by her step-mother and a couple of men. She gets emotionally and physically involved with the Head of State of the Federal Republic of Nigeria to whom she is employed as house help. She loses her son temporarily to him when she turns down his passionate marriage proposal, marries another man but breaks with him because she could not accept a polygamous marriage. She suffers a miscarriage and finally marries another man. A combination of all of these traumatic experiences causes her mental breakdown. But perhaps one of the most graphic representations of her predicament is her stepmother's literal cancellation of her face. In spite of all her travails, Okekwe succeeds in creating a notable character in Zita-Zita. She is delineated as strong-willed, assertive and fearless, though respectful and humble.

On a more epistemological plane Zita-Zita's condition occasions an interrogation of the norms of identity definition. From the beginning she is presented as an ineffable girl anxious to please and live up to her father's idealism. She tries very hard to be right, to please her stepmother in spite of her wickedness towards her. Failing to efface her identity through murder, Ekenma literally deforms or deletes her seat of physical identity. The physical begins to constrain and entrap the psychological—the ugly and revolting mask oppresses the beauty within. This conflict between physical and internal identities imposes a barrier between who she really is and her physical look, a battle between individual and socially constructed identities. Madness now becomes a psychological expression of that disagreement with the social mapping of identity. Her otherwise admirable and beautiful personality is entrapped in a grossly deformed visage. Outward appearance intersects and subverts internal reality. And it is the external that is most haunting because society writes her first, or at least instantly—by the outward appearance. It is the surface that eventually, more or less, takes over the inside and what results is 'madness,' an aberrant behavior matching an aberrant physical appearance.

This entrapment in an ugly face, metaphoric of the debased society in which they live and are named, contrasts Afiadu's more domestic entrapment and neurosis. Without a psychologically present and loving husband, childless and enamoured with the bogus trappings socially available to her by virtue of her social position, Afiadu is like a woman in a mask. Unlike Zita-Zita, whose ugly mask envelops the goodness within, Afiadu's pretty mask houses an ugly interior. Although she is socially powerful she is lacking in agency for she is passive and utterly dependent on her husband. In a hopeless bid for self-inscription she finds expression along inhuman and anti-social tributaries.

Okekwe actually utilizes the enviable status of First Lady to explore three differently constituted female identities. In spite of the very oppressive masculinity of Michael Igini, the tyrannical Head of State, Aku, as First Lady, refuses to submit her agency but consistently asserts her will as a self-determined subject. She holds tenaciously to her principles and commitment to the handicapped children in spite of her husband's hostility. Unlike Zita-Zita she is a tough, articulate and less emotional personality. On the other hand, faced with the glamour and trappings of the position of First Lady, Zita-Zita, a more emotional and humble lady, decidedly turns her back on them and re-possesses her personality by turning down Michael's marriage proposal. However, Afiadu, a more materialistic character, hankers after the trammels of power only to get entrapped in a loveless and emotionally empty marriage. She represents the kind of woman thematized in much feminist criticism as a victim of domestic repression. She is denied all avenues of self-expression so she turns inwards, in search of alternative media, to abuse her stepson, become alcoholic, lachrymal and finally a murderer. Okekwe here seems to be saying to the regular feminists that the contemporary African woman is only entrapped domestically if she chooses to be. Zita-Zita and Aku are delineated as self-determined subjects who, by their agency, refuse to be entrapped by the male, while Afiadu is portrayed as a pathetic and virtually empty personality whose ephemerality deprives her of all agency.

On the theme of female sexuality Okekwe endorses a position that is counter-discursive to the radical feminist position which disparages what it construes as patriarchal control and compulsory heterosexuality. She endorses heterosexuality and vilifies promiscuity, homosexuality and lesbianism. The admirable women and men enjoy wholesome heterosexual relationships, a condition which she conceives as normal. This implies a validation of the cultural script on sexuality. Such aberrant habits as homosexuality and lesbianism are unequivocally renounced. However, in the explicitness of her sex scenes Okekwe also seems to be contesting the cultural script which relegates such issues as women's sexual pleasure to the very private domain. Osofisan notes that in this respect "the customary diffidence and traditional squeamishness about the matter of sex are over" (*The Guardian* 2003: 39.) With regards to lesbianism Nfah-Abbenyi narrates her experience at the 17th Annual African Literature Association Conference in 1991 when the issue of lesbianism was raised in respect of Calixthe Beyala's works. She notes that "the reaction of most of the African women in the audience fluctuated between indifference, anger, aggressivity, and even outright contempt." The consensus, as impatiently posited by the chair of the panel, is that the women of Africa "have other pressing and more important "problems" to worry about" (29). This seems to be Okekwe's position for the two instances of lesbianism and homosexuality are anathematized outright. In the assault on Frederick McDermott by Kenneth it is not the rape or violation of personality that is problematized but the revulsion at being touched by another man. Okekwe states that "Frederick was not grouchy. He was simply deadened by the horror of the quantum of filth injected into him. He was shocked and nauseous like someone fed to the brim with shit." (*Fumes and Cymbals*: 209). Kenneth is described as an abnormal man who "went through the back of the male instead of the front of a female" (275). It is not coincidental that only Kenneth, the homosexual, dies among all the members of Black, Black Birds who kidnapped and violated McDermott. And Lori Menakaya's lesbianism is equally offensive to Okekwe's sensibility. Lori is portrayed as an uppity, arrogant and self-righteous character, and in the end she is murdered rather inconsequentially because of her 'unwholesome' sexuality. Okekwe seems to punish these people for their 'abnormal' sexuality. She describes Kenneth's homosexuality as "his offence, it cost him his life" (275). Ekenma's and Ahaemesi's calamities, and even that of Michael Jnr, derive from their lack of sexual restraint and fidelity. With sexuality as the agenda Okekwe's narrative is obviously moralistic: punishing sexual immorality by killing off all deviants but rewarding all conformists.

Arising from the theme of sexuality is the issue of the female body which Western feminism tends to subvert in its construction of that body as weak and entrapping. It declaims sexual dichotomies and rather than explore and acknowledge the physical and physiological differences aspires to elide them by reading the bodies as fundamentally identical. In this pursuit the female body is construed as inadequate while the male's is idealized; the female body is disavowed and renounced, setting the woman against herself. In critiquing the representation of the female body by Simone de Beauvoir in *The Second Sex* Signe Arnfred observes that "Its capacity for pregnancy, childbirth, and lactation is *never* seen as a positive potential, as a source of pleasure or pride, but only and always as a curse, a drag, and a burden" (2002). Thus motherhood becomes identified as one of the major physical maladies which the female must subvert. It is conceived as the ultimate tool with which the male dominates and enslaves the female body and consigns it to the domestic sphere. However, according to Arnfred, "This is motherhood as seen by (European) men; not motherhood as seen by (African) women" (2002). In Okekwe's 'African-woman's sight' the female body is beautiful and motherhood is in fact the ideal of femaleness and the greatest medium of empowerment. Nfah-Abennyi observes that "Whereas many Western women may view multiple childbirth as both oppressive and restrictive ... most African women find empowerment in their children and families" (24). Obviously subscribing to this cultural script Okekwe glorifies motherhood and practically identifies it as godly. As exemplified in the words of Aku, easily the most admirable and empowered female in the narratives, motherhood is empowering and honorific and is an approximation of the divine creative essence:

> God has made us co-creators with him and co-workers in his vineyard. So he made us hold seeds for nine months in our wombs for him... It's a great honour ... We can shape the minds and characters of our children and our husbands, these people we hold and nurture in our wombs. (*Zita-Zita*, 152)

Thus Okekwe's most admirable females, Aku and Zita-Zita, have experienced multiple childbirth and are not in any way oppressed or domesticated by that. They are good mothers who love and cherish their children, women who are not at war with their bodies but are comfortable and empowered within and without the domestic space. The weakest and most pathetic ones, Afiadu and Ekenma, are notably childless.

It is the practice of Western feminists and their non-Western acolytes to focus and isolate one or more, usually insignificant, issues concerning non-Western women and then problematize it or them out of all reasonable proportions. Conceitedly, they silence the more oppressive, but obviously least attractive to the West, concerns of these women. Okekwe veraciously ignores most of these favorites of Western feminism, such as female circumcision and polygamy, but focuses on the oppressive political and social landscape on which her people exist. And rather than deploy the postcolonialist and feminist pervasively confrontational gender and sexuality polemics she nuances gender in a discourse that is more reformative, progressive and revolutionary, and more contemporaneous. She addresses the sufferings of her people, a suffering which she does not trivialize, abstract, metaphorize or undermine by subscribing to the gender hysterics of feminism which, according to Ogunyemi, "concentrates on patriarchy, analyzing it, attacking it, detecting its tentacles in the most unlikely places" (69). Okekwe subscribes to the form of feminism differently labeled by many African women but commonly characterized by shared ideals. Named 'Womanism' by Chikwenye Okonjo Ogunyemi and 'Stiwanism' by Omolara Ogundipe-Leslie (1994) this peculiar movement advocates the sharing of experiences amongst the sexes and aims at integrating, rather than dividing the sexes. This is evident in "the dynamism of wholeness and self-healing that one sees in the positive, integrative endings of womanist novels" (Ogunyemi 72).

Okekwe's strategy is not 'gender-is-the-agenda' narrative wherein characters are constituted and named by their gender, or defined in accordance with obvious contestation of their socially or culturally constructed or assigned sex-based roles. Rather, by eliding or being apparently gender indifferent she does speak volumes for gender equity. Rather than subscribe to gender balance by narrating oppressive gender inequities, she subscribes to gender balance by narrating cordial gender equities. This allows her to further the womanist agenda and to rub thematic shoulders with some of Africa's most renowned male writers in the sheer currency and intensity of her social reformist campaign. Fired by this urgent zeal, she ignores undue mythification and metaphorization, a narrative technique particularly typified in the creative writings of Femi Osofisan and early Wole Soyinka, wherein narratives are set in fictitious landscapes, topicality compromised by circuitous plots and labyrinthine innuendoes and proverbs. Okekwe does not only set her story in concrete and oppressively contemporary and recognizable settings—Lagos, Onitsha, Ibadan, Aso Rock in Abuja, *et cetera*—she also recreates characters and events obviously modeled after very controversial real prototypes. Thus her textuality is characterized by an uncanny intertextuality, a conflation of non-fictive familiar and notorious texts unto her narrative which not only displays the acuity of her social consciousness but a determination to assail the imperceptibility or distancing of the reader by making her/him encounter recognizable texts and people.

Promise Okekwe creatively articulates in her fiction the position in the theorizing of many non-Western 'feminist' scholars regarding feminism and gender discourse in non-Western societies. She demonstrates the inappositeness of applying the Western model to contemporary Nigeria where the socio-political and economic landscape is peculiar. Thus she subscribes to the peculiarity of contemporary Nigerian society rather than the popular postcolonial critical practice of inclusiveness and literary commodification which engenders representations along Western scripted matrixes.

Notes

1. See Bill Ashcroft *et al* in *The Empire Writes Back: Theory and Practice in Post-colonial Literatures*, 1989: 2.
2. Buchi Emecheta, for instance, seems to recommend, even in some of her fiction, that African women follow her example and emigrate from the sexually oppressive postcolony to the liberating Enlightened West.
3. For instance, Mireille's in Mariama Bâ's *Scarlet Song*, Elizabeth's in Bessie Head's *A Question of Power*, Nnu Ego's in Buchi Emecheta's *The Joys of Motherhood*, et cetera.

Works Cited

Amadiume, Ifi. *Male Daughters and Female Husbands: Gender and Sex in an African Society*. London: Zed Press, 1987.

Appiah, Kwame Anthony. "Is the Post- in Postmodernism the Post- in Postcolonial?" *Critical Inquiry* 17, 2 (Winter 1991): 336-357.

Arnfred, Signe. "Simone de Beauvoir in Africa: "Woman = The Second Sex?" Issues of African Feminist Thought." *Jenda: A Journal of Culture and African Women Studies*, (2002) 2, 1. [http://.jendajournal.com/jenda/vol2.1/toc2.1.htm]

Ashcroft, Bill, Gareth Griffiths, and Helen Tiffin. *The Empire Writes Back: Theory and Practice in Post-colonial Literatures*. London: Routledge, 1989.

Bâ, Mariama. *Scarlet Song*. (Trans. Dorothy S. Blair). Essex: Longman, 1986.

Clech Lam, Maivan. "Feeling Foreign in Feminism." *Signs* 19, 4 (Summer 1994): 865-893.

Elaine Showalter. *The Female Malady: Woman, Madness and English Culture, 1830-1980*, London: Virago, 1985.

Emecheta, Buchi. *Joys of Motherhood*. New York: George Braziller, 1979.

Goodman, Lizbeth. *Literature and Gender*. London: Routledge, 1996.

Head, Bessie. *A Question of Power*. Oxford: Heinemann, 1974.

Kumah, Carolyn. "African Women and Literature." *West Africa Review* Vol. 2, No. 1. [http://www.icaap.org/iuicode?101.2.15]

McClintock, Anne. "The Angel of Progress: Pitfalls of the Term 'Post-colonialism.' " *Social Text* (Spring 1992): 1-15.

Mishra, Vijay and Bob Hodge. "What is Post(-)colonialism?" *Colonial Discourse and Post-colonial Theory*. Eds. Patrick Williams and Laura Chrisman. New York: Columbia University Press, 1994.

Mohanty, Chandra Talpade. "Under Western Eyes: Feminist Scholarship and Colonial Discourses." *The Postcolonial Studies Reader*. Eds. Bill Ashcroft, Gareth Griffiths and Helen Tiffin. London and New York: Routledge. 1995, 2001: 259- 263.

Mukherjee, Arun. "Whose Post-Colonialism and whose Postmodernism?" *World Literature Written in English* 30, 2 (autumn 1990): 1-9.

Nfah-Abbenyi, Juliana Makuchi. *Gender in African Women's Writing: Identity, Sexuality and Difference*. Bloomington and Indianapolis: Indiana University Press, 1997.

Njubi, N. Francis. "African Intellectuals in the Belly of the Beast: Migration, Identity and the Politics of Exile." *Mots Pluriels*, no. 20, 2002. [http://www.arts.uwa.cdu.au/MotsPluriels/MP2002fnn.html]

Ogundipe-Leslie, Omolara. *Re-Creating Ourselves: African Women and Critical Transformations*. Trenton, New Jersey: Africa World Press, 1994.

Ogunyemi, Chikwenye Okonjo. "Womanism: The Dynamics of the Contemporary Black Female Novel in English." *Signs* 11, 1 (Autumn 1985): 63-80.

Okekwe, Promise. *Hall of Memories*. Lagos: Oracle Books Limited, 2001.

—. *Zita-Zita*. Lagos: Oracle Books Limited, 2002.

—. *Fumes and Cymbals*. Lagos: Oracle Books Limited, 2002.

Osofisan, Femi. "Eagles in the Age of Unacknowledged Muse." Lagos: *The Guardian*, (Feb. 22, March 1, and March 8, 2003).

Ouloguem, Yambo. *Bound to Violence* (Trans. Ralph Manheim). London, 1968.

Oyewumi, Oyeronke. *The Invention of Women: Making an African Sense of Western Gender Discourses*. Minneapolis: University of Minnesota Press, 1997.

Parmar, Pratibha and Valerie Amos. "Challenging Imperial Feminism." *Feminist Review* 17 (Autumn 1984).

Schulze-Engler, Frank. "The Politics of Postcolonial Theory." *Acolit* (Special Issue) No. 3: *Postcolonial Theory and the Emergence of a Global Society*. Eds. Gordon Collier,

Dieter Riemenschneider and Frank Schulze-Engler. Frankfurt and Maim, 1998: 31-36.

Stanovsky, Derek. "Fela and His Wives: The Import of a Postcolonial Masculinity." http://social.chass.ncsu.edu/jouvert/v2i1/stan.htm.

Trinh, T. Minha. "Writing Postcoloniality and Feminism." In: *The Postcolonial Studies Reader*. Eds. Bill Ashcroft, Gareth Griffiths, Helen Tiffin. 1995, 2001: 264-268.

Chapter 4

The Fragmented Heritage in the Reconstitution of Home: Assia Djebar's *L'amour, la fantasia*

Najat Rahman

---

*"Everything is clearer
and nearer to us
than the words we choose
to speak of it."*
—Adonis, Al-Kitab 53

"I have become to myself the country of destitution."
—St. Augustine, cited in *Fantasia: An Algerian Cavalcade* 216

*"Fiction and the history of actual events converge toward the same
nothingness; the knowledge revealed by the hypothesis was construed.
Knowledge of the impossibility of knowing precedes the act of consciousness that tries to reach it."*
—Paul de Man, *Blindness and Insight* 75

In *L'amour, la fantasia*, Assia Djebar writes of her desire to redress the absence of home: "I do not claim here to be either a story-teller or a scribe. On the territory of dispossession, I would that I could sing."[1] Djebar's prose seeks literary forms that can face and efface dispossession, which is the cause of the longing for home and the promise that it implies.[2] For this writer, literary texts are ultimately "wagers on lastingness," and "embody *le dur désir de durer* [the difficult desire to endure]" (Steiner 57). In addition to its particular temporality, the literary text also impacts the physical nature of the human body. As Steiner further indicates, "the meaning of poetry and the music of those meanings, which we call metrics, are also of the human body" (Steiner 9). Thus Djebar evokes the physicality and rhythm of writing to reinforce the link between writing and possession, even as she announces the impossibility of such possession: "When the hand writes...carefully bending forward...crouching, swaying to and fro...[it does so] as in an act of love. When reading, the eyes take their time, delight in caressing the curves, while the calligraphy suggests the rhythm of the scansion: as if the writing marked the beginning and the end of possession" (Djebar 180).

Writing is the limit for Djebar; it is a threshold where possession may become possible in the inherent act of dispossession that is writing. But the question of what form the writing takes points to the failures of writing home, a kind of writing that keeps taking place only to mark its own materiality. It is nonetheless the physicality of writing that embodies possibility, and rhythmically engulfs the maternal duplicitous cry of welcome, protest, love, and violence that Djebar wants to reveal.

Similarly, reading, marked by the caressing gaze of desire, always proceeds "as if," in order not only to possess meaning and intelligibility from writing, but also to mark the possibility of survival. Maurice Blanchot, in his reading of Kafka, entertains literature as possibility, and states: "...art can succeed where knowledge fails: because it is and is not true enough to become the way, and too unreal to change into an obstacle" (Blanchot, *The Work of Fire* 19). Blanchot continues:

> Art is an as if. Everything happens as if we were in the presence of truth, but this presence is not one, that is why it does not forbid us to go forward. Art claims knowledge when knowledge is a step leading to eternal life, and it claims non-knowledge when knowledge is an obstacle drawn up in front of this life. It changes its meaning and its sign. It destroys itself while it survives. That is its imposture, but that is also its greatest dignity, that same that justifies the saying 'Writing is a form of prayer'" (ibid.).

It is from this duplicity of writing [and its duality as disappearance of the maternal oral cry and its survival in writing] that Djebar begins, that is, from the inherited *cri* already embedded there in *écriture*.

Writing for Djebar remains that hand extended by the father, a borrowed hand, and a hand possessed. This ambivalent hand is a severed fragment from the past, one that cannot be completely claimed nor can it appropriate the present even as it seeks self-possession; it is always at once overtaken and violated. Following Djebar, one wonders where possession "beyond beginning and end" is demarcated within writing. One also gropes for where Djebar's text begins and ends, where the boundaries are drawn between epigraph, epilogue, text, and pre-text. Not only does her work resist a founding moment from which to begin despite the profusion of dates, it also refuses closure.

This article considers the fragment in Djebar's heritage as key to the reconstitution of home in writing and as a facet of discontinuity. Djebar gathers fragments of the past, handed to her primarily by a paternal heritage, which she translates through her own fragmentary writing. Writing through the fragment marks absence in her reconstruction and struggle against the effacement of the maternal past. Even though writing gives voice, this voice remains nonetheless a "hieroglyph of a wild, collective voice" (Djebar 56). The fashioning of this voice in her project of reconstruction is what Djebar foregrounds as fiction. For Djebar, the fragment, as written remnant of an effaced past, allows for the possibility of testimony.

The link of home to writing is seen in Djebar's inheritance of *écriture* as linguistic exile. This articulation of the home challenges its restitution by nationalist modes of reading. If we consider the French language that the father passes on to his daughter, which allows her to write forbidden love letters, and later to read fragmentary written accounts of the French chroniclers on the conquest of Algeria, then this heritage is not a heritage in one's language or in one's mode of expression, but rather an unexpected inheritance of conquest and violence given out lovingly to the female child by the father. It is also the image of the father as symbol of order inherited with the language. George Steiner suggests that language is always inherited along with the figure of the father: "Our language inheritance is the father figure, the proponent figure of speech, which threatens to devour the autonomy, the novelty, the immediacy to ourselves (the idiolect) towards which our feelings, thoughts and needs strive" (Steiner 108).

Writing is presented as a forbidden inheritance for females by the social order of the father. And yet, Djebar suggests, it is liberating in its unveiling, allows one freedom of movement, and the words flow into inaccessible passages. Writing also makes it possible to reconstruct the past, and have a glimpse of this past as it disappears.

To probe the implications of a literary project that seeks reconstruction of home from the fragments of the past will allow us to delve into the enactment of writing as home for Djebar in a narrative of a particularly complicated identity. Djebar not only 'fragments' her text through writing in various genres, coupling love and war, and making ambivalent use of the French language, she also writes a text that is really a composite of intertextual fragments.[3]

L'AMOUR, LA FANTASIA AS A WORK OF TRANSLATION

Being a historian, Djebar sees the historian as a translator who reads the past with the present, in order to probe the discontinuities of the constructed past. Thus translation would disrupt, rather than interpret, the presumed continuity. Just like Walter Benjamin, she conceives of the past as fragmentary, accessible only through moments of crisis: "The past can be seized only as an image which flashes at the instant when it can be recognized and is never seen again...For every image of the past that is not recognized by the present as one of its own concerns threatens to disappear irretrievably" (Benjamin 225). The past is only accessed when the fleeting image, which threatens to disappear, is acknowledged, in other words, testified to, as testimony. Likewise, translation's historicity enables a questioning of the status of the "original," where history is neither a recollection of a state before fragmentation nor a subjective consciousness of this fragmentation. And it is translation as a fragment of a fragment that bears the tension of the necessity of witnessing and the impossibility of doing so. Benjamin's notion of translation as a broken fragment is useful for Djebar, because it follows the logic of heritage rather than of identity. It also presents the translator as a historian, one committed to the vanquished past and to those struggling in the present.

Djebar's *L'amour, la fantasia* is thus a work of translation (translating the fragments of the past into the present, the historical into the personal, and the literary and the oral into the written, etc.).[4] More importantly, it performs itself as displacement.[5] In crossing borders of language, time, national cultures, genres, and strict gender demarcations, it crosses forbidden limits. But the limits themselves become the writing of imprecated borders. Djebar interlocks fragment and narrative, history and translation, testimony and fiction. Inherited generic differences are destabilized, if not undone. The first *roman* [novel] of a projected quartet, *L'amour, La fantasia* is at once an autobiography, a historical narrative of the effacement of Algerian history under French colonization, a rewriting of French archives, and a transcription of oral testimonies by Algerian women. Paradoxically, her work announces itself as 'fictional' testimonial. In a soliloquy, she ruminates:

> My fiction is this attempt at autobiography, weighed down under the oppressive burden of my heritage. Shall I sink beneath the weight? [...] But the tribal legend crisscross the empty spaces, and the imagination crouches in the silence when loving words of the unwritten mother-tongue remain "unspoken" language conveyed like the inaudible babbling of a nameless, haggard mummer...How shall I find the strength to tear off my veil, unless I have to use it to bandage the running sore nearby which words exude?" (Djebar 218)

Implied in this narrative is the impossibility of speaking from the "inside," that is to say, in one's own mother tongue. The testimony is on absence as the burden of heritage. The writer nonetheless attempts to translate this silence and absence in her reconstruction of the past. The testimony is unveiled as a duplicitous intervention, for it is not the speaking subject that testifies but her language, the imposed French language handed to her by a father wearing a European suit and a fez, as she, a "little girl [goes] to school for the first time...walking hand in hand with her father" (Djebar 3). Thus problems of testimony, reconstruction, narration, and writing are situated at the level of language as a symbolic system that allows for naming, appropriation and representation. It is "a language which, in attempting to witness, cannot escape the repetitive gesture of violence: "*Le viol, non dit, ne sera pas violé*" [Violation unspoken will not be violated] (Djebar 226). There is a central emporium: if one represents, one risks reproducing, however slightly, the gesture of violence. But, if one does not speak, one risks erasing the traces. Throughout, Djebar foregrounds her role, posing her testimonies as apodictic questions: "Are these the ghosts of the raped, flitting over the piled-up corpses? Is it the spirit of an unacknowledged love, felt only in an intuitive sense of guilt?" (Djebar 16) The distanced fascination of the writers who write for Paris about the war is not only acknowledged by Djebar, perhaps she shares them as well. She asks: "What if this fascination also paralyzed the threatened camp?" (ibid.) And: "But why, above the corpses that will rot on successive battlefields, does this first Algerian campaign reverberate with the sounds of an obscene copulation?" (Djebar 19).

Not unlike the work of linguistic translation, Djebar's writing threatens the security of borders. Steiner reflects on the destabilizing force of the process of translation: "Translated into saying...the conceptual process, the deed of imagining can abolish, reverse, or confound all categories (themselves embedded in language) of identity and of temporality. Speech can change the rules under which it operates in the course of its operation..." (Steiner 54). The passage of writing entrusted to the translator is not only unstable, but is potentially also a violent one. The translator in Djebar's text, who carries a letter of peace, eventually dies from bearing the written words: "Any document written by 'the other' proves fatal, since it is a sign of compromise" (Djebar 33). Just as the written words are perceived as a sign of political compromise, so is writing by women seen to compromise them. Djebar foregrounds her position as translator: "This language was formerly used to entomb my people; when I write it today I feel like the messenger of old, who bore a sealed missive which might sentence him to death or to the dungeon...." (Djebar 215). For her to use the language of the "former enemy" complicates her work of testimony further and breaks down the frontiers of this passage of translation.

Djebar violates the prohibition against "laying bare one's self;" she "attempt[s] an autobiography in the former enemy's language" (ibid.), in order to carry out her project of reconstruction. To reconstitute the effaced horror of the Algerian past, she relies on the fragmented accounts written in letters by French fighters and observers. These accounts were written in the same French language that silenced the Algerians and which she now uses. Despite its wounds, French is nonetheless her access to these fragments and to writing. Her re-appropriation of these fragments allows her to reread the traces of a writing that has been erased. This further allows her to rewrite the story of Algerians centering on women. Her reading of these French accounts further destabilizes the said accounts, wrenching from them their process of effacement. To this French writing, she attempts to integrate Arabic oral accounts by women. The disjunction created between her fictionalized rewriting and the concealments of the letters reveals the fictional nature of these autobiographical letters, and her own fictional reconstruction becomes, perhaps, a more significant historical narrative.

This narrative presents itself as a writing that interrogates and reflects on the act of writing, all the while aware of the fiction of referentiality and the confrontation with the other language.[6] The narrator who poses as a self-conscious "witness" does not refrain from mingling the personal story with the historical narrative of the Algerian people, and making them indissociable. This past is not singular. It is personal. It is the past of her childhood, and that of the collective, namely, the 1830 French invasion of Algeria, and the 1954 Algerian war of liberation.

LOVE, FANTASIA, AND HISTORY

There is an inextricable link between love (*amour*) and warring (*fantasia*) through the figure of the father.[7] The first part of the text, entitled "The Capture of the City or Love Letters," already imbricates love in the historical events of war. The father's love is relayed through the gift of writing, and is expressed in writing.[8] At the same time, her father prohibits writing love letters. The writer's early personal and historical accounts are brought together, and are indissociable. The dominant theme of love is depicted against warring, for love, which is always there, precedes any warring. Thus *amour* precedes *fantasia* in naming this text. It is however a love that remains undisclosed. Djebar is forced to share in this love, if only to simply identify her own love for Algeria. She states: "It is as if these parading warriors...are mourning their unrequited love for my Algeria. I should first and foremost be moved by...the suffering of the anonymous victims, which their writings resurrect; but I am strangely haunted by the agitation of the killers, by their obsessional unease" (Djebar 57).

Love is intertwined in a letter, in the written words. But, paradoxically, it is in the words of the "other" that she attempts to write this love: "Love, if I managed to write it down, would approach a critical point: there where lies the risk of exhuming buried cries, those of yesterday and as well as those of a hundred years ago"[9] (Djebar 63). This attempt at writing love would allow her to "exhume the buried cries" of the dead. Love is already there in writing, as the ambivalent cry: "Love is the cry, the persistent pain which feeds upon itself, while only a glimpse is vouchsafed of the horizon of happiness" (Djebar 107).

Djebar musters ammunition in the form of many languages for women denied an expression of love or desire: "French for secret missives; Arabic for our stifled aspirations towards God-the-father... Lybico-Berber, which takes us back to the pagan idols-mother-gods of pre-Islamic Mecca. The fourth language, for all females, young or old, cloistered or half-emancipated, remains that of the body..." (Djebar 180). Djebar asserts that the body is invisible without words. At the same time, writing serves as another veiling of the body, a veiling that makes the body invisible in its visibility. Writing in the language of the other also changes one's perception of and relation to the body: "Writing the enemy's language is more than just a matter of scribbling down a muttered monologue under your very nose; to use this alphabet involves placing your elbow some distance in front of you to form a bulwark; however, in this twisted position, the writing is washed back to you" (Djebar 215). Writing as hiding becomes writing as unveiling in the appropriation of French. As Clarisse Zimra suggests, "[w]oman becomes a textual trope of absence, even when on display" (Zimra 70). And the body is also at stake in writing as it is unveiled. It is exposed in its enactment of love, in its cries, as the writing recalls the voices of the past. Writing itself is as much about evading individual effacement as it is about the survival of collective memory.

> *"L'amour, ses cris" ("s'écrit"):* my hand as I write in French makes the pun on love affairs that are aired; all my body does is to move forward, stripped naked, and when it discovers the ululations of my ancestresses on the battlefields of old, it finds that it is itself at stake: it is no longer a question of writing only to survive (Djebar 214).

The French language, which allows the writing of love, is also for Djebar the language through which violence speaks. It is ambivalently constructed as violation and freedom, and home and exile. Her paternal inheritance of this language both liberates and exiles her. It liberates her from the confinement of a patriarchal tradition, but it exiles her from the women of her own culture: "French... the language that my father had been at pains for me to learn, serves as a go-between, and from now a double, contradictory sign reigns over my initiation..." (Djebar 4). French lifts the burden of the inherited taboos, but it also implies dissociation from others of her tribe: "Once I had discovered the meaning of the words—those same words that are revealed to the unveiled body—I cut myself adrift" (Djebar 5). The image of cutting adrift in this discourse is indissociable from the symbolism of the ship of the invading French. Djebar further reminds us that the oral source of the French language for the colonized is violence; it is the language of law courts, words of accusation, and legal procedure (Djebar 215). Writing in French becomes at once a way of inheriting this colonial violence and resisting it. She states: "Words that are explicit become such boastings as the braggart uses; and elected silence implies resistance still intact" (Djebar 178). Thus the veiling of language allows her to resist, and affords her the opportunity to write under a pseudonym about the women in her country and about the war, as well as "affirm" herself, just like in the forbidden love letters written by the young women, "[a]s if the French language suddenly had eyes, and lent them me to see into liberty..." (Djebar 181).

STRUCTURAL FRAGMENTATION

Intertextuality structures *L'amour, la fantasia* along paternal figures (Donadey 107). Fromentin's words frame this novel, while the three main sections are divided into very short pieces, introduced each by an epigraph. The first opens with an epigraph from Barchou de Penhoën, followed by an account of the author's father taking her to school. Ibn Khaldun opens the second. One epigraph to the third section, "Voices from the Past," is from St. Augustine, and the other is from Ludwig van Beethoven. This third section is structured as a musical composition, and subdivided into five movements, where each movement begins with a "voice" and ends with "embraces."

An ending fragment further follows each section. The first part, for instance, is concluded with an italicized fragment of poetry, "Deletion," embedded within an alternation of plain text and italicized passages that marks ruptures as borders for the personal and historical. It speaks of fragments where "faint images flake off from the rock of Time" (Djebar 46). Djebar seeks to capture these forgotten, "liberating," moments that Walter Benjamin has spoken of: "And for a fleeting moment, I glimpse the mirror-image of the foreign inscription, reflected in Arabic letters, writ from right to left in the mirror of suffering; the letters fade into pictures of the mountainous Hoggar in prehistoric times..." (ibid.). The ephemeral image of Hoggar emerging from the fading letters is one of suffering and effacement, inherited in the maternal figure of Hoggar as 'other.' The image is the absence and disappearance of writing, its otherness and foreignness, but reflected in Arabic letters.

The difficulty of reading this writing that reflects the effacement of the maternal figure lies in the fact that it also requires impossible rigor and a certain vulnerability: "To read this writing, I must lean over backwards, plunge my face into the shadows, closely examine the vaulted roof of rock...lend an ear to whispers that rise up from time out of mind...Alone, stripped bare, unveiled, I face these images of darkness..." (ibid.). Not unlike the task of writing, the process of reading unveils the reader as well. Djebar, who reads the divine command, "Read," made in the cave as the Angel Gabriel unveiled the Qur'anic revelation to Muhammad, is exempted from the ritual of female veiling. When the familial matriarchs question her mother as to why the young girl is not veiled, the mother answers "she reads," which in spoken Arabic also means "she studies." Reading provides for revelation, and for her it is that of her own body. This revelation is also mediated through the body.

> This language, which I learn, demands the correct posture for the body, on which the memory rests for its support. The childish hand... begins to write. "Read!" The fingers laboring on the tablet send back the signs to the body, which is simultaneously reader and servant. The lips having finished their muttering, the hand will once more do the washing, proceeding to wipe out what is written on the tablet: this is the moment of absolution, like touching the hem of death's garment. Again, it is the turn of writing, and the circle is completed (Djebar 184).

Reading approximates prayer, a prayer that is incidentally a series of ritualized body movements accompanying Qur'anic recitals. Reading is performative, submitting to the command "Read" by reading it.[10] In Djebar's formulation, the repetitive move, from reading to writing, is predicated on erasure, erasure that provides absolution, protection not only for the reader but also for the writing itself.[11]

HERITAGE

Djebar sees her heritage as fractured, divided between a paternal heritage where love recedes and a maternal heritage always in retreat: "How are the sounds of the past to be met as they emerge from the well of bygone centuries? ... And my body reverberates with sounds from the endless landslide of generations of my lineage" (Djebar 46). Heritage is expressed in the familiar familial tropes. The beginning of her narrative juxtaposes the paternal father passing on to her the French language and the mythical mother deleting it.

Juxtaposition is again evident between Hoggar and Abraham whose ballad "The Ballad of Abraham," is situated towards the end of the text. It is a fragment of the overall heritage she invokes, which points to the convergences and separations of paternal traditions inherited. This heritage offers her the opportunity for dialogue through song: "Tradition would seem to decree that entry through its gate is by submission, not by love. Love, which the most simple of settings might inflame, appears dangerous. There remains music" (Djebar 169). Music is perhaps that exceptional excess that is allowed a cultural space. It is also a response to longing, a possibility, and a "promise."[12]

Djebar offers a reading of the ballad of Abraham, seeing the primacy of love in the story of Ibraham. She also sees love in the story of Muhammad, a love rendered secondary to submission, if not altogether irrelevant in traditional Islam. This primacy of submission is inherited from the figure of Abraham, Abraham the paradigmatic father, the father of Arabs and Jews, the one whose legacy is to disinherit. He dispossesses and exiles one son as well as acquiesces to the sacrifice of his son Isaac.[13] But Ishmael is forever the remainder, and in the texts of Djebar he is connected to music.[14] Djebar reads this story of Abraham differently. It is the submission of Isaac that makes it compelling for her: "I loved the simplicity of Isaac's song" (Djebar 171). But the story is never that simple, since it valorizes submission over love and points to that threatening possibility of foreclosing one's future for one's past. It is this inherited cultural moment that will lead Djebar to point to the ruptures of her inheritance and to attempt a new reading of this story.

Her narrative is framed with the father, whether it is her Algerian father, the literary fathers Augustine and Ibn Khaldun, or the French figures, such as Fromentin or Pélissier. It is an inheritance usually bestowed on males, and she is aware of her privilege to receive it as a female. St. Augustine's epigraph in the third section occurs after five hundred years of Roman occupation of his home-land, when he writes his autobiography in Latin. Both father of the Catholic Church and father of the Western autobiography, St. Augustine, like Djebar, writes his story in the dominant language of the 'other' (Djebar 241-42): "And his writing presses into service, in all innocence, the same language as Caesar or Sulla, writers and generals of the successful 'African Campaign'" (Djebar 215). Djebar inscribes her work in this Latin heritage that precedes the Arabic one.

Another great figure that Djebar claims for her heritage is the famous historian Ibn Khaldun, who opens the second section, "The cries of the fantasia." He also writes his autobiography in the dominant Arabic language. In opening this section, there seems to be an implicit comparison between the violence of the Arab conquerors and the violence of the French occupation.

> As with Augustine, it matters little to him that he writes in a language introduced into the land of his fathers by conquest and accompanied by bloodshed! A language imposed by rape as much as by love...Ibn Khaldun is now nearly seventy years of age: after an encounter with Tamerlane—his last exploit—he prepares to die in exile in Egypt. He suddenly obeys a yearning to turn back on himself: and he becomes the subject and object of a dispassionate autopsy (Djebar 216).

Djebar claims the lineage of St. Augustine and Ibn Khaldun, not only because they wrote in the language of their conquerors and did violence to writing, but also because they are fathers of the forms of autobiography and history that she has inherited and is employing. She names them as her own, as fellow compatriots, so as not to be exiled. Djebar proclaims that speaking of one's self outside the language of the ancestors exiles one. But, the language of the ancestors when written is always a borrowed one (Djebar 178).

Djebar also claims the inheritance of the French language, the writing of the French chroniclers. Inheritance becomes simultaneously liberating and dead weight. It is a language that she not only masters but exploits poetically, so that it yields beautiful passages around her own disinheritance: "The French language could offer me all its inexhaustible treasures, but not a single one of its terms of endearment would be destined for my use..." (Djebar 27). Commenting on the voluminous amount of print written by so many fighting men and on the fact that linguistic representation is itself violent, she writes: "And words themselves become a decoration...words will become their most effective weapons. Hordes of interpreters, geographers, ethnographers...will form a pyramid to hide the initial violence from view" (Djebar 45).

Djebar recognizes that she bears an inescapably ambivalent heritage that includes the paternal heritage of the French figures and the language passed on by her father: "For my part, even when I am composing the most commonplace of sentences, my writing is immediately caught in the snare of the old war between two peoples. So I swing like a pendulum from images of war (but always in the past) to the expression of a contradictory, ambiguous love" (Djebar 216). This is the closest articulation of what she means by love, a love in the present that is replete with contradictions. Her narrative as well alternates between present and past where her accounts of the French and Algerians are brought together and are intertwined.

Djebar announces another father figure, the 19th century painter Eugène Fromentin, the official painter of the conquest of Algeria, as strategic for mediating her move from "fact" to "fiction." Fromentin is important for her literary intervention as she relies on his travel notes in her rewriting: "I intervene to greet the painter who has accompanied me...like a second father figure...Fromentin offers me an unexpected hand, the hand of an unknown woman he was never able to draw" (Djebar 226). This is the severed hand that she takes from him in order to write. Djebar wonders about the effect of this hand on the painter who spent more time writing than painting: "Is it the feel of this object in his hand which transforms him from a painter of Algerian hunting scenes into the writer depicting death in words? ...As if the story passed on to him could only find its final form in words..." (Djebar 167).

Djebar repeats the recounting of this fragment from Fromentin's travelogue, which tells of him picking up a severed hand of an unknown woman and throwing it away. This is the unexpected hand that she takes from him. In this repetition, Djebar adds: "...Fromentin picks up out of the dust the severed hand of an anonymous Algerian woman. He throws it down again in his path. Later I seize on this living hand, hand of mutilation and of memory, and I attempt to bring it the *qalam* [pen]" (Djebar 226). This retrieval of the hand from Fromentin, which is severed, then rejected, then reappropriated by Djebar as instrument of writing, enables her to rewrite the story of the mutilated Algeria, by using the Arabic *qalam*. Djebar's gesture of picking up the hand becomes an act of testimony, by writing the Arabic traces and attempting to liberate the gendered through inscription. The borrowed hand, which is a significant recurring frame of this novel, is a starting point for writing and for possession, since it is through the hand that one appropriates the world. And yet the hand being severed also testifies to the inability to narrate what is not narratable.

The novel opens and closes on a citation from Fromentin's, *Une Année dans le Sahel*: "A heart-rending cry arose—I can hear it still as I write to you—then the air was rent with screams, then pandemonium broke loose..." (Djebar 1). She, as well, is able to hear these intermittent cries through writing. The ominous last lines that close her novel are an oral reworking of Fromentin's citation: "I wait ...foreseeing the inevitable moment when the mare's hoof will strike down any woman who dares to stand up freely...Yes, in spite of the tumult of my people all around, I already hear, even before it arises and pierces the harsh sky, I hear the death cry in the Fantasia" (Djebar 227). In these words, she links the "inevitable" future of Algeria to its past and present where violent warring and subjugation of women prevail over unspoken love.

Pélissier also grants Djebar a paternal inheritance of writing, just like her father first gave her the inheritance of the French language. The narrator is "moved by an impulse" to express gratitude to the one that handed her the report, the "butcher-recorder": "After the...brutal killing...he is overcome with remorse and describes the slaughter he has organized. I venture to thank him ...for having indulged in a whim to immortalize them in a description of their rigid carcasses... For having looked on the enemy otherwise than as a horde of zealots..." (Djebar 78). Her expression of gratitude seeks to emphasize the threat of complete effacement without writing and recording. In rendering a tribute to their remorseful killer, as disingenuous as she deems it, she inescapably commits violence against the memories of victims. In the gesture of gratitude, she has to momentarily forget the victims in order to remember him. She grants this "silent witness" authority in this privileged status [of a silent witness], and to herself an ambivalent authority as witness of this testimony (Djebar 79). And yet it is her own tribe that falls victim to Pélissier's act. Her own act of reconstruction is revealed to be apodictic in its violent ambivalence and necessity.

Writing, including the description of the incident, can potentially grant her "voice," one that is not dissociated from what it hears: "one hundred years later... I find the strength to speak. Before I catch the sound of my own voice I can hear the death-rattles, the moans of those immured in the Dahra Mountains...they provide my orchestral accompaniment" (Djebar 217). Djebar recognizes that she ultimately shares in this long violent legacy, even as she attempts to redress it.

The voice is also a cry that is always present, in the violence of the French and the imposition of the French language, not to mention the silence of the women: "I am alternately the besieged foreigner and the native swaggering off to die, so there is seemingly endless strife between the spoken and the written word" (Djebar 215). Despite the strife, or because of it, there is an embedding of orality and writing. The play on *cri* and *écriture* undermines the dichotomy between orality and writing and points to the dialogism between the oral and the written. For Djebar, writing is the other language; it is language as 'other'. She is aware of the inherent contradiction in her project. She wants to represent silence of women and of the dead. But, how does one attempt to render a voice? She asks: "Can I pretend to live these voices?" (Djebar 226). While she nonetheless attempts it through self-conscious fragmentation and foregrounding of narrative, she simultaneously announces its impossibility.

Writing becomes a way to respond to and redress the amorous aphasia of her veiled and silent "sisters" (Djebar 142). She redeems writing, which allows her to hear the women's silent cries of protest. Writing also discloses and grants voice: "Writing does not silence the voice, but awakens it, above all to resurrect so many vanquished sisters" (Djebar 204). The veil stretches beyond covering the face or body, it also covers the voice: "To refuse to veil one's voice and start 'shouting', that was really indecent, real dissidence. For the silence of all others suddenly lost its charm and revealed itself for what it was: a prison without reprieve" (Djebar 204). Djebar attempts to reclaim the cry/voice in writing.

Writing is also linked to being for Djebar: "The half-emancipated girl imagines she is calling on his [the father's] presence to bear witness: 'You see, I'm writing, and there's no harm in it...It's simply a way of saying I exist...!'" (Djebar 58). It is also a way of demarcating being: "By keeping up a dialogue with this presence that haunted me [presence of the father], my writing became an attempt, or a temptation, to set the limits on my own silence..." (Djebar 61). But, inversely, the language in which she writes is absenting: "...the [French] words I use convey no flesh-and-blood reality. I learn...lists of flowers...that I shall never smell...In this respect, all vocabulary expresses what is missing in my life...I do not realize...that, in the conflict between these two worlds, lies an incipient vertigo" (Djebar 185).

TESTIMONY

Djebar's work, preoccupied as it is with the figure of the father, is also grounded in the oral testimonies of the Algerian women. She adds a fragment on Pauline Rolland, an 1848 revolutionary, who was deported to Algeria. Although she is not Algerian, she nonetheless is counted as an ancestor because of her struggle: "Her true heirs...the chorus of anonymous women of today... could pay homage to her with that ancestral cry of triumph, the ululation of convulsive sisterhood!" (Djebar 223). Through this ending story, Djebar reveals a heritage imbricated not only in orality and writing but in cultural and linguistic terms as well.

She sustains the tension and ambivalence of inheritance to the end. The epigraph to the last section, which the story of Rolland begins, includes two definitions of cry, a cry of misfortune, *tzarl-rit*, and a cry of happiness. The French words that she employs to conjure the voices of the women are the same ones that divide her from them. Djebar cannot access her heritage, except through a language imposed, that which is written and which does violence to her retreating oral heritage. While this language may set her apart from the other women, it also reinforces the gender dynamics of reticence: "I cohabit with the French language: I may quarrel with it, I may have bursts of affection...If I deliberately provoke an outburst, it is...because I am vaguely aware of having been forced into a "marriage" too young, rather like the little girls of my town who are 'bespoke' in their earliest childhood" (Djebar 213).

When Djebar writes, she insists on the necessity of the language of the 'other' for witnessing. She problematizes the valorization of ocular testimony, since the usual association of the notions of testimony and witnessing are with seeing, hearing, living, and do not include writing. She not only includes, she also foregrounds writing. There is always an excess of what the witness can see or hear or live: "I...read as if I were shrouded in the ancestral veil; with my one free eye perusing the page, where is written more than the eye-witness sees, more than can be heard" (Djebar 209). She renders problematic her role of "witness," pointing to its many limitations: "Can I, twenty years later, claim to revive these stifled voices? And speak for them?" (Djebar 202). This is no longer an immediate "eye-witness" account, but testimony [read narrative] that is always necessarily retrospective and after the fact. In a sense, it is impotent since the stakes are no longer the same when one belatedly testifies: "I, in my turn, write, using this language, but more than one hundred and fifty years later" (Djebar 7). So the problem of memory and language that underlie fictionality are there. This fictionality, however, is often denied in testimonial narratives.

Testimony reveals a double structure: the witness testifies not only to the perceived, lived, heard-of "event," but also to his/her own reliability. The witness testifies essentially to his/her own potency to tell the "truth," to his/her generative power.[15] There is a sense of impotency for the witness in this belatedness: "What ghosts will be conjured up when in this absence of expressions of love (love received, 'love' imposed), I see reflection of my own barrenness, my own aphasia" (Djebar 202). Just like translation, the compelling need for testimony is accompanied by the foreknowledge of the failure to do so. Djebar sees the testimonial writing of the French officials and the love letters written by young Algerian women as futile. These young women write because of their confinement; "...they mark their marasmus with their own identity in an attempt to rise above their pathetic plight" (Djebar 45). The accounts of the French fighters depict "invaders who imagine they are taking the Impregnable City, but who wander aimlessly in the undergrowth of their own disquiet" (Djebar 45).

Djebar's text seems poignantly aware of how narration and representation cannot escape fictionalization, falsification, and transformation of what one is trying to see. Claiming all generic identities, she claims also their fiction.[16]

Djebar recognizes that she can work with only traces of writing, hence she stays with them in rewriting the history as her story. But this "reconstruction" remains fragmentary in its excess, and hallucinatory in its movements. She reveals testimony as always fleeting and forgotten (Djebar 116). It cannot provide a totalizing narrative, hence the valorization of the fragment even in this paradoxical "narrative." Testimony for Djebar seems to be an inheritance, an exhumed memory that one inhabits and whose aftermath one lives (Djebar 92).

Notes

1. The historical account of this text begins with the capture of Algiers in 1830 and extends to the War of Independence of 1954-62. For covering the War of Conquest, Djebar relies on her archival research and obscure fragments of eye-witness accounts written at the time by participants in the war who wrote either for publication or simply to their own families. The oral testimonies of the women who participated in the struggle form the basis for covering the War of Independence. See the original in Assia Djebar. *L'amour, la fantasia*. Paris: Éditions Albin Michel, 1995. Prémiere édition: Jean-Claude Lattès, 1985.

2. Goerge Steiner, in his emphasis on music as granting "real presence," cites Pierre Jean Jouve, the French poet and essayist, who defines "the promise" as "the concrete universal of the challenging and consoling experience of the unfulfilled" and situates it in music (Steiner 19). For Steiner, literary texts are not unlike the musical composition (Steiner 27).

3. This anticipates her other writing projects where she writes in an intertextual manner, retracing the other writing in its fragments and incorporating it in her writing. In *Loin de Médine* she reads the historical accounts of the early Islamic century, those of Ibn Hashem, Ibn Saad, and Tabari, a period which begins with the death of the prophet Muhammad in order to "resurrect" these forgotten women that traverse the early (and later accounts of Islam).

4. She follows from the traditions of Arabic translations of the ancient Greek manuscripts, especially those commentaries of Ibn Rushd (or Averroes) on Aristotle, to reveal a notion of translation that allows for intertextuality rather than a limited notion of mimesis.

5. In Latin, *translatio* suggests displacement through its meaning of "carrying over."

6. She implicates her own autobiographical project in the inherent contradictions and fictionality of language itself. Writing is also linked to the anonymity of the self in the venture of autobiography. "While I thought I was undertaking a 'journey through myself', I find I am simply choosing another veil. While I intended every step forward to make me more clearly identifiable, I find myself progressively sucked down into the anonymity of those women of old, my ancestors!" (Djebar 217). The project of autobiography itself resists the anonymity practiced by and required of an Arab woman.

7. Fantasia is from the Arabic *fantaziya* which signifies "ostentation" and which is associated with warring. It designates more specifically "a set of virtuoso movements on horseback executed at a gallop, accompanied by loud cries and culminating in rifle shots" (See Dorothy S. Blair, "Introduction," *Fantasia: An Algerian*

Cavalcade n.p.). It also alludes to an improvisational musical composition. It is in the third part of the novel where the musical references are most insistent and which is divided into five "movements."

8. The cultural transgression of the father, who at one point writes the mother and not the family, hence an open declaration of love, is significant for her since love is articulated but always in the language of the conquerors, a language paradoxically imposed and liberating. Her mother's transgression is by referring to her husband by his name. The name of the father, Taher, becomes more pure (*taher*) through this transgressive cultural act that contaminates the mother.

9. Djebar seems to make an implicit reference to the pre-Islamic *qasida* through the desert journey motif. The pre-Islamic poetic words would also constitute for her a paternal heritage if not a "language of the other."

10. The Qur'an even etymologically suggests that which is to be read, placing the emphasis on reading rather than writing.

11. In Jacques Derrida's discussion of Freud's mystic pad, writing always attempts to safeguard itself. Derrida suggests: "There is no writing which does not devise some means of protection, to protect against itself, against the writing by which the "subject" is himself threatened as he lets himself be written: as he exposes himself." (Derrida, "Freud and the Scene of Writing 224, emphasis is his) Whereas the layer of celluloid shields the wax paper, Djebar has many veiling techniques including her own pseudonym. Derrida further writes: "the trace is the erasure of selfhood, of one's own presence, and is constituted by the threat or anguish of its irremediable disappearance, of the disappearance of its disappearance. An inerasable trace is not a trace, it is a full presence..." (Derrida 230).

12. Steiner"s central claim in his book is that "the experience of aesthetic meaning in particular, that of literature, of the arts, of musical form, infers the necessary possibility of this 'real presence'" (3).

13. There is a tendency in popular Islamic belief to view Ishmael as the one that Abraham set out to sacrifice.

14. This will connect Ishmael to music in *Loin de Médine*, as the possibility for a new beginning.

15. Testimonials strangely foreground the sexuality of the witness, predicating the ability to testify with one's generative possibilities. See, for instance, Ghassan Kanafani's *Men in the Sun* where Abu al-Khaizaran the guide, the survivor, and witness, who is further associated with the Palestinian national liberation movement, is named and identified as castrated. See also *The Last of the Just* where Krémer, the sympathetic humanist, the witness from the window, has one testicle. It is also noteworthy that Deuteronomy rejects detesticled males as non-Jews; and those with one testicle cannot enter the house of God. "He whose testicles are crushed or whose male member is cut off shall not enter the assembly of the lord" (See Deuteronomy 23:1). One's ability to proliferate the continuity of the father through one's progeny and words is the implied measurement of the witness.

16. Genre testifies to its own corpus of works and assumes that individual texts testify to their communality with other texts.

Works Cited

Benjamin, Walter. *Illuminations: Essays and Reflections*. Edited and introduced by Hannah Arendt. New York: Schocken Books, 1969.

Blanchot, Maurice. *The Work of Fire*. Trans. Charlotte Mandell. Stanford: Stanford University Press, 1995.

Chalala, Elie. "The Silence of Arab Intellectuals on Algeria's Killing Fields." *Al-Jadid* 21 (1997): 38.

De Man, Paul. *Blindness and Insight: Essays in the Rhetoric of Contemporary Criticism*. Minneapolis: University of Minnesota Press, 1988.

—-. *The Resistance to Theory*. Foreword by Wlad Godzich. Minneapolis: University of Minnesota Press, 1986.

Derrida, Jacques. "Freud and the Scene of Writing." *Writing and Difference*. Translated and introduced by Alan Bass. Chicago: The University of Chicago Press, 1978.

—-. "From Des Tours de Babel." Trans. Joseph F. Graham. In Rainer Schulte and John Biguenet, Eds. *Theories of Translation: An Anthology of Essays from Dryden to Derrida*. Chicago: University of Chicago, 1992.

Djebar, Assia. *Fantasia: An Algerian Cavalcade*. Trans. Dorothy S. Blair. Portsmouth, NH: Heinemann, 1993.

Donadey, Anne. "Assia Djebar's Poetics of Subversion," *L'Esprit Créateur* 33 (1993): 107.

Felman, Shoshana and Dori Laub, MD. *Testimony: Crises of Witnessing in Literature, Psychoanalysis and History*. New York: Routledge, 1992.

Kanafani, Ghassan. *Men in the Sun: and other Palestinian stories*. Trans. Hilary Kilpatrick. Cairo: The American University of Cairo Press, 1978.

Marx, Karl. *The Eighteenth Brumaire of Louis Bonaparte*. New York: International Publishers, 1963.

Niranjana, Tejaswini. *Siting Translation: History, Post-Structuralism, and the Colonial Context*. Berkeley: University of California University Press, 1992.

Schwarz-Bart, André. *Le Dernier des Justes*. Paris: Éditions du Seuil, 1959.

Steiner, George. *Real Presences*. Chicago: University of Chicago Press, 1991.

Zimra, Clarisse. "Writing Woman: The Novels of Assia Djebar," *SubStance* 21 (1992): 70.

PART TWO

RUMBLES OF RACE IN GENDER AND SEXUALITY MATTERS

The African Diaspora Factors of Race and Racism,
and Social and Racial Injustices

Chapter 5

The Issue Is Race: Gender and Sexuality in Dany Laferrière's North-American Autobiography

Ada Uzoamaka Azodo

Sexuality is subject to shifting history, economics, politics, and culture.[1] Those are closely the words in which Senegalese woman writer Ken Bugul, a notable voice in African second wave feminism, contests in *The Abandoned Baobab*, the first of a four-part autobiographical writing, the erroneous reduction of the complexities of sexual destinies and practices to traditionalist and normative definitions, according to which, gender and sexuality are fixed and natural phenomena. The author arrived at her poignant lucidity in the course of her own feelings of worthlessness in Europe, due to exile, isolation, alienation, and loneliness, and her subsequent resort to all kinds of desperate sexual practices in attempt to regain her equilibrium—night stands, strip-tease, nudity, lesbianism, bisexuality, and prostitution for money. Bugul states: « *Dans tout exode, il y a alteration de l'echelle des valeurs* » (*Le Baobab fou* 65). ["In every exodus there is a change in the sets of values" (*The Abandoned Baobab* 51)]. In feminist terms, Andrea Dworkin and Catherine MacKinnon would say that Ken Bugul was sexually "objectified" by white men who saw her as a "gender female," and would add that subsequently Ken Bugul viewed her self as "a thing" in service to men. It is unavoidable situation of things for women like Bugul, MacKinnon would again say, for most of such women "live as fish in water," and like fish that thrive on and derive nourishment and sustenance from water these women are glued to men. It is a bad situation for all women, nonetheless, because women are and will continue to be prohibited from exercising their rights of self-determination and self-expression, in one unhyphenated word, their humanity (1989, 124).

The issue of human rights above, or more poignantly, women's rights, derived from Ken Bugul's affirmations of the evil effects of neocolonialism on the postcolonial subject, recalls John D'Emilio's own and similar observation about the erroneous myth, widely accepted in gay movements, of the "eternal homosexual." D'Emilio states:

> The argument runs something like this: gay men and lesbians always were and always will be. We are everywhere; not just now, but throughout history, in all societies and all periods. This myth served a positive political function in the first years of gay liberation.

> In the early 1970s, when we battled an ideology that either denied
> our existence or defined us as psychopathic individuals or freaks of
> nature, it was empowering to assert that "we are everywhere." But,
> in recent years, it has confined us as surely as the most homophobic
> medical theories, and locked our movement in place" (Lancaster &
> Leonardo 1997: 170).

D'Emilio then goes on, like Bugul, to posit that gender and sexuality evolve with
history, adding that in history capitalism has led to the possibility of certain men
and women becoming gays and lesbians, thus sustaining gay identity.[2] D'Emilio
states:

> Here I wish to challenge this myth. I want to argue that gay men
> and lesbians have *not* always existed. Instead, they are a product of
> history; and have come into existence in a specific era. Their emer-
> gence is associated with the relations of capitalism: it has been the
> historical development of capitalism—more specifically, its free
> labor system—that has allowed large numbers of men and women
> in the late twentieth century to call themselves gay, to see themselves
> as part of a community of similar men and women, and to organize
> politically on the basis of that identity (ibid.).

D'Emilio argues further that more and more people will become gay, due to
capitalism's ambiguous relationship with the family. Capitalism has "gradually
undermined the material basis of the nuclear family by taking away the economic functions that cemented the ties between family members," contrary to
the capitalist ideology of society that "has enshrined the family as the source
of love, affection and emotional security, the place where our need for stable,
intimate human relations was satisfied" ("Capitalism and Gay Identity"). This
ambivalence of capitalism, to be against family values and yet at the same time
foster family as a nurturing and emotional satisfaction center, has made it possible for gays to change tactics as they grow in numerical and spiritual strength:

> Capitalism has created the material conditions for homosexual
> desire to express itself as a central component of some individuals'
> lives; now, our political movements are changing consciousness,
> creating the ideological conditions that make it easier for people to
> make that choice (Lancaster & Leonardo 1997: 175).

What is more, adds D'Emilio, more and more people will become gay, due to
evolving historical process of capitalism in the West:

> A corollary of this argument is that we are *not* a fixed social minor-
> ity composed for all time of a certain percentage of the population.
> *There are more of us* than one hundred years ago, more of us than
> forty years ago. And there may well be more gay men and lesbians in
> the future. Claims made by gays and nongays that sexual orientation
> is fixed at an early age, that large numbers of visible gay men and
> lesbians in society, the media, and the schools will have no influ-
> ence on the sexual identities of the young, are wrong. Capitalism

has created the material conditions for homosexual desire to express itself as a central component of some individuals' lives; now, our political movements are changing consciousness, creating the ideological conditions that make it easier for people to make that choice (Lancaster, Roger & di Leonardo 1997: 175).

Clearly, Bugul and D'Emilio have one thing in common; both authors opine that history has a lot to do with the evolution of human sexual desire and views of gender. Ken Bugul arrived at her lucidity from personal insights from her experiences of multiple gender and sexuality in Europe during her sojourn there in the 60s. We have said that before. John D'Emilio, for his part, arrived at his own enlightenment from his own gay identity, and from observations about gay life, thanks to his vantage point at the direction of United States National Gay and Lesbian Headquarters.

When the focus is on postcolonial subjects in the African diaspora, as this study intends to do, racially subjugated individuals and a collectivity suffering feelings of *déracinement* in exile as they cross boundaries of traditional morality to express their feelings of exasperation and desperation of the moment, we begin to see assertions that lend credence to the belief that psychoanalysis is an inevitable part of the exploration of people in exile; they are wandering peoples. Clearly, theirs are journeys into otherness, journeys that engender sexual and gender inequities, which lead to gender and sexual behavior modifications, cultural schizophrenia, confused identities, and ethnic and racial bigotry.

The implicit assertion above that imperialism, racism, and oppressive regimes of power impact gender and sexual destinies, if persuasive, has implications for our present study; it can help us to articulate the convoluted intermingling of race, gender, and sexuality in Haitian Dany Laferrière's writings. Dany Laferrière is important in this study then, due to his contribution of the racial factor to gender and sexuality discourses in African and African disapora literatures.

Laferrière's four autobiographical novels on the North-American reality— *Comment faire l'amour avec un Nègre sans se fatiguer* (1985); *Chronique de la dérive douce* (1985); *Éroshima, mon amour* (1987), and *Cette grenade dans la main du jeune Nègre, est-il une arme où un fruit?* (1993)—treat the author's own tribulations in exile, in particular, and the anguish of Haitian immigrants in Montreal, Canada, in general. The Haitian minorities in Canada are composed of individuals who perform gender and sexual identities imposed on them by the dominant group that has reinvented them, and made their inclusion irrelevant.[3] In the first novel, translated into English as *How to Make Love to a Negro*, the diaspora author-narrator and his African roommate Buba spend their time practicing voodoo, reading the Koran, playing jazz and blues music, searching for a job, or having sex with white blonds, and this to avenge into the bargain insults on their human dignity and centuries of denigration of the black race, and talking with glee about it. It is these sexual escapades and yearnings for freedom and justice by two aggrieved black men in Montreal that constitute the contents of this first novel. The subsequent three novels would take up again and again, in varying degrees and locales, the subject themes of the first.

Clearly, the issue in these autobiographical novels is discussion of our common humanity from the angle of race, gender, and sexuality. Consequently, constructionist understanding of gender and sexuality, as espoused on the pages of this chapter, is opposed to biologist and essentialist notions of gender and sexuality. It sees racial beliefs of self-as-norm as reeking havoc one on the other. Racism condones derogatory and humiliating views of the "Other," and leads to social injustices and violence. Laferrière's subversive texts explode gender and sexuality myths based on race. It also explodes cultural constructions and knowledge based on racial inferiority and superiority complexes, which affect notions of class and ethnicity in untold ways.

This study will demonstrate that gender and sexuality transformations occur with transnational border crossings, reducing issues of masculinity and femininity, gender and sexuality, to a question of race. According to Laferrière, once you leave your home, relevant factors of the racial equation change. In the circumstance, the relational binary in Haiti is no longer *noir/mulâtre* [black/mulatto], but rather the more expansive *noir/race* [black/race].[4] This change in register, this change in orientation from ethnic to racial categories, Laferrière argues, affects all aspects of human relations, including class, sex, gender, and race.

* * *

Relevant as a theoretical framework for our present study is Judith Butler's essay, "Gender is Burning: Questions of Appropriation and Subversion" (McClintock, Mufti, and Shohat 1997: 381-395). It is a re-examination of the marginalization of sexual minorities by the dominant heterosexual group, and attempts by the marginalized minorities to resist gender and sexual oppressions. Butler's essay provides us the necessary intellectual light to explore the similarity between the yearnings, tribulations, and challenges faced by sexual and racial minority groups of all times.

First, Butler states that the burning questions of race, sex, and gender should be taken up by all oppressed groups and subverted, that is, used in such a way that the original aims of the oppressors are exorcized, reversed, or even displaced. Butler adds that not only should the offensive words be used—nigger, Negro, black—they should be repeated in novel ways that can only "induce a destructive repetition compulsion" as a means of responding affirmatively to violations.

Second, employing Louis Althuser's notion of interpellation as laid out in "Ideology and Ideological State Apparatuses," Butler argues that the individual becomes a social subject, thanks to formative and performative state apparatuses of law, which engender a new being, by "hailing" and "interpelling" the individual, unilaterally, thanks to its power to do so. The state power subjects the individual to fear, although recognizing him as a social person. It is the fear and reprimand embedded in the call that affects the social subject adversely. In other words, the state forms the individual to respond to police summons, engendering at once the spirit of conformity to societal rules and the fear that nonconformity might result in sanctions. There would be absolutely no problem with a law-abiding citizen, if the law were always just and fair. Unfortunately, that is not always the case. Then again, there is also the possibility of "bad subjects," but these have not been taken into consideration in the kind of disobedience to the law that Althuser considers here.

Third, Althuser's argument in a Jacques Lacan-type structural analysis holds that sometimes "a relation of misrecognition persists between the law and the subject it compels." (McClintock, Mufti, and Shohat 1997: 382). The coercion by the law, continues Butler, could result in disobedience on the part of the one called, for not only will the law be refused, it might be "ruptured, forced into a rearticulating that calls into question the monotheistic force of its own unilateral operation"(ibid.):

> Where the uniformity of the subject is expected, where the behavioral conformity of the subject is commanded, the refusal of the law might be produced in the form of the parodic inhabiting of conformity that subtly calls into question the legitimacy of the command, a repetition of the law into hyperbole, a rearticulating of the law against the authority of the one who delivers it (ibid.).[5]

Thus, there are two cardinal ways that an individual might contest the power of the state or law to hail it. His resistance is seen as passive when it happens at the lower level of disobedience, rebellion, or refusal to obey the law. However, at a higher level of rebellion, the rebel could go all out, using all within reach to (re)affirm self. Again, says Butler:

> Here the performative, the call by the law that seeks to produce a lawful subject, produces a set of consequences that exceed and confound what appears to be the disciplining intention motivating the law. Interpellation, thus loses its status as a simple performative, an act of discourse, with the power to create that to which it refers, *and creates more than it ever meant to, signifying in excess of any intended referent* (McClintock, Mufti, and Shohat 382; *my emphasis*).

Butler observes that not only is the subject modified by the call when it happens, a name is also invented, constructed, and imposed on it by others, with neither its choice nor consent, hence the subject is at once violated, but also enabled to take the law into its hands for self-defense, having been drawn into the vicious cycle and forced to assume its agency to oppose the imposition of a name, what Gyatari Chaktravorty Spivak has called "enabling violation."

Butler then further argues that the subject is "implicated," in the power relations' structure, of revenge and name-calling:

> If one comes into the discursive life through being called or hailed in injurious terms, how might one occupy the interpellation by which

one is already occupied to direct the possibilities of resignification against the aims of violation? (ibid.).

And that brings us to the fourth point, namely, that a situation of ambivalence in the power relations occurs, as the constant repetition of "messages implied in one's being" results in subversive uses of violations imposed on one. "Race," "Sex" and "Gender," Butler adds, become valid terms of reference when read in light of the postmodernist "isms," respectively of racism, sexism, and heterosexism, all of which spell oppressive regimes of power. The subject wounded in its person by such oppressive interpellations responds by "appropriating" the language learned from the oppressors, and "abrogating" their normative values as well:

> Precisely because such terms have been produced and constrained within such regimes, they ought to be repeated in directions that reverse and displace their aims. One does not stand at an instrumental distance from the terms by which one experiences violation. Occupied by such terms and yet occupying them oneself risks complicity, a repetition, a relapse into injury, but it is also the occasion to work the mobilizing power of injury, of an interpellation one never chose. Where we might understand violation as a trauma that can only induce a destructive repetition compulsion (and surely this is a powerful consequence of violation), it seems equally possible to acknowledge the force of repetition as the very condition of an affirmative response to violation. *The compulsion to repeat an injury is not necessarily the compulsion to repeat the injury in the same way or to stay fully within the traumatic orbit of that injury. The force of repetition in language may be the paradoxical condition by which a certain agency—not linked to a fiction of the ego as master of circumstance—is derived from the* impossibility *of choice* (McClintock, Mufti, and Shohat 383; *my emphasis*).

Butler's eloquent observation of the situation of ambivalence in the power relations between the interpellator and the one hailed reiterates the fluid, shifting, and contradictory nature of the subject in postmodernist and postcolonial times. Accordingly, the subject is constructed, and refuses to be determined by those constructions. Hence the ambivalence, the difference between the construction and resistance to it, makes it possible to rework the very terms of the subjectivation, whether it succeeds or fails: "There is no subject prior to its construction, and neither is the subject determined by those constructions," states Butler (ibid.).[6]

Evidently, it is in the nature of law to be constantly reinterpreted, adds Butler, for it is more of a continuing conversation between the citizen and the state, and less of a set of rigid state rules that individuals have to follow. Butler cites Friedrich Nietzsche in *On the Genealogy of Morals*:

> The purpose of 'Law' is absolutely the last thing to employ in the history of the origin of law; on the contrary, (...) *the cause of the origin*

of a thing and its eventual utility, its actual employment and place in a system of purposes, lies worlds apart; whatever exists, having somehow come into being, is again and again reinterpreted to new ends, taken over, transformed and redirected (McClintock, Mufti, and Shohat, 381; *my emphasis*).

Clearly, Butler's theory on appropriation and subversion of gender and sexuality norms elucidates our own thinking about racial minorities, in particular reference to peoples of African descent, who are constantly oppressed and drawn into gender, sexual, and racial inequities and humiliation.

* * *

The case of the Haitian immigrants in Montreal in Laferrière's four autobiographical writings under study here, narrates not just the author's personal struggles to become a writer, be known, and have economic independence, but also the ability of his people, as Laferrière once stated in an interview, "to face the past and the daring to open the closets and take out the skeletons" (*Callaloo*, 22.4, 917). Laferrière's use of homosexual terms of "skeletons" and "closets" in talking about his people's Odyssey in Montreal, Canada, hints the similarity between sexual and racial oppressions, and the isolation, loneliness, seclusion, alienation, and oppression of gender and sexual discriminations. The notion of "coming out" destroys the social structure that categorizes people in rigid gender, sexual, and racial terms. Laferrière's autobiographical writings are indeed about the pride of self and nation. It is his unilateral response to individual wound and collective hurt. It is for these reasons that he assumes the responsibility to defend and illustrate his race, challenge the widely held erroneous myth of black sexual promiscuity, and employ novel writing as an arm of protestation, contestation, and revenge.

DEFENSE AND ILLUSTRATION OF THE BLACK RACE

You're Not Born Black,
You Get That Way.
　　　　　　　　　　　—Dany Laferrière, *Cette grenade...* 117.
Il est bon que l'ordre des choses soit bousculé de temps en temps
　　　　　　　　　　　—Dany Laferrière, *Cette grenade...*, 91.
[It is good to shake up the order of things from time to time; my translation*]*

Cette grenade dans la main du jeune Nègre est-elle une arme ou un fruit? [This grenade in the Hand of the Young Negro is it an Arm or a Fruit?], Laferrière's second novel, is a compact piece of writing whose exploitation of notions of gender as the most immediate factor in the lives of postcolonial subjects, records its author's experiences as he travels through the length and breathe of North America. Laferrière explores notions of gender in framing his story and his own and his people's experiences in exile, fostering the ideology that gender is not equal to sex. It is society or a particular culture that is responsible for creating notions of masculinity and femininity. For example, he asserts, Black men's promiscuity has nothing to do with so-called natural masculine aggression, innate sex drives, nor urges of testosterone, as essentialists would have people believe. They have nothing to do with femininity and female biology. On the contrary, all is due to race. The constructionist in Laferrière contends that the Black man is not intrinsically more inherently sexually aggressive, not even more violent than men of other races. Yet in North America black people have been painted "black," and "violent," to the extent that they have begun to perform those imposed identities, that is act out, intentionally or unintentionally, the names by which they are called. It is therefore the structural elements of the state/national/regional apparatuses that are responsible for the sexual and gender transformations and inequities apparent in individual behaviors in society. This emphasis on the social creation of gender identities enables us to affirm what we believe is Laferrière's position, namely, that racial assumption and practices are wrong and need to be changed through awareness. They are not natural and should not be condoned, for the common good.

Laferrière asserts, first, that one is not born black, but becomes one—the loan translation from Simone de Beauvoir's expression, "One is not born a woman, but becomes one," is eloquent. Second, he adds that it is important to periodically question the normative epistemologies of the status quo. He resists the perpetuation of the black person's identity as inferior, a wrongful belief, which has led to the feminization of the black race, where the white race is held as superior and male.

In another of his autobiographical writings, *Chronique...*, which explores several aspects of racism that the black person encounters on the North American continent, Laferrière advocates the repetition of racial clichés and slurs attached to the black race—promiscuity, black (read evil), Jazz, (read lack of developed language), what Judith Butler has referred to above as "destructive repetition compulsion," in order to draw attention to their oppressiveness (50). It is the phenomena of ghettorization and urbanization that are at the root of casting blacks and whites respectively as inferior and superior. This feminization and masculinization of the races, has led to social and racial injustices against black people. Clearly, the dominant culture naturalizes itself as the norm and the original economic and political power, and deals with members of their group to the exclusion of the "other" seen as inferior. According to Gustav d'Eichtal: "*Le noir me paraît être la race femme / Dans la famille humaine, comme le blanc / Est la race mâle'.* [The Black appears to me as the female race in the human family, like the white / Is the male race] (*Lettres sur la race noire*, 183). Applied to Laferrière's American autobiography, the black race is demeaned, hence the author takes to writing to defend and illustrate the black race.

And this leads to the second, and perhaps more important point. Laferrière's resistance, along with that of his race, seem to suggest that the invention and name calling of the black race as feminine and inferior, are performative, that is to say, political. Clearly, the black race must fight to rid itself of the pejorative names attached to it, for such names internalized affect adversely not only male/female relations but also white/black relations too. Laferrière warns the human race to take care of its minorities and other oppressed of the earth, because when they rise from their oppression, they could become worse than the present perpetrators of racial and sexual injustices, given their extreme suffering. It goes without saying that the black race will return to ascendancy, he opines, and has indeed started to do so, by appropriating the racial insults and turning them on their heads. He nonetheless refuses to accept that the black person is in any way different from the white race uniquely on the racial score. Laferrière denies that black is equal to inferiority, violence or promiscuity. On the other hand, his countering of tacit essentialist approval of normative notions of femininity and masculinity spells belief and hope for the transformation and modification of society.

CHALLENGE OF THE MYTH OF THE NEGRO AS A SEX MACHINE

> *Sexe + race = politique*
> —Dany Laferrière, *Je suis fatigué* [I am tired] 77

The examination of racial issues in feminine and masculine terms in Laferrière's writings leads directly to the exploration of gender and sexual politics. Clearly, sex is not equal to gender. This differentiation elucidates characterization and identification in Laferrière's writings, and empowers the reader to observe that if characters act differently from the natural characteristics and gender roles traditionally attributed to them, it is because of the emotional contexts of their life in their society. Hence, some of the black characters with the male sex have displayed passive and feminine characteristics of submission, whereas conversely those with the female sex have manifested masculine and aggressive tendencies in sexual matters. It all has to do with prevalent notions of race in society.

The cliché of the *Nègre grand baiseur* [Black Mother Fucker] allows us to see gender and sexuality as categories of analysis in this study. Laferrière debunks the myth of the Negro as a sex machine, for he reiterates in *Cette grenade...*, that the discourse is not about sex alone, but also the dignity of the black person. He asks this rhetorical question: « *Est-il possible qu'un écrivain noir, puisse écrire, un jour, sur une autre chose que le sexe ? C'est possible, s'il n'est plus un écrivain* (*Cette grenade...* 82). [Is it possible that a black writer will one day write on any other topic but sex? It is possible, if he ceases to be a writer]. The implication here, underlined with the use of the subjunctive tense in the question that spells probability, almost disbelief, is that the author doubts that the sexual abuse of Africans and their descendants will ever cease. It will take the writer renouncing his art for that to happen!

Furthermore, subverting the myth that Black men can never give up a chance to take a white woman to bed, the author-narrator accepts and takes to bed a white girl who attempts to proposition him. As a matter of principle, and with utter sarcasm, he explains, he never refuses sexual advances from white girls, rather he takes advantage of them, as so many oppressed Black men do, to avenge centuries of oppression, and continuing (*Cette grenade*...124-125). This radical stance, this seeing sex as a weapon of revenge, demonstrates his and his race's aversion to being called "black," when that term connotes inferior, promiscuous, and other. He questions the identification of sex with race, blackness to promiscuity, and blackness to femininity. On the contrary, he sees it as mere politics, dirty racial politics at that.

Clearly, this boils down to Judith Butler's assertion that gender and sexual identities are subject to the individual's (and group's) performativity. The problematizing of the sexual-racial-gender equation through a deep ambivalence also recalls Judith Butler's assertion that "identification is always an ambivalent process."[7]

Laferrière then calls to question the norm reserved by whites to name blacks in *Comment faire l'amour...* [*How to Make Love to a Negro*], where the author-narrator nicknames his upstairs black neighbor Beelzebub. He thinks the profuse and derogatory name-calling is befitting in his neighbor's case, because the neighbor has the practice of copulating with white girls even in the most unwholesome summer hot temperatures. This linking of sex and race, by calling a fellow black man a black devil in those peculiar circumstances, just as a white man would do, subverts a favorite racial slur of the dominant race. Notice that in world mythology Beelzebub is the chief of all devils, the fiercest Seraphim of Lucifer's satanic constellation, the Prince of Flies, the Satan of Greed, and the supreme Head of the Infernal Empire.

Significantly, for a long time after the first novel appeared in publication, many among Lafferière's reading public, black and white, did not accept that the book was written by a black writer, until the author's appearance on Canadian television. The confusion stemmed simply from the author's impudence in appropriating racial slurs normally reserved for blacks and flinging them back on whites and blacks alike, with impunity. Clearly, the author amply demonstrates the danger in name calling according to one's particular whim or fancy.

Laferrière also confounds gender ambivalence with racial ambivalence when he refers to sexual encounters between blacks and whites and/or Asians as bomb explosions, hence the provocative title of his third book, *Éroshima*. "Éros" is that by which the so-called black sky-high libido is identified, and "Hiroshima" is "the Japanese city of hell," thanks to the nuclear bombing of that city during the Second World War. Together, in one word, the neologism suggests war and violence, a veritable bomb explosion, in interracial amorous relationships. At stake is a political vision for whites and blacks in the future.

Nonetheless, the situation remains ambivalent and unstable, for although black men sleep with blond women in war and violence, the black men also realize that they will never enter the white women's world, caught in the middle, as they are, between the ghetto (read the slave ship) and the palace (read Britannica). Observe that black men make love to white women who despise them, but the white women cannot pass up the opportunity to make love to black men whom they see as sex studs. Although the white women despise the black men, the latter nonetheless take advantage of the blonds that offer themselves to them, as a means of avenging all the racial and social injustices suffered by individual blacks and the black race at the hands of the white race.

Indeed, Laferrière calls into question claims of normality and originality by which gender, sexual, and racial oppressions sometimes operate. Although the narrator is biologically of the male sex, yet he is able to swap the social gender identity attached to males for another when it suits his personal and racial yearnings, even if it means playing the submissive sexual and gender roles normally assigned to the female.[8] In *Éroshima*, for example, the author-narrator allows himself to be "kept" by a Japanese woman journalist in her apartment for a fortnight, a 'Nancy boy,' or 'Miss Nancy,' in gay slang term, like a well-cared-for woman and mistress. Indeed, he is like a 'catamite,' meaning "a boy kept as lover by a pederast," term coined from the name of the Trojan boy, Ganymede, whom, reportedly in Greek mythology Zeus carried off to serve him as a lover and personal cupbearer. When the journalist goes away for business, the author-narrator stays back in her apartment, as a mistress would do. Yet, all the time, he sees his black penis as a phallus, a veritable weapon of revenge, for inflicting humiliation and suffering, through love making, to the "white" oppressor, represented by the Asian woman. His sexual orgies in the journalist's home are his opportunity to get back at the white race. It makes no great difference that she is of the yellow race and not a traditional "white." That fact is not important for his purposes.

Notice that this tendency to adorn conflicting, complex, alternate, and ambivalent gender and sexual identities exhibited by the author-narrator is in keeping with postcolonial and wandering peoples. When they are not merely "hunters" and "warriors" in an African bush, who switch their gender roles according to the circumstances of the occasion, such as war or rite of passage, they can be postmodern oppressed subjects crisscrossing boundaries and international frontiers of race, class, and culture. In the African diaspora, the issue is more about race, racism, and homophobia, whereas on the continent it is relatively easy to castigate patriarchy for certain oppressions against women and females in general.

Certain conflicting questions come to mind. Is the black person necessarily driven by uncontrollable passion and limited to sexual urges? Is it indeed true that the black man has an overwhelming, and proverbial sexual prowess? On the other hand, is the white man's libido as low as it is said to be? Is the white woman really a male compared to a black man, and always a female compared to the white man? Where does the black woman fit in, as a male or female? Does her gender alter depending on association with black male, white male, white female, and fellow black woman? Laferrière seeks to understand these gender and sexual questions always linked to race. He also wants to understand his own personal, or any black male's, so-called high-level of libido. Does black libido come from the effects of the scorching sun in the Tropics or perhaps from nursing at the mother's breast well into the seventh year of life?[9] Observe that the number seven in mythological terms spells totality, eternity.

If indeed black libido comes from the effects of the sun in the Tropics or the fact that mothers breast-feed their offspring for a long time, why do the Miz Shakespeares and Miz Literatures, blonds and stereotypical representatives of the white culture, as Laferrière opines, flock to the ghettos to seek out black men, instead of accepting the sexual advances of men of their own kind? Why do the white girls feel good to bring in food, cook it, and serve poor black men in their hovel in this novel? The meal over, why do they also wash plates, in rotten sinks, for these penniless black men, men who relax and watch television, and all the time without the blonds feeling that they should not be serving male individuals of the black race that they so despise? Are these merely gestures of femininity on the part of the girls or do the girls see themselves as "masculine" and thus merely condescending towards the black men whom they see as "females" and inferior?

There is no gainsaying that Laferrière exploits his privilege of an artist to create exceptional characters, including the narrator, characters who mirror complexity, refuse to be bound by societal limits that grant them one unitary identity, characters who shift their gender and sexual identities as their representational whims change.

What you see may be a mirage and may not be real. The transgressive question to ask is, at what point do questions of sex and gender become issues of race and politics?

NOVEL WRITING AS POLITICAL STRATEGY

Following the exploration of black racial identity, and racial/sexual politics is Laferrière's preoccupation with class, race, and culture in his writings. The society performing and the ideal performed by the individual, appear at loggerheads.[10] Importantly, Laferrière explores color in racial/sexual politics. Blond women seek out black men. Yet black women cannot go anywhere with black men, for these latter look down upon black women, prefer blonds, thanks to the ingraining in their psyche of the superiority of whiteness. Black men and women dream of becoming real, in order to end their poverty, homophobia, and racist delegitimization, in order to integrate into society.

Why, the author-narrator asks, is the black man seen as a woman in the eyes of the dominant race? Turning the gender discrimination against blacks on its head, he sees it as an insult to the white woman, rather than to the black man. The black man takes advantage of the situation to avoid paying his bills when the waiter chooses to give it to the white man whom he sees as his client and not to the black male whom he takes merely as the white man's companion. Vicariously, opines Laferrière, the black woman profits from the situation, since her black partner is spared some change in his pocket.[11]

In his first novel, *How to Make Love to a Negro,* Laferrière declares war against racism, and sexual and gender discriminations; it is his only chance to regain his humanity (115-116, 117).[12] In *Cette grenade...* he deals with inter-racial sex, and expatiates on his reasons for becoming a writer, by seeing himself as the griot of the black race. He is the spokesperson of the youth, including the white ones (38), and affirms by so doing his humanity (122). Thanks to his writing, he believes, it has become fashionable to discuss the black race, and consequently the status of the black race has been elevated. "*Depuis que j'ai publié ce livre, les NÈGRES sont devenus à la mode. On n'a jamais tant parlé des Nègres (Cette grenade... 48).* [Since the publication of my book, Negroes have come into vogue. People do not stop talking about Negroes]. Clearly, in Laferrière's production of realness, the subject repeats and mimes the legitimizing norms by which it has been degraded.

In addition, the media comes under castigation, because it is the media in the print pages and television that invariably fosters humiliating images of black immigrants as poor, undeveloped, promiscuous, and backward. Laferrière takes head on the issue of AIDS in African and the rest of the world, which is a favorite news item of the mass media, recalling the controversy surrounding the origin of the disease in the world. Was it a Western experiment on monkeys in the African rain forests? Was it a concoction to rid Western urban cities of the menace of homosexuals? The result today, however, is a pandemic, which, ironically, is again ravaging Africa more that any other region of the world. His Afrocentric, albeit sarcastic, interpretation of the situation is that the black race is suffering more than any other race, because only they understand the beauty of sex. On the other hand, the white race is not promiscuous, does not appreciate the beauty of sex, and so has found it in itself to taint sex with disease.[13] Clearly, Dany Laferrière appropriates fiction writing as a subversive weapon. Thanks to the use he has made of sex, he outruns the society that rejects him, captures its attention, and forces it to buy his literary production, pay him to eat, clothe, and lodge him.

Still, Africa and its diaspora as a whole continue to live in a fool's paradise, he lucidly suggests. Haitian art, for example, which continues to paint idyllic landscapes of lush greenery and beauty, shows a people still living in a fool's paradise and needing to wake up to the realities of the present world (*Cette grenade...,* 116). The African world still faces the challenges of the myth of white superiority.

CONCLUSION

This study of Dany Laferrière's North American autobiography has attempted to enlarge issues of gender and sexuality beyond the narrow confines of femininity and masculinity, homosexuality and heterosexuality, and all the in-betweens, imbuing them with race issues. It has demonstrated that issues of gender and sexuality are more often than not fundamentally about what our individuality is. Yet because they go beyond issues of biological determinism to embrace those of societal ways and manner of constructing identities and ideologies, they tell stories about our beings and the collectivity. Through justifying, complicating, and expanding the notion of sex and gender into the African diaspora, bringing it to the racial and international levels, this study has analyzed some of the deeply held beliefs that gender is natural rather than cultural, and that heterosexuality is normal and homosexuality and other sexualities abnormal. With unusual boldness, Laferrière has shaken up the status quo, shocking the reader and the wide world with his blatant and unabashed revelation of sex and gender biases at the racial level. Evidently, race goes hand in hand with gender and sexuality matters as other categories of difference, often leading to political, social, and economic injustices. In order to control racism, social views of human gender and sexuality must improve.

Notes

1. The other three autobiographical novels are, in order of publication, *Cendres et Braises* [Ashes and Embers, 1994], *Riwan, ou le chemin de sable* (1999), and *La Folie et la Mort* [Madness and Death, 2000].

    Ken Bugul also adds later:

    > Et cela m'arrangeait. Le désespoir de vivre menait à tout. Pourquoi n'avoir pas prévu la réaction de la femme noire au néocolonialisme? Contenir le soudeur des pulsions qui assurent en partie l'équilibre, l'épanouissement du soi défini (*Le Baobab fou* 113)

    > [And it suited me. The despair of living led everywhere [sic; to everything]. Why hadn't they foreseen the Black Woman's reaction to neocolonialism? One must absorb the muteness of the drives that partly ensure equilibrium, the blossoming of the defined self (*The Abandoned Baobab* 96-97)].

2. John D'Emilio is the author of *Sexual Politics, Sexual Communities: the Making of a Homosexual Minority in the United States,* 1940-1970 (Chicago, 1983); *Making Trouble: Essays on Gay History, Politics, and the University* (Routledge, 1992); and, with Estelle Freedman, *Intimate Matters: a History of Sexuality in America* (Harper and Row, 1988). He is also the Director of the Policy Institute of the National Gay and Lesbian Task Force. He states in "Capitalism and Gay Identity": "I have argued that lesbian and gay identity and communities are historically created, the result of a process of capitalist development that has spanned many generations " (Lancaster, Roger & di Leonardo 1997: 169).

3. See Dany Laferrière, *Je suis fatigué,* 77.

4. The Haitian immigrant has thus a historical and sociological background that foregrounds Laferrière's autobiographical texts. In exile in North America, the Haitian immigrant wants "to arrive," (*démeler*), that is, climb the social ladder to prominence or at least to economic sufficiency (Chierici 1991). Flore Zéphir also sees the new immigrants as present-day "maroons," who practice "*marronage,*" that is defiance in the face of political, social, and economic oppression. Laferrière numbers

among these illustrious Haitian artists in exile from the Duvalier regime's post-independence era mayhem, and has become the voice of the voiceless. Through subversion of the Western monologic, abrogation of the norm, and appropriation of the technique of writing, Laferrière has attempted to achieve self-salvation and defense and illustration of his race.

5. See also *Dangerous Liaisons*, 383. Butler states:

> On the contrary, precisely because such terms have been produced and contained within such regimes, they ought to be repeated in directions that reverse and displace their originating aims. One does not stand at an instrumental distance from the terms by which one experiences violation. Occupied by such terms and yet occupying them oneself risks complicity, a repetition, a relapse into injury, but it is also the occasion to work the mobilizing power of injury, of an interpellation one never chose. Where one might understand violation as a trauma that can only induce a destructive repetition compulsion (and surely this is a powerful consequence of violation), it seems equally possible to acknowledge the force of repetition as the very condition of an affirmative response to violation."

6. Butler also adds:

> It is always the nexus, the non-space of cultural collision, in which the demand to resignify or repeat the very terms that constitute the "we" cannot be summarily refused, but neither can they be followed in strict obedience (McClintock, Mufti, and Shohat, 383).

7. Judith Butler states:

> Identifying with a gender under contemporary regimes of power involves identifying with a set of norms that are and are not realizable and whose power and status precede the identification by which they are insistently approximated (McClintock, Mufti, and Shohat 385).

8. Judith Butler would say that he performs his gender and sexuality, demonstrating that appearances are deceptive and might really be mere illusions.

9. Laferrière asks:
> Ce désir insatiable du corps
> que j'ai est-il dû au fait que
> j'ai grandi sous les Tropiques
> ou est-ce parce que ma mère m'a
> allaité jusqu'à l'âge de sept ans ? (*Chronique...* 8)
> [This craving for the body
> Is it due to the fact that
> I grew up in the Tropics
> Or is it because my mother had
> Suckled me up to the age of seven?]

10. Evidently, Judith Butler would say that the blond girls' gestures towards the black men, whom they choose to go to bed with are "performative, not rentative," since the white girls would not do one tenth what they do for the black men for the white male students they study with at McGill University, Montreal.

11. Laferrière states:

> J'ai remarqué que chaque fois que je mange avec un blanc, immanquablement, c'est à lui qu'on remet l'addition. Le Nègre est l'équivalent d'une femme aux yeux des serveurs. Ce qui doit être une insulte suprême pour une blanche (*Cette grenade*...111).

> [I have noticed that every time I eat with a white man, invariably it is he that gets the bill. The black man is the equivalent of a woman in the eyes of the servers. That should be an insult of the first order to a white woman].

12. These are Laferrière's own words about how he began to write:

> I'm typing like crazy. The Remington is having a ball. Words are squirting out everywhere. I type. I can't take it any more. I type. I'm at the end of my ribbon. I finish. I crash out on the table next to the typewriter with my head on my arms. (...) My novel is a handsome hunk of hope. My only chance. Take It (*How to Make Love to a Negro*) (115-116, 117).

13. Laferrière says:

> Ce n'est pas le sexe qui a inventé le sida. C'est le dégoût du sexe qui l'a crée. Son dégoût occidental. Et qui paie les pots cassés aujourd'hui ? Encore le tiers-monde (...). Le tiers-monde existe aussi en Amérique du Nord. Ce sont les ghettos où les filles-mères confondent encore la cocaïne (plutôt le crack) et le lait en poudre. L'enfant naîtra aveugle, drogué, malade. Pourtant, il ne mourra pas de cela, mais d'une balle à la tête au coin de 125th Street et Broadway (*Cette grenade*... 27).

> [Sex did not invent AIDS. It is the disgust of sex that created it. Western distaste of it. And who is paying the price today? Still the Third World (...). The Third World also exists in North America. They are ghettos where girl-mothers still mistake cocaine (read crack) for powdered milk. Her child will be born blind, drugged, and ill. Yet, he will not die from that, but by a bullet to the head at the corner of 125th street and Broadway].

Works Cited

Althuser, Louis. *Lenin and Philosophy and Other Essays*. New York: Monthly Review Press, 1972. "Freud and Lacan," 18-22; "Ideology and Ideological State Apparatuses," 170-177.

Bauer, J. *Les minorités au Québec*. Boréal, 1994.

Bugul, Ken. *The Abandoned Baobab*. Chicago: Lawrence Hill Books, 1991.

—-. *Cendre et Braises*. Paris: L'Harmattan, 1994.

—-. *Riwan, ou le chemin de sable*. Paris : Présence Africaine, 1999.

—-. *La Foie et la Mort*. Paris : Présence Africaine, 2000.

Chierici, Rose-Marie Cassagnol. *Demele: Making It: Migration and Adaptation among Haitian Boat People in the United States*. New York: AMS Press, 1991.

Dejean, P. Français. *Les Haïtiens au Québec*. Montréal: Presses de l'OQAM, 1978.

D'Emilio, John. "Capitalism and Gay Identity." Chapter 11. In: Roger N. Lancaster & Micaela di Leonardo. Eds. *The Gender and Sexuality Reader: Culture, History, Political Economy*. New York and London: Routledge, 1997.

Dubuisson, W. *Immigration et intégration sociale des Haïtiens au Québec*. Sherbrooke: Naaman, 1987.

Ferguson, James. *PAPA DOC, BABY DOC: Haiti and the Duvaliers*. New York: Basil Blackwell Publishing, 1988(1987).

Fiori, E. *Le Haïtiens de Montréal et la nature: Pratiques et représentations d'Haïti au Québec*. Montréal, 1996.

Frenette, Y. *Perception et vécu du racisme par les imigrantes et immigrants haïtiens au Québec*. Montréal: Université de Montréal, 1985.

Gairdner, William D. *The War Against the Family: A Parent Speaks Out on the Political, Economic, and Social Policies That Threaten Us All*. Toronto : Stoddart Publishing Company, 1993 (1992).

Heinl, Robert Debs, and Namey Gordon Heinl. *Written in Blood: The Story of the Haitian People: 1492-1972*. Boston: Houghton Mifflin Company, 1978.

Herbert, Eugenia W. *Iron, Gender and Power: Rituals of Transformation in African Souelies*. Bloomingotn and Indianapolis: Indiana Univ. Press, 1993.

Hernton, Calvin C. *Sex and Racism in America*. London, Toronto, Sydney, and Auckland: Anchor Books, Double Day, 1988 (1965)

Hurbon, Laënnec. *Comprendre Haïti: essai sur l'État, la nation, la culture*. Paris: Karthala, 1987.

Konferenzen, D. *Minorities: Community and Identity*. Berlin: Springer-Verlag, 1983.

Labelle, Micheline. *Idéologie de couleur et classes sociales en Haïti*. Montréal: Presses universitaires de Montréal, 1978.

Laferrière, Dany. *Comment faire l'amour avec un nègre sans se fatiguer*. Montréal: VLB, 1985.

—-. *Éroshima*. Montréal: VLB, 1987.

—-. *Cette grenade dans la main du jeune Nègre est-il une arme ou un fruit ?* Montréal : VLB, 1993.

—-. *Chronique de la dérive douce*. Montréal: VLB, 1994.

—-. *Je suis fatigué*. Montréal: Lanctôt, 2001.

Lancaster, Roger N. & Micaela di Leonardo. Eds. *The Gender and Sexuality Reader: Culture, History, Political Economy*. New York and London: Routledge, 1997.

Mackinnon, Catharine. *Toward a Feminist Theory of the State*. Cambridge, M. A.: Harvard University Press, 1989.

McClintock Anne, Aamir Mufti, and Ella Shohat. Eds. *Dangerous Liaisons: Gender, Nation, and Postcolonial Perspectives*. Minneapolis and London: University of Minnesota Press, 1991.

Magloire, Eddy. *Regards sur la minorité ethnique haïtienne aux États-Unis*. Québec: Éditions Naaman, 1984.

Marchand, R. *Immigration et adaptation des Haïtiens à Montréal* : Montréal: Université de Montréal, 1981.

Murray, Stephen O. and Will Roscoe. Eds. *Boy-Wives and Female Husbands: Studies in African Homosexualities*. New York: St Martin's Press, 1998.

Miller, Jake C. *The Plight of Haitian Refugees*. New York, Philadelphia, Toronto: Praeger Special Studies, 1984.

Nfah-Abbenyi, Juliana, Makuchi. *Gender in African Women's Writing: Identity, Sexuality, and Difference*. Bloomington and Indianapolis: Indiana University Press, 1999.

Nicholls, David. *From Dessalines to Duvalier: Race, Colour and National Independence in Haiti*. New York: Cambridge University Press, 1979.

Nussbaum, Martha C. *Sex and Social Justice*. New York: Oxford University Press, 1999.

—-. "Objectification," Chapter 8. In: *Sex and Social Justice*. New York: Oxford University Press, 1999.

Reid-Pharr, Robert F. *Black Gay Man*. New York and London: New York University Press, 2001.

Robinson, Sally. *Engendering the Subject: Gender and Self-Representation in Contemporary Women's Fiction*. Albany: State University of New York Press, 1991.

Tremblay, P-A. *La discrimination envers les minorités visibles au Québec*. Chicoutimi : Presses de l'Université du Québec, 1991.

West, D.J. *Homosexualité*. London and Belgium: Gerald Duckworth and Co. Ltd./ Charles Dessart (nd.).

Wiegman, Robyn, and Elena Glasberg. *Literature and Gender: Thinking Critically Through Fiction, Poetry, and Drama*. New York and Harlow: Longman, 1999.

Wilentz, A. *The Rainy Season: Haiti since Duvalier*. New York: Simon and Schuster, 1989.

Williams, D. *Les Noirs de Montréal*. Montréal: VLB Éditeur, 1998.

Wood, John C. *When Men Are Women: Manhood among Gabra Nomads of East Africa*. Madison: the Univ. of Wisconsin Press, 1999.

Zéphir, Flore. *Haitian Immigrants in Black America: A Sociological and Sociolinguistic Portrait*. Westport, Conn. and London: Bergen and Garvey, 1996. 27-28.

Chapter 6

Building Alternative Communities: Race and Female Sexual Agency in Calixthe Beyala's *Amours sauvages*

Stacy E. Fifer

In patriarchal societies, community identity and male control of female sexuality are inseparable. Female sexuality is constructed as dangerous in these communities, a threat to the group identity that anchors communal consciousness. As such, it is controlled through a variety of means including marriage customs, taboos against sex outside of marriage for women, and even through the prohibition against inter-racial relationships and marriage in order to keep women from crossing communal borders. In Calixthe Beyala's recent novel *Amours sauvages* (1999), visions of a new community where women are no longer oppressed because of their race or by men and patriarchal customs are accompanied by assertions of a female sexual agency free of racial and gender oppression. In the novel, this kind of female sexual agency becomes an essential requirement for the attainment of social equality for both sexes and all races, indicating that a healthy community necessarily includes a subversion of patriarchal controls of female sexuality. The story of Beyala's protagonist offers a vision of how one woman may subvert patriarchal norms and control her sexuality outside of these norms without suffering the social repercussions that usually accompany them. Before analyzing how Beyala's protagonist succeeds in this subversion, some terms need to be defined to begin a discussion about female sexual agency and community.

In this chapter, the identity of Beyala's protagonist, her subjecthood, and agency are central themes. The term "identity" is used to designate the kind of cultural identity Stuart Hall elucidates in "Cultural Identity and Diaspora." Hall explains that cultural identity is "a matter of 'becoming' as well as of 'being'" and that "identities are the names we give to the different ways we are positioned by, and position ourselves within, the narratives of the past" (Hall 1994: 394). In this sense, "...cultural identity is not a fixed essence... [n]ot an essence but a *positioning*" (Hall 395). The term "subject" replaces "individual" in post-structural vocabulary in order to clarify that people are not "unified, autonomous individuals exercising free will" (Scott 1992: 34). "Agency," then, refers to their ability to act within certain situations. As Joan Scott reminds us, people are subjects who are constituted discursively and whose "agency is created through situations and statuses conferred on them." She goes on to quote Adams and

Minson: "Being a subject means 'subject to definite conditions of existence, conditions of endowment of agents and conditions of exercise'" (Scott quoting Adams and Minson, ibid.). Thus, agency for subjects does not constitute an unlimited number of choices for action, but choices for action that are (over) determined by the cultural context in which the subject lives.

Racist patriarchal (colonial) constructions of black female sexuality have long attempted to define black women as sexual savages whose sexual appetite is unparalleled (Gilman 1985: 213). Within this construction, the only status conferred on black women as subjects is that of a sexual being whose agency is defined by her excessive sexual appetite. In the specific context of patriarchal sub-Saharan cultures, female sexuality is subject to control through traditions and rites such as those mentioned above. Here again, sexual agency is extremely limited for women because it must conform to the status conferred on women by patriarchal ideology. This chapter will focus on how the protagonist of *Amours sauvages* establishes female sexual agency in terms that subvert the dominant patriarchal matrix whose norms severely limit black female sexual agency in both white and black communities.

Any discussion of community identity in the post-colonial context also elicits the theoretical and sociological writings of Frantz Fanon. Throughout Fanon's work, he calls for the development of a "new humanism" (Fanon 1967: 9), a new human community that would include all men, regardless of color, as equals. In *Black Skin, White Masks*, Fanon states that he wants to free both black and white men from the prejudice of color, to establish "a world of reciprocal recognitions" (Fanon 218). He expresses a similar view at the end of *The Wretched of the Earth* when he makes a plea to his fellow comrades in arms fighting for liberation: "For Europe, for ourselves and for humanity, comrades, we must turn over a new leaf, we must work out new concepts, and try to set afoot a new man" (Fanon 1966: 255). Here, Fanon imagines a new community for the whole of humanity. His "new humanism" is described as a humanism of inclusion, one that directly opposes the colonial construction of an exclusionary humanism meant only for white Europeans.

Yet, Fanon's vision of inclusion has been questioned by several feminist critics who find a misogynist discourse underlying his writings about the black man and his alienation and those addressing the development of a communal consciousness that would promote the inclusion of all members of a new nation. It is important to note that while Fanon expresses the desire to move towards a "new humanism" for all of mankind, the majority of his writings about community address post-colonial nation building and the development of a national consciousness and national culture for these new nations. Thus, before arriving at his "new humanism," Fanon recognizes that in his historical context, colonized and formerly colonized peoples must first achieve independence and successful nationhood, a nationhood that embraces the needs and best interests of "the mass of the people" (*Wretched*, 121) of each nation. This is where some post-colonial feminist critics have taken issue with Fanon. They assert that Fanon's nationalism is one governed by patriarchal ideology and is not, therefore, concerned with the needs and best interests of women. According to these critics, for Fanon, "the mass of the people" is composed of a group whose normative subject is male. Specifically, critics such as Anne McClintock, Gwen Bergner, Diana Fuss, and Rey Chow have all demonstrated a male bias in Fanon's treatment of women of color and/or white women, identifying particular discursive problems with how Fanon attributes or fails to attribute agency to the woman of color in his writings.

In particular, McClintock and Chow find that while Fanon does attribute agency to women of color in his writings, it is a very limited agency. In McClintock's analysis of Fanon's sociological writings about the Algerian resistance, she concludes that the agency he grants to women is an "agency by designation" (McClintock 1999: 291) at the behest of male revolutionaries fighting for liberation from colonial domination. She reads Fanon as taking "pains to point out that women's militancy does not precede the national revolution. Algerian women are not self-motivating agents, nor do they have prior histories or consciousness of revolt from which to draw" (McClintock 290). The male revolutionary's call for female participation in the national resistance defines her agency within the community. McClintock asserts that "Feminist agency, then, is contained by and subordinated to national agency" (McClintock 293).

For Chow, Fanon provides an uneven analysis both of the woman of color and the white man and of the man of color and the white woman. She asserts that Fanon condemns the woman of color for her desire of the white man because he reads it as a desire for "lactification" of the race, which he insists "must be understood once and for all [as] a question of saving the race" (*Black Skin*, 54-55). At the same time, in a supposedly parallel analysis, Fanon attributes the man of color's desire for the white woman to his alienation and ambivalent identification with both the white and black communities that are the result of colonial assimilationist discourse. Thus, Chow asserts that, for Fanon, the man of color is a victim of psychological alienation, whereas the woman of color is judged as betraying her race. The motivations of the woman of color are seen as an act of betrayal to her racial community. Chow concludes that Fanon constructs "a female sexual agency that is entirely predictable and already understood, conscious or unconscious" (Alessandrini 1999: 45) that is at the same time the only kind of agency he grants to the woman of color.

McClintock's and Chow's analyses both demonstrate that Fanon does not exclude black women from agency; he only limits that agency severely in his writings. The two critics show separate instances of Fanon's attribution of agency to women of color. Each analysis has merit and, taken together, they illustrate that for Fanon, black women do exert agency in both the social and sexual spheres of their communities. However, that limited agency attributed to them under patriarchal domination is oppressive since it maintains a social hierarchy in which women are placed at the bottom of the social ladder.

This chapter explores how Calixthe Beyala proposes an alternative pro-feminist community in *Amours sauvages* without narrowly limiting the agency, sexual or otherwise, of any of its members. First, a more detailed discussion of Rey Chow's critique of Fanon is in order to clarify some of the links she makes between race, female sexuality, community, and Fanon's writings. Next, the majority of this paper will examine how the protagonist of *Amours sauvages* is able to position herself outside of the dominant patriarchal and racial borders of the communities in which she lives without compromising her acceptance in her community of origin. Finally, the construction of Beyala's new community will be analyzed through the lens of Fanon's vision of community, the one that works "towards a new humanism" (*Black Skin*, 9) as well as the one that has been attacked by many feminist critics as exclusionary of women.

Since Beyala's construction of an alternative community is based on miscegenation and the literal birthing of this new community through the adoption of a mixed-race child, this analysis will borrow certain terms from Rey Chow's feminist critique of an apparent prohibition against miscegenation in Fanon's writings about inter-racial relationships. In addition, the discussion of some of the finer points of her analysis will be important for understanding Fanon's own linking of community formation and female sexuality.

Chow's article explicitly links the issues of sexuality, female agency, and community. In her discussion of community, she notes that community formation is always implicitly based on exclusion and inclusion, or what she terms "admittance." She defines three meanings of "admittance" in her articulation of the "politics of admittance." The first is the "basic, physical sense of admittance, of being allowed to enter certain spaces." The second refers to "a permission to enter in the abstract, through the act that we will call validation," and the third is "admittance in the sense of a confession" (Alessandrini 35). Discussing community formation in the context of identity politics, Chow uses these three understandings of the term "admittance" to define how subjects are included (read "admitted") in certain communities while being excluded from others.

To address the issue of admittance in the post-colonial context, Chow looks at Fanon's writings and poses the question that drives the rest of her discussion: "how is community articulated in relation to race and to sexuality?" (Alessandrini 36). She notes that, for Fanon, admittance is always based on racial identities. Since he is writing against the colonial order, an order that excludes him from certain communities because of his race, he envisions an escape from this order through the establishment of post-colonial national communities based on racial and ethnic divisions. In analyzing the connection between female sexuality and community formation, Chow looks to Fanon's representations of black female sexuality and concludes:

> Fanon's descriptions of women do not depart significantly from the traditional masculinist view that equated women with sex. In contrast to men, who are defined by violence and ambivalence, Fanon's construction of womanhood is a construction through notions of

sexual chastity, purity, fidelity, depravity, and perversion (Alessandrini 46).

By describing Fanon's gender bias, Chow is able to locate how he positions female sexuality and its threat of miscegenation as a site of potential danger to his own concept of a post-colonial national community. Chow states,

> If the creation of a postcolonial national community is at least in part about the empowerment of the formerly colonized through the systematic preservation of their racial and ethnic specificities, then such an empowerment could easily be imagined to be threatened by miscegenation, the sexual intermixing among the races. Such sexual intermixing leads to a kind of reproduction that is racially impure, and thus to a hybridization of the elements of the community concerned (ibid.).

Here Chow highlights the fact that women literally have the potential to give birth to a new kind of community not envisioned by Fanon. Thus, she explains that Fanon's gender bias is the result of the threat of unbounded female sexuality to, what she calls, the male intellectual's concept of community (Alessandrini 48). Women could disrupt "a pure grouping" by giving "rise to alternative groups of people whose origins are all bastardized and whose *communal bond* can henceforth not be based on the purity of their status as black or white" (Alessandrini 47).

Amours sauvages offers a representation of the alternative community Chow discusses above: an "alternative kind of community, a community in which the immanence and specificity of corporeality would coexist with a democratic, open-ended notion of collectivity" (ibid.). *Amour sauvages* recounts the power of female sexuality to build a new community. The struggles of Ève-Marie, the protagonist, in her inter-racial relationship help her face the stereotypes that try to define her and control her sexuality in both the white French community and the black African micro-community of Belleville in which she lives in order to eliminate the threat of miscegenation. In the end, the protagonist succeeds in establishing an identity that she chooses for herself, outside of the stereotypes, by controlling her own sexuality. Her new subject position places her in a space in which she begins to construct a new community that exceeds racial communal boundaries and the gender oppression she experiences in those communities.

Before analyzing the role Ève-Marie's sexuality plays in her community, it is important to first identify the levels of admittance allowed the protagonist to determine how she is included in the communities around her or excluded from them. Ève-Marie experiences a double alienation, in the sense that she faces exclusion based at once on race and gender. She is excluded from the larger white community of France, due to her race. However, she is admitted into the community of poor immigrants living in Belleville. Yet, in both communities, her gender excludes her from the dominant patriarchal structures that dictate the limits of acceptable behavior. Thus, she is admitted into the white French community, where she is physically present, but receives no validation from that community. In the Belleville immigrant community, she receives admittance in that she is also allowed into the community physically and receives validation from it based on her willingness to adhere to the patriarchal norms of her black society. However, due to Ève-Marie's challenges to the dominant order of her society, such a validation remains in flux throughout the duration of her quest for an acceptable alternative cultural identity.

The principal battle of Ève-Marie's subversion of communal norms is the fight to live her life outside the purview of the gaze of both the white man and the black man that positions her as a sexual object of exchange. The struggle is intensified for this black woman because she works as a prostitute upon arriving in France and eventually marries Pléthore, one of her white clients. She will have to rely on what she calls her "constructions of an independent woman" (Beyala 1999: 107)[1] to maintain an identity that resists the two male gazes attempting to define her within the constructions of racial and patriarchal stereotypes. Placing herself outside of these stereotypes will then allow her to begin forming an alternative community free from racial and gender oppression.

One of the stereotypes Ève-Marie must shatter is the colonial stereotype of the licentious black woman with a "'primitive' sexual appetite" (Gilman 213). At the beginning of the narrative, we learn that upon arriving in France, the only work she finds is as a prostitute in Mr. Thirty Percent's bar where she is called Ms. Good Surprise. Beyala's initial positioning of her protagonist as a prostitute is somewhat ironic and subversive at the same time. As Gwen Bergner notes, in the colonial race-sex economy, men view women as objects of exchange and try to control their sexuality through both the incest taboo and the miscegenation taboo (Bergner 81). Working as a prostitute, Ève-Marie would seem to fit perfectly, in a stereotypical sense, into the colonial race-sex economy, because she sells her sexuality as a commodity. Ironically, her choice to work as a prostitute situates her in the exact colonial stereotype that tries to define black women as sexually deviant. Sander Gilman shows how colonial discourse linked the black female with images of uncontrolled sexuality and stereotyped her as a prostitute (Gilman 229). However, the narrative of *Amours sauvages* does not portray Ève-Marie as a stereotypical prostitute who yields to the domination of men as a sexual commodity. Instead, she is represented as an individual, not as a type, who gains economic independence through prostitution. Although this portrayal does not negate masculine desires, it does position Ève-Marie as an individual subject with her own needs and desires.

The character of the prostitute is always a subversive one in Beyala's work. Odile Cazenave's study of a new generation of female African novelists identifies Beyala's prostitute protagonists as models of a new woman, who will help create a new society for the future. In her discussion of the functions of the prostitute in Beyala's earlier novels[2] Cazenave notes:

> Beyala uses a procedure that differs from that of most male writers, accentuating the similarities between prostitutes and other women

> rather than their differences...The female writer approaches the char-
> acter with empathetic examination; the prostitute is a woman with
> traits common to all women...Far from avoiding any identification
> with her reader..., [Beyala] pushes the reader to identify with [the
> prostitute protagonist]. Each [prostitute protagonist] embodies a
> model of clairvoyance that is symbolic of the new woman and of the
> potential new society (Cazenave 1996: 61).

Although Cazenave's comments do not directly address *Amours sauvages*, they may certainly be applied to it. Ève-Marie is the protagonist with whom the reader identifies. She is not represented as a type as has traditionally been the case for prostitutes in literature (Horn and Pringle 1984: 2). The plot does not focus on the stereotypical reform of a prostitute or descent of a good girl into prostitution, but rather on the love story of Ève-Marie and Pléthore and the difficulties they must surmount to build a successful inter-racial relation-ship outside of sexual commodification. Thus, represented as an individual, Ève-Marie's character subverts the dual stereotypes attached to her as a black woman and a prostitute by attaining financial independence outside of prosti-tution, establishing her subjectivity in a relationship in which she controls her own sexuality, and by overcoming the challenges of social determinism that help entrench her in the colonial stereotype.

First, to begin to dispel the stereotyping of the black female prostitute, Ève-Marie explains her reason for engaging in prostitution as a purely economic need. On one level, she separates the praxis and commodification of prostitu-tion from her identity formation and understands that her job permits her to be economically independent. It is true that she lives in an economically deprived neighborhood that stands in stark contrast to the luxury of other well-to-do neighborhoods in Paris, but she is able to afford an apartment, pay her bills, and eat well. Prostitution is the job that allows Ève-Marie a degree of the economic independence she desires.

Once Ève-Marie marries Pléthore and is able to work legally in France, she leaves the brothel to work as a cleaning lady for a gynecologist. One may read this as an indication that she is cleansing herself of her past profession. However, more importantly, her change in profession corresponds to the "success" reflected by her name and status change: "I was no longer Ms. Good Surprise, but Mrs. Ève-Marie Gerbaud" (Beyala 17). Thus, her marriage provides her with an opportunity to escape the identity attached to the name "Ms. Good Surprise" and to develop a new identity and a new economic independence.

One possible reading of this change may be that she gains legitimacy in France as the wife of a Frenchman. However, I contend that this reading is inadequate because it ignores certain aspects of Ève-Marie and Pléthore's rela-tionship. For example, the traditional economic hierarchy attached to male and female roles is reversed in their case. Ève-Marie supports Pléthore with her job because he is a struggling writer and she believes he has the talent to succeed as an artist. While he stays home to write, Ève-Marie works to support the couple.

Yet, her economic independence is also a question of personal satisfaction. Soon after her marriage, she leaves her job with the doctor to pursue the more ambitious goal of opening a *marquis*, a clandestine restaurant, in their apartment. The text of the first advertising cards she makes associates her marquis with the birth of the new woman and society that Beyala's prostitute protagonists typically represent:

> *Eat as you do at home, with Ève-Marie,*
> *first Lady of the universe,*
> *as indicated by her family name.* (Beyala 35)

The opening of her own restaurant symbolizes her development as an independent woman, what she calls her "constructions of an independent woman," which is not based on her position as the wife of a Frenchman. The Biblical reference to the myth of the first woman, Eve, indicates that Ève-Marie is creating a new world in which she will be the first woman of a new society. Yet, Ève is also linked to Marie, or Mary, the virginal mother who births a new religion and, thus, a new social order. In her protagonist's name, Beyala links sinner and virgin to create the mother of an alternative society free of oppression. Ève-Marie's marquis is a first step toward her liberation from the dominant social order that will allow her to begin establishing a new kind of community. When Ève-Marie leaves her life as a prostitute, which had once been her only path to economic independence, she founds an economic autonomy outside of prostitution, which in turn allows her to begin to create a social independence.

Second, to affirm her subjectivity outside of commodification and take control of her sexuality, Ève-Marie accepts Pléthore's marriage proposal. He asks her to marry him one day when he is fed up with his writing. At first, she reacts angrily to his proposal even though she had been dreaming and hoping that Pléthore would do just that. Initially, she believes that he must be mocking her, and the rest of the crowd in the bar echoes her reaction. But Pléthore defends his intention: "I want to marry Ève-Marie!" (Beyala 35). The men in the bar pronounce him crazy, and the women determine that he is impotent (ibid.). Ève-Marie describes the dramatic scene that follows in this way:

> Pléthore grabbed me by the wrist: "I'll marry you, Ève-Marie!" He swept me along behind him crowing triumphantly: "I'll marry you, Ève-Marie. In the name of the father!" We went through the bar under the astounded look of those who had been postulating about the meaning of Pléthore's behavior: "I'll marry you, Ève-Marie!" As soon as we began to climb the stairs, Mr. Thirty Percent said: "It's thirty percent!" But that was a given!
>
> In the minuscule pink bedroom where I worked, I discovered slow and rhythmic delirious happiness with Pléthore, furiously roaring tides, the red glow of seas, yellow and blue azures, and some "I'll marry you, Ève-Maries." Drowning, we murmured the vow of the

oriflammes, "I love you!". That Sunday, we gave birth to each other
while the muses of pleasure lit embers in the earth and explained to
us secrets of which we were ignorant (Beyala 15).

During this scene, Pléthore proves that he is serious about wanting to marry
Ève-Marie by demonstrating that he is not impotent. Paradoxically, the act con-
firming his intentions occurs in the space of Ève-Marie's prostitution. Yet, her
description of the event classifies it as a sexual encounter between lovers and not
between a prostitute and her client. They discover "slow and rhythmic deliri-
ous happiness," and whisper "I love you" to each other. Nevertheless, Mr. Thirty
Percent claims his usual thirty percent from the two lovers regardless of the
atypical circumstances of their sexual encounter. So, while Mr. Thirty Percent's
demands indicate that their union can only be a matter of commerce, Pléthore
proves to her that he sees her outside of the commodification of her body.

Third, Ève-Marie transcends her own self-defeating prejudices that affirm
the dominant colonial stereotype of black woman as erotic object through the
unfolding of three significant events in the novel and the development of two
of her relationships. These events and relationships are linked because they all
concern male abuse or violence against females and involve the repression of
Ève-Marie's former profession as a prostitute. They help shape her behavior and
rejection of Pléthore after he cheats on her. Throughout the novel, they slowly
elucidate Ève-Marie's own psychological struggle to escape the stereotype as
well as give her the strength she needs to build a successful inter-racial relationship with her husband. Together they serve as a period of apprenticeship for
Ève-Marie to break out of the colonial stereotype.

The first event is the discovery of an unidentified woman whose body is
found in front of Pléthore and Ève-Marie's apartment. The murdered woman,
whom Ève-Marie names Ms. Nobody, preoccupies the protagonist because she
is sure that the woman was killed by "a man who does not like women" (Beyala
59). The event disturbs Ève-Marie, because in her view the unknown woman
represents all women who are victims of male violence. The dead, unknown
woman becomes a martyr for Ève-Marie, who hears "faint cries coming from the
trees as if thousands of women were suffering in there" (Beyala, 48) when she
thinks of Ms. Nobody. The latter is a metonymy for Ève-Marie's own possible
victimization, as well as that of all other women, at the hands of men.

The second occurs when, just days after the discovery of Ms. Nobody's
body, Ève-Marie catches Pléthore in the act of having sex with a white neighbor,
Flora-Flore. Since the beginning of their marriage, Ève-Marie and Pléthore have
never discussed their prior relationship as prostitute/client. As a result of this
repression, she doubts Pléthore's intentions towards her when she discovers his
betrayal. In her emotional pain, Ève-Marie begins to wonder if he could go even
further than adultery and be the killer of Ms. Nobody. Ève-Marie determines
that since Pléthore is disrespectful towards her as a woman, he belongs in the
category of "men who do not like women." In this state of mind, Ève-Marie

associates Ms. Nobody's pain with her own pain as a woman betrayed by the man she loves. She wonders if she really knows him at all:

> First of all, who was Pléthore? He had told me that he didn't have any family, and I had believed him. He had told me that he loved me, and I had believed that. Which did not stop him from betraying me disgracefully. "Let's see if it isn't him who, after having taken advantage of Ms. Nobody, would have killed her so that she would not reveal their affair!" I said to myself (Beyala 53).

Pléthore's betrayal puts everything into question for Ève-Marie because it threatens her destiny, her dream of creating a new identity and community in this post-colonial society. By sleeping with another woman, Pléthore strips Ève-Marie of her sense of control and independence in their relationship. As a result of the new doubts that dominate Ève-Marie's thoughts, she also questions Pléthore's ability to love her as a black woman and not the stereotypes she is working to escape: "And what if he had only been attracted by exoticism and then once satisfied by all there was to take, enjoy, eat, drink, he got tired of it?" (ibid.). She feels the pressure of the colonial stereotype, their racial difference, and the continued haunting presence of her prostitution that has been repressed in their relationship until the moment when these doubts overwhelm her. Thus, Pléthore's infidelity topples Ève-Marie's fragile foundation for an inscription that tries to move past colonial stereotypes. Instead, she laments: "Doubt invaded me, prejudices replaced emotions" (ibid.). By concluding that Pléthore is no different from any of the other white men who continue to place black women in the colonial stereotype, Ève-Marie distances herself from the pain of having discovered Pléthore's infidelity. She chooses to believe that it is impossible for a white man to love a black woman in the first place, especially one who is a former prostitute. In this way, she reinscribes herself in prior tropes that had (over) determined her socially before her marriage with Pléthore. As a consequence of her coping mechanism, she effaces her sexual identity and, as we shall see next, begins to submit to the colonial stereotype of black women.

Third, embracing these prejudices to ease the pain of conjugal deception, Ève-Marie begins a sexual relationship with Michel, a racist neighborhood grocer, who views her as an erotic object to be possessed. In her pain, she submits to the colonial stereotype that haunts her after Pléthore's betrayal. Although Michel hates "Negroes, Arabs, and Jews," Ève-Marie explains that: "With my enormous cushiony breasts, my midnight skin and my hair like a baseball hat, I symbolized the exception that confirms the rule" (Beyala, 11). Thus, she recognizes that Michel places her within the colonial race-sex economy in which white men desire the forbidden other and want to have control of the sexual commodification of this other. His attraction to her "enormous cushiony breasts" and her "big butt" (ibid.) and his gestures that demonstrate his belief that she will be easily seduced, point to the colonial stereotype Sander Gilman describes. He shows how black women came to be seen by Europeans as possessing an uncontrollable sexual drive through the image of the Hottentot Venus with her so-called "primitive" genitalia (Gilman 213). Michel's desire for Ève-Marie's enormous breasts and huge buttocks is linked to her race and gives her an "excessive" sexual presence, similar to the "primitive" genitalia of the Hottentot Venus. When Michel propositions Ève-Marie, he believes he can seduce her with an apple "like the serpent of Eden" (ibid.). Thus, he connects what he considers to be her "excessive" sexual presence as a sign that she must also have an "excessive" sexual appetite and, therefore, would want to have sex with him for the negligible gift of an apple.

In the above quote, Ève-Marie describes Michel as being the stereotype of white, male desire—the serpent of Eden who thinks he can seduce her with an apple. Her reference again positions her as the first woman of a new community and, just like Eve, if she were to accept Michel's offer, she would destroy the new community she is trying to build as an independent woman. She would fall back into the colonial stereotype, becoming a sexual object to be exchanged within the colonial race-sex economy. However, when Ève-Marie discovers Pléthore's infidelity and begins to doubt her "constructions of an independent woman," she accepts Michel's offer to have sex, as if to become the erotic object she believes she may have been for Pléthore. During their encounter, Ève-Marie describes her feelings: "I was torn in half, tormented by contradictory sensations. Pleasure and disgust fought for parts of my person" (Beyala, 64). And again, when she returns to him once more before her reconciliation with Pléthore, she recalls her murderous feelings: "...I wanted to kill Michel" (Beyala, 90). Thus, although she takes on the colonial stereotype of the black female, she experiences pleasure and disgust during their encounters: pleasure at maintaining a certain control over her sexuality, because she chooses to become this object, and disgust at his complete lack of tenderness (Beyala, 64) and his revolting person. Her desire to kill him expresses her need to dominate the stereotype she chooses to become by sleeping with him. She wants to erase her fall from "Eden" and re-establish the start of a new community, a goal she will accomplish with the help of Flora-Flore.

Fourth, Ève-Marie's friendship with Flora-Flore, the white neighbor with whom she catches Pléthore having sex, places Ève-Marie in the role of mentor for a woman searching to escape the painful physical and emotional abuse of her marriage. The two women become friends when, after having sex with Pléthore, Flora-Flore attempts to make peace with Ève-Marie explaining "I'm begging you. I regret what happened. I just wanted to feel a little bit of true tenderness. Jean-Pierre Pierre is violent and you know it, Ève-Marie" (Beyala 56). Eventually, Ève-Marie feels sorry for this young woman and the two establish a unique friendship. Their relationship provides a space for both to explore the pleasure of true friendship between women. While Flora-Flore reveals the truth about her relationship with Jean-Pierre Pierre little by little, Ève-Marie is there to offer her advice, maternal love, and protection from the abusive power men sometimes have over women. In Ève-Marie's role as mentor to Flora-Flore, the protagonist proves to be a model of strength and independence as she tries to teach her neighbor how to prevent male abuse. She nurtures her friend, showing her how to become an independent woman even when her own independence is put in doubt. For Ève-Marie, the relationship allows her to question and confirm the identity she is constructing for herself, that of an independent woman who defies cultural taboos and the traditional definitions of her role as a black woman in society to begin building a new community. The fact that Ève-Marie provides mothering and love for a white woman also helps her to begin breaking down racial barriers that inform her position within the community of Belleville and the black African community.

Finally, Ève-Marie's struggle to break free of the colonial stereotype comes to a head when Flora-Flore reveals to her that it was Jean-Pierre Pierre who killed Ms. Nobody, a woman he had been using to torture Flora-Flore emotionally to "educate her and cultivate her jealousy" (Beyala 103). She explains:

> ...they screwed in front of me and laughed at my sadness...they tied each others' hands behind their backs, whipped each other and got off on pain...That night, they wanted to play rapist-strangler with his victim. And it turned out badly (Beyala 103-104).

With the double revelation that "Ms. Nobody...was, in the end, nobody" (Beyala 133) and that Pléthore was not guilty of what Ève-Marie had thought to be an atrocious crime against an innocent woman, the protagonist has a series of realizations that emerge as a result of what she learns from all of the events and relationships described above:

> I had suspected Pléthore of this murder, why?...the confused sickness that had devoured my brain was exposed to daylight. Why? Because he was white? Because he symbolized white superiority? The black complex? The black anti-complex? The thousands of abuses of confidence? The ten thousand treasons? Slavery and submission? Our couple – like millions like it – carried in its breast, the seed of unconfessed historic dissonances. I had loved Pléthore like a slave loves her master, with mistrust. I had feared, without admitting it to myself, that he was only attracted by my exoticism and by those sexual prejudices that accompany the existence of black women, enclose them, and determine their relations to the world. Without realizing it, I had taken his infidelity as a pretext to make him pay for the brutality of humanity (Beyala 103).

Ève-Marie realizes that she had been letting the colonial stereotype define her in ways she had not even noticed. The psychological colonization she has undergone has always been present in her feelings for Pléthore, even if she does not recognize it. The social structure of dominance of white men over black women that is a large part of her alienation from white French society remains a threat to her even after she thinks she has established her independence, and it is reinforced by the brutal act of Jean-Pierre Pierre. Although she does not connect her realizations to her relationship with Michel, that relationship certainly reflects the depth of her psychological colonization. In it, she accepts all of the "sexual prejudices...that determine the relationships of black women in the world."

After Pléthore's betrayal, Ève-Marie rejects him even though he repeatedly attempts to prove his love for her. She changes the locks just after the incident of infidelity and refuses his attempts to reconcile with her, although she clearly misses him and longs to be with him. Her doubts that link him, in turn, to the white male gaze make it impossible for them to have a loving relationship between two individuals. Her own alienation, resulting partially from the "sexual prejudices that accompany the existence of black women" (ibid.), was impeding her from trusting Pléthore again. The realization that Pléthore is innocent convinces her to allow his return home where together they confront the stereotypes of the black female as eroticized sexual object and white man as someone who sees black women only in this sexualized position, stereotypes that Ève-Marie has been allowing to define their inter-racial relationship. The renewal of their commitment to each other places Ève-Marie firmly back in her "constructions of an independent woman."

The colonial stereotype is not the only obstacle that stands between her and her "destiny." The black African community in Belleville, the community that gives her validation on the basis of race, also attempts to define her sexuality by policing her sexual behavior. The policing is meant to uphold the patriarchal values of the black African Muslim community in Belleville which views inter-racial marriage as taboo and encourages polygamous marriages. However, the policing is carried out by a group of black African women who monitor Ève-Marie's relationship, not by the men in the community. This kind of policing is one of the hallmarks of patriarchal domination: "the domination of man is only fully established when the woman appears to be the only one responsible for her situation as a victim"[3] (Godelier 1976: 16). Thus, in taking responsibility for their domination, these women strive to uphold the ideals and practices of their Islamic cultures from home, even though they do not all come from the same country in Africa. Thus, they seek out women who adopt behaviors that are seen as stereotypically "white" or "European" to the black African Muslim community. The perceived rule-breakers are then labeled as deviant, and the women who work to protect the borders of their racial and religious community discourage their "white" behaviors in an attempt to restore the conformity of practices within that community.

Ève-Marie's marriage to Pléthore is considered an outrage by the group of black African women who police other women's sexual behavior. Pléthore's infidelity provides an occasion for these women to try bringing Ève-Marie back within the borders of the community. Both her reaction to the betrayal and her marriage to Pléthore are the subject of the scolding remarks of the African women. When Ève-Marie discovers Pléthore with Flora-Flore, she feels so ashamed that she decides to run through the neighborhood spreading news of the scandal. She explains: "It was my way of preventing the putrid comments I was expecting from people" (Beyala 50). When she arrives at a local bar with her news, a group of African women approaches her:

> A procession of Negresses advanced step by step, hunched up in colored boubous, waving their hands, hooting: "It is not allowed to do things like this!" I wanted to flee, but Mama Suzanne, M'am Myriam, M'am Térésa, M'am Soumia and many other uprooted women who were aware of my misfortunes, were already bumping into me with their behinds. "You are covering us with shame, my dear!" they yelled.... "A Negress who behaves like a white woman, never heard of it! And again: "What difference does it make to be cheated on, huh?" We're not dead because of it! Right, girls!"...They laughed and cursed the attraction for sin, this absolute desire to break taboos that pushed a white man and a black woman to flaunt themselves, to play at evil to the point of entering into marriage (Beyala 50-51).

In this scene, the African women admonish Ève-Marie for behavior that crosses the line of what is normal or acceptable within their community. Their comments are representative of a sustained effort throughout the book to bring Ève-Marie back within the borders of the community and pressure her to submit to a conformist group identity. Her decision to spread the news of her conjugal deception betrays the patriarchal values of their community as it subverts male control of female sexuality by questioning the male's right to choose a sexual partner at will. Ève-Marie calls that right into question, because she finds Pléthore's behavior unacceptable, and wants the entire Belleville community to know. The African women, who try to regulate women's behavior for the benefit of the African men in their community, threaten Ève-Marie's admittance within that community by accusing her of acting like a white woman. Her loyalty to their cultural values is called into question because she does not accept her husband's infidelity as the women who scold her have done in the context of their own marriages. The group of African women takes this opportunity to remind Ève-Marie that her suffering is predictable, because she has already committed a taboo by marrying Pléthore. Her disregard for the rules of the community places her on the border of admittance.

However, Ève-Marie wants to escape the gaze of the black man that would define her as a sexual object to be held within the borders of the black African community. This gaze, in turn, is over-determined by the black man's position as object of the white man's gaze, rendering her escape even more difficult. Her commentary about the policing of the group of African women demonstrates her determination to build a new community and to move past the unwritten rules that she feels constrict her ability to be independent. When reproached by the African women who try to bring her back within the borders of the community, the narrator thinks:

> They had seen some hurtful affairs in their careers as cuckolded wives. They had lived sordid family intrigues and village pettiness. To hear them talk, they were great politicians in the matter: they took such details seriously, but used and abused protocols that allowed them to make the bloodiest wars proper (Beyala 51).

Ève-Marie's commentary reflects her desire to define the terms of her own relationships with men outside the norms of the community. The conjugal reality of the other women in her community, as she describes it, represents a life of deception that Ève-Marie is not willing to accept. Pléthore's infidelity raises questions about his love for her and in order to be independent, Ève-Marie wants to feel confident in the fact that she and her mate are truly in love. Her reaction, just like her advice to Flora-Flore about how to be an independent woman, expresses her own desire to become independent by escaping the domination of men and defining her position in her relationship with her husband on her own terms.

As noted earlier, Ève-Marie's escape from the authority of the black man may come at a price – that of non-validation from the black African community in Belleville. Although she is working to build a new community, she does not want her new identity to exclude her from her original community of validation. Throughout the narrative, she wrestles with opposing desires: to break free from the constraints of the black African community and to maintain admittance, in the sense of validation, within that community. After a particular confrontation with the African women policing her, she wonders if she will be able to reconcile her two desires: "Did aspiring to total love mean losing my African woman's soul?" (Beyala 60). Before Pléthore's betrayal, she believed she did not question her ability to maintain her Africanness and experience true love with a white man. However, after he cheats on her, the two desires seem to be in opposition with each other.

Her questioning and doubts about Pléthore's ability to love her as a black woman and not see her in the role of the colonial stereotype, made even more difficult given her past profession, influence her struggle for independence from the role of women in her community. When she feels that the foundation of her "constructions of an independent woman" is in jeopardy and that she may lose admittance to her black African community, she attempts to reintegrate into the African community by adopting the discourse of the African women who police her behavior. By doing so, she appears to embrace the patriarchal values of the black African community in Belleville and even seems to be complicit with the group of African women who police the sexuality of other African women. She explains: "...I wanted these returns to the palm trees because they were reassuring. They allowed me to condemn my love of Pléthore. The sight of a black-white couple in the street gave me ulcers" (Beyala 108). Thus, by adopting the normative behaviors of women in the black African community, Ève-Marie distances herself from the pain of Pléthore's betrayal and the resulting loss of her independence. She admits, "I was demolishing my own constructions of an independent woman" (Beyala 107). She inserts herself into a superficially protective social construct, one that ultimately remains distinctive from the subjectivity she embraces throughout the rest of the novel. So, her escape from the gaze of the black male that tries to maintain patriarchal domination in the black African society through the enforcement of specific behaviors fails briefly.

When Ève-Marie accepts Pléthore back into her life, she must resolve the seemingly inherent conflict between her independence from the rules governing women's sexuality in the black African community in Belleville and her desire to retain a sense of validation in that community. Ève-Marie achieves this unlikely balance, thanks to her talent as a writer and Pléthore's commitment to her. She finds validation from her community outside of the typical role of black African women when she begins writing a novel. The news of her artistic endeavor excites her poor African clientele. Bassonga, a "tirailleur sénégalais" who frequents her marquis, exclaims: "What is the world coming to, huh, if women write their stories?" (Beyala 111). He acknowledges that the world, with its values and borders, changes when women pick up their pens to tell stories from a woman's perspective. However, the majority of her clients react with gratitude: "They hugged me and congratulated me: 'Bravo and thank you for everything!' as if I were a heroine who had just saved the people from certain death" (Beyala 113). By writing, Ève-Marie undertakes a European-dominated enterprise in order to give voice to the African experience. Even if Ève-Marie's writing exceeds the patriarchal imperatives of her community as Bassonga's comment suggests, her work is seen more as a threat to the dominant white French community and is, therefore, acceptable in terms of African success in France. Thus, Ève-Marie is applauded as a victor while subverting male dominance in her own community.

Her admittance to the black African community of Belleville is assured at the end of the novel when she receives a letter from a potential publisher informing her of the "immense interest" of her manuscript, regretting that they will not be able to publish it, due to their overbooked program (Beyala 130). Although the letter is obviously a rejection form letter, the black African community in Belleville views it as a major victory for Africa and for Africans. They parade around the neighborhood shouting: "We won!" (Beyala 132). The letter, in their opinion, signals recognition of their community by those in charge of "the realities of social determinism" (Beyala 127) and it is seen, thus, as a sort of admittance to the dominant social matrix. This admittance is, however, ironic since it represents a moment of conformity with the white French community. Still, for Ève-Marie, it represents her successful subversion of the patriarchal values of her own community. Bassonga, the "tirailleur sénégalais" who did not approve of a woman writing when Ève-Marie first announced her book project, changes his attitude completely and tells her: "Do you know that if there had been ten women like you...Africa would not be where it is...It's true...We would be a respected people today; and feared by the concert of nations" (Beyala 131). The letter is a certificate of recognition for Ève-Marie's success as an independent woman. For the inhabitants of her neighborhood, it demonstrates that the white French culture that excludes many of the members of their own community recognizes Ève-Marie through her contribution to the arts. While this implies that the community demonstrates a continuation of subconscious ideological domination by the white French community, Ève-Marie still successfully subverts patriarchal norms in her own community. She sums up her own feelings while watching the spectacle around her:

> ...I felt big, big and large, capable of nestling all emotions in my arms. Because it was me, the woman, the prostitute, the black woman who had succeeded in this undertaking, because the idea of writing was born from my senses, from my guts, from my heart, from my head, it came out all alone, not by accident, but from me (Beyala 133).

This achievement, viewed as extraordinary for a black woman who was previously a prostitute, wins Ève-Marie validation in her community. The act of writing allows her to redefine herself. She successfully breaks free of the stereotypes attached to "the woman, the prostitute, the black woman" and still manages to maintain validation from the black African community. Thus, she moves freely back and forth across the borders of her community, because she has created a new position, a new woman.

Ève-Marie's "constructions of an independent woman" find their own solid foundation at the end of the novel. At first, she worries because her reconciliation with Pléthore does not guarantee that their relationship will be successful. Even though they love each other, she is afraid that social pressure could still force them apart. Ève-Marie reveals how she intends to measure the success of their relationship when she asks Pléthore for reassurance about their chances together: "Do you think that we will grow old together?... I don't know any mixed couples who have finished their lives side by side" (Beyala, 120). Ève-Marie now knows that Pléthore loves her as an individual, not as the stereotype of the exotic black woman and that the major obstacle to their relationship is social pressure. His response to her questioning acknowledges the uphill battle they face in their life together:

> Pléthore explained to me that he would never drift far from me, that he would never cease loving me. He didn't know what form our love would take because, up until then, the social imagination had not explored miscegenation on a big scale. He was convinced that, without being leaders, we could remodel public tastes by mixing private needs so that they adapt to each other.
>
> In any case, he concluded, I refuse to see our differences of color and culture as a problem (Beyala 120-121).

Pléthore's comments here leave the reader to imagine, with him, what form their love will take. It is clear, however, that Pléthore has become Ève-Marie's partner in the construction of her "destiny," or the creation of a new post-colonial community in which neither race nor gender are excluding factors.

At the end of the novel, Ève-Marie's success in building her destiny is represented by two significant symbols. First, we learn that she and Pléthore do grow old together. As the narrator concludes her story, she jumps forward in time to her present day, allowing the reader a glimpse at the "end" of the story. The comments of others reveal their success: "You and Pléthore are truly exceptional. We don't know any mixed couples who have hung in there for so long!" (Beyala 158). They have measured up to Ève-Marie's test for success: they remain together into their old age.

Second, before the narration jumps forward in time, the reader learns the end of Flora-Flore's story, one that has significant implications for the establishment of Ève-Marie's new community. Flora-Flore has given birth to a baby boy, Edgar, conceived when she had a brief affair with one of Ève-Marie's friends from Senegal. When the baby is born, she claims that Jean-Pierre Pierre is the father although he is obviously a child of mixed race. Several months later, Jean-Pierre Pierre brings the baby to Ève-Marie's apartment to confront her about the paternity of the baby. When Ève-Marie convinces Jean-Pierre Pierre that Edgar is an inter-racial child because Flora-Flore "lived with us too much," he responds, saying "You are responsible for me being legally cuckolded. Therefore, I leave this child to you until he whitens up!" (Beyala 150). So, Edgar comes under the care of Ève-Marie who, unable to have children of her own, immediately claims him as her own: "…if Jean-Pierre Pierre decided to take Edgar back, it would consequently crush my bones until they turned into dust…Because Edgar, without being my past, was already my future" (Beyala 151). Ève-Marie does keep Edgar, because Flora-Flore dies soon afterward, presumably from injuries received from her husband. Thus, Ève-Marie and Pléthore raise this inter-racial baby as their own son. He is yet another symbol of his mother's establishment of a successful hybrid identity.

In terms of Fanon's conceptualizations of community, the alternative community proposed by Beyala in *Amours sauvages* accomplishes one of his expressed goals: it moves towards a "new humanism" (*Black Skin*, 9) in which the establishment of "a world of reciprocal recognitions" (*Black Skin*, 218) between the races becomes possible. However, in Fanon's writings about the woman of color and those about post-colonial nation-building, woman is only granted a mediated agency: the sexual agency that Chow describes and the agency by designation described by McClintock. Through these two feminist critiques of Fanon's construction of limited female agency, the contrast between the agency he constructs for women and the agency Beyala constructs for women in her alternative community comes into focus. Beyala creates both a social and sexual agency that do not suffer the limitations of either racial or patriarchal restrictions for her protagonist in the black African community of Belleville. In this community, Ève-Marie opens her own business, allowing her to support herself, even outside of her troubled marriage. She is never trapped within the construct of female dependence on male economic support. In addition, when she takes up her pen and begins to write, this act symbolically places her in a position to exert an agency that is not subject to the same patriarchal rules and conditions as other women in her community. The validation implicit in this new position allows Ève-Marie to subvert patriarchal norms in another important way: her choice of sexual partner no longer brings reprisals for non-conformity from her community; she exerts sexual agency outside of the borders of her community and does so without endangering her admittance inside that community.

Alongside the fact that Ève-Marie does not receive validation from the white French community because she no longer needs it, Beyala succeeds in deconstructing deeply entrenched stereotypes about a black female prostitute in a post-colonial community. This breaking down of the colonial stereotype about black female sexuality is what allows Ève-Marie to break the miscegenation taboo and build a successful relationship with her husband outside of white French norms as well.

Thus, in a way, Beyala's alternative community, like Fanon's "new humanism" for all communities, begins in the post-colonial community of color. It is from within this community that she and Pléthore can serve as a model for both communities to work towards "a new humanism." This idea is affirmed by Pléthore: "He was convinced that, without being leaders, we could remodel public tastes by mixing private needs so that they adapt to each other" (Beyala 121). The difference between Beyala's fictional construction of this community and Fanon's theoretical vision of this community is that in Beyala's, women may exert an agency that allows them to break free of patriarchal domination. Fanon envisions his post-colonial community with a normative male subject giving women either sexual agency within their communities or "agency by designation." Most importantly, in Beyala's novel, it becomes clear that women must be in control of their own sexuality in order for an alternative community to be successful, one in which racial and gender oppression is eliminated. Women must be full social and sexual partners able to exert sexual agency without being confined within communal borders by patriarchal or racial controls of their sexuality.

Notes

1. All translations of *Amours sauvages* are mine.
2. Here, Cazenave discusses the function of the characters Ateba, Tanga, and Megri from *The Sun Hath Looked Upon Me, Your Name Shall Be Tanga*, and *Seul le diable le savait* respectively.
3. My translation.

Works Cited

Accad, Evelyne. "Rebellion, Maturity, and the Social Context: Arab Women' Contribution to Literature." *Arab Women: Old Boundaries, New Frontiers*. Judith Tucker. Ed. Bloomington: Indiana University Press, 1993: 224-253.

Adams, Parveen and Jeff Minson. "The Subject of Feminism" in *The Woman in Question*, Parveen Adams and Elizabeth Cowie, eds. Cambridge, Mass.: The MIT Press, 1990: 81-101.

Beyala, Calixthe. *Amours sauvages*. Berlin: Éditions J'ai lu, 1999.

Bergner, Gwen. "Who is that Masked Woman? or The Role of Gender in Fanon's *Black-Skin, White Masks*." PMLA 110 (1995): 75-88.

Cazenave, Odile. *Rebellious Women: The New Generation of Female African Novelists*. Boulder: Lynne Rienner Publishers, 2000.

Chow, Rey. "The Politics of Admittance: Female Sexual Agency, Miscegenation, and the Formation of Community in Frantz Fanon" in *Frantz Fanon: Critical Perspectives*, Anthony Alessandrini, Ed. New York: Routledge, 1999: 34-56.

Fanon, Frantz. *Wretched of the Earth* (trans. Constance Farrington). New York: Grove Press, 1966.

—-. *Black Skin, White Masks*, trans. C.L. Markmann. New York: Grove Press, 1967.

Fuss, Diana. "Interior Colonies: Frantz Fanon and the Politics of Identification." In: *Rethinking Fanon: The Continuing Dialogue*. Ed. Nigel C. Gibson. New York: Humanity Books, 1990: 294-328.

Gallimore, Rangira Béatrice. *L'Œuvre romanesque de Calixthe Beyala*. Paris: L'Harmattan, 1997.

Gilman, Sander L. "Black Bodies, White Bodies: Toward an Iconography of Female Sexuality in Late Nineteenth Century Art, Medicine, and Literature" in *Critical Inquiry* 12, no. 1 (Autumn 1985): 204-42.

Godelier, Maurice. "Le sexe comme fondement ultime de l'ordre social et cosmique chez les Baruya de Nouvelle-Guinée." In: "Le problème des formes et des fondements de domination masculine," *Cahiers du CERM*, no. 128, (1976): 1-36.

Hammonds, Evelyn M. "Toward a Genealogy of Black Female Sexuality: The Problematic of Silence." in *Feminist Genealogies, Colonial Legacies, Democratic Futures*. M. Jacqui Alexander and Chandra Talpade Mohanty. Eds. Routledge: New York, 1997: 170-182.

Hall, Stuart. "Cultural Identity and Diaspora." In: *Colonial Discourse and Postcolonial Theory*. P. Williams and L. Chrisman, Eds. New York: Columbia University Press, 1994: 392-403.

Horn, Pierre L. and Pringle, Mary Beth, Eds. *The Image of the Prostitute in Modern Literature*. New York: Frederick Ungar Publishing Co., 1984.

Little, Roger. *Between Totem and Taboo: Black Man, White Woman in Francographic Literature*. Exeter: University of Exeter Press, 2001.

McClintock, Anne. "Fanon and Gender Agency" in *Rethinking Fanon: The Continuing Dialogue*, Nigel C. Gibson, Ed. New York: Humanity Books, 1990: 283-293.

Scott, Joan W. "Experience" in *Feminists Theorize the Political*, Judith Butler and Joan W. Scott, Eds. New York: Routledge, 1992: 22-40.

Chapter 7

Feminine Transgression and Crossing Over: Maryse Condé's *I, Tituba, Black Witch of Salem*

Amy Lee

———————

Maya Angelou's poem "Africa" presents a personal rendition of the personae's motherland:

> Thus she had lain
> sugarcane sweet
> deserts her hair
> golden her feet
> mountains her breasts
> two Niles her tears.

Beginning with a tone of mourning, the poem depicts the hurt and oppression suffered by the richly nurturing motherland, which finally reaches self awareness and strength, and marches its people to a brighter future. This rendition of "Africa" the motherland is a vivid portrayal of Africa's recent history in terms of its relationship with the colonial powers, and its people's sentiments. The allusion to a female nurturing richness is not only true of the land's identity in the eyes of its subjects, but also ironically true of its being exploited by the colonial powers. The colonizers which "churched her with Jesus" and "bled her with guns" have assumed a dominant masculine position, whereas Africa, the colonized, is the virgin land violated by the phallic exertion of foreign dominance. This gender differentiation of masculine vs feminine is very often used as the tool to symbolize superior versus subordinate power distribution among different cultural groups.

This feminized other, whether in terms of gender, racial, sexual, and class identities, is thus allocated the negative pole of a binary opposition where the unmarked entity is always the masculine, the norm and the positive identity. The mark of the feminine, in all these different binary oppositions, can perhaps be best summarized by their silences. Virginia Woolf, in her exploratory essay of early 20th century, has hit the nail on the head when she mentions that the female character is a strange creature being over-represented and under-represented at the same time. Her persona in *A Room of One's Own* searches historical and biographical records of famous women only to discover that while there are plenty of heroines in literature penned by men, they seldom speak for themselves. Talking about colonization and cultural domination, Spivak asks the famous question: "can the subaltern speak?" again highlighting the need of a voice in order for individual subjectivity to be. The ability to speak, the existence of a position from which to speak, as well as having a language of their own are the top priorities of the marginalized to come to themselves.

The attempt to find a voice, a position and a language of its own has increasingly been a major endeavor of the black female literature in the past few decades. In many ways a response to Woolf's urge for women to reclaim a tradition of their own writing, black female writers have also engaged in constructing their own literary history, tracing its genesis and development all the way back to an origin of oral narratives. In the course of this collective striving to build a story of their own, what is revealed is not only the treasure of a group of black female story-tellers, but also unique stories and ways of telling them. Writing away the misconceived stereotypes of the silent black female, the African diaspora writing has unearthed voices, languages, images and stories which are engaged in a complex dialogue with representations from their former colonizers.

While Woolf finds that the female writing talent needs at least a room and five hundred pounds for its free expression, the African diaspora poses a very different context for its female writers. The matrilineal pattern of identification and literary legacy is particularly strong not only because of the pool of feminine talent, but probably also because the masculine has been feminized in the colonial discourse. Colonized African men have not been given a chance to assume a protective role to their fellow women and children, thus women have been left to fend for themselves in their struggle for subjectivity and even for survival. Narratives by black female writers become a site of struggle where the individuals strive for a presence, a voice, and a position beyond the multiple jeopardy they have been forced to occupy by their racial, gender, sexual, and class identities.

A black feminist ideology, therefore, should not, and cannot, be an ideology of victims. Deborah King writes in "Multiple Jeopardy, Multiple Consciousness: The Context of Black Feminist Ideology" that an ideal black womanhood is one of strength and distinct visibility, against the multiple oppression black women face: "racism, sexism, and classism" (King 237), sometimes even within liberation movements. While I very much agree with this individuation in terms of experiences and identity, I would like to add that to achieve all these, a unique language of their own is essential. Black women not only have to speak, but they also have to steer clear of the language of the oppressors, which will only put them in the oppressed position once more. To reinvent themselves, they have to reinvent a language first. It is with an aim to examine a manifestation of this special language that I turn to Maryse Condé's 1986 novel, *I, Tituba, Black Witch of Salem*, to read the pregnant feminine text which empowers black women's self-representation.

Tituba is a historical figure who has gone down in history as "a slave originating from the West Indies and probably practicing 'voodoo'" (210). During the 17ᵗʰ century, in the small village of Salem in Massachusetts, an outbreak of mysterious hysterical diseases among the women had led to the church's suspicion of witchcraft. It was thought that among the villagers, there were people who were in league with the devil to undermine the church's authority over the population. What resulted were a massive witch-hunt, trials, confessions, and executions. Records of the trials were voluminous but nothing much was devoted to someone like Tituba, who was black, a woman, and a slave. Condé's fictional biography of such a personality captures very well the possible frustration felt by such a person if she really exists:

> There would be no mention of my age or my personality. I would be ignored. As early as the end of the seventeenth century, petitions would be circulated, judgments made, rehabilitating the victims, restoring their honor, and returning their property to their descendants. I would never be included! Tituba would be condemned forever! There would never, ever, be a careful, sensitive biography recreating my life and its suffering. (110)

Indeed, Tituba will serve as a prime example of a woman suffering from what King would call multiple jeopardy, as she is the most powerless in terms of class, race, gender, and even sexuality.

As an answer to this existential void of an imaginary personality, Condé creates in the imagined realm what is not recorded in history. When asked about the invention of Tituba, Condé confesses that: "being a black person, having a certain past, having a certain history behind me, I want to explore that realm and of course I do it with my imagination and with my intuition" (201). The writing of this fictional biography of a real person who is not much recorded in official history is therefore not just an innocent act of filling in a gap left in/by history, but is a highly deliberate act stemming from the writer's consciousness of her own cultural and historical identity. In an interview with Ann Scarboro, Condé says:

> For a black person from the West Indies or from Africa, whatever, for somebody from the diaspora, I repeat it is a kind of challenge to find out exactly what was there before. It is not history for the sake of history. It is searching for one's self, searching for one's identity, searching for one's origin in order to better understand oneself. (203-4)

Her act of reconstructing a personal history for Tituba is therefore a journey undertaken to experience the self, rather than a mission to historical authenticity. Tituba has assumed a voice and spoken through the words of Maryse Condé; what is this voice and how does it speak to us?

Angela Davis in her forward to the English translation of the novel writes:

> Tituba engages in recurring meditations on her relationship – as a black woman – to feminism. In this sense, her voice can be viewed as

the voice of a suppressed black feminist tradition, one that women
of African descent are presently reconstituting – in fiction, criticism,
history, and popular culture. (xii)

Whether we call Tituba a feminist is not important. But her re-emerged voice
which speaks of a multiple consciousness through its pregnant words reverses the
negation associated with femininity. The reconstruction of Tituba's story puts
focus on her vigorous sexuality, her transgressive ways of communication, and
her capacity to form female-bonds which become the core of her fight in establishing a self beyond the restrictions of a patriarchal racist society. *I, Tituba, Black
Witch of Salem* is a feminine text which illustrates in its form, its content, and its
imagery how being feminine can be an empowerment and not a liability.

Even before the proper story of Tituba's life starts to unfold, the text starts
its seducing narrative thread by playing with our understanding of authorship.
Maryse Condé, in her capacity as the author of the text, writes: "Tituba and I
lived for a year in the closest of terms. During our endless conversations she told
me things she had confided to nobody else." While seeming to assure readers of
authenticity or exclusiveness of the information revealed, this ironically highlights the impossibility of such an endeavor, and in turn the fabricatedness of
this narrative. The impossibility of such a relationship, one between a long dead
subject and an author who has not much historical facts to go upon, challenges
the readers to deviate from the traditional qualities of a biography such as fidelity, clarity, objectivity, and the reliance on proved facts when reading the text
to follow. The transgressiveness of these two women's relationship heralds the
unfolding of a world not conforming to patriarchal meanings.

Categorization of the narrative, for one, seems impossible. With the name
of Maryse Condé as the author, and her claim that Tituba has confided in her
personally, the label of biography seems to apply. Yet the very first page of the
content greets us with "Abena, my mother, was raped by an English sailor" (3),
undoubtedly the voice of Tituba the subject. Moreover, this auto/biography
does not end when Tituba's life comes to an end. Tituba is executed as a revolutionary, and her final words in the story proper are: "I was the last to be taken
to the gallows. All around me strange trees were bristling with strange fruit"
(172). Not only is it difficult to imagine the author being present at Tituba's
execution three centuries ago; the image of new life bursting forth in "strange
trees were bristling with strange fruit" immediately frames Tituba's death with
new meaning. Life and death within the space of this narrative does not adhere
to conventional understanding.

This transgression beyond patriarchal understanding is confirmed in the
epilogue, when Tituba's voice appears again even after her mortal life: "And that
is the story of my life. Such a bitter, bitter story" (175). The already dead Tituba
says: "My real story starts where this one leaves off and it has no end" (175). The
real story, the one which has never been told before, not even simplified in the
words of patriarchal historiography, is a story of different substance, nature, and
texture. The epilogue, which is usually a brief section after the main narrative

to round up the loose ends of the narrative proper, is here instead undermining the centrality of the main narrative. It embodies a "real" story, but a story which subverts the linear progression of conventional life narratives, and a story which celebrates change, as Tituba takes different "mortal form" (178) for fun: an *anoli*, a fighting cock, a bird, or a goat. Tituba's life after life is overflowing, and interpenetrable with nature.

This power to penetrate is present right from the beginning when a shared consciousness between two women is given as the genesis of the tale. Two women sharing even the most intimate thoughts so that they are interchangeable, conceive an unprecedented identity which goes beyond conventional parameters of a self. Heterosexual liaison might give birth to mortal life, but woman-woman bond gives birth to the kind of unending life Tituba claims in her narrative. *I, Tituba, Black Witch of Salem* is possible because women identify with women across time, space, and differences and form a matrilineal consciousness more fertile than heterosexuality. Feminine same-sex liaison, in its multiple and transgressive forms, evades the stigma of absence imposed by patriarchy, and brings forth buried females subjectivities in defiance of restrictions present only in man-centered world. Tituba's story celebrates feminine sexuality, which gives life and defies death, through the various women bonds.

Mother and daughter's "natural" bond in Tituba's life was cut short when her biological mother, Abena, was hanged in Tituba's childhood. Severance of this primary connection does not render Tituba helpless, though. There is no lack of surrogate mothers in the community whom Tituba can depend on for orientation and for self realization. Women who have no direct or familial connection to Tituba, even women who do not belong with her community, enrich Tituba's life simply by being there. Mama Yaya, a Nago woman whose family members have been tortured to death, takes care of the seven-year-old Tituba after her mother dies and teaches her the languages of life:

> Mama Yaya taught me about herbs. Those for inducing sleep. Those for healing wounds and ulcers. Those for loosening the tongues of thieves. Those that calm epileptics and plunge them into blissful rest. Those that put words of hope on the lips of the angry, the desperate, and the suicidal. (9)

The ability to identify and use these healing plants is a door into another dimension of life. Mama Yaya's tutelage is an act of life-granting fertility.

Apart from learning to heal, Tituba is also initiated into what she calls the upper spheres of knowledge, communication with the other worlds: the world of the dead and the world of the non-human beings. An ability to maintain contact with the deceased gives almost absolute freedom to Tituba because the threshold of mortality no longer bounds her world. Being able to assume different animal shapes also liberates her from the confines of the human carcass. Although Mama Yaya is not Tituba's biological mother, she has given her life, moreover life which transgresses boundaries. Judah White, a friend of Mama

Yaya, grants Tituba a new life not only in helping abort her unwanted baby, but also in creating a new sensibility in Tituba: "I returned to Boston a little reassured, having learned to see friends in the black cat, the owl, the ladybird, and the mockingbird, creatures that I had never paid attention to previously."(52) What these unrelated women have done for Tituba is the begetting of a fertile life which cannot be stopped or contained.

Ironically echoing Chodorow's concept of reproduction of mothering, Tituba's course of life also mirrors a pattern of mothering other creatures like herself. In service with the Parris household, she takes pity on Goodwife Parris and little Elizabeth because these two submissive female remind her of the marginalized position she inhabits. Herself a highly sexual being, she shows unwilling sympathy to the Salem Village teenage girls who are forced to lead a puritanical and pleasure-less life. Even after her mortal life has expired, she continues her mothering through the choice of a Creole girl Samantha as her successor. Tituba's personal narrative of her life is a chain of women connecting to other women, protecting one another, nurturing one another, and mutually mothering each other. This matriarchal network goes beyond linearity and demonstrates its fertility through a rhizome-like path, evading pre-set routes and rules.

The enormous feminine energy of this network of females can also be seen in its transgressive and aggressive paths of communication. In *I, Tituba, Black Witch of Salem*, Tituba identifies not only with women who mother her or women whom she mothers; her spectrum of identification spreads across age groups, across the threshold between life and death, and beyond accepted sexual orientations. She is able to talk to Abena and Mama Yaya even when they have crossed over to the other side of life, and she is equally capable of making Samantha, her chosen successor, understand her. The after-life Tituba says:

> [T]his child of mine has learned to recognize my presence in the twitching of an animal's coat, the crackling of a fire between four stones, the rainbow-hued babbling of the river, and the sound of the wind as it whistles through the great trees on the hills. (179)

Although already passed out of the mortal world, Tituba shows that the feminine presence can freely break into the living world and manifests herself in the most lively and permanent activities within nature.

Among the feminine energy portrayed in her life story, the most powerful, defiant, and fearless one driving Tituba's subjectivity all along is her sexuality. Within the context of the patriarchal heterosexual hegemony, the feminine is placed as the permanent subordinate of the masculine. Feminine sexuality is silent, a lack, submissive, and shapeless, merely a complement to the powerful aggressive maleness. Yet Tituba's voice is founded on the very subversion of such a representation. Although conceived as a result of a sexual violence imposed on her mother, Tituba has no fear of her own sexuality and is happy with the harmony in her own "curves and protuberances" (15). Even in the most difficult times in her life, she has never ceased to enjoy bodily pleasure with her men: John Indian, Benjamin Cohen d'Azavedo, and Iphigene. Her sexual being is an aspect of herself that transects various identity marginalization, for it refuses to be silenced no matter what kind of oppression is exerting force on Tituba.

The flamboyance of this sexuality can be seen in the centrality of the taboo relationships Tituba has with other women. She is in the "closest of terms" with a female writer 300 years her posterior; her encounter with Hester in jail is fiery in many ways:

> That night Hester lay down beside me, as she did sometimes. I laid my head on the quiet water lily of her cheek and held her tight. Surprisingly, a feeling of pleasure slowly flooded over me. Can you feel pleasure from hugging a body similar to your own? ... Was Hester showing me another kind of bodily pleasure? (122)

Tituba is no stranger to bodily pleasure, but with Hester the experience opens up a whole chain of events because she has acquired an alternative perspective through this most familiar bodily experience. Intimacy with Hester, at many different levels, leads to a discovery not only of new physical fulfillment, but of cultural and emotional empowerment beyond that of heterosexism.

For besides the suggested sexual intimacy between the two, Hester and Tituba have also shared the feminine experience of being pregnant. Hester in jail inhabits the same miraculous position, which Tituba has tasted, of harboring another life inside her body. She shares with Tituba the joy of companionship and understanding from her baby, but also the responsibility and pain of life for two people. Hester's intimacy with Tituba, therefore, is not just two women's bodily contact, but also a communion of life across generations. In their free time, the white Hester asks for stories and details of Tituba's home town for the enjoyment of her unborn daughter; while her determination to die with her daughter gives Tituba new confidence concerning her previous abortion. Seeing Hester and her determination, Tituba is assured that she has acted correctly and true to herself when she had an abortion.

Pregnant with alternative meanings, the feminine text crosses the parameters of gender, sexuality, life and death barrier which constitute the meaning of a male-dominant world. Tituba's story has multiple beginnings and no proper closure: Condé's claim of an impossible intimacy with the long dead subject, and the sexual violence on the deck of *Christ the King* which gives birth to Tituba, a being of between-worlds; and the voice of the already dead Tituba remarks that her story has no end. Instead she says: "My people will keep my memory in their hearts and have no need for the written word. It's in their heads. In their hearts and in their heads" (176). Tituba's story is no official history contained in a volume, but a song which is all-present:

> I hear it from one end of the island to the other, from North Point to Silver Sands, from Bridgetown to Bottom Bay. It runs along the

> ridge of the hills. It is poised on the top of the heliconia. The other
> day I heard a boy four or five years old humming it. (175)

The fluid, feminine text defies thresholds meaningful in the male-dominant consciousness, and disseminates via channels beyond the grip of patriarchy.

This feminine text, however, is not a self-marginalized loner isolated from the rational narration of the masculine language. Instead, it obtains nourishment by referring to and reinterpreting canon masculine texts. Tituba's cross-cultural encounter with Hester in jail, their emotional and perhaps sexual intimacy, and their communication across the threshold of death are all remaking of values and beliefs held sacred in the patriarchal canon. Here in this feminine textual space, skin color is irrelevant, adultery becomes liberation, sexual deviance becomes a bond of individuals, and witchcraft heals and cares. Hester is remodeled and revealed to be a feminist who assumes responsibility over her actions and takes full control of her own life. She is no longer the embodiment of silent submission, for her actions are revealed to be pregnant with other values and meanings which the patriarchal text is incapable of understanding.

The fertility of this feminine text can further be seen in one of the crucial conversation between Tituba and Hester. Tituba is to be put on trial for liaising with the devil and practicing witchcraft, and Hester is preparing her to face the court:

> Give names, give names! If you do you'll become the same as they
> are with a heart full of filth! If some of them have wronged you in
> person, then take your revenge, if that's what you want. Otherwise
> give them an element of doubt and, believe me, they'll know how
> to fill in the blanks! At the right moment shout: 'Oh, I can't see any
> more! I've gone blind!' And you'll have pulled the trick off. (100)

A "trick" is the right strategy to adopt because the accusation and the court are also a trick. The patriarchal narrative demands one truth, that which is revealed and proved by the most powerful voice. The narrative Hester has suggested, however, refuses to give one truth but does not withdraw from the right to tell, either. The essence of this confession is the unusual power of the feminine. Instead of being the multiple-jeopardized being within the clutches of white male power, Tituba's confession defies convention and covers new ground unanticipated by masculine discourse.

Taken out of its original root of privacy and darkness in the catholic tradition, Tituba's public confession sheds the burden of secrecy and absence of individuality. By taking public stand and speaking in her own voice, Tituba has changed the confession into her personal performance, full with her own agenda and her own signature. The power of this feminine confession is complex:

> Yes, I was going to take my revenge. I was going to denounce them
> and from the pinnacle of these powers they accorded me I was going
> to unleash the storm, whip up the sea with waves as high as walls, and
> toss the beams of the houses and barns into the air like straws. (93)

The publicity of the confession transfers the control of narration from the confessant to the confessor, thus Tituba has the chance to tell her own story, in her own words, and follows her own logic. Confessional story-telling can be an assumption of subjectivity, as Hester "would have used that tribunal to shout her hatred of society and to curse her accusers in return" (106). Once again, the feminine text contains infinite possibilities inherent in the fertility of female sexuality.

Feminization is a tool used by the dominant to contain the subordinates and to keep them under. Yet in *I, Tituba, Black Witch of Salem*, the feminine is shown again and again to be an ingenious presence capable of reversing the existing power distribution and manifestation. Abena, Mama Yaya, Judah White, Tituba, Hester, John Indian, Iphigene, and even Benjamin have all suffered the brand of feminization because they are the marginal beings in a society which is defined by a racist, sexist, classist, and xenophobic ideology. Instead of fighting against the dominant ideology on the same grounds and striving for the upper position, these individuals in their own ways have embraced the feminine position, but seek to create alternative possibilities inherent in its otherness.

What is finally unfolded in the novel is this feminine otherness manifesting itself in the nourishing and fertile drive of the sexual, giving birth to meanings in completely different ways from the masculine. The fictional reconstruction of Tituba's life and death not only celebrates this feminine power, but the subjectivity guiding us through *I, Tituba, Black Witch of Salem* can be seen as a primary example of the sexually driven being who defies all oppressions on her multiple-disadvantaged position through her ever-renewed libidinal energy. Her sexual being, above all social, historical and cultural restrictions, defies categorization and breaks free from ideological confinement. The patriarchal church calls it witchcraft and condemns it because it cannot understand the mechanism by which the feminine achieves meaning. The feminine, however, exemplified by the transgressive behaviors of Tituba, continues forward into the realm of the invisible by its own creative strategy of crossing over, making meaning as it moves along.

Works Cited

Angelou, Maya. "Africa." Mr. Africa Poetry Lounge. April 2, 2003. http://www.ctadams.com/mayaangelou21.html.

Condé, Maryse. *I, Tituba, Black Witch of Salem* (translated by Richard Philcox). Charlottesville: University Press of Virginia, 1992.

Davis, Angela. "Foreword." *I, Tituba, Black Witch of Salem*. Charlottesville: University Press of Virginia, 1992, xi-xiii.

King, Deborah. "Multiple Jeopardy, Multiple Consciousness: The Context of a Black Feminist Ideology." *Feminist Social Thought: A Reader*. Diana Tietjens Meyers, Ed. New York: Routledge, 1997, 220-242.

Scarboro, Armstrong. "Afterword." *I, Tituba, Black Witch of Salem*. Charlottesville: University Press of Virginia, 1992, 187-225.

PART THREE

CONTESTATIONS, PROTESTATIONS, AND REPRESENTATIONS

Performance, Corporeal Practices, and Individual Life Styles

Chapter 8

Woman-Woman Marriage in Igboland

Egodi Uchendu

A century ago marriage was a mark of responsibility and a symbol of adulthood in Igboland.[1] It was a group affair and one that involved two unrelated kinship groups. It qualified the actors for full participation in the community and served as a means of forging political, military, and economic alliances. Paulme calls it the imperfect means of concluding alliances (1971: 3). The essence of marriage in Igboland in the pre-colonial and early colonial periods was not necessarily to unite two lovers, though this could be possible, but primarily to establish a legal basis for procreation, which given its emphasis on having children the Igbo regarded as an obligation to the ancestors. This was based on the understanding that those born owe the debt of begetting others.

Different types of marriages existed in pre-colonial Igboland. They included the normal marriage contract involving two exogamous families; marriage through pawning, which allowed fathers to use their daughters as collateral for loans, but which was abolished during the colonial period by British legislation; concubinage; and marriage by abduction, practiced in Anioma, in which financially constrained young suitors abducted girls of their choice for marriage. This was done with the consent of the girls' parents, although not necessarily of the girls. Two other forms of marriage that existed at the time were marriage by exchange and woman-woman marriage. Local rulers and very influential men contracted marriage by exchange for the purpose of establishing political, military, or economic links (Talbot 1967: 193). Marriage by exchange required two men exchanging their daughters in marriage in order to form alliances necessary for the political prestige and the military strength of the chief contractors who often were lineage or community heads.

Woman-woman marriage, the concern of this chapter, was a recognized and legal form of marriage in pre-colonial Igbo society (also observed among the Kalabari of the Niger Delta (Talbot 1967: 196)). Woman-woman marriage was contracted for social and economic reasons. In many cases, women who married fellow women were either barren or had passed the childbearing age without begetting a male child. Others were wealthy and influential women who married fellow women as a means of celebrating their wealth and for economic gains. Woman-woman marriage as a mark of wealth, and, for economic and social advancement was popular in parts of Igboland in the second half of the nineteenth century (Ekejiuba 1967: 637; Amadiume 1987: 31).

The over-riding goal for woman-woman marriage in Igboland was for women to have children through other women for inheritance purposes. A barren widow in Igboland or one who had no male child for her deceased husband had no claim to the deceased's property. If, however, she had married a wife and had a male child from her, she would inherit from the husband through the male child born for her by her wife. Moreover, the fear that the man's homestead would become extinct in the absence of a surviving male child would no longer exist. This chapter considers the origin of woman-woman marriage in Igboland, its nature and relevance in the past and at present, and the changes that have occurred within the institution. In discussing marriage in Igbo society, it should be borne in mind that any form of marriage in Igboland was less a matter of the particular person's concerned, but, rather a social arrangement to ensure that a new generation appears to take over from the present one, and that its members were brought up to fill smoothly the various established places (Price 1954: 23).

ORIGIN OF WOMAN-WOMAN MARRIAGE IN IGBOLAND

Little is known about the origin of woman-woman marriage in Igboland. Individuals interviewed on this practice spoke of its antiquity but could not state when exactly it came into existence. If it is considered that a normal marriage contract has generally been between a man and a woman, we can conclude that the existence of woman-woman marriage or its evolution in Igboland, most likely, must have been the product of cultural innovation that took place within the people's tradition. Social systems and cultural practices, as Henn points out, were not static during the pre-colonial period, due to the interpenetration of different societies and a history of long distance trade with other cultural groups (1984: 1). That woman-woman marriage existed among the Kalabari (an Ijaw sub-group in the Niger Delta) by the first decade of the twentieth century lends credence to the claim of interpenetration of societies. It is very plausible that the Igbo borrowed woman-woman marriage from the Kalabari or vise versa. Surprisingly, the practice is not known to have existed during the same period among other Ijaw groups of the Niger Delta as it did among the Kalabari, suggesting that the Kalabari could have borrowed it from the Igbo. How then did woman-woman marriage evolve in Igboland?

The earliest known Igbo legend that spoke of the existence of woman-woman marriage was that recounted to Talbot between 1914 and 1915 when he was gathering information on the indigenous customs of groups in southeastern Nigeria (1967: 92-93). The tradition was woven around two female deities in Igboland, Ogugu and Wiyeke. According to the story, Ogugu, the chief female deity in Ohambele and neighboring towns in the Owerri District, was popular for giving children to its female worshippers. In another town, Akwete, resided another female deity, Wiyeke. At one point, for undisclosed reasons, Wiyeke courted Ogugu as her wife. Ogugu agreed to the marriage on the condition that Wiyeke would come and live with her at Ohambele. Wiyeke accepted the condition and thus joined Ogugu as one of the female deities of Ohambele, assuming the status of Ogugu's husband. The reason for this legend, which seems to give credibility and divine sanction to woman-woman marriage in Igboland, is unknown. However, woman-woman marriage was popular in towns in the old Owerri and Aba Districts and in most parts of northern Igboland, around the Awka, Udi and Nsukka areas before the 1930s.[2] In addition to the religious sanction given this form of marriage using the legend of Ogugu and Wiyeke, certain social values made woman-woman marriage acceptable to the Igbo and could have led to its institutionalization in Igboland.

The Igbo mainstay in the pre-colonial period was agriculture and women were its backbone. Successful Igbo men were known for the number of their yam barns and the overall turnout of their farm produce. As a result, the Igbo favored polygynist marriages, because they allowed them to have as many wives as possible. The wives, and sometimes, along with the children, made up a man's labor force. Men who for any reason were unable to marry more than one woman were in some cases assisted in acquiring a second wife by their first wives. A woman would marry a wife and give to the husband to be his second wife in order to ease her domestic burden as well as to have assistance with farm work. It was partly because of this practice that Price wrote that any African marriage was a social investment, absorbing some resources and with prospects of replacing them at last (1954). Although polygyny provided a man with additional outlets for sexual gratification, it was also a status symbol and an investment that enabled him to expand his agricultural output, the proceeds of which he could utilize in acquiring social titles that entitled him to an honored place in his community. Women who married wives for their husbands for the reasons stated above engaged in woman-woman marriages, which because of its various advantages to the men in particular gained the support and approval of the society.

A second factor that possibly led to the evolution of woman-woman marriage in Igboland was the high value the Igbo placed on children and especially on the male child. It was the belief of the people that male children were indispensable for the continuation of the ancestral line and for retaining a family's ownership of whatever belonged to it. The reality of family extinction cannot be ducked where children are not forthcoming (Mere 1973: 93). Such a situation was regarded as an abomination. The Igbo family was the most fundamental and the primary social institution that for reasons of sheer survival must be sustained through the male child. It is for this reason that Igbo women expressed their desire for children with this song:

> Olisa nye m nwa nye m ego
> Olisa nye m nwa nye m ego
> karia I ga awo m nwa wo m ego
> mgbe nwa m toro ego m abia

mgbe nwa m toro ego m abia

[*God give me a child and give me money*
God give me a child and give me money
Instead of denying me a child deny me money
When my child grows up, money will come
When my child grows up, money will come].

The importance attached to children was also reflected in the names they were given, for instance, *Nwabueze* (a child bestows kingship), *Nwabuba* (a child is wealth), and Nwakuba (a child is of more value than wealth), for male children; and Nwakaego (a child is of more value than money) for female children.

Barren women and women who gave birth to only daughters made efforts to marry wives to have children, preferably sons, for them. This was particularly so since the social status of an Igbo woman was partly hinged on her ability to reproduce and give birth to male children, besides her economic success and organizational abilities. In spite of her other achievements, a childless woman in pre-colonial Igboland was certainly disadvantaged and was often pitied for her plight. Her inability to reproduce was looked upon as a curse while she was sometimes treated with ignominy. To make women's social distinctions obvious in pre-colonial and early colonial Igboland, a wife might not wear anything valuable until after the birth of her first child, while a childless woman would not dress her head in the elaborate manner allowed only to mothers (Talbot 1967). Women, therefore, resorted to woman-woman marriages as a way of getting out of the dilemma of barrenness or the plight of giving birth to only female children as well as other economic and social disadvantages. The Igbo were not alone in their love for sons. In traditional Korean culture, the desire for many sons existed although it did not derive from the need to preserve the family structure but rather to secure more manpower (Joungwon Kim 1977: 25-26).

Closely linked to the high value placed on children as a factor for woman-woman marriage, was the system of inheritance in Igboland. In all parts of Igboland, women inherited from a deceased spouse if they had given birth to a male child in his name. Inheritance passed from father to son and never from father to daughter or from husband to wife. The latter applied also in Ohafia, Afikpo and Ihechiowa, communities that were (and still are) matrilineal. The exception in matrilineal groups was that the property of a deceased man first of all went to his brothers from the same mother and then to his sisters by the same mother, in their order of seniority, and finally to the children, male and female, of his eldest sister by the same mother (Chubb 1961: 22). This was only possible if there was enough to go round. Among the patrilineal communities, a wife who had a son could only hope to share in his son's inheritance, but not necessarily to inherit directly from her husband. Her husband's brothers had a better chance of inheriting his property than the wife. It is in the system of inheritance that the Igbo markedly differ from the Yoruba and the Hausa-Fulani of southern and northern Nigeria respectively, the other two major ethnic groups in the country.

In these groups, the indigenous culture and the entrenchment of Islam some centuries ago gave women rights of inheritance, though limited. Such female rights of inheritance did not exist in Igboland.

In pre-colonial Igboland when no authority existed above that of the male elders of a community, Igbo women had little opportunity for redress when confronted with cultural practices that discriminated against them such as the inheritance rights. To circumvent their plight, women married fellow women to have children for them. It was only through this medium that a childless widow could claim any form of inheritance from her husband's family. Where a widow had daughters, one of the daughters might remain unmarried in the hope that she would have a son for the family. Any son she gave birth to was accepted in the family as her father's and the deceased's property rightly became his. Through this arrangement, the daughter succeeds in retaining the property of the father and ensured that her father's family did not treat her widowed mother shabbily.

Retaining a daughter in the family to raise male children for her parents was widely indulged in by the Igbo on both sides of the Niger. In Nnobi in the 1920s, a father recalled his daughter from her husband's home for this purpose (Amadiume 1987: 32-33). A father wishing to retain one of his daughters at home to have male children for him presented locally-tapped wine to his immediate male family members and informed them of his decision. From then onwards the matter was accepted and the lady in question would be treated as a man for the rest of her life, having from that day acquired ascribed male status. This was the idea behind the existence of "male daughters" in parts of Igboland. Sometimes, too, fathers kept their most beloved daughter at home in order not to part with them.

The communalistic nature of the Igbo society must have contributed to the institutionalization of woman-woman marriage in Igboland. Pre-colonial Igbo society placed emphasis on the community rather than the individual. Consequently, moral obligations were regulated by the demands of the moral codes, tradition, and custom of the people and not by the exercise of individual judgment and conscience. The individual's responsibility in the society was very clear and never shirked, because social expectations and values were commonly observed and the social ethos of any Igbo community was jealously guarded (Ilogu 1974: 22). This made it difficult for a woman to take a stand, which the wider society might consider incompatible with the over-all good of the people. The childless woman who failed to marry a wife to have children on her behalf, therefore, stood the chance of living a very lonely life and forfeiting the comfort of being properly looked after in her old age. In general, woman-woman marriages featured more prominently then when the idea of *in vitro* fertilization, and, child adoption were unknown to the Igbo. It met needs in the society that these options are meeting today.

Woman-woman marriage in the pre-colonial and early colonial periods was contracted like normal marriages. Potential wives were sought for from distant communities from those of the would-be female husbands. The conditions under which women accepted to be wives to fellow women at the time are unknown to the present writer, due to the paucity of documented materials on the matter, but inferences can be made based on the situation prevailing in the present.

Female husbands paid the bride-wealth of their wives as men did when marrying women. Having a wife had its advantages. Besides the prospect of begetting children through another person, it enhanced the status of a daughter and qualified some to become heads of households. This was particularly so where a female husband herself had had children. In a society where gender inequality prevailed and women lacked the political and social powers men enjoyed, woman-woman marriage was an avenue for appropriating certain masculine privileges. It was an arrangement that had economic, social, and political benefits for women. In Nnobi, Onitsha, Ossomari and some other Igbo communities, there was a direct link between the accumulation of wives by women, the acquisition of wealth, and the exercise of power and authority by women (Amadiume 1987: 45; Ekejiuba 1967: 637-8). A female husband found a man to meet the sexual needs of her wife but she played the role of mother to her, and claimed her services from which she increased her wealth and affluence. The marriage was undoubtedly economically rewarding hence some wealthy women married as many as nine wives. The exploitative nature of this relationship was the reason why the people of Nnobi regarded it as *Igba ohu*, that is, slavery.

A woman who had a wife enjoyed the status and customary rights of a husband over his wife, as would a man. The wife on her part was also accorded her customary rights in the society, while the children were not subjected to any political or social disadvantage on the basis of their parentage or of the circumstances of their birth. They were accepted as belonging jointly to the female husband and her wife but the children inherited property from the husband of their mother's female spouse or her father, if she had no husband.

Woman-woman marriage suffered a set back midway through the colonial period, primarily due to Christian missionary activities in Igboland. Early Igbo converts to Christianity were encouraged to ignore and distance themselves from local marriage customs that had no parallel either in the Bible or in the British family system. Polygyny among church members was frowned upon and the Roman Catholic Mission, in particular, denied communion to polygynists (Mba 1982: 53). The displeasure with which the Church handled polygyny was also visited on woman-woman marriage (Price 1954). Consequently, the preponderance of woman-woman marriage gradually whittled down in Igboland. Until the 1980s, persons negating Church ordinances conducted themselves with utmost discretion and were careful not to flaunt actions that were unacceptable to the Church. Women with wives concealed them and the knowledge of their existence, in order to protect themselves as well as the male consorts of their female wives.[3] But, women who were unwilling to go underground left the orthodox Churches for syncretism that was more accommodating of woman-

woman marriage and other indigenous cultural practices.[4] Excluding the attitude of the Christian Churches to woman-woman marriage, modernization contributed to the dwindling of the practice. Also, within the last two decades, the gradual conversion of some Igbo people to Islam became another factor challenging its existence in Igboland; Igbo Muslims regard it as loathsome.[5]

WOMAN-WOMAN MARRIAGE IN CONTEMPORARY IGBO SOCIETY

The incidents of woman-woman marriage in Igboland in the last decade may be construed as a resuscitation of the practice. But, it is still not enjoying the popularity attached to it in the pre-colonial and early colonial periods when it was described as "the custom of the time" (Ekejiuba 1967: 637). From the rough estimate done for the purpose of this discussion, it was discovered that persons who in one way or the other are presently involved in woman-woman marriage--either as female husbands, female wives, or as male consorts to female wives--are not highly educated. Many, actually, did not progress beyond the primary school level. The majority of the female wives were discovered to be dropouts from the primary school or not to have attempted school at all.

Woman-woman marriage in contemporary Igbo society is still contracted like any man-woman marriage. This implies that a female wife is sought for and wooed as any young girl would, but in most cases not by, and for, a man but by friends of the prospective female husband for the latter.[6] Interviews with some of the female husbands reveal that women wishing to marry fellow women appeal to their female friends to search for a suitable girl for them. They do this because many young women would not willingly accept a marriage proposal from a fellow woman. In Amawbia, before a woman undertakes to marry another woman, she first kills a goat for her community, an act that confers on her the status of a man. With her ascribed male status, she proceeds to marry a fellow woman.[7]

To ensure the chances of getting a willing wife, individuals assisting an intending female husband search for young girls with one social disability or the other and whose chances of marrying men of their choices seem to have been impaired or are slim as a result of their disability. It is this assumed social disability that intermediaries emphasize and use to cajole young girls into woman-woman marriage relationships. In the case of Justina of Obollo-eke and of Regina of Ovoko, their wives are from very poor homes and completely uneducated. Justina's wife was born in 1969 to a father who until his death believed that girls should not be educated because such an investment financially drained their natal families, which also stopped benefiting from the investment once the girls are married. With this idea, Priscilla and her sisters were not sent to school. A decade after the death of their father, Priscilla's mother abandoned her children and went into prostitution, a socially unacceptable profession in most of Igboland. After the death of the father and the desertion of the mother, Priscilla was hard put to fend for herself. This predicament and her slight physical challenge from rickets rendered her a prime candidate for woman-woman marriage.

Priscilla's female husband, on her part, became blind in 1989. Prior to her loss of sight, she was a successful small-scale businesswoman. She reported that since losing her sight, members of her family have not been forthcoming with the sort of help she needed. Her husband, a professional farmer, who earlier married a second wife, because of Justina's childlessness, sought medical help for her until her loss of sight was confirmed irreversible. The Nigerian society today has no credible social services for handicapped people. Justina's alternative was to look for a fellow female to assist her. Her best option was a female spouse who would show more commitment than a hired assistant and who might possibly give her the children she was unable to have. By the time of our interview, the two women had lived together for ten years, producing a girl and three surviving boys.

Regina's wife also was from a poor family. Her parents, subsistence farmers, did not generate enough income to enable them appropriately care for their children or train them for any vocation. Ngozi was still in her twenties when I met her, but has given birth to two girls and a boy, the oldest of whom was six years old by the time of our interview. Her female husband is not entirely childless. Of the thirteen children she gave birth to, a male and two females survived and these have all married. Regina's main reason for marrying was to have companions who would run errands for her and stay home with her in case of any happenstance. It has always been her desire, she confessed, to have another male child, since, as she pointed out, "a lone tree does not make a forest."[8] Both Regina and Justina justify their marriage with the argument that lonely persons die early. Woman-woman relationship, to them, among other benefits, is a panacea for loneliness.

The third case of female husband/female wife relationship encountered in the course of fieldwork involves Chioma from Ovoko whose female husband is from Uzo-Uwani, all in northern Igboland. Chioma was an unmarried expectant mother when she was wooed for marriage. The Igbo, even up till the present, are not very accommodating of pregnancy outside marriage although young girls enjoy pre-marital sexual relationships. While such adventure may not be too welcome, many parents will overlook it as long as it does not result in conception. Among the Nsukka Igbo, girls were culturally allowed discreet sexual adventure until they married, after which time such a conduct was censured.[9] For a young and unmarried girl like Chioma to be compromised in that manner was enough to impair her chances of marriage to a suitor of her choice, in spite of the fact that she completed her primary education. Chioma's predicament is best appreciated when considered that she is one of seven siblings whose father died and whose mother is a petty trader. Chioma's female husband is a middle-age unmarried and childless professional prostitute. She married Chioma both to have children for her and to enhance her social standing in her community. That Chioma was already pregnant by the time of their marriage was a bonus for her. She gained Chioma as a wife, Chioma's baby as her child, and consequently assumed the privilege of being the head of her own household.

The cases discussed above reveal some of the variegated reasons for woman-woman marriage in the present time. This form of marriage has extended beyond having children for childless women and women without male issues to include serving as a medium for companionship for lonely or aging women; finding an aide for the handicapped, a service that the state should provide; and acquiring mourners in preparation for one's death.[10]

To demonstrate the declining popularity of the alliance in the present time, women aspiring to be female husbands do not marry wives from their communities or from places where they are well known. Girls are sought from distant towns and in some instances are not informed of the true nature of the relationship, that is, that they would be wives to fellow women. A male accomplice is usually presented as the person interested in the girl while the actual "husband" remains concealed except to the parents or guardians of the girl. Ironically, in the cases of woman-woman marriages encountered, all the female wives had lost their biological fathers and surrogate fathers approved their marriages, attracted by the material benefits associated with it. It is worth investigating how supportive one's biological father will be of such a marriage.

Certain parents who accepted their daughter's woman-woman relationship appealed to the female husbands not to disclose the true nature of the relationship, to conceal as much as possible their identity as the "husband" of their daughters. This suggests that among those directly or indirectly involved in establishing the contract, woman-woman relationship is something of an anomaly, even though it had social and other benefits for the chief actors. Perhaps, this feeling is caused by the prominence of heterosexual marriages in Igboland and the Christian doctrine that disapproved of woman-woman marriage. Nevertheless, it is the family members of a female wife who are most eager to conceal the details of the marriage. When asked why she married Priscilla, Justina quickly corrected me and replied that she is not the one marrying Priscilla but her husband's brother. This was before she conceded some information on their marriage.

The man who is brought forward during the marriage negotiations in many cases will eventually be responsible for the sexual needs of the wife. From this, we can regard woman-woman marriage as a partnership between a female husband and a male consort for the good of the former. All expenses for the marriage rites, however, are borne by the female husband. Once the bride-wealth is paid the young wife is released by her family to join her husband in accordance with the system of patrilocal residence practiced in Igboland. Some female wives were considerably surprised on realizing that their actual husbands are women. Since Igbo wives live with whoever paid their bride-wealth, such wives will under no circumstance remain in their parents' home unless their marriages have been dissolved. Meanwhile, the major actors in the contract would not allow a wife to back out of the contract without evidence of serious provocation from the female husband.

Woman-woman marriage in Igboland does not connote the existence of sexual relationship among women similar to lesbianism. It is by no means a homosexual affair and cannot also be regarded as a plain heterosexual union. Where a female husband did not arrange for a male consort for her wife, she allows her the freedom to choose a man of her choice to mate with. In parts of Abia State, such as Umuahia, wives of female husbands are allowed to choose men of their choice for their sexual fulfillment, but it must not be an individual with questionable character. In Nsukka and its environs, it is the female husband who selects the man to do the honors. Care is taken to ensure that whoever is chosen for this role has an acceptable public image and is neither a social outcast nor a profligate. Some married female husbands like Regina may give their wives to their husbands to meet her sexual needs, but not as a co-wife. Unmarried female husbands would choose a man from their extended family or from elsewhere for their wives. The male consorts must visit the women in their female husband's homes.

There is a difference between a woman marrying a wife for her husband and marrying for herself. If she is marrying for her husband, she will accept and treat the new wife as a co-wife. The children from the union will be strictly her husband's. Where she is marrying for herself, even if the husband accepts to take care of the sexual needs of her wife, he has no claim to her and her children will belong jointly to the two women in the relationship. The husband may neither rebuke nor discipline the wife's wife. Also, he will have no obligations to either the new wife or to her family. His relationship with the new wife strictly remains a sexual one. Some husbands, like Justina's, refuse being involved in such an arrangement. In that case, their wives look elsewhere for male consorts for their wives, in this case exhibiting power over them as a male husband would over a wife. It is the duty of the female husband to control and discipline her wife. Acts of indiscretion on the part of the wife is reported to a female husband who also supervises the social conduct of the former to ensure that it conforms to the norms of their society.

Rules, which apply to normal customary marriage contracts in Igboland, apply in woman-woman relationships. For instance, Igbo culture permits a woman to stick strictly to one man. It is frowned upon if a female wife moves from one man to the other. To check against possible misconduct many female husbands restrict their wives to one man by choosing that man themselves.

Female husbands have their own obligations to their wives and to their wives' families. It is their responsibility to take care of their wives as a man would his wife. In the second half of the 19th century, female husbands were wealthy and influential women. This does not appear to be the case in the present Igbo society. Of all those interviewed, only Chioma's husband and Gladys, an administrative staff in a federal University, would be regarded as somewhat materially comfortable. Since most of the female wives had little or no formal training, their female husbands are responsible for their maintenance. Some of the female husbands interviewed started a mini business for their wives to make them financially independent. The profit from such ventures, however, is not such to guarantee the complete sustenance of the women without extra provision from their female husbands. Even in these cases, part of what a wife realizes goes to her husband. Other female husbands simply co-opted their wives in their own businesses instead of starting them on an entirely new line of business. If we go by this observation, woman-woman relationships can also be regarded as a symbiotic partnership among women.

The normal relationship between in-laws exists between female husbands and the parents or families of their female spouses. Thus, whenever anything crops up in the family of a female wife, the female husband is informed and she dutifully performs the appropriate roles required. Where an in-law dies, a female husband, on notification, arranges for a condolence visit and provides whatever is customarily required under such circumstances. Anytime a female wife puts to bed, the female husband notifies her parents and receives the mother for the post-natal confinement, at the end of which she sends her home with lots of presents. During visits to the family of the wife, the wife's male consort may accompany her female husband but this is done to protect the real stakeholders in the relationship.

That woman-woman marriage is at present practiced largely by the uneducated and semi-educated in Igboland reveals the traditional inclinations of those involved. They have largely remained unaffected by the popularity of child adoption and the successes of *in vitro* conception in the country. This group, in particular, are wary of adopting children clandestinely abandoned, or given up for adoption by their mothers, for the simple reason that they cannot say with certainty what the child's progenitors are like. The circumstances under which children are abandoned in the society have created the suspicion in many that all cannot be well with either or both parents of that child. To make sure that one's child has a good background, very culturally inclined women who need children prefer to them through woman-woman marriages than through adoption. Another reason why people are unwilling to adopt children is the fear that some of these babies may have congenital problems that may not be obvious at birth. Also, the mother of a baby given up for adoption may be infected with AIDS, which can easily be transmitted to the baby.[11] More importantly, the cost of medical treatments for conception and services leading to *in vitro* fertilization is far beyond what lower class members of the society can afford.

CONSTRAINTS ON WOMAN-WOMAN MARRIAGE

Reasons have been adduced for the existence of woman-woman marriages in Igboland. In spite of the advantages and the arguments in favor of this form of marriage, it has its share of abuses. The relationship indirectly encourages a discreet form of polygamy with its social ills and abuses of women. It is also an avenue for unbridled prostitution among young women who are wives to fellow women. It is not in all cases that female husbands carefully regulate the sexual activities of their youthful wives. Thus, some wives are allowed to meet any man they want as long as they have children for their husbands.[12] Giving men access to more than one woman and vise versa promotes the spread of sexually transmitted diseases, especially AIDS, which already is a scourge in Africa.

Woman-woman marriage relationship, in many instances, allows some women to disregard the sanctity of marriage. Would-be female husbands, in their determination to promote their interest, sometimes fail to show concern for the interests of women whose husbands they co-opt to act as sexual partners to their wives. Regina was asked what would happen if a wife objects to her husband meeting the sexual needs of another woman and she retorted that the wife should quit the marriage and find another husband.

Woman-woman marriages have their share of risks like other human relationships. There is no guarantee of permanence in the relationship, just as it is in some male-female marriages. Female husbands do send away their wives for failing to give birth to a male child. Also, female wives could become targets of unwanted sexual harassment from the male spouses of their female husbands. This puts them in an uncomfortable situation and may degenerate into hostility from the man. Added to this is the confusion that results in the family when a male head feels neglected by his wife and blames this on her female wife. Some aggrieved men transfer their frustration to their wives' female spouses and may make life unpleasant for them. This was the situation in Nnennaya and Love's marriage before its dissolution. In this case, Nnennaya's husband maltreated Love, the wife, and her children.[13] When Love's predicament became unbearable, she left the marriage with only the youngest of her four children.

Indeed, it is not in all instances that female spouses co-exist peaceably. Intractable problems between them sometimes result in a wife secretly absconding with all, some, or none of her kids. Once she returns to her family, the female husband loses all claims to her and to the children she absconded with because, in the first instance, the two women jointly claim the children. In such a development, the female husband loses most of, if not all, her investments in the relationship. What some female husbands do when they become aware of deep-seated problems in the marriage is to get their wives a separate accommodation while the contract remains in force. This occurred in Regina and Ngozi's marriage. Since their separation, Ngozi only visits with Regina. Whenever she puts to bed and has weaned the child, Regina takes it away and continues the mothering role. As a result of this arrangement Ngozi's children have formed a much closer bond with Regina instead of with Ngozi, their biological mother, and consequently started regarding their real mother as merely a friend of the family. This fact points to another feature of the relationship: the possibility of transferring of natural affection from one's biological parent to a surrogate even when the two are living in proximity to each other.

Children of same-sex couples resent their parent's relationship when they grow up and become aware of the nature of the relationship. Some become rebellious to their mother's female spouse as a means of registering their displeasure and the embarrassment they feel over the union, especially for being victims of peer group ridicule. We may not at present ascertain the depth of their psychological trauma, but it is not in doubt that the relationship is traumatic for children.

In conclusion, despite its somewhat exploitative nature and the potential for abuse of power by women over fellow women, woman-woman marriage remains one avenue through which Igbo women take care of their social problems within the limits of their culture and its strong patriarchal structure.

Notes

1. The Igbo are found in southern Nigeria. Igboland is divided unequally into two by the River Niger. The Igbo heartland, which covers a larger territorial area, is found in southeastern Nigeria while the smaller Igbo territory, preferably known as Anioma, is found in the southwest.

2. Information on woman-woman marriage in Igboland came from interviews and discussions with the following: Regina Nweke, c. 65 years, Ohagu, Ovoko; Justina Obianyido, c. 60 years, Obollo-eke; Priscilla Obianyido, 35 years, Obollo-eke; Mr. O. Igwegbe, 44 years, Director (Administration), Nigerian Supreme Council for Islamic Affairs, Owerri; Eucharia Nweke, 32 years, Ohagu, Ovoko; Mama Uma, 66 years, Ohafia; Nwannedi Ogbu, 80 years, Okiuga, Umuahia; Mr. and Mrs. J. and C. Ogbu, 49 and 39 years, Ihechiowa; Ogochukwu Chukwu, 25 years, Abatete; Uloma Ani, 42 years, Udi; Dr. C. Nwocha, Reproductive Physiologist, University of Nigeria; and Mrs. N. M. Awachie, 43 years, Awka. The interviews were conducted between March and October 2003. All the interviews were tape-recorded.

3. An observation I made in early 1980s.

4. Interview with Justina Obianyido.

5. Interview with Mr. O. Igwegbe.

6. Interview with Regina Nweke.

7. *Sunday Champion*, November 17, 2002, pp. 24 - 26.

8. Interview with Regina Nweke.

9. This information came from a discussion with Dr. M. U. Ozo, 78 years, Retired Chief Health Consultant, Enugu, in September 1997.

10. Interviews with Regina Nweke, Eucharia Nweke, and Nwannedi Ogbu.

11. Discussion with Dr. C. Nwocha.

12. Discussion with Ogochukwu Chukwu.

13. Interview with Nwannedi Ogbu.

Works Cited

Amadiume, Ifi. *Male Daughters and Female Husbands*. New Jersey: Zed Press, 1987.

Chubb, L. T. *Ibo Land Tenure*. Ibadan: Ibadan University Press, 1961.

Ekejiuba, F. "*Omu* Okwei, The Merchant Queen of Ossomari: A Biographical Sketch." *Journal of the Historical Society of Nigeria*. Vol. 3. No. 4, 1967.

Henn, Jeanne. "Women in the Economy: Past, Present, and Future." In: Paulme, D. Ed. *Women of Tropical Africa*. Berkeley: University of California Press, 1984.

Ilogu, E. *Christianity and Igbo Culture*. New York: Nok Publishers, 1972.

Kim, J. Ed. *Korean Cultural Heritage: Traditional Lifestyles*. Vol. 4., Seoul: The Korea Foundation, 1977.

Mba, Nina. *Nigerian Women Mobilized*. Berkeley: University of California Press, 1982.

Mere, Ada. "Social Values Heritage of the Igbo." *Ikenga,* Vol. 2, No. 1, 1973.

Paulme, D. "Introduction." In: Paulme, D. Ed. *Women of Tropical Africa*. Berkeley: University of California Press, 1971.

Price, Thomas. *African Marriage*. London: SCM Press, 1954.

Talbot, P. A. *Tribes of the Niger Delta*. London: Frank Cass, 1967.

Uchendu, Egodi. "Anioma Women and the Nigerian Civil War, 1966-1979," Unpublished Ph.D. Thesis, University of Nigeria, 2002.

UNICEF. *National Baseline Survey of Positive and Harmful Traditional Practices Affecting Women and Girls in Nigeria*, 1998.

Chapter 9

Uncovering Incest in Father/Daughter Relationships: Displacement and Distancing Strategies in Buchi Emecheta's *The Family* and Evelyne Mpoudi Ngolle's *Sous la cendre le feu*

Jill Eagling

As Barbara Sheldon has remarked in a recent work, "There is hardly any comprehensive study on fathers and daughters in literature comparable to the studies which exist for mothers and daughters."[1] According to Sheldon, who focuses on Western literature, with the recent disintegration of the traditional nuclear family and the concurrent importance of the father as a subject of study, "it is strange that the father and his relationship to the daughter have received relatively little attention from literary critics. Many of them, so intent on dealing with patriarchy, have neglected the father."[2] Sheldon also cites Gisela Moffit who wrote a book on fathers and daughters in German novels of the 1970s: "[D]aughters and fathers have been the step-children of Western empirical research and scholarship. While much research on the family has been conducted in recent years, most of it has centred around the mother-daughter, mother-son, or father-son dyads, making fathers the 'forgotten parents' and daughters 'the forgotten offspring.'"[3]

If such is the situation with regard to writing, both fictional and critical, in the West, to what extent is the father/daughter relationship considered in African writing? Although fewer examples of literary explorations spring to mind than those focusing on the mother/daughter relationship,[4] nevertheless there are novels which feature a father/daughter relationship,[5] although critics generally have ignored this area of debate. Indeed, it is generally true to say that very few critics have dealt with either the mother/daughter relationship or the father/daughter relationship in African fiction by women writers.[6] Despite the lack of critical attention in this domain, the father/daughter relationship, even where it is not a major aspect of a particular work is nevertheless significant, as I shall seek to demonstrate in two novels, Buchi Emecheta's *The Family* (1990) and Evelyne Mpoudi Nolle's *Sous la cendre le feu* (1990).[7]

Buchi Emecheta's *The Family* focuses on the issue of incest and the betrayal of the father by the daughter in one particular family and the ramifications of the abuse of power. The dictionary definition of incest is "the crime of sexual intercourse or cohabitation between persons related within the degrees within which marriage is prohibited."[8] It must be acknowledged, however, that the particular forms of the incest taboo, in relation to the sort of behavior which is forbidden, to whom it applies and how it is dealt with, vary depending upon the particular culture or society.[9] In discussing the issue of incest I adopt Emily Driver and Audrey Droise's definition in the introduction to their work on child sexual abuse, as:

> the sexual molestation of a child by any person whom that child sees as a figure of trust or authority – parents, relatives (whether natural or adoptive), family friends [...] etc. We see the questions of blood-relationship and taboo as red herrings which obscure the central issue: the irresponsible exploitation of children's ignorance, trust and obedience. Incest is the sexual abuse of power.[10]

Such a definition acknowledges that it is the question of the abuse of trust, rather than just one of blood ties, with its concomitant abuse of power, which is significant in such abuse. Apparently Emecheta first conceived the idea of treating such a subject when, after giving a college lecture, a number of girls went to her room afterwards and disclosed to her that they had been sexually abused by their fathers.[11] Emecheta had already dealt with the subject of rape in her novel *The Rape of Shavi* as well as in *Destination Biafra*, but in *The Family* she transposes the random, violent anonymity of rape described in these earlier works into an exploration of sexual abuse which is perpetrated by a close family member, one that may be more calculated and accompanied by a personal betrayal by someone in a position of trust. Another new venture for Emecheta is the fact that she is dealing with a West Indian family rather than her more usual Nigerian protagonists, although some of the latter are also presented. However, the theme of migration is not new and has been broached in several of her novels including *Second Class Citizen* (1974) and *Kehinde* (1994) in these cases emigration from Nigeria to England.

The novel opens as Gwendolen, a young Jamaican girl, aged five, is readying herself to say farewell to her father, Winston Brillianton, who is leaving to work abroad in England, "the moder kontry" as it is referred to in the novel. Shortly afterwards he sends for his wife Sonia, who assures Gwendolen that she too will be sent for as soon as they are able to afford to do so. In the meantime, she is to live with her Grandmother Naomi, Sonia's mother, in Granville, a very poor area of Jamaica where they endure a constant battle for survival. During this time Gwendolen is kept busy helping her grandmother, with little time or money for schooling, her parents neglecting to send money as time goes by. A constant companion and occasional lover of her grandmother, Uncle Johnny, who has always acted kindly towards Gwendolen, enters her bed one night when Naomi has fallen asleep and rapes her when she is still only ten years old. Some years later she is eventually sent for by her parents and is at first overjoyed to find herself welcomed into the midst of her family, even though she is expected to work hard helping her mother with the housework and bringing up her younger brothers and sister born in England. When Sonia returns to Jamaica a few years later because she learns that her own mother is sick, Gwendolen is left in charge of the family and her father sexually abuses his daughter. She becomes pregnant and everyone believes the father to be a young Greek boy, Emmanuel. Her father's sudden death, and her mother's refusal to visit her, leave her no choice but to make an independent life for herself with her newly born baby girl, with the support of Emmanuel and an eventual reconciliation with her mother.

As can be seen from this synopsis of the novel, Gwendolen's young life is marked by affliction, both in her native Jamaica and in her adoptive country, England. The unfortunate circumstances are not only caused by the two acts of incest, but also by being abandoned by both parents while still only a young girl. Gwendolen is not too affected by her father's departure because he is away much of the time working anyway, but when her mother also leaves, she feels abandoned and alone, especially as her mother does not seem dismayed at the prospect of leaving her daughter: "it looked as if her Mammy was happy to leave her behind, giving the impression she was not really wanted"(18). Many Caribbean novels stress the close relationship enjoyed between grandmother and granddaughter and it appears to be normal practice for the grandmother to assume the mother role without causing any problems for the child.[12] However, in Gwendolen's case, her relationship with her grandmother is not particularly close, the latter mainly preoccupied by the daily battle for survival and thus unable to lavish too much care and attention on her charge. Additionally, she is betrayed by her uncle Johnny, who is very much like a father figure to her and liked and respected by everyone she cares for. Her confusion is therefore all the more pronounced when she is subjected to his sexual assault. Gwendolen's description of his actions underlines his use of force, a hand over her mouth, combined with persuasion, accompanied by his assurance that he will protect and care for her. Moreover, he plays on Gwendolen's loneliness and sense of abandonment by her parents: "Your Mammy gone na England to join your Daddy. Dem no want you dere, but me look after you, right? [...] Don't tell nobody, because they'll say you're a bad gal" (22). In these words we see the same blending of threats and promise of protection. When her ordeal is over Gwendolen runs outside and asks "Mammy, why you no take me with you?"(22). Such a question, directly after the incident of incest, appears to be an indictment by the author of an act of mother/daughter betrayal.

Emecheta's treatment of incest points to many of the traditional motifs surrounding this subject, especially those concerning the psychological make-up of the victim. According to sociological literature, victims of sexual abuse are prone to self-blame and guilt. As a consequence of these two factors they are less likely to be able to speak out against their aggressor. In the case of Gwendolen's rape by her Uncle Johnny, she feels both confused and guilty. She is confused when, the morning after the rape, her Uncle arrives earlier than usual to help her Grandmother on her bee-farm, acting perfectly normally. Gwendolen cannot understand this if what her Uncle had done to her the previous night was wrong. She starts to feel guilty without understanding why, except that she thought that "everyone would blame her if they knew her secret" (25), especially as everyone seemed to think so highly of him. After submitting to repeated acts of sexual assault, Gwendolen runs away to her paternal grandmother, but receiving a lukewarm reception, her dark skin being too black for her light relative, she decides to return and tell her Grandmother Naomi about Uncle Johnny's behavior. Although Naomi is outraged, and he is ostracised by most of the community, at the same time Gwendolen is blamed and suspected of complicity. Her grandmother starts to criticise her behavior incessantly, hinting that she was herself the cause of Uncle Johnny's attentions. She wants to know "why she always rolled her backside when she moved about" and "How come Uncle Johnny did not trouble the other girls?" (36). Her grandmother misses her friend's company and especially his help, so loneliness and tiredness provoke harsh treatment towards Gwendolen, with constant beatings and public humiliations about her bedwetting, which appears to worsen after Johnny's unwelcome attentions. Gwendolen's suffering from a trusted adult's sexual interference is therefore compounded by her grandmother's treatment: she feels totally betrayed by the adult world.

When Gwendolen first hears that she is finally to join her parents in England, she believes that all her problems will dissolve and that she will be able to "be herself – happy, trusting, Gwendolen again" (39). However, there are signs at her initial meeting with her father at the airport that they will have problems. Winston finds it difficult to recognise that Gwendolen is indeed his daughter and is ill at ease at his daughter's enthusiastic greeting. He "was surprised and uneasy at the antics of this little girl, who was his daughter and whom he was beginning to realize he had to work hard and wake up fatherly feelings towards" (49). When she arrives back at her parents' home, her mother also finds difficulty in relating to a daughter who she also perceives as an adult. To underline the discrepancy in her parents' conception of her, Gwendolen is described as reverting to childlike behavior on seeing both her father and her mother: "Gwendolen cried as she rushed into her mother's open arms. She felt reborn. She felt as if she was entering into her mother's womb again" (52).

The emphasis by Gwendolen's parents on her adult looks foreshadows their treatment of her as older than her years. Sonia sees in her daughter someone who will lighten her domestic tasks, while Winston begins to regard her in a new light, based on sexual attraction rather than fatherly devotion. Moreover, her mother recognizes her husband's new interest in her daughter when she arrives home one day to find her enjoying a joke with her father. Sonia is furious: "'June-June, why you sit dere laughing with your Daddy and Ronald? Me give you work fe do, before me go to market. You sit dere laughing with men, eh, Marm?' Anger blazed in every word" (87). Sonia's outbursts at the appearance of closeness between father and daughter is provoked by jealousy and hence also feelings of inadequacy. Gwendolen is dismayed to discover that her mother is giving her "the eye of suspicion Granny Naomi gave her a long time ago in Granville" (88). She wants to forget her past and cannot understand her mother's attitude as "Daddies did not hurt their daughters" (ibid). From that time onwards Gwendolen becomes more cautious and slowly her trust and confidence which had started to increase in England begin to waver.

Upon Sonia's departure for Jamaica, Gwendolen assumes her mother's role in the home and it is at this time that her father makes his sexual demands manifest when he enters her bed one night. He attempts to excuse his intentions towards his daughter by describing her as a "woman teasing a lover" (144). The fact that Gwendolen also resembles her mother, not just physically but in her mental make-up, adds to his temptation. She was "the type of woman he favoured, small, vulnerable, just like his Sonia" (ibid). Evidently he is attracted to weaker women and needs to be in a position of power. Nevertheless, he expects Gwendolen to "fight him off like any other woman. Because she was like any other woman to him. She was almost grown before she came back into his life" (ibid). He is embroiled in the gendered discourse of his upbringing where women are expected to resist a man's attentions and in this way perpetuate his sexual anticipation. However, Winston's remembrance of that night is different to Gwendolen's version of events. According to him, Gwendolen is easily persuaded to consent to the sexual act, but Gwendolen recollects that "She could not scream, because though he begged, he covered her mouth with that strong hand of his" (145). She remembers also getting into trouble if you told of what happened. Winston's egotism is apparent when he discovers his daughter is not a virgin, evident in his outcry: "'You allow men to do this to you before, June-June?' the enraged father cried. He thought he was going to be the first. What a disappointment" (ibid). In this way the narrator stresses the contradictions inherent in Winston's attitude, the double standard between his own conduct and what he expects from his daughter. Moreover, such an attitude underlines how Gwendolen is being induced to take on the "wifely" role, as Winston plays the part of the jealous "husband" who is devastated that she does not fulfil the standards of sexual chastity he expects. The hypocrisy behind this double standard is made clear when, the following day, Gwendolen is forced to listen to her father preach against the sins of the world, such as the evils of adultery: "No one knew why the easy-going Winston, whose tiny wife Sonia could bully him into silence at home, talked so brutally about women whenever he took the pulpit" (113). There is a hint here of a deep-seated misogyny which may result from a poor self-image and lack of authority, certainly in respect to his wife. However, his lack of interpersonal skills is no hindrance to him in his role as declaimer of the faith when he is given the power to speak and to be heard without interruption.

In contrast, Gwendolen copes by retreating into herself, as she had done in Granville, accepting her father's sexual attentions without resistance, "suffering his anger and guilt" (146). He becomes like a stranger to her "And for this somebody else, she had to lie very still, because she had no solid and protective Daddy to shield her any more" (ibid). Just as she had suffered from guilt when sexually abused in Jamaica, she feels guilty once more for being unable to stop her father. In fact, her reaction to this new rape is shown to be governed by her previous treatment by Johnny, how he had insisted that "Every gal done done it. Dat's why they're girls" (145). Just as she did in Granville, she feels isolated, unable to confide in anyone, and runs away. She also fears that if she were to tell, her father might be put in prison, causing her family to disintegrate. Thus, to some extent at least, the first act of sexual abuse governs her reactions to the second, and there are other parallels. When the social worker is trying to uncover the circumstances of Gwendolen's pregnancy, Sonia tells her that Gwendolen rolls her waist inside as well as outside the house. This is reminiscent of her Grandmother's reference to Gwendolen's walking in a certain manner inside as well as outside the house and intimates Sonia's unvoiced and probably unacknowledged suspicions about her husband.

In describing Gwendolen's reaction to incest, especially her decision to run away in both cases, Emecheta is again reinforcing sociological findings.[13] Whereas in Granville, Gwendolen is forced to return to her Grandmother Naomi's because her other grandmother did not offer her a warm welcome, in London she receives more sympathetic treatment in a mental institution. There she is given more personal autonomy than ever before, counselled as to her options, and is allowed to decide whether she wishes to see her parents. She is also not forced to name the father of her child. When her parents do eventually visit her, she describes her father "standing as solid as an oak by the window. His standing there radiated dependability and solidity all rolled into one. A father any girl should be proud of. But he did not even come near to her. She did not look into his eyes for fear of what she would see" (190). The first part of Gwendolen's description is based on wish-fulfilment, an attempt to fill the vacuum of her own needs, as she imagines her father as someone she can rely on, couched in an image resonant of the English countryside, surely one from which she would be estranged living in the urban sprawl of London. Whether this is a poor choice of language by the author or whether the narrator is intimating that Gwendolen's idealized vision of her father is far removed from reality, or both, is not clear. She knows instinctively, however, that no solace awaits her in her father's eyes, which is why she averts her gaze. Moreover, it is significant that her father does not speak to her once. His guilt is reflected in a total breakdown in communication.

Sonia's unvoiced suspicions of her husband are uppermost in her mind when she hears the news of Winston's death in a gas explosion. According to his friend, Mr Ilochina, Winston had insisted on testing the gas himself even though he was aware of the dangers, as if he had wanted to die. The suggestion is that Winston has committed suicide through the guilt he feels as a result of his treatment of his daughter. His wife, who has failed to voice her suspicions when he was alive, can no longer avoid the truth when she finally visits Gwendolen and her new baby daughter, who is the image of Winston. After making her peace with her daughter, accompanied by her Nigerian friend, Mrs Odowis, she walks home. Unable any longer to repress her rage, she draws a knife from her bag and plunges it repeatedly into a bag of refuse. The knife with which Sonia had intended to attack her daughter is instead used to ritually re-enact her husband's death.

It is clear from the above discussion that Emecheta has included many of the points made in theoretical works on incest, such as family dysfunction and issues of consent, as well as questions of blame and guilt. In such works, family dysfunction primarily concerns the conduct of the mother, rather than that of the father, a mother who may be emotionally cold towards her daughter or physically absent from the family. As the authors of one study on incest have stated, "In the clinical literature [...] the theme of maternal absence is emphasized almost to the exclusion of anything else."[14] In such cases the eldest daughter is relied upon for housework, child care and emotional support. According to these same authors: "For the daughter, the duty to fulfil her father's sexual demands may evolve almost as an extension of her role as 'little mother' in the family."[15] This is precisely what happens in Emecheta's novel to the point that the roles of Gwendolen and Sonia are reversed. As Gwendolen takes on her mother's role, Sonia is cosseted and treated like a child in Granville after suffering a nervous breakdown. While there, she "did not have to worry about her meals, her family's meals, their washing, their bed-making and the children's bed-wetting" (134). It could be argued though that even before Sonia's physical absence, there is an emotional void in her relationship with her daughter, and her rather selfish attitude towards Gwendolen is contrasted to her good friend and neighbour, the Nigerian Mrs Odowis, who is a strong and capable mother. In this depiction therefore Emecheta is furthering the process whereby women are often considered blameworthy when incestuous sexual relations develop.[16]

Although Emecheta upholds much of the sociological data concerning incest on a fictional level, she does break from such sources in depicting a protagonist who has successfully overcome such an ordeal. By the novel's end Gwendolen seems to have accepted the tragedy of her young life and willingly accepts her child. She welcomes her mother back into her life, and is taught to read by Emmanuel, who remains a good friend. She appears to be living an independent and fulfilled life to the extent that one critic comments that "[t]he novel ends perhaps too optimistically for an incest victim."[17] Although it is true that Gwendolen does show a remarkable resilience, one assumes that Emecheta wishes to combat the negativity of the sexually abused child condemned to victimhood. Another commentator feels that: "The image of Gwendolen as a single, liberated, self-sufficient, healthy mother is too pat and at odds with the profoundly disturbing image of the fatherless black child or the commonplace wandering madwoman."[18] This criticism of Emecheta's positioning of her heroine seems over-stated, for she in no way presents the arrival of Gwendolen's baby in this manner. Gwendolen's baby may be fatherless but it is intimated in the novel that Emmanuel will act as a father figure, while the baby is certainly the source of Gwendolen's sense of achievement. Nor is there any image of a "wandering madwoman" in the novel. Although, admittedly, Gwendolen runs away from home and does indeed wander aimlessly for a day until she seeks a night's sleep on a park bench, such a description seems unjustified. Even though she is sent to a home for the mentally sick, it is clear that her mental health is never in jeopardy and while there she is treated in a warm and friendly manner and, more importantly, she is given some freedom of choice in controlling her destiny as already discussed. Finally, one might also query the suggestion that the image of a "wandering madwoman" is commonplace. This remark is then not further contextualized. Is Ogunyemi referring to fictionalized accounts and, if so, from what region? Certainly not in the African and Caribbean literatures in which traditions this novel is based. If one were to criticize Emecheta's lack of *vraisemblance* in this novel, what strikes me as even more exaggerated, and which has not been raised by such commentators is the melodramatic way in which Winston meets his death, thereby avoiding issues of confrontation and reconciliation with his wife and daughter.

There is some clinical support for Emecheta's optimistic vision of a survivor of incest. In a work which includes biographical accounts of women sexually abused as young children, the authors comment that these women "do not present themselves as the doomed 'victims' that one is accustomed to see in the traditional incest literature; instead, they speak for the resilience and creativity that all of us can share in overcoming the cruelty of sexual abuse."[19] Unlike the protagonist in Toni Morrison's novel, *The Bluest Eye*, Pecola, who descends into madness after being sexually assaulted by her father, Gwendolen does not become mad, but instead thrives in a "home for the mentally sick" where she is "mothered" by Ama, the Ghanaian nurse.

In *The Family* the process of naming is suggestive of fractured relationships, as well as Gwendolen's very fragile identity. The novel opens with the words: "She was christened Gwendolen. But her Mommy could not pronounce it, neither could her Daddy or his people" (9). One critic on this novel suggests that

> a palpable symptom of Gwendolen's entrapment within the patri-
> archal culture that legitimates her rape is the parental gift of grand
> deception embodied in her name. The text opens with the lie that
> all but erases Gwendolen's identity, rendering her an easy target of
> patriarchal reconstruction.[20]

This comment appears to be somewhat flawed. Nowhere in the novel is it suggested that Gwendolen's rape is "legitimated" or in any way excused, although as I have suggested, her plight does not always receive full and compassionate understanding. Moreover, this "patriarchal culture" is not so applicable to the Jamaican situation which might be more appropriately considered "matriarchal," although the author may be referring to the situation in England. Certainly, Gwendolen is seen in a position of weakness, but this is principally because of the powerlessness of a child before an adult rather than oppressive male/female relationships. Nevertheless, I agree with this critic that the process of naming draws attention to Gwendolen's fractured identity and it most certainly suggests cultural alienation.

Ironically, in England, the name of Gwendolen is equally reflective of alien-ation because it is the one recognized by officialdom, both by the air-hostess and by the school, and therefore one with which Gwendolen must come to terms. However, she and her family still have difficulty in its pronunciation, her mother introducing her to the landlord as "Grandalee," which he also then mispronounces. It is evident that Gwendolen's already fragile sense of identity must seem even more precarious to her as a result of the confusion surrounding her name. This is reflected by her strong desire to make sure that her daughter will not suffer the same fate: "One thing she was sure of, her daughter was not going to be given a foreign name which she could not pronounce" (209-10). She asks the Ghanaian nurse for help in choosing her baby's name, one which would encapsulate the idea that the child was her friend, her mother, her sister and her hope. The nurse suggests the Yoruba name "Iyamide," which means all these things and, additionally, "anything-nice-you-can-think-of-in-a-woman's-form" (210). What pleases Gwendolen the most is that she finds her daughter's name easy to pronounce, although ironically it is a "foreign" Nigerian name and both Gwendolen and her family have difficulty in pronouncing such names. It may be that with the choice of this name the narrator is suggesting some kind of a diaspora reconnection, especially in view of the fact that both Sonia and Winston have close relationships with African friends, Sonia with Mrs Odowis and Winston with Mr Ilochina. Additionally, Emecheta has dedicated her novel "To that woman in the Diaspora who refused to sever her umbilical cord with Africa." It is noticeable that the nurse rejects the idea that Gwendolen name her daughter after her father. The father/daughter bond is not to be perpetuated in the act of naming.

Emecheta's decision to set *The Family* in Jamaica, then in England and to choose West Indian protagonists raises interesting questions. Is Emecheta's distancing herself from her usual choice of Nigerian characters an attempt to avoid criticism from her Nigerian compatriots if she were to discuss incest in the context of African society?[21] There are several other markers in the text which suggest that Emecheta's decision is not coincidental. For example, the narrator frames the incest story into a larger historical dimension of diaspora relationships. Winston attempts to discover if such incestuous desires are manifest in other cultures when, learning about the practice of polygamy in African societies, he asks his Nigerian friend, Azu Ilochina, whether Nigerian men ever marry their daughters. His friend quickly comprehends the significance of this question and is appalled. However, he intimates that Winston is the victim of circumstances beyond his control when he asks himself "What had slavery done to a nice brother like this?" (143). In this way Mr Ilochina intimates that incest is not a natural occurrence in African societies, but has been introduced into diaspora communities by the havoc wrought on familial relationships by slavery. He further dismisses the possibility of incest in African societies with an economic argument when he tells Winston that "A daughter belonged to the father, her bride price was his. If the daughter was chaste, it would enhance her father's position and make him richer. So why should a father wish to ruin his own wealth?" (142-43).[22] To further illustrate the incest taboo, he recalls a story told him by his mother about a man who had committed incest with his daughter and who was beaten into a pulp by the women from his village. Such a man is considered as sinning against the Earth and "If he is not discovered, he will surely be killed by an Earth force like thunder, you know, natural electricity, drowning, just an Earth force" (144). Although, with this tale of incest Mr Ilochina is contradicting himself, for it does relate an actual incident of incest in African society which he claims does not occur, nevertheless, it is intimated that it is an isolated incident, and in fact the tale takes on the dimension of an oral myth told for purposes of moral edification.

To further explore the possibilities surrounding Emecheta's decision to distance her somewhat from African culture in this novel, it is noticeable that when Gwendolen chooses a name for her child she chooses a Nigerian name. Although her reasons are both pragmatic (a name that she can at least pronounce) and symbolic (she aspires to a close relationship with her daughter and hopes she may yet find solace in her relationship with her mother), nevertheless this decision has further ramifications. By adopting the name suggested by the Ghanaian nurse and agreeing with the nurse's advice not to name the child after her father, it is as if Gwendolen is adopted into a world of matriarchal values. In choosing her daughter's name, Gwendolen is stressing the importance of the mother/daughter relationship and distancing herself from the paternal line which has so nearly destroyed her. In adopting an African name Gwendolen is also rejecting the world of diaspora alienation in which she has grown up. This is further emphasised when, confronted by the social worker regarding his daughter's pregnancy, Winston is sure Gwendolen will not betray him by telling about the incest, that she will be unable to confide in a mother because that "closeness between African mother and daughter had been lost during the slave passage"(170). The reasoning behind this is difficult to follow, for although slavery certainly separated men from their families, it was normal for mothers and children to remain together. Whatever the intention, what appears to be suggested is that Gwendolen and her family's problems are due to historical factors. The many contradictions inherent in the text and the displacements regarding incest utilized by Emecheta in *The Family* are indicative of her ambivalence towards this subject.

The Cameroonian writer, Mpoudi Ngolle's novel *Sous la cendre le feu* is set in Douala, in Southern Cameroon and focuses on a family's attempts to come to terms with a man's rape of his stepdaughter. The narrative is told from the perspective of the wife, Mina, a 30-year-old, well-educated and reasonably affluent young woman, who is attempting to dislodge from her subconscious her knowledge of this event. When her husband Djibril and her daughter Fanny, visit her in hospital and the latter asks her mother if it is true that she is mad, the narrator is forced to confront the nature of her illness. Her psychiatrist, a Dr. Lobé, assures her that once she recovers her memory she will recover from her depressed state. As Mina delves back into her past the reader learns how, after a fleeting romance during the last year of high school, she becomes pregnant by a medical student, Joel, who refuses to acknowledge any responsibility. Immediately afterwards she meets Djibril, who is about ten years older than her and working as a lawyer. They fall in love and decide to marry whereupon he vows to recognize her unborn child as his own. The child, Fanny, is followed by three more children, but later Mina discovers that Djibril has raped Fanny while she was visiting him after school in his office. Unable to cope with what Fanny tells her, she collapses and is sent to recover in hospital.

The two father/daughter relationships in this novel, that between Mina, the narrator, and her father and that between Mina's daughter, Fanny, and her stepfather, Djibril, are close and loving, but both are linked to traumatic events following an illicit sexual relationship. By confiding in her psychiatrist her childhood memories Mina is able to uncover not only incidents concerning her father, but also those from her recent past which affect her husband and her daughter, both of which Mina regards as acts of personal betrayal. In fact, the recounting of Mina's memories to her psychiatrist forms most of the narrative, occasionally interrupted by visits from her husband and her children. Dr Lobé himself plays the role of a father figure. He is someone Mina trusts absolutely and in whom she is able to confide without reservation.

Mina's relationship with her biological father, most of which is told in flashback, is ambiguous. Although he encourages her in her studies, he also professes that "*ses diplômes ne lui serviront à rien*" (15) [her diplomas won't be of any use to her], and tells her that her first consideration should be marriage. Mina, who is fifteen years old at the time, realises from that moment that: "*la femme n'était et ne serait jamais chez elle nulle part: chez ses parents, elle est une passante. Chez son mari, elle est susceptible d'être mise à la porte au gré du mari ou même de sa belle-famille*" (16) [a woman did not have and never would have a place she could call her own: in her parents' home she is only passing through. In her husband's home she is likely to be shown the door at the whim of her husband or even that of her family-in-law]. Such an acknowledgement induces Mina to become resigned to suffer her fate, an attitude that may account for her inability to cope when faced with her husband's incestuous actions.

Both father/daughter relationships involve the betrayal of a child. Mina feels personally betrayed when she discovers that her father is having an affair. As a child, Mina had looked upon him in the same way that she looked upon the Christian God, the "father of the church," as someone who was infallible. Such an idealized image is finally shattered when she witnesses a domestic row involving her father, his lover and her mother. Mina feels totally betrayed by her father: "*cette révélation, sans réhabiliter ma mère à mes yeux, avait détruit mon père-dieu*" (88) [this revelation, without causing me to think any better of my mother, had destroyed my god-like father]. The shock of this disclosure causes Mina to suffer from a crippling fear expressing itself physiologically in stomach cramps and headaches. She also loses weight but no ailment is discovered, although the doctor believes it may be due to impending puberty. Mina never confronts her father or even confides in him her insecurities, and this may be why she is never able to deal with this upset and why she continues to suffer its mental and physical effects into adulthood. Mina's illness is therefore linked to sexual undercurrents, not only caused by discovering the reason for her parents' marital problems, but by the onset of puberty and her own awakening sexuality.

In the case of the second father/daughter relationship depicted, it is Mina's child Fanny who is betrayed, although Mina is also deceived by her husband. Mina's illness, recurring periodically at moments of stress, returns when Fanny tells her that she has been raped by her stepfather while still only twelve years old. Mina collapses at this time and is taken to hospital. As she realises later, unable to cope with what her daughter was telling her, she *"l'avai[t] enfoui au plus profond [d'elle]-même, pour ne jamais le révéler à personne, [elle] l'y avai[t] tellement enfermé que [s]a propre mémoire se refusait à le laisser remonter à la surface"* (190) [had hidden it in the deepest parts of herself, so as never to reveal it to anyone, she had shut it away to such an extent that her own memory refused to let it resurface]. Moreover, Mina feels she must accept some blame, for instead of believing her sister when told how Djibril had also tried to rape her; she instead takes her husband's side and blames her sister for trying to seduce him. In answer to Dr. Lobé's probing about whether she is sure that Djibril has committed incest with his own daughter, Mina denies this, telling the doctor that Fanny is not Djibril's biological daughter. Mina's denial of actual incest may be interpreted as another instance of her repressing what has happened, or at least displacing it onto something that is less shocking to her, so that she is able to deal with it. In the definition of incest I have previously cited, it is stated that the perpetrator of the sexual assault does not have to be a biological relation. It is the abuse of power and the breaking of a position of trust which is important and of course, as far as Fanny is concerned, Djibril is the only father she has ever known.

Mina further diminishes the seriousness of Djibril's conduct towards their daughter in blaming herself for Fanny's distress, believing her inability to deal with her daughter's disclosure has been the primary cause of Fanny's suffering, rather than the sexual attack itself. Mina is not even sure that Fanny resents her father's conduct, that she might have accepted it *"avec un naturel identique à celui qui entourerait n'importe quelle autre marque d'affection entre un père et sa fille"* (200) [quite naturally as one associated with no matter what other token of affection between a father and his daughter] if she had not reacted so dramatically. Mina seems to be intent, once again, on deceiving herself, for it was she who had noticed a change in Fanny's conduct after her father's sexual abuse. Even before she admits to the doctor, or to herself, Djibril's actions, she had perceived Fanny to be silent and self-absorbed. It is clear that Mina's reaction to her daughter's confidences and her subsequent breakdown would add to Mina's troubles, but it seems logical to deduce that Fanny's trauma is the result of her rape rather than her mother's reaction to it.

Mina does, however, realise that she must discover why Djibril has betrayed their daughter's trust for she is sure that Djibril loves Fanny: *"Il a élevé plus encore que moi cette fillette, qui était sa joie. [...] Qu'a-t-il bien pu se produire pour que Djibril ait oublié que Fanny était sa fille?"* (199) [He had shouldered more of the responsibility than I in raising this young daughter who was his pride and joy. [...] What could have happened to cause Djibril to forget that Fanny was his daughter?] The explanation is given at a family conference when Djibril explains how one of his friends persuaded him to see a *féticheur*[23] in order to try and make his business more profitable. The *féticheur* had promised Djibril that he would become very rich if he agreed to fulfil certain requirements, one of which was to hand over a sum of money to the *féticheur* and another, to sleep with a pre-pubescent girl from his family. Mina is very disturbed that her husband could think of doing such a thing for money and Djibril reassures her that he had tried to withdraw from the agreement and he had only failed to do so because he had been visited that same day by Fanny's biological father, Joel, who wished to claim his daughter. Djibril assures Mina that he would never have perpetrated such an act against Fanny if Joel had not arrived and threatened to take his wife and daughter away from him. According to Djibril it was this visit that *"a ouvert dans [s]a tête la breche par laquelle l'idee démoniaque s'est infiltrée ensuite"* (204) [caused his mind to be open to the demonic idea which then took hold of him].

At this point in the narrative, the reader's response may, like Mina's, be one of disbelief as Djibril's excuses for his conduct seem to lack any sort of logic. If, as he states, he only decided to follow through with the *féticheur's* instructions because of Joel's threats, surely his actions would only serve to underline his unsuitability as a surrogate father. A more moral and circumspect attitude towards his daughter would have ensured that no reproach could be levelled against him. Mina's response to Djibril's excuses is to pity him despite herself and she also remembers her gratitude towards him twelve years previously when she was pregnant and abandoned. In addition, she is determined that Fanny's biological father should not destroy her family. Mina's reasoning also seems to lack logic in this instance. She forgets that Djibril did not marry her out of pity but because he was in love with her. Furthermore, although she might justly resent Joel's reappearance in her life at this time and his ludicrous demands, nevertheless she forgets that it is Djibril's conduct which has threatened to destroy their family, not Joel's.

There are two competing discourses, traditional and Western, suggested in *Sous la cendre le feu* as to how to best resolve the family's problems and reintegrate Djibril back into the family; Mina believes that Fanny would suffer more should she decide to divorce Djibril. In order to try and free Djibril from the spell he is under, his uncle suggests visiting a Marabout but Mina's parents, as practising Christians, vigorously reject this proposition and instead insist on the ministrations of their priest. In this case, it is the Western religion which gains the upper hand, the entire family visiting the village of Mina's parents and their family priest where they all pray together. The novel then ends with the following description:

Dehors, les tam-tams déchaînés roulaient déjà dans un rythme endiablé;
mes enfants perdus au milieu des autres enfants du village, regardaient,
émerveillés, les danseurs et les batteurs de tam-tam, tous ces signes d'un
monde qui leur était inconnu, et qu'ils semblaient regretter de ne pas
connaître. Fanny, en nous voyant arriver, courut se placer entre Djibril
et moi, et, nous prenant chacun par la main, nous entraîna vers le cercle
formé par les danseurs (207).

[Outside the wild drums were beating to a furious rhythm; my children, lost in the midst of the other village children, were looking,
filled with wonder, at the dancers and the drum beaters, all those
signs of a world unknown to them and which they seemed sorry
not to know. Fanny, seeing us arrive, ran and placed herself between
Djibril and I, and, holding both our hands, led us towards the circle
formed by the dancers.]

The above scene appears rather clichéd for several reasons. Above all, perhaps, because it presents the obligatory "happy ending" even though such a prospect seems highly unlikely given the events depicted. Additionally, there is an inti- mation that if only, as a family, they could return to their cultural origins, every- thing else would fall into place. Certainly, Mina's and Djibril's children seem totally at ease in the communal gathering, in fact they are "lost in the midst of the other village children" (207), lost, because indistinguishable from them, suggesting total reintegration. Even Fanny is no longer morose and suspicious, but makes a gesture of reconciliation to her parents as all the villagers form a harmonious circle. Not only is the ending of the novel unlikely given Fanny's earlier distress, it is highly romanticized.

The presence of two parallel discourses in the novel, traditional and Western, are thus adhered to in varying degrees by the different protagonists although the above scene, with the priest's ministrations and the traditional dance seem to betoken a certain successful syncretism. However, the author has previously suggested that Mina and Djibril, who have received a Western-type education, do not subscribe to tradition. In their search for a "cure" for Mina's "madness," traditional remedies in the form of a visit to a traditional healer are rejected by them, Mina referring to such practices as "*obscurantistes*" (90) [reac- tionary]. Mina's parents are convinced that Djibril's relatives must have put a spell on Mina and therefore believe that "Western" medicine would be ineffec- tual. However, the narrator has previously stated that, as practising Christians, Mina's parents reject a visit to the healer in the case of Djibril's misconduct. Additionally, Djibril himself describes a visit to a *féticheur*, yet purportedly does not subscribe to such practices. Such a lack of consistency in character motiva- tion produces less than credible protagonists.

Of interest in this novel, however, is the way Mpoudi Ngolle explores the question of the applicability of Western psychiatric medicine in the treat- ment of her African protagonists. In contrast to the Zimbabwean writer Tsitsi Dangarembga's novel *Nervous Conditions*, such a possibility is dismissed by the

Western psychiatrists approached by Nyasha's parents. That particular novel is set in the 1960s, whereas *Sous la cendre le feu* appears to be set in 1980s Cameroon. Evidently, allowing for variation in country, the depiction of psychiatric medicine has radically altered. Mina's psychiatrist is African, not European and she is in a well-equipped, modern, neuro-psychological hospital where Freudian ideas are deemed to be applicable to African patients. Mina herself raises this issue with her doctor, remarking that she thought that concepts such as the subconscious were *"des histoires de Blancs, et que les Noirs n'avaient rien à voir avec toutes ces complications psychologiques"* (91) [a story made up by white people and which did not concern black people with all its psychological complications].[24] Mina also insists that something like the Oedipus complex would be unthinkable in an African context, but Dr Lobé responds with his belief that there is no fundamental difference between people because of their race, although socio-cultural factors are influential. In a traditional context a child who is looked after by many people makes it less likely that he or she would have the possibility, or even the need, to become fixated on one parent, yet he believes that modern society is changing so quickly, with the family module becoming more and more westernised, that there is no longer a great difference between these cultures.[25]

As if to elaborate on the ways in which the socio-cultural environment is influential in family relationships, Mpoudi Ngolle presents a "modern" family which has obviously undergone quite a strong Western influence, particularly in the education of its two principal protagonists, Mina and Djibril. Mina, although a housewife and mother, wants to improve her educational qualifications and spends long periods of time away from her family in order to do so when Djibril becomes the primary child carer. He shows less willingness to undertake domestic and child rearing tasks, however, under increasing disapproval from both spouses' families and the influence of his business colleagues. Is Mpoudi Ngolle suggesting that such practices of child rearing are more likely to lead to incestuous desires on the part of the father towards his daughter?[26] Certainly Djibril is uncomfortable that Fanny has no compunction about being in a state of undress in his presence and he asks Mina to talk to their daughter about this. Conversely, however, the motivation for incest presented in the novel is not sexual but purportedly financial initially, and then as a means of a desperate attempt by a father to stake a claim of "ownership" of his daughter, an act lacking in any logic, due to the taboo nature of incest.

Although incest is obviously central to the plot of *Sous la cendre le feu*, it is not well integrated into the novel's structure either in relation to plot or characterization, possibly as a result of the author's discomfort with the subject. Certainly, the way in which Mpoudi Ngolle delineates the problems of mental illness and incest may be an attempt to depict the hybridity inherent in the sociological structures of a rapidly changing post-colonial society. What is less credible is the way in which she attempts to render the treatment of incest in an African context more realistic by introducing a cultural African authenticity to it, yet instead eroticizes it, perhaps with the Western reader in mind, with the introduction of the whole episode of the *féticheur*. Although such events are not beyond the realms of possibility, this aspect of the novel lacks feasibility and appears contrived. Accordingly, it might be claimed that the author's treatment of such a serious matter as that of incest tends to trivialize it rather than contribute anything meaningful to the debate.

Although in both father/daughter relationships the daughter is betrayed by the father, in the first relationship to be depicted, it is Mina's mother who suffers the primary betrayal due to her husband's infidelity. She is, however, prepared to forgive her husband. Mina, the daughter, who also feels betrayed, could be said to have unrealistic expectations when she compares her father to "God the father," but perhaps the pertinent question here is: why does she have such an idealised vision of her father in the first place? In a novel which is structured around the concept of the repression of Mina's subconscious, Mina's obsession regarding her father may be a manifestation of the Electra complex. In less psychoanalytical terms, her idealized vision of her father may stem from the inequitable nature of male/female relations in her society that she is made aware of as a young girl. In the second father/daughter relationship, Mina herself is betrayed by her husband, in the first instance in the attempted rape of her sister and finally, in the rape of her daughter. Just as Mina's mother has done before her, Mina makes excuses for her husband when she takes his side against her sister and, in the incest on her daughter, she makes allowances for him. The reasons for such indulgence towards their respective husbands are present in the sub-text which suggests that a woman has little choice in the patriarchal society into which she has been born.

Indeed, it is evident that Mina is made aware of the inequitable nature of gender relations in her society by her encounter with several authoritative "father" figures. She rejects the option of an abortion as an unmarried pregnant woman, citing the judgemental attitude of her local priest, completely lacking in charity a young woman parishioner who died while undergoing an abortion. Another possibility is for Mina to take advantage of a presidential decree obliging any young man who is responsible for making a minor pregnant, to marry her. If the young man refuses, he is sent to jail for six years. Mina also rejects this solution, likening such forced marriages to "*deux jeunes gens qu'on traînait devant le maire comme des bœufs à l'abattoir*" (40) [two young people being dragged in front of the mayor like cattle to the slaughter]. Such an authoritarian presidential edict points to a paternalistic attitude towards young women, who are assumed to be incapable of coping with such problems. It seems that neither the Catholic priest, in his position of "father of the community," nor the President, in his position as "father of the nation," is able to provide Mina with the resolution of her dilemma. When Mina meets Djibril she feels that all her problems are solved. The meeting of the two young people is described in terms of a *coup de foudre*. The unlikely nature of their romance, combined with the difference in their ages, does not augur well for a reciprocal adult relationship, but rather suggests yet another unsatisfactory paternal relationship.

Father/daughter relationships in the two novels discussed are governed by conflicts of varying degrees due to many different factors. The framework of my discussion has been built around two major themes: patriarchy and incest. As in my discussion of patriarchy, the treatment of incest in these novels is framed by an exploration of hegemonic relationships, notably the father's power over the daughter. As stated in Herman and Hirschman's study of incest:

> Because a child is powerless in relation to an adult, she is not free to refuse a sexual advance. Therefore, any sexual relationship between the two must necessarily take on some of the coercive characteristics of a rape, even if, as is usually the case, the adult uses positive enticements rather than force to establish the relationship."[27]

Emecheta's treatment of incest in *The Family* is somewhat ambivalent, especially in the distancing techniques she uses in her discussion of this taboo subject. Much of the detail in relation to incest appears to be based on sociological readings, perhaps not surprisingly given her training in sociology, one of its major determinants being the lack of a strong mother figure, both emotionally and physically. In suggesting that this may be a primary cause of father/daughter incest, Emecheta is implicating herself in a discussion which feminist sociologists are now contesting, seeing it as yet another patriarchal ruse to apportion blame to the woman. Certainly, however, Emecheta does depict a victim of incest who finds the strength to rise above the abuse she has suffered and in this way, she presents us with a protagonist who has been able to overturn the power structure of familial relationships and to make them work to her own advantage. The novel's conclusion posits a new kind of society, one in which despotic "fathers" are not welcome. It presents a different kind of family unit, one which consists of a mother and daughter and a non-biological father who, although not married to Gwendolen, and unlikely to be so, nevertheless is a powerful presence in his daughter's life.

Mpoudi Ngolle's novel *Sous la cendre le feu* is a "confessional" narrative which features as part of a psychoanalytic exploration of the effects of incest on a family. The description of Mina's repressed memories and her unravelling of them work as a narrative device to hold the reader's attention. Intertwined with this narrative are allusions to "traditional" culture which are eroticized in their presentation, as in the episode of the *féticheur*. In this way the author appears to commodify incest rather than exploring it in an insightful manner. Mina's "cure" appears perfunctory and although it provides a resolution to the question posed at the novel's beginning, namely the cause of her "madness," the author does not then seek to probe the question of incest in a serious manner or to suggest its wider ramifications in the hierarchies of power which she delineates. Her protagonist, Mina is never able to subsequently satisfactorily resolve the issues that beset her despite being pronounced "cured" and although her husband is chastened, little has changed and the obligatory "happy ending" seems highly superficial.

The two novels referred to depict father/daughter relationships which are concerned to some extent with questions of power. Intersecting with relations of power are issues of gender whereby "daughters" attempt to assert themselves independently from their fathers. In Emecheta's *The Family* the father exploits his daughter's emotional needs and his physical strength. He has no idea that Gwendolen has already been subjected to the ordeal of sexual abuse in her past and is therefore conditioned to hopelessness, making his conquest of her all the more possible. However, an escape from this unhealthy situation is possible because of sexual desire which takes place outside the father's influence. In Mpoudi Ngolle's *Sous la cendre le feu* issues of power are never satisfactorily resolved. The psychiatric discourse contained in the novel is one which puts power into the hands of the physician, a representative of the patriarchal establishment, however benevolent, but this power is never attained by its female protagonists. At the novel's end it appears that the power dynamics in the family are not radically altered, or even questioned.

Both of the novels discussed explore the father/daughter relationship from different perspectives and in different modes, from a more serious investigation in *The Family* to a more melodramatic sensationalism in *Sous la cendre le feu*. However, a common feature of both of these novels is the endemic nature of patriarchy, whether traditional or Western.[28] In them patriarchy has been represented at the level of "father" of the family, the community, the medical establishment and the Church. However, patriarchal ideology can be contested, and in both novels studied there is an overt, or at the very least, a veiled, challenging of the "rule" of the Father.

Incest is a taboo practiced in most cultures, and I have noted how both Emecheta and Mpoudi Ngolle have developed distancing strategies towards it. In *The Family,* Emecheta displaces the whole discussion on to another culture; in *Sous la cendre le feu,* Mpoudi Ngolle uses the technique of psychological displacement encapsulated in her heroine's breakdown and then her refusal to fully acknowledge its origin in incest. In depicting such controversial issues African women writers are extending the frontiers of the subjects they are prepared to broach, conscious of the fact that market demands render such forbidden topics tempting for their readers. However, their contrived resolutions suggest that they are circumscribed to a certain extent, whether by their own inhibitions, or whether they perceive that any radical treatment of such subjects would receive harsh criticism, especially in their own societies.

Notes

1. Barbara H. Sheldon, "Introduction" to *Daughters and Fathers in Feminist Novels* (Frankfurt: Peter Lang, 1997), 11-15, 11.
2. Ibid., 12.

3. Sheldon, 12, citing Gisela Moffit, *Bonds and Bondage: Daughter-Father Relationships in the Father Memoirs of German-Speaking Women Writers of the 1970s* (New York: Peter Lang, 1993), 8.

4. Two such examples are Nozipo Maraire's *Zenzele* (1996) and Yvonne Vera's *Butterfly Burning* (1998).

5. Noteworthy among these are, in Anglophone Africa, Tsitsi Dangarembga's *Nervous Conditions* (1988) and, in Francophone Africa, Aminata Sow Fall's *L'Ex-père de la nation* (1987).

6. One exception is Cazenave's *Femmes rebelles* which includes a brief study of the father/daughter relationship in Mpoudi Ngolle's *Sous la cendre le feu*, 167-68, 170-71. For a brief enquiry into the father/daughter relationship in Aka's *Les Haillons de l'amour*, see Pierre N'Da, "Transgressions, Dévergondage Textuel et Stratégie Iconoclaste dans le Roman Négro-Africain" in Amadou Koné, Ed., *Lumières Africaines: Nouveaux propos sur la littérature et le cinéma africains* (New Orleans: University Press of the South, Inc., 1997), 75-87, 77.

7. Buchi Emecheta, *The Family* (New York: George Braziller, 1990) and Evelyne Mpoudi Nolle, *Sous la cendre le feu* [The Fire under the Ashes] (Paris: L'Harmattan, 1990). All page references, inserted in the text, refer to these editions.

8. *Shorter Oxford English Dictionary.*

9. Judith Lewis Herman with Lisa Hirschman, *Father-Daughter Incest* (Cambridge, Mass. and London: Harvard University Press, 1981), 50.

10. Emily Driver and Audrey Droisen, Eds. *Child Sexual Abuse: Feminist Perspectives* (London: Macmillan Education Ltd, 1989), 18.

11. Marie L. Umeh tells of this story in her "Introduction: (En)Gendering African Womanhood: Locating Sexual Politics in Igbo Society and Across Boundaries." In: *Emerging Perspectives on Buchi Emecheta*, Ed. Marie Umeh, xxxiii-xlii, xxx, also Endnote no. 8, xl. Apparently during a lecture to Umeh's students at The City University of New York in March 1991, Emecheta informed them that eight out of ten of the students who spoke to her had been sexually abused.

12. A pertinent example is the francophone novel *Pluie et vent sur Télumée Miracle* by Simone Schwarz-Bart (Paris: Editions du Seuil, 1972) where the relationship between grandmother and granddaughter is extremely close. In fact, in this instance, the mother entrusts her daughter to the grandmother in order to prevent a possible incident of incest at a later date: "*Le premier soin de ma mère fut de m'éloigner, d'écarter ma petite chair de dix ans pour s'éviter de la peine, quelques années plus tard, de danser sur le ventre qui l'aurait trahie,*" 46 [My mother's first concern was to send me away, remove my little ten-year-old flesh in order to save herself the trouble, a few years later, of trampling on the womb that betrayed her].

13. Herman with Hirschman, *Father-Daughter Incest*, 93. In a survey of stories by 40 incest victims, most of them in Massachusetts, 13 had attempted to run away.

14. Ibid., 45.

15. Ibid.

16. For more details, see Janet Liebman Jacobs, "Reassessing Mother Blame In Incest" In: *Signs: Journal of Women in Culture and Society* 30.3 (1990): 500-14.

17. Christine Sizemore, "The London Novels of Buchi Emecheta," In: *Emerging Perspectives on Buchi Emecheta*, 367-85, 377. She cites the work of Herman with Hirschman, whom I have already referred to, in reaching this decision.

18. Ogunyemi, *Africa Wo/Man Palava*, 278.

19. Driver and Droisen,Eds., *Child Sexual Abuse*, 2.

20. Tuzyline Jita Allan, "Trajectories of Rape in Buchi Emecheta's Novels," 222.

21. Other commentators suggest that Emecheta is distancing herself from describing incest abuse in African cultures by this device. See, for example, Christine W. Sizemore's "The London Novels of Buchi Emecheta," 367-85, 374; also Allan's "Trajectories of Rape in Buchi Emecheta's Novels," 221; Ogunyemi even comments that Emecheta's action "is hardly a sisterly move for a writer reaching out to the African diaspora to claim kin," *Africa Wo/Man Palava*, 271.

22. Emecheta has spoken about how the "African father will not have sex with his daughter, because he knows that he will then be cheated of the bride price. If she is a virgin on the wedding night, he will get more palm wine and more money. The West Indians have no bride price, but the father thinks that the child is his daughter and loves him, and therefore she will not say anything [about incest]. In both cases the man regards his daughter as his property," in "The Dilemma of Being in between Two Cultures," in Raoul Granqvist and John Stotesbury, Interviewers and Eds., *African Voices: Interviews with Thirteen African Writers* (Sydney: Dangaroo Press, 1989), 17-20, 20. Herman/Hirschman's comments are also relevant here when they cite Claude Levi-Strauss's *The Elementary Structures of Kinship* (1949): "The prohibition of incest is less a rule prohibiting marriage with the mother, sister, or daughter, than a rule obliging the mother, sister, or daughter to be given to others. It is the supreme rule of the gift, and it is clearly this aspect, too often unrecognized, which allows its nature to be understood." Cited on page 50.

23. *Prêtre des religions traditionnelles (animistes) en Afrique. Le féticheur joue le rôle de médecin et de l'éducateur* [A priest of traditional religions (animist) in Africa. The féticheur plays the role of doctor and educator]. Cited in *Le Robert: Dictionnaire de la langue française*. Tome IV, 480.

24. In a conversation with Mary Childers, bell hooks, an African-American feminist and critic, has suggested that we do not have to see white people as inventing psychoanalysis – many processes that we name as psychoanalytic we can find in other cultures, so-called archaic or primitive cultures, that use the same processes in therapeutic rituals. Is not to name something as psychoanalysis therefore not to have invented it?" in "A Conversation about Race and Class" in Marianne Hirsch & Evelyne Fox Keller, Eds. *Conflicts in Feminism* (New York and London: Routledge, 1990), 60-81, 65.

25. For the applicability of Freudian theory, more especially the Oedipan complex, to the African situation, see Marie Cécile and Edmond Ortigues, *Oedipe africain* (Paris: Plon 10/18, 1976). See also Awa Thiam, *Le Continent noir* (Paris: Tierce, 1987), particularly her Chapter "Freud et le continent 'noir' Afrique," 79-84. Thiam did not believe in the applicability of the Oedipal complex to the African situation at the time her work was published (1987), citing such factors as the extended African family, polygamy and the parents' choice of marriage partners for their children in a traditional context although she believed that it could not be ruled out in the future. See also Nicki Hitchcott's article, "African Oedipus?" which attempts to determine the applicability of Freud's theories of sexuality, particularly femininity, to an African context and in which she parallels Freud's theory of the castration complex to clitoridectomy in the construction of a woman's sexual identity. Hitchcott critiques the Ortigues' rejection of "their female case-histories

in favor of an almost exclusively men-centred study" which "recalls Freud's remarks concerning what he considered to be the inaccessibility (or rather the impenetrability) of femininity." *Paragraph* 16.1 (1993): 59-67, 61, 64. See also Chapter 5, "La psychanalyse en Afrique" in Michel Cornaton, *Pouvoir et sexualité dans le roman africain* (Paris: L'Harmattan, 1990). 45-53.

26. If this is indeed the view of Mpoudi Ngolle, then this reasoning is also shared by the Nigerian critic, Ogunyemi, in her work *Africa Wo/Man Palava*. Responding to Nancy Chodorow's proposal that men should take an equal share in parenting, Ogunyemi believes that such "theories fail to tackle the harrowing problem of incest, which arises from unhealthy intimacy between father and daughter in the confining nuclear family." Moreover, Ogunyemi further posits that the Nigerian woman "would prefer to be given the wherewithal to make her parenting successful and empowering rather than have men share the parenting, eroding the space that gives her authority." *Africa Wo/Man Palava*, 78.

27. Herman with Hirschman, *Father-Daughter Incest*, 27.

28. In an article entitled "Ecritures romanesques féminines: L'art et la loi des Pères," Romuald-Blaise Fonkoua explores the writing of African and Caribbean francophone women writers and concludes that the prevailing discourse is that of "la loi des Pères." *Nouvelles Ecritures féminines. Notre Librairie* 117 (1994): 112-25, 113.

Works Cited

Allan, Tuzyline Jita. "Trajectories of Rape in Buchi Emecheta's Novels." In: *Emerging Perspectives on Buchi Emecheta*. Ed. Marie L. Umeh. Trenton, N.J.: Africa World Press, 1996. 207-25

Cazenave, Odile. *Femmes rebelles: naissance d'un nouveau roman africain au féminin*. Paris: L'Harmattan, 1996.

Childers, Mary with bell hooks. "A Conversation about Race and Class." *Conflicts in Feminism*. Eds. Marianne Hirsch & Evelyne Fox Keller. New York and London: Routledge, 1990. 60-81.

Cornaton, Michel. *Pouvoir et sexualité dans le roman africain*. Paris: L'Harmattan, 1990.

Dangarembga, Tsitsi. *Nervous Conditions*. London: The Women's Press, 1988.

Driver, Emily and Audrey Droisen. Eds. *Child Sexual Abuse: Feminist Perspectives*. London: Macmillan Education, 1989.

Emecheta, Buchi. *The Family*. New York: George Braziller, 1990.

Fonkua, Romuald-Blaise. "Ecritures romanesques féminines: l'art et la loi des Pères." *Nouvelles Ecritures féminines. Notre Librairie* 117 (1994): 112-25.

Granqvist, Raoul and John Stotesbury. Eds. *African Voices: Interviews with Thirteen African Writers*. Dangaroo Press, Sydney, 1989. Papers from the Second Stockholm Conference for African Writers, Uppsala, Sweden, 11-16 April 1986.

Herman, Judith Lewis with Lisa Hirschman. *Father-Daughter Incest*. Cambridge, Mass. and London, England: Harvard University Press, 1981.

Hitchcott, Nicki. "African Oedipus?" *Paragraph* 16.1 (1993): 59-67.

Jacobs, Janet Liebman. "Reassessing Mother Blame in Incest." *Signs: Journal of Women in Culture and Society* 30.3 (1990): 500-514.

Mairaire, Nozipo. *Zenzele: A Letter for My Daughter*. London: Phoenix, 1996.

N'Da, Pierre. "Transgressions, Dévergondage Textuel et Stratégie Iconoclaste dans le Roman Négro-Africain." *Lumières Africaines: Nouveaux propos sur la littérature et le cinéma africains.* Ed. Amadou Koné. New Orleans: University Press of the South, Inc., 1997. 75-87.

Ogunyemi, Chikwenye Okonjo. *Africa Wo/Man Palaver: The Nigerian Novel by Women.* Chicago: University Press of Chicago, 1996.

Ortigues, Edmond and Marie Cécile. *L'Oedipe africain.* Paris: Plon 10/18, 1976.

Schwarz-Bart, Simone. *Pluie et vent sur Télumée Miracle.* Paris: Editions du Seuil, 1972.

Sheldon, Barbara H. *Daughters and Fathers in Feminist Novels.* European University Studies, Series 14 Anglo-Saxon Language and Literature, Vol. 334. Frankfurt: Peter Lang, 1997.

Sizemore, Christine W. "The London Novels of Buchi Emecheta." In: *Emerging Perspectives on Buchi Emecheta.* Trenton, N.J.: African World Press, 1996. 367-85.

Sow Fall, Aminata. *L'Ex-père de la nation* [The Former Father of the Nation]. Paris: L'Harmattan, 1987.

Thiam, Awa. *Le Continent noir.* Paris: Tierce, 1987.

Umeh, Marie Linton, Ed. "Introduction, (En)Gendering African Womanhood: Locating Sexual Politics in Igbo Society and across Boundaries." In: *Emerging Perspectives on Buchi Emecheta.* Trenton, NJ: African World Press, 1996. xxxiii-xlii.

Vera, Yvonne. *Butterfly Burning.* Harare: Baobab Books, 1998.

Chapter 10

Représentation(s) de l'excision dans le roman ivoirien : des *Soleils des indépendances* (1968) d'Ahmadou Kourouma à *Rebelle* (1998) de Fatou Kéita

Bernadette K. Kassi

« Dieu [a] créé [les femmes] avec un clitoris. Pourquoi, et
au nom de quoi, un simple être humain p[eu]t-il décider
que l'œuvre [divine] [est] imparfaite? »

- Fatou Kéita[1]

INTRODUCTION

L e roman est reconnu, selon Marthe Robert, pour « s'empare[r] de secteurs de plus en plus vastes de l'expérience humaine dont il donne une reproduction en l'interprétant à la façon du moraliste, de l'historien, du théologien, du philosophe » (1972: 14). Même si des auteurs comme Gustave Flaubert, James Joyce et Franz Kafka ont permis au roman de s'affirmer avant tout comme fait esthétique et que, de nos jours, « le développement des sciences humaines a assigné d'autres domaines à l'activité romanesque » (Raymond 2000: 21), le fait est que le roman continue de « respire[r] l'air de son temps » (15). Il le fait à un point tel qu'il est possible de dire, à la suite d'Edwin Hamblet, que la littérature est parfois la meilleure façon de jauger le niveau de civilisation d'un peuple (1987: 6), sans pour autant se laisser emporter par un « réalisme béat », inspiré de la célèbre phrase, « le roman est un miroir que l'on traîne le long du chemin », attribuée à l'écrivain français Henri Beyle, alias Stendhal (1783-1842).

Cela est d'autant plus vrai pour la gent féminine, l'autre moitié de l'humanité, dont les représentations littéraires—diverses, plurielles et contrastées au fil des siècles—ont souvent exprimé un écart entre le réel et le fictionnel. Longtemps sublimées, mystifiées et mythifiées par les écrits du sexe opposé—pensons, dans le cas de l'Afrique noire, au poème « Femme noire » de Senghor (1945) —, les femmes ont été décrites, depuis que l'Objet s'est fait Sujet d'écriture en Afrique et plus particulièrement en terre d'*Éburnie*[2], sous leurs plus réalistes atours et contours.

Mais qu'en est-il du phénomène de l'excision[3] que d'aucuns taxent de « *mutilation* sexuelle féminine » et que nous désignons par « marque corporelle féminine », dans un premier temps, par souci d'objectivité. Aujourd'hui dépourvue de son aura spirituelle et initiatique—surtout lorsqu'elle est pratiquée en zone urbaine ou transatlantique (par la diaspora) —, l'excision ne cesse de susciter les passions les plus vives, même si plusieurs dispositions légales, nationales et internationales, ont déjà été prises pour son abolition. Le parlement ivoirien a adopté une telle loi dans le courant de l'année 1998, pour respecter justement la ratification de plusieurs conventions dont celles relatives à l'élimination des violences faites aux femmes et aux enfants[4].

Pourtant, une brève revue du corpus romanesque subsaharien francophone révèle, contre toute attente, que rares sont les écrivains et écrivaines francophones qui aient abordé la question d'une façon ou d'une autre. En effet, jusqu'en 1998, la production littéraire traitant de l'excision compte moins d'une dizaine d'auteurs[5], parmi lesquels Ahmadou Kourouma et Fatou Kéita sur lesquels nous reviendrons. Quant aux autres romanciers, à l'exception de Calixthe Beyala[6], même quand ils abordent le sujet, c'est souvent au détour d'une description ou d'une allusion, sans pour autant porter un regard critique sur la pratique. Comme s'ils redoutaient de dénoncer le caractère désuet de cette coutume et surtout le danger qu'il représente pour la moitié de l'humanité.

Le plus surprenant, c'est de constater, à ce sujet, le silence « coupable » dans leurs œuvres de plusieurs romancières considérées pourtant comme des pionnières de la littérature féminine d'Afrique francophone (Mariama Bâ, Aminata Sow Fall, Werewere Liking, pour ne citer que celles-là).. Lilyan Kesteloot rapporte justement que « sur le plan littéraire, les seuls échos féminins connus à ce combat précis pour la réappropriation du corps dans son aspect le plus élémentaire furent ceux de Calixthe Beyala et d'A. Maïga Ka » (2001: 281-82).

Il importe de s'interroger sur les raisons d'une telle désaffection, d'une telle indifférence à l'égard d'une cause qui n'en demeure pas moins importante eu égard au nombre de victimes qu'elle engendre et aux passions qu'elle soulève, puisqu'elle jugule des *a priori* à la fois religieux, juridique et socioculturel. Il est vrai que l'objet d'écriture ne doit pas être imposé aux écrivains par respect pour leur sacro-saint liberté d'expression et pour cette « nécessité intérieure » (Boni 1998: 6) utile à l'écriture. Mais l'écrivain, quel que soit son sexe, ne doit-il pas être aussi cette « bouche des malheurs qui n'ont point de bouche » et « [s]a voix, [être] la liberté de celles qui s'affaissent au cachot du désespoir » (Césaire 1983: 22) ?

Notre corpus s'étale sur trois décennies (de 1968 à 1998 inclusivement) et se compose des deux romans ivoiriens qui, durant cette période, font largement mention de l'excision dans leur trame narrative : *Les Soleils des indépendances* (1968) d'Ahmadou Kourouma et *Rebelle* (1998) de Fatou Kéita. Kourouma est considéré comme l'un des grands écrivains de la Côte d'Ivoire, voire de l'Afrique et même de l'espace francophone[7]. Sa bibliographie impressionnante, qui lui a valu plusieurs prix nationaux et internationaux, n'est plus à présenter. En ce qui concerne Kéita, elle est l'une des figures montantes de cette même littérature et aime « raconter ce que tout le monde préfère taire » selon Érik Orsenna (1998). Elle compte à son actif plusieurs romans de jeunesse, couronnés par les Prix ACCT (Agence de la Francophonie, 1994), UNESCO (1997)..., et *Rebelle*, son premier roman.

Il s'agira de voir quelles sont les représentations de l'excision que ces deux auteurs donnent à lire. Autrement dit, comment cette question est-elle perçue et traitée—en terme de stratégies narratives, textuelles—dans leurs romans retenus au corpus. Et surtout, quels éclairages et perspectives d'avenir proposent-ils, à trente ans d'intervalle (1968-1998), face à ce « fléau » toujours contemporain? Le choix du corpus est également motivé par la critique au féminin qui permettra de rendre compte de l'impact d'une quelconque *valence différentielle* des sexes, puisque les deux auteurs sont de sexes opposés. Nous tiendrons compte à la fois du programme narratif des personnages et de l'énonciation du discours social en filigrane.

Il va sans dire que notre propos n'est pas tant de prendre position ou de condamner que de nous interroger sur les tenants et aboutissants de cette marque corporelle « polysémique »—à plus d'un titre—que la sociologue Martine Lefeuvre-Déotte réduit à une « écriture de la loi ancestrale sur le corps des initiés » (1997: 22). En effet, notre désir de neutralité abonde dans le même sens que le sociologue et économiste Alain Caillé qui estime, dans *La démission des clercs*, que « les sciences sociales [et les sciences humaines] ne sont susceptibles d'une certaine justesse que pour autant qu'elles poursuivent la *Justice* [...] [qu'elles portent] plainte [...] surtout là où tout le monde se tait [et] envisage[nt] l'absolution, ou les circonstances atténuantes là où tout le monde condamne... » (1993: 278-79).

Notre contribution s'articulera autour de trois axes : rappeler, d'abord, les fondements ontologiques et socioculturels de l'excision, avant de préciser les liens entre ces représentations de l'excision et la texture (stratégies narratives, voire textuelles) qu'arborent les deux romans, sans oublier les positions idéologiques des instances narratrices sur la question.

EXCISION: FONDEMENTS ONTOLOGIQUES ET SOCIOCULTURELS

Ce premier point nous permettra de définir l'excision et d'en donner les différents types, puis de rappeler ses représentations sociales généralement admises (dans les sociétés pratiquantes).

Définition et type d'excisions

L'excision, qui fait partie des « altérations réductrices » selon les taxinomies des mutilations sexuelles féminines d'inspiration médicale (Erlich 1991), est appelée aussi « circoncision féminine » dans la terminologie internationale. Depuis quelques années, l'UNICEF a adopté l'appellation de *mutilations génitales féminines (MGF)* (Herzberger-Fofana 2000) pour désigner toutes ces marques, ces blessures corporelles féminines.

Au début des années 1990, environ 80 millions de femmes subissent des MGF. Elles sont originaires d'une centaine de sociétés, elles-mêmes réparties dans plus de 50 États principalement africains situés « dans une vaste zone intertropicale transcontinentale allant, à l'ouest, du Sénégal au Cameroun et, à l'est, de l'Égypte à la Tanzanie » (Erlich 1991: 25). Dans le cas de la Côte d'Ivoire, seules les sociétés situées dans certaines régions du Nord (Malinké, Bambara, etc., communément appelés « Dioula »), et de l'Ouest (Gouro, Guéré, etc.) du pays sont concernées par la question. Mais étant donné les nombreuses migrations interrégionales, au fil des ans, on retrouve des cas d'excision dans les autres régions du pays (le Sud, le Centre et l'Est), même si elle n'y était pas pratiquée auparavant.

Il existe plusieurs taxinomies des pratiques de l'excision. Cette analyse s'inspire de celle de Michel Erlich qui propose une typologie tripartite de ces pratiques, en fonction de leur degré vulnérant :

Type I : l'« excision *a minima* » limitée à l'ablation du capuchon clitoridien, également appelée « circoncision sunna » en raison de sa fréquence dans certaines sociétés musulmanes. C'est la moins grave.

Type II : l'« excision commune » qui comporte l'ablation plus ou moins étendue du clitoris et des petites lèvres. Pratiquée dans de nombreuses sociétés animistes, musulmanes et chrétiennes, c'est la plus répandue et la plus courante d'entre elles.

Type III : l'« infibulation », également appelée « circoncision pharaonique » au Soudan et « circoncision soudanaise » en Égypte, comporte une excision de type II assortie d'une fermeture presque complète de l'orifice vaginal par suture et accolement cicatriciel des grandes lèvres, pour laisser passer le flux menstruel. Ce dernier type est géographiquement limité en Afrique du Nord-Est, Soudan, Érythrée, la Corne de l'Afrique (Somalie, Djibouti, Éthiopie) et exceptionnellement au Mali et au Nigéria du Nord.

Toutes ces opérations se pratiquent dès la naissance jusqu'à l'âge adulte, avec une préférence pour les intervalles de 2 à 4, de 7 à 12 ans. Erlich oppose schématiquement les opérations des sociétés païennes – pré-pubertaires, collectives, ritualisées, intégrées à des initiations de type *rite de passage* – à celles des sociétés musulmanes et chrétiennes, individuelles, peu ritualisées, parfois médicalisées (1991: 45-46). Cette précision nous conduit de plain-pied dans les représentations sociales ou les fondements socioculturels de l'excision.

Fondements socioculturels de l'excision

Les pratiques de l'excision sont souvent justifiées par les mythologies dont les plus célèbres, en ce qui concerne l'Afrique noire, demeurent les séquences des cosmogonies dogon et bambara qui « exaltent la castration primordiale » (Erlich 1991: 12). Il appert de ces récits mythiques que naissent uniquement des êtres androgynes et que seules les altérations sexuelles, la circoncision pour l'homme et l'excision pour la femme, peuvent permettre la distinction des sexes, des genres.

De plus, ces « mythes [cosmogoniques] insistent [en général] sur le jaillisse-ment désordonné de l'énergie créatrice imputable à l'élément féminin heureuse-ment maîtrisable par le pouvoir régulateur des hommes » (Mbow 1999: 72). L'excision, en tant que moyen de cette régulation, apparaît donc comme une nécessité vitale dont l'inexistence pourrait être fatale pour les contrevenantes : « [le] destin [de la femme] s'accomplit par une socialisation matérialisée par le mariage qui neutralise les forces obscures par une sexualité féconde et assure à la femme protection et stabilité sous tutelle masculine » (*ibid.*). Vu son ancrage dans l'imaginaire socioculturel, seul le passage de ce rite, la réussite de cette épreuve qualifiante (au sens sémiotique du terme) octroie aux héroïnes « l'agrégation à une communauté », celle des femmes. D'où l'anxiété des deux mères du corpus à l'idée que leur fille respective ne réussisse pas les épreuves de ce rite. Les croyances autour de l'excision ont également été associées à un pré-tendu caractère religieux, basé sur d'hypothétiques origines sémitiques démen-ties, entre autres, par Awa Thiam dans son essai *Parole aux Négresses* (1978)[8].

L'autre argument fréquemment brandi pour la pérennité de l'excision est la maîtrise de la libido féminine qu'elle infère : une femme non excisée serait une adepte inévitable du dévergondage sexuel. Cette idée est tellement bien ancrée dans les mœurs des sociétés pratiquantes que même plusieurs femmes en sont convaincues. C'est le cas de cette Malienne, licenciée en Sciences économiques, interrogée par Awa Thiam dans *Parole aux Négresses* :

> - J'ai été, dans mon enfance, excisée. [...] Aujourd'hui, je m'estime satisfaite de cette opération que l'on m'a fait subir : l'excision. En effet, si je soutiens un tel argument, c'est parce qu'elle a rempli sa fonction à mon niveau. Voilà quatre ans que je suis divorcée, et pas une seule fois, je n'ai ressenti le désir de courir après un homme, ou tout simplement l'absence de rapports sexuels comme un manque, un manque vital. Cela fait apparaître dans une certaine mesure la fonction de l'excision : elle permet à la femme d'être maîtresse de son corps (1978 : 88).

En somme, les motivations légitimant l'excision sont très souvent « purement et simplement irrationnelles » et traduisent « une certaine conception et vision du monde », qui indexe le clitoris comme élément perturbateur de l'ordre social :

> Les Mossi du Burkina Faso, les Dogon et Bambara du Mali croient que le clitoris constitue un danger pour l'enfant au moment de sa mise au monde. En Éthiopie, selon les populations, un clitoris non coupé finira par prendre les mêmes proportions que le sexe d'un homme. Là, il s'agit d'affirmer l'identité féminine. Mais d'un autre côté, on peut percevoir le clitoris entrer en rivalité avec la verge. Ce que les Bambara veulent exprimer dans sa forme extrême lorsqu'ils affirment que le poison qui sort du clitoris non excisé peut être mortel pour l'homme (Mbow 1999: 74).

Comment ces indices sociaux s'inscrivent-ils dans les textes romanesques ? Autrement dit, que transpirent *les Soleils des Indépendances* et *Rebelle* à propos de l'excision ?

EXCISION ET TEXTURE ROMANESQUE (STRATÉGIES NARRATIVES ET TEXTUELLES)

La narration des deux romans du corpus est assumée par un narrateur extrahétérodiégétique ou narrateur omniscient. La focalisation est par contre variable dans les deux cas. En ce qui concerne les séquences traitant de l'excision, elles sont prises en charge, de ce point de vue, tantôt par ce narrateur-témoin, tantôt par les personnages principaux respectifs, ou encore par les personnages incarnant la Tradition (les mères, la famille élargie, les exciseuses, etc.). Il est intéressant de voir jusqu'à quel point les représentations sociales de l'excision sont explicites, que le schéma culturel est reproduit dans les textes : seule les dépositaires de la Tradition, de cette coutume, peuvent en parler.

Dans les *Soleils des indépendances*, même si le narrateur évoque Salimata dans les deux premiers chapitres, c'est au troisième chapitre (« le cou chargé de carcans hérissés de sortilèges comme le sont de piquants acérés, les colliers du chien chasseur de cynocéphales ») que la question de l'excision est introduite par un *indice* (Barthes 1985: 167-206). Il s'agit de la nuit désagréable que Salimata a passé avec son « éhonté de mari » (Kourouma 1970: 31) « que rien [...] ne préoccupait, rien n'[...]empêchait de dormir, ni l'impuissance, ni les pleurs de Salimata, ni le manquement aux devoirs conjugaux » (*ibid.*). Sa mauvaise humeur favorise l'affluence d'un flot de souvenirs, surtout regrettables, dans son esprit (*ibid.*). Salimata est alors en focalisation sujet sur elle-même, pour emprunter la terminologie de Pierre Vitoux (1982: 359-68). Elle associe l'excision à une expérience tout aussi douloureuse, le viol; les deux étant une aliénation du corps de la femme : « Et le viol! Ses couleurs aussi, ses douleurs, ses crispations. Le viol! Dans le sang et les douleurs de l'excision » (Kourouma 1970: 31). Chez Kourouma, l'une ne vient pas sans l'autre. Ce qui marque une différence d'avec le traitement opéré dans *Rebelle* de Fatou Kéita.

Dans ce deuxième roman du corpus, la question de l'excision occupe une place de choix et est évoquée dès le premier chapitre (sur les trente que compte le texte). La suite du récit (surtout les chapitres trois à cinq) est composée d'autant d'occasions pour l'instance narratrice de mettre en scène les péripéties de la petite Malimouna aux prises avec cette pratique. Mais contrairement à Salimata, qui accepte de subir ce rite initiatique, Malimouna, malgré son jeune âge, refuse de s'y soumettre (Kéita 1998: 15). Elle arrivera à ses fins grâce à la manipulation d'un détail textuel, au sens d'indice, autour duquel s'organise sa rébellion : la connaissance du secret sur la lubricité de l'exciseuse Dimikéla. Malimouna a surpris cette femme, dépositaire de la Tradition et si austère de réputation, en flagrant délit d'ébats amoureux lui étant apparemment proscrits (*ibid.*: 9-10). Grâce à cette information, Malimouna subira une parodie d'excision avec la caution de Dimikéla qui voulait acheter ainsi le silence de la jeune fille. Leur secret sera sauf jusqu'à la nuit de noces de Malimouna : à 14 ans, son père Louma l'a mariée contre son gré à son vieil et riche associé Sando. Plus tard, la découverte de son état de non excisée, cette nuit-là, coûtera à la jeune héroïne l'arrachement à sa terre natale, l'opprobre jeté sur sa mère, Matou, et sa mise en quarantaine dans le village.

Les deux romans sont toutefois très prolixes en ce qui concerne le déroulement de la cérémonie. Leurs descriptions sont, à quelque nuance près, vraisemblables et confirment que seule l'excision de **type II** y est pratiquée. Ces tableaux culturels, comparables à des séquences d'essais ethnologiques, sont souvent précédés de la conception que les instances narratrices ont de la pratique de l'excision. La focalisation est alors déléguée aux personnages qui incarnent la Tradition, en l'occurrence les mères ou les exciseuses. Le dialogue que la mère de Salimata entame avec elle est très éloquent à ce propos : « l'excision est la rupture, elle démarque, elle met fin aux années d'équivoque, d'impureté de jeune fille et après elle vient la vie de femme (Kourouma 1970: 32-33) » ou « le clitoris [est] considéré comme l'impureté, la confusion, l'imperfection » (*ibid.*: 34).

Toutes choses qui confirment les représentations sociales couramment admises évoquées plus haut.

POSITIONS IDÉOLOGIQUES (DISCOURS SOCIAL)

La pratique de l'excision, en tant qu'habitus demeure si importante que, dans les cultures concernées, ne pas s'y soumettre conduit à une marginalisation. Dans les deux textes, cette cause est entendue, car les sociotextes présentent des structures sociales qui légitiment cette pratique : « les règles y étaient établies, et personne ne les remettait en cause, chacun connaissant son rôle et sa place dans la communauté » (Kourouma 1970: 5). C'est pourquoi Salimata, jeune fille, n'éprouve aucune résistance à subir cette épreuve qui fera d'elle une « vraie femme ». Elle rend sa mère très malheureuse, d'ailleurs, lorsqu'elle ne revient pas du camp avec ses camarades d'initiation, à cause de sa défaillance physique durant l'opération.

Quant à Matou, la mère de Malimouna, elle jure d'éviter l'opprobre à sa fille, fut-ce à son cœur défendant, car c'est désastreux de se dérober à l'excision, cette « épreuve si capitale dans la vie d'une femme » (Kéita 1998: 18). Dimikéla, l'exciseuse, abonde dans le même sens, lorsqu'elle rappelle à Malimouna « qu'une femme qui ne subit pas cette épreuve ne peut être maîtresse de son corps et ne peut devenir qu'une dévergondée » (*ibid.*: 21). Un discours assez paradoxal pour la jeune Malimouna qui ne manque pas de le rappeler à l'exciseuse Dimikéla : « Si je ne le fais pas, est-ce que je me comporterai comme toi avec Seynou? » (ibid.). Une réaction qui annonce les points de divergence entre les positions idéologiques des deux romans sur la question de l'excision.

Salimata ou quand le viol « légitime » l'excision

Kourouma est l'un des rares romanciers francophones[9] à avoir accordé autant d'importance à l'excision dans une œuvre fictive au point d'en faire l'un des éléments—sinon l'élément catalyseur principal—de la trame narrative : l'excision favorise le viol et conduit à la stérilité de Salimata, privant ainsi Fama, le prince de Togobala, de descendants.

Cette attention ne suffit pas à faire de lui un « chantre » ou un « abolitionniste » de l'excision, même s'il met à nu en quelque sorte les conséquences psychologiques de l'épreuve. En effet, Salimata est traumatisée par cette expérience, jusque dans sa vie d'adulte : « Sa tête gronda comme battue, agitée par un essaim de souvenirs. L'excision! Les scènes, ses odeurs, les couleurs de l'excision » (Kourouma 1970: 31). Le malaise qu'on éprouve à situer Kourouma à l'un ou l'autre pôle est exacerbé par des réflexions quelque peu sexistes sur le rôle de la femme dans la société : « [B]alayer, épousseter, laver, placer ceci, déplacer cela seyaient mieux à une femme [porteuse de pagne] » (*Kourouma* 67) ; « la soumission de femme, sa servitude sont les Commandements d'Allah, absolument essentiels parce que se muant en force, en valeur, en grâce, en qualité » (*Kourouma* 44).

De plus, pourquoi avoir associé le viol à l'excision? Est-ce pour atténuer les effets négatifs de cette pratique, tant est qu'il serait dans une logique de dénonciation de cette altération sexuelle? Malgré ce fait, il est difficile de le considérer comme un abolitionniste de l'excision.

Malimouna ou la « conscience féminine » contre l'excision

Quant à la jeune Malimouna, elle fait preuve, assez tôt, d'une conscience lucide de son corps, surtout de son clitoris, « ce petit bout d'elle-même […] qu'elle savait à présent qu'il était en effet très doux au toucher » (Kéita 1998: 33), comme le lui avait confié son amie Sanita, la citadine (Kéita 18). Elle est tellement attachée à cette caractéristique féminine, à l'importance que revêt la présence de cet organe qu'elle ose partager avec sa mère, d'abord, avec Dimikéla l'exciseuse, ensuite, son désir de se soustraire au rite initiatique de l'excision, au grand dam de ces deux chantres de l'excision. En effet, selon la terminologie de Fatou Sarr (1999 : 80), ces deux femmes sont des « culturalistes » par opposition aux « abolitionnistes ». Les premières rejettent toute répression de l'excision par respect des valeurs traditionnelles, les secondes considèrent les mutilations génitales comme une violence faite à la femme, une atteinte à son intégrité avec un impact néfaste sur sa santé.

L'idéologie « rebelle » en filigrane dans ce roman de Kéita s'immisce insidieusement dans le discours dominant afin d'en démonter les postulats. C'est ainsi que, contrairement à Salimata de Kourouma qui, « malmenée par la douleur, avait rencontré le malheur » sur le champ de l'excision et en est devenu stérile, Malimouna enfreint les règles ancestrales, avec la complicité de l'exciseuse, garante de la perpétuation de cette tradition. L'héroïne agit ainsi sans que cela n'altère son identité féminine, comme le prévoient les mythes cosmogoniques, ne la prive de certaines capacités féminines, dont la maternité, et de vertus universelles telles la fidélité, pour ne citer que ces exemples. En effet, elle a eu des rapports sexuels normaux, s'est mariée et a donné naissance à de beaux enfants. En plus, « c'était une femme rangée et une mère exemplaire » (Kéita 1998: 219).

Les arguments avancés à l'envi pour justifier cette mainmise « patriarcale » sur le corps féminin sont battus en brèche par le parcours narratif du principal protagoniste. L'instance narratrice indique une autre voie à suivre, celle de la révolte que le titre *Rebelle*, tout à fait programmatique, permet d'envisager *a priori*. De plus, l'implication sociale effective de Malimouna dans un cadre associatif (Association d'Aide à la Femme en Difficulté) pour le mieux-être des femmes, qui comprend la lutte pour la cessation de l'excision, informe le lecteur quant à la position adoptée par ce roman de Fatou Kéita dans le débat sur l'excision : à savoir, celle d'une remise en cause des habitus, d'un recadrage de la perception de cette pratique ancestrale, par les femmes elles-mêmes, d'abord, et par le reste de la société également. En effet, ces propos plein d'humour de Malimouna sont sans équivoque à ce sujet :

> Dieu avait créé [les femmes] avec un clitoris. Pourquoi, et au nom de quoi, un simple être humain pouvait-il décider que l'œuvre du « Tout-Puissant » était imparfaite? Comment pouvait-on croire à la fois en Dieu et en de telles absurdités? Certes, il y avait des erreurs de la nature qui faisaient que certains êtres naissaient avec des malformations, des infirmités, mais de là à faire croire que la moitié de la population mondiale—c'est-à-dire toutes les femmes de la terre—avait une même malformation! Il y avait une exagération dont elles se rendaient compte. [...] leur retirer cet organe singulièrement érogène qui, autrement, ne pouvait que les entraîner à la luxure et à la débauche... Mais tout ceci était faux [...]. Pourquoi, après tout, avait-on peur de la sexualité féminine? Pourquoi une femme ne devait-elle pas ressentir le même plaisir qu'un homme? On disait la femme faible, mais qu'en était-il des hommes auxquels, dans certaines cultures, il fallait cacher toutes les parties du corps féminin, y compris les cheveux, de peur de susciter chez eux des réactions incontrôlables? Qui donc, finalement, était incontrôlable, l'homme ou la femme? (Kéita 218-19)

CONCLUSION

À l'instar de *Présence Africaine* qui a consacré plus d'un dossier à la problématique de l'excision (n° 141, 1987; n° 160, 1999), compte tenu de la forte médiatisation de « l'affaire de l'exciseuse de Paris », et en réaction « aux analyses à l'emporte-pièce » du genre « l'excision serait un fait culturel rétrograde africain, dont l'Afrique devrait faire à présent l'économie et le monde civilisé serait là pour le lui rappeler » (1999: 29), nous avons voulu nous mettre à l'écoute de ces voix romanesques pour mieux comprendre ce phénomène. Nous comptions éviter ainsi le piège de l'ethnocentrisme.

Le constat global est que le traitement de ce problème a évolué positivement d'un roman à un autre même si, dans les deux cas, l'excision est perçue négativement par les deux protagonistes principales : la première, Salimata, à cause des conséquences désastreuses (stérilité) sur sa vie de couple, et la seconde, Malimouna, pour le principe de conserver son intégrité physique.

Cette analyse non exhaustive, révèle, d'une part, que le salut des femmes face à l'excision est passé de l'acceptation-résignation (Salimata) à la révolte (Malimouna). Les deux auteurs admettent implicitement, toutefois, l'ancrage profond de cette pratique dans les habitus de ces sociétés. Néanmoins, l'immensité des obstacles surtout socioculturels à franchir—pour celles qui le désirent—n'est pas insurmontable, du point de vue de la romancière, mais passe forcément par la sensibilisation aux conséquences néfastes de l'excision sur le plan médical, et par l'éducation, car « [l]a volonté de purifier, de préserver la chasteté, la dignité de la femme en contrôlant sa sexualité est une véritable forme de violence exercée sur la liberté, le corps et la psychologie de la femme. Mais puisque elle-même se trouve au cœur de la perpétuation de certains rites comme l'excision, seule son éducation peut constituer le facteur décisif de la transformation sociale » (Mbow 1999: 72).

D'autre part, Fatou Keita innove en dotant l'héroïne à exciser—même très jeune —, d'une conscience de sa féminité et donc de son identité, et d'une volonté farouche de défendre son intégrité au détriment de « l'honneur » de sa famille. Est-ce donc le primat du sujet (féminin) sur le collectif ? Toutefois, « le roman de notre temps ét[ant] rongé par les remises en question et les incertitudes de l'esprit moderne » (Raymond 2000: 21), le projet ainsi proposé n'est-il pas utopique, d'autant plus que certains acquis de cette lutte contre les mutilations génitales féminines sont remis en cause[10] ?

Notes

1. Fatou Kéita, *Rebelle*, Paris/Abidjan, Présence Africaine/NÉI, 1998, p. 218.
2. Terme désignant la Côte d'Ivoire.
3. Le terme *excision* est employé ici dans un sens générique pour désigner toutes ces marques corporelles initiatiques ou non subies par les femmes.
4. Voir Herzberger-Fofana, plus précisément le chapitre sept, pour plus de précision sur la politique des États africains à ce sujet.
5. Annette Mbaye d'Erneville, Aïcha Fofana, Kesso Barry, Aminata Ka Maïga, Ndiaye Boury, Ahmadou Kourouma, Calixthe Beyala, Fatou Kéita.
6. En plus de dénoncer toute forme d'exploitation du corps féminin par le système patriarcal, Beyala propose une autre interprétation de la fonction de l'excision : dans son roman *Tu t'appelleras Tanga* (1988), elle met l'accent sur l'aspect mercantile de la pratique de l'excision.
7. Défini comme une « réalité non exclusivement géographique ni même linguistique, mais aussi culturelle [car] elle réunit tous ceux qui, de près ou de loin, éprouvent ou expriment une certaine appartenance à la langue française ou aux cultures francophones » (Têtu 1997: 14).
8. Grâce aux témoignages d'érudits musulmans dépositaires du savoir de cette religion et culture musulmane, à ceux d'illustres historiens, Awa Thiam a réussi à démontrer dans son essai que les origines de l'excision sont loin d'être religieuses. De plus, plu-

sieurs travaux d'envergure confirment le fait que « l'excision existerait depuis plus de 2 500 ans avant l'apparition de l'Islam et du christianisme » (Jean Pliya 1998: 3). Lire aussi à ce propos le dossier préparé par Pierrette Herzberger-Fofana sur les « Mutilations Génitales Féminines » (2000).

9.   C'est ainsi, même si, selon Lylian Kesteloot, seul le Somalien Nuruddin Farah (*Sardines*, 1981) a su « rendre compte de la condition féminine jusque dans sa souffrance la plus aiguë et les révoltes les plus radicales. Il dépasse sur ce point toutes les tentatives (méritoires, certes) des écrivains francophones » (2001: 282).

10.   En effet, le projet de code de statut personnel islamique du Collectif islamique pour la réforme du code de la famille (CIRCOF), au Sénégal, proposait en juillet 2003 « l'abrogation de la loi de 1999 contre l'excision » (Arab 2003: 2).

Works Cited

Arab, Adel. « Droits-Sénégal : Les femmes rejettent le projet de code de statut personnel islamique ». *Inter Press Service News Agency*. 3 juil. 2003. Dakar. 11 août 2003 <http://www.ipsnews.net/fr/print.asp ?idnews=1716>

Bâ, Mariama. *Une si longue lettre*. Dakar : Nouvelles Éditions Africaines (NÉA), 1979.

---. *Un chant écarlate*. Dakar: NÉA, 1981.

Barry, Kesso. *Kesso, princesse peuhle*. Paris : Seghers, 1988.

Barthes, Roland. « Introduction à l'analyse structurale des récits ». *L'aventure sémiologique*. Paris : Seuil, 1985 : 167-206.

Beyala, Calixthe. *Tu t'appelleras Tanga*. Paris : Albin Michel, 1988.

Boni, Tanella. « Écritures et savoirs : écrire en Afrique a-t-il un sens? ». *Mots pluriels Revue électronique de Lettres*. (8 octobre 1998), University of Western Australia. 08 juillet 2003 <http://www.arts.uwa.edu.au/MotsPluriels/MP898tb1.html>

Boury, Ndiaye. *Collier de chevilles*. Dakar : NÉA, 1983.

Caillé, Alain. *La démission des Clercs*. Paris: La Découverte, 1993.

Césaire, Aimé. *Cahier d'un retour au pays natal*. Paris: Éditions Présence Africaine, 1983 [©1947].

Collectif. « Dossier Excision ». *Présence Africaine* 141 (1987): 161-80.

Dossier : Excision. Présence Africaine nº 160, Paris : Éditions Présence Africaine, 1999.

Erlich, Michel. *Les mutilations sexuelles*. Paris : Presses Universitaires de France, 1991.

Flaubert, Gustave. *Madame Bovary*. Paris : Société Les Belles lettres, 1945.

Fonfana, Aicha. *Mariage, on copie*. Bamako : Jamana, 1994.

Hamblet, Edwin. *La littérature canadienne francophone*. Paris: Hatier, 1987.

Herzberger-Fofana, Henriette. « Dossier. Les Mutilations Génitales Féminines (MGF) ». *Lire les femmes écrivains et les littératures africaines*. juillet 2000. University of Western Australia. 07 juillet 2003 <http://www.arts.uwa.edu.au/AFLIT/MGF1.html>

Joyce, James. *Ulysses*. New York: Modern Library, 1934.

Ka Maïga, Aminata. *La Voie du Salut suivi de Le Miroir de la vie*. Paris : Présence Africaine, 1985.

Kafka, Franz. *Le procès*, traduction de Alexandre Vialatte. Paris : Gallimard, 1972.

Kéita, Fatou. *Rebelle*. Abidjan/Paris: Nouvelles Éditions Ivoiriennes/Présence Africaine, 1998.

Kesteloot, Lylian. *Histoire de la littérature négro-africaine. Histoire littéraire de la franco-phonie*. Paris : Karthala/AUF, 2001.

Kourouma, Ahmadou. *Les Soleils des indépendances*. Paris: Seuil, 1970 [©1968].

Lefeuvre-Déotte, Martine. *L'excision en procès : un différend culturel?* Paris/Montréal: L'Harmattan, 1997.

Liking, Werewere, *Elle sera de jaspe et de corail. Journal d'une misovire....* Paris : L'Harmattan, 1983.

Mbaye D'Erneville, Annette. *La bague de cuivre et d'argent*. Dakar : NÉA, 1983.

Mbow, Penda. « Pénaliser un fait culturel : quelle solution à l'excision? ». *Présence Africaine* 160 (1999).

Orsenna, Érik. « Quatrième de couverture ». *Rebelle*. Abidjan/Paris: Nouvelles Éditions Ivoiriennes/Présence Africaine, 1998.

Pliya, Jean. « L'excision dans les sociétés africaines ». *Le Matinal*. 4 novembre 1998.

Robert, Marthe. *Roman des origines et origines du roman*. Paris: Grasset, 1972.

Raymond, Michel. *Le roman*, 2e édition. Paris: Armand Colin/HER, 2000.

Sarr, Fatou. « De la survivance d'un mode de pensée archaïque au contrôle de la sexualité féminine : la question de l'excision ». *Présence Africaine* 160 (1999).

Senghor, S. Léopold. « Femme noire ». *Chants d'ombre*. Paris : Seuil, 1945.

Sow Fall, Aminata. *Le revenant*. Dakar : NÉA, 1976.

---. *La grève des Bàttu ou les déchets humains*. Dakar : NÉA, 1979.

Stendhal. *Le rouge et le noir*. Paris : Aubry, 1943.

Tétu, Michel. *Qu'est-ce que la francophonie?* Paris: Hachette-Edicef, 1997.

Thiam, Awa. *La parole aux Négresses*. Paris: Gonthier/Denöel, 1978.

Vitoux, Pierre. « Le jeu de la focalisation ». *Poétique* 51 (1982): 359-68.

Editor's Recapitulation
Representation(s) of Excision in the Ivorian Novel: From Ahmadou Kourouma's *The Suns of Independence* (1968) to Fatou Keita's *Rebellious Woman* (1998)

Bernadette K. Kassi

"God created women with a clitoris. Why, and in the name of what, can an ordinary human being decide that the divine work is imperfect?"

—Fatou Keita

Bernadette Kassi begins with Martha Robert's assertion according to which the novel continues to evolve into larger and larger areas of human experience, which it then reproduces, through interpretation from several points of view: moral, historical, theological, and philosophical (1972: 14). Although earlier novelists like Gustave Flaubert, James Joyce, and Frantz Kafka had focused on the aesthetic aspects of the novel, continues Kassi, yet today the discipline of the Humanities has assigned other roles to the novel, namely, that of reflecting its era and society (Raymond 2000: 21). Literature, says Edwin Hamblet, is, sometimes, the best way to determine the level of civilization of a given people (1987:6), without necessarily adopting hook, line, and sinker realism à la Stendhal, for the nineteenth-century French realist, also known as Henri Beyle, has often been quoted as having said that every novel is a faithful mirror of its society.

This assertion is all the more true in the case of women, that other half of humanity, adds Kassi, which has been represented in literature over the centuries in diverse, plural, and contrasted forms, such that the gap between the real and the fictional is significant. Women have for long been sublimated, mystified, and rendered mythical by phallocentric writings. In the case of African literature in which woman as Object has become the Subject of writing, women have often been unrealistically portrayed in male-dominated literature, if one takes Senghor's poem, "Femme noire," as an example of this kind of sublimation, mystification, and mythologizing of women. And this is particularly the case in the West African country of the Ivory Coast.

Regarding excision today, which is often termed "genital mutilation," a term coined by the United Nations, and which for the sake of objectivity Kassi calls "body marks," excision has all but lost the spiritual and initiatory aura attached to it, especially when it is practiced in urban areas or in the African diaspora.

Nonetheless, the practice continues to receive critics' passionate attention, despite several legal depositions, nationally and internationally, calling for its abolition. In 1998, the Ivorian parliament adopted a law abolishing excision, in keeping with several other laws worldwide calling for the elimination of violence towards women and children.

However, the silence of African literary artists on the subject of excision is baffling, especially those female writers that one could call pioneers of literature on women—Mariama Bâ, Aminata Sow Fall, Werewere Liking, etc. In 1998, only about ten Francophone authors, including Maïga Ka (1985), Kesso Barry (1988), Calixthe Beyala, and, of course, the two authors under study here in this chapter, Ahmadou Kourouma and Fatou Kéita, have dealt with excision. Even then, it is only Calixthe Beyala and A. Maïga Ka of the other authors, other than Kourouma and Kéita, who have focused on excision as such in their writing, instead of merely making cursory mention of it (Kesteloot 2001: 281-82). Why is there this dearth, one would ask, if not due to the legal, religious, and socio-cultural implications of the subject of excision?

In this study, it will be necessary to try to establish the reasons for the neglect and the indifference with regard to a cause that remains valid, due to the number of women that continue to fall victim to it, due to the passion it engenders, and which *a priori* impacts religious, legal, and socio-cultural domains. True, one may not impose on the writer her or his subject, due to her or his inalienable freedom of choice of subject and style of expression (Boni 1991: 6). Yet every writer, regardless of her or his sex, should also be, in the words of the famous Martiniquan poet Aimé Césaire, "la bouche des malheurs qui n'ont point de bouche" and "[s]a voix [être] la liberté de celles qui s'affaissent au cachot du désespoir" (1983: 22) ["the mouth of those calamities that have no mouth," and "(his) voice the freedom for those who break down in the prison holes of despair"]. (See Aimé Césaire. *Notebook of a Return to the Native Land* 13 (translated and edited by Clayton Eshleman and Annette Smith. Middleton, Conn.: Wesleyan University Press).

This chapter will study excision in African literature from 1968-1998, specifically the narrative (textual) representation of excision in *Les Soleils des indépendences* by Ahmadou Kourouma (1968), and *Rebelle* by Fatou Kéita (1998), in order to determine future prognosis of the practice. Both authors are very well known; on one hand Kourouma for his long standing reputation as one of the greatest Ivorian writers, his impressive bibliography which has won national and international literary prizes; and on the other hand up and coming Kéita for her controversial writings (Orsenna 1998), her novels for young adults [these have also won literary prizes of the Francophone world (1994) and the UNESCO (1998)], and *Rebelle*, her first novel.

In this chapter, Kassi attempts to see how each of the two authors represents excision in fictional writing, that is the style of presentation, and the insights and perspectives for the future brought to bear on this subject. Although the writings of both authors are separated by three whole decades (1968-1998), yet the issue of excision remains contemporary. Second, from a gynocentric point of view, this study will seek to determine the dichotomy between male and female views of the subject. Note that Kourouma is male, whereas Kéita is female. The strategy will be to follow the narrative and also the implicit social ramifications.

It goes without saying that this chapter has no intention of taking a position, or of condemning anything or anyone (see Alain Caillé 1993: 278-79). On the contrary, the goal is to interrogate the ins and outs of these body marks with multiple names, which sociologist Martina Lefeuvre-Déotte has referred to as "the inscription of ancestral law on the bodies of the initiates" (1997: 22).

The following three imperatives are in order in this study: recall of the ontological and socio-cultural foundations of excision; the links between the representations of excision and the texture (read narrative, textual strategies) of the two novels under study, and the narrative ideological positions on the issue of excision.

EXCISION: ITS ONTOLOGICAL AND SOCIO-CULTURAL FOUNDATIONS

To begin with, what is excision? What are the different types of excision? How do they generally present in societies that practice excision?

Definition and Types of Excision

According to the medical taxonomies of female sexual mutilations, inspired by Michel Erlich's work (1991), excision, also known as female circumcision in international circles, is part of the general body of over-simplistic transformations of the woman's body. For many years now UNICEF has adopted the appellation *female genital mutilation* (FGM) (Herzberger-Fonfana 2000) to refer to all these marks and wounds on the female body.

In the early 1990s, about 80 million women were excised in about 100 societies in more than 50 states principally located in sub-Saharan Africa (Erlich 1991: 25). In the Ivory Coast, excision is practiced by the Northern ethnic groups, the Malinké and Bambara tribes, etc., commonly referred to as the Dioula, and in the West by the Guoro, Guéré, etc. However, pockets of Ivorian groups that practice excision, who did not always do so before, can also be found in the South, the East, and the Centre, due to years of interregional migrations.

There are many terms for the description of excision, but this study will treat three broad types recommended by Michel Erlich, types which reflect the degree of the cutting:

Type 1: *Minimal Excision*, the least invasive of all the types of excision, is limited to the removal of the hood of the clitoris; it is also called "Sunna circumcision," given that it is frequently practiced in certain Islamic societies.

Type 11: *Ordinary Excision*, the most wide-spread and the most common of all types of excision, this involves a more or less extended removal of the clitoris and the small labia, and is practiced in many animist, Islamic, and Christian societies.

Type 111: *Infibulation*, also known as "pharonic circumcision" in the Sudan and in Egypt as the "Sudanese circumcision," involves all of the **Type 11** along with a near-complete closure of the vaginal orifice and the scaring of the big labia, except for a small outlet for the menstrual fluid to get out. Geographically speaking, this type of excision is prevalent in North-Eastern Africa, the Sudan, Eritrea, and in the Horn of Africa—Somalia, Djibouti, and Ethiopia—, with particular frequency in Mali and Northern Nigeria.

These types of circumcision can take place anywhere from childhood to adulthood, usually and preferably between ages 2-4 years, and 7-12 years. There are two broad categories of excision, according to Erlich who makes a distinction between those tied to ceremonies of initiation, pre-puberty rites of passage, community and ritual practices in traditional societies; and the others having to do with Moslem and Christian traditions, which are often done for individual or personal reasons, and which are barely tied to any kind of ritual, and sometimes carried out as medical procedures (1991:45-46). But, what are the social representations and the sociocultural foundations for excision?

Sociocultural Foundations of Excision

The practice of excision is justified in black Africa by mythologies, notably the Dogon and Bambara myths of origin, according to which humans are born androgynous and only male and female transformations, circumcision for men and excision for women, can help to finally distinguish the individual sexually and by gender.

The same myths also insist that woman is created wild, full of uncontrollable female creative energy which only the male principle can check and control (Mbow 1999:72). Hence the belief that excision is a necessity for women, and that those girls who do not get excised are in true mortal danger (ibid.). What is more, marriage allows the neutralization of the evil forces, through a fertile sexuality under the control of a man. According to the socio-cultural imaginary then, only marriage, protection, and stability under a man can save a woman from these perceived dangers. One does not become a woman in the community without this operation. Thus, the two mothers in the texts under study in this chapter are forever anxious that their daughters pass through this rite of passage, successfully. Some groups have as well adduced a religious reason for excision, fielding the hypothesis that excision has some Semitic origins. However, Awa Thiam, among many other scholars, has discredited the validity of such a claim in her essay, *Parole aux Négresses* (1978).

The third argument often adduced to explain the persistence of excision is woman's need to be saved from her high libido, her excessive sex drive which, without excision, is uncontrollable. This belief is so wide spread in communities that practice excision that many women have come to believe it too, as Awa Thiam has noted in an interview with a Malian woman with a university degree in Economics, interrogated and recorded in her book *Parole aux Negresses* (1978:88).

In sum, reasons for excision are, to say the least, irrational, pure and simple; they go with world views, which point at the clitoris as an element of social disorder. These beliefs are alive and well among the Mossi of Burkina Faso, the Dogon and Bambara of Mali, and are existent in Ethiopia too (Mbow 1999:74).

How do our two authors, Kourouma and Fatou, treat excision in their novels, respectively *Les Soleils des Indépendences* and *Rebelle*?

EXCISION AND FICTIONAL TEXTURE (NARRATIVE AND TEXTUAL STRATEGIES)

The two authors, Kourouma and Kéita, both make use of an omniscient narrator; however the focus is variable in each writer. In the relevant passages or sections of the novels, excision is seen from time to time through the omniscient narrator-observer, sometimes through the major characters, and at other times through the characters that assure traditional or generational continuity—mothers, the extended family, or the sage women who carry out the operations of excision, etc.

It is interesting to note the extent to which the social representations of excision are made explicit in the texts, reproducing the natural ambiance, and allowing only the trustees of tradition and custom to talk about it.

Les Soleils des indépendences: The major character Salimata is present in the first two chapters, but it is in the third that excision comes up, thanks to a *sign* (Barthes 1985: 167-206); Salimata associates excision to marital rape earlier experienced at the hands of her husband. Rape and excision both spell invasion of the female body, in her view. In Kourouma's novel, rape and excision go hand in hand, for both are associated with pain, blood, tension, and contraction, all of which are in contrast to Kéita's treatment of excision in her own novel.

Rebelle: In this novel composed of thirty chapters, excision is evoked right from the first chapter, and continues, particularly in chapters 3-5, which treat the details of this practice for the heroine Malimouna. Excision is a matter of choice in this novel, contrary to Salimata's case in Kourouma's novel. Salimata accepts the rite of passage in *Les Soleils des indépendences*, but Malimouna in Kéita's novel, *Rebelle*, does not accept excision and refuses to undergo the rite of passage, although young, thanks to a narrative detail presented as a *sign*: the knowledge of the secret of the sage woman Dimikéla's lustfulness. Malimouna stumbled on Dimikéla, also a well-known staunch guardian of tradition, openly and without shame savoring with a man an amorous encounter forbidden to her, Malimouna (Kéita 1998: 9-10). To buy Malimouna's silence, the excision woman enters into a duplicity with Malimouna in which the excision woman 'fakes' the operation on her. Their secret duplicity would remain inviolable until Malimouna's wedding night. At the age of 14 years, her father Louman had married her to a wealthy old associate of his, Sando. When the deceit is finally uncovered, the heroine Malimouna and her family suffer shame and she is ostracized in her village.

All the same, both novels are verbose in their description of the ceremony. The two descriptions, which sound like ethnological material, are close, true to life, and show that only **Type 11** form of excision is practiced. The cultural scenes, which read like sequences of ethnological essays, are often preceded by the author or narrator's ideological conception of the practice of excision. Women who perform the operation and women who maintain generational continuity, like the mothers or the women who carry out the operation, are often the authorial personas. Salimata's mother explains to her what the operation is all about, adding that it saves a woman from unstable and impure days of girlhood, transforming her into a real woman (Kourouma 1970: 32-33). The clitoris is represented as impure, a source of confusion and abject imperfection (Kourouma 1970: 34).

IDEOLOGICAL POSITIONS (SOCIAL DISCOURSE)

The practice of excision as a habitus remains so significant that in the cultures where it takes place, one is marginalized merely from refusing to undergo the operation. In the two texts studied, it is evident that social structures in place legitimize the practice. That explains why Salimata shows no resistance to undergoing this rite of passage that should turn her into a "real woman." Her mother is, however, distressed when Salimata does not return with her age mates from the excision camp, due to her blackout during the operation.

As for Matou, Malimouna's mother, she swears to see to the success of her own daughter, even against this daughter's will; it is an operation that is just that important a rite of passage in the life of a girl (Kéita 1998: 18). Dimikéla, the sage woman, also instructs Malimouna on the importance of excision as a controlling element in the sexually wild nature of the woman. Malimouna, having witnessed the excision woman Dimikéla's delight with her lover wonders aloud if the excision would not rob her of her own delight with her own man Seynou (1998: 21). This reaction from Malimouna marks the point of ideological difference between the two novels on the subject of excision.

Salimata, or when Rape "legitimizes" Excision

Kourouma is one of the rare male Francophone writers, who has made excision one, if not *the*, principal thematic subject of his novel. According to Kourouma, it is excision that makes rape possible, and leads to Salimata's sterility, thus preventing Fama, the Prince of Togobala, from having descendants.

Just because Kourouma shows the psychological consequences of excision does not make him an "abolitionist" of excision. Salimata is traumatized by her childhood experience well into adulthood (Kourouma 1970: 31). Nonetheless, his sexist views on the role of the African woman, dictated by the commandments of Allah, to submit to the man, and wearing her pagne, to sweep, dust, wash, pick up, and move this and that, make it difficult to position him in the eyes of many critics (44, 67).

Then again, why associate rape with excision? Is it so as to attenuate the negative effects of this practice, making it possible to denounce sexual transformations? Even with that argument, it is still difficult to see Kourouma as an abolitionist of excision.

Malimouna or the "Feminine Consciousness" against Excision

As for Kéita's heroine Malimouna, very early in life, she manifests consciousness of her body, particularly of her clitoris, thanks to her city friend Sanita who showed her how pleasant it is to the touch (1998:18; 33). She is so attached to this little organ of her body that she shares with her mother and the sage woman, such that she is prepared not to take part in the rite of passage, to the great displeasure of these two 'pillars' of excision, whom Fatou Sarr has called "culturalists," as opposed to "abolitionists," (1999: 80). The ones consider genital mutilations as violence done to a woman, and a shot at her integrity with a nefarious impact on her health, whereas the others reject all repressions of excision out of respect for traditional values.

The "rebel" ideology, implicit in the discussion of excision in Kéita's novel, insidiously enters into the primary discussion, in order to destroy its axioms. That is why, contrary to Kourouma's Salimata, who becomes sterile on the excision grounds, Malimouna goes against traditional laws, in complicity with the sage woman, who ordinarily maintains tradition. Malimouna does not change her feminine identity, her feminine qualities as stipulated by cosmogonic myths, such as motherhood, nor does she contravene such a universal value as fidelity to her man, etc. Malimouna was able to have normal sexual relations with a man, got married and had beautiful children, and has been a well-adjusted woman and an exemplary mother (1998: 219).

The arguments often readily advanced to justify "patriarchal" domination of the female body are instantly erased by the narrative journey of the principal protagonist. The rhetorical title, *Rebelle a priori* prescribes revolt as the alternative approach to the practice of excision. What is more, Malimouna's adherence to the Association for Battered Women, which seeks the better-being of women and the cessation of excision, shows the authorial position on the subject of excision. Fatou Kéita would like women to reconsider habitus, and change perception of this traditional practice, first by women, to be followed subsequently by the rest of the society.

With humor, Kéita asks why anyone would suppose that God is capable of imperfect work when it is God that created woman. Why do societies think that women—which count as much as 50% of humanity—can all have a particular imperfection? Why, Kéita asks, do societies want to cut this erotic part of woman? Why are people afraid of female sexuality? Why men are they afraid of controlling themselves and so seek to cover up women from head to toe? Ironically, concludes Kéita, men still view women as the weaker sex ....!? (218-219).

In conclusion, this study has attempted to examine the issue of excision, in order to better understand the phenomenon of excision, through the study of the two novels, and in that way steer clear of falling into the trap of ethnocentrism. But, excision certainly remains a hot topic in Africa. Little wonder that *Présence Africaine* has devoted many numbers of its illustrious journal to excision (no. 141, 1987; no. 160, 1999). Both heroines, Kourouma's Salimata and her acceptance-resignation stance and Kéita's Malimouna and her revolt, view excision negatively; Salimata's view is due to its disastrous consequences on a married couple (sterility) and Malimouna's view is due to her principled belief in her inalienable right to conserve her physical integrity. Both authors, Kourouma and Kéita, demonstrate implicitly the prevalence of the subject of excision in the social fabric of their society. For Kéita, the huge problem posed by excision is not insurmountable, and can be achieved through education; making the populace aware of the health problems it poses, and the fact that the mere wish to violently control a woman's chastity and dignity by physical force is violence against her liberty, body, and psychology. Now the education of the woman is cardinal and paramount, given that women perpetuate the practice of excision (Mbow 1999: 72). In this wise, Malimouna's consciousness of her body and female identity right from an early age, and her adamancy to defend her integrity at the risk of falling out with her family, augurs well for the future for women. Yet is it a mere utopia to suppose that things might change when the modern era is so unstable and so full of constant shifts in positions, which do not spare laws already put in place against forms of female genital mutilations?

- Ada Uzoamaka Azodo

PART FOUR

SOCIAL CONSTRUCTIONS OF HOMOSEXUAL, LESBIAN, BISEXUAL, AND TRANSVESTITE IDENTITIES

Gay Male and Female Bodies and the Politics of Gender and Sexual Identity and Representation

Chapter 11

"She doesn't know the truth about me": "[T]he shaping presence" of the Closet in Amma Darko's *Beyond the Horizon*

M. Catherine Jonet

This essay brings two twentieth-century figures alongside each other. It brings the image and the mythology of the homosexual closet—that cultural space where homosexuality is supposed to quietly subsist on the edges and out of sight of dominant society—next to the image and the mythology of the West African woman trafficked into prostitution in Western Europe. She, too, is supposed to quietly exist at the periphery and beyond the view of society and its culturally sanctified "norms." Neither of these figures are generally thought of as inhabiting approximate locations. Neither is expected to intersect, much less parallel. But, these figures do intersect and parallel in Amma Darko's novel, *Beyond the Horizon*. They intersect and parallel in such a way that their cultural subject positions reveal how exploitation is built on secrets, acts of shaming, and the dispossession of certain identities for a society's own reward. It is one thing to discuss the disadvantages, the presence and issues surrounding the prostituting of West African women in Germany, but it is another to discuss the privileges and gains others receive by locating these women in that exploited, unspoken of, and maligned positionality. Darko's novel does speak of it. She does address the matrix of exploitation that dares not speak its name.

The representation of homosexual identities in West African fiction is almost non-existent. Cultural and legal practices not only keep homosexuality closeted, but they also keep it unarticulated and unexpressed. Moreover, discourses in many West African nations attribute homosexuality to colonialism. While constructions of "gay" identities in sub-Saharan Africa are linked to the performance of such identities in the West, the claim that homosexuality is a colonialist project participates in the cultural and legal suppression of both same-sex desire and homosexual identities in West Africa. More often than not, it is *homophobia*—not homosexuality—that is the attribute of colonialism. The colonial project rendered indigenous identities, practices, and gender relations that did not fit its own paradigms suspect, abnormal, unwanted, and often outlawed. Homophobia has become naturalized. It is now normalized and operates in many cultures, ethnic groups, and nations where before the colonial project and its suppression might not have been singled out as such a foundational discourse. Suparna Bhaskaran provides evidence of the normalizing of homosexuality in India in her article, "The Politics of Penetration: Section 377 of the Indian Penal Code" when she examines Gandhian socialist, Janak Raj Jai's attempts to maintain the criminalization of homosexuality: "[he] defended a colonial sexual code as 'Indian tradition'" (16). The defense of "colonial sexual codes" and mores as "Indian tradition" reveals the extent to which colonial ideologies become naturalized and possibly continue to manage terms of debate through their prolonged mobilization. They also show, as Manisha Sethi states: "to be queer in India was not so queer after all. Until the British arrived that is" (17).

The absence of same-sex identities and representations in West African fiction is part and parcel of cultural paradigms that unwittingly link themselves to colonial legacies. The absence also keeps homosexuality a mostly unarticulated subject position in the West African experience. It is shunned. It is quieted. It is put in the (colonial) closet. However, the silence surrounding homosexuality in West African fiction and culture is not only tethered to homosexuality, it is also mapped on to other bodies.

West African fiction that engages the African experience of Europe and other parts of the West—to name only two areas—opens a space to encounter homosexuality and the ways in which it is positioned and embodied in Western society. This encounter can also shed light on the circumstances of particular West African identities in Europe and in Africa. The positioning of homosexuality in Western culture can be put in service of postcolonial projects that would use it to mediate representations of un-named and un-acknowledge subject positions. While cultural and legal practices in the West also curtail and sanction the expression of same-sex desires and homosexual identities, the existence of homosexual networks and communities—especially after the beginning of the gay liberation movement in the U.S. with the Stonewall riots in 1969—allow for the expression and participation of same-sex desires and homosexual subject positions. However, even with the appearance of "out" homosexuals and the cultural work that centers on the full participation of homosexuals in the United States and Western European countries, there are few—if any—queer people whose lives are not shaped or affected in some way by the closet.

The closet, a post-Stonewall term used to designate multiple subject positions in regard to the homosexual experience that range from the concealment of one's sexuality (to be "in" the closet or to be in denial of one's homosexuality, "closet case") to its public avowal (to be "out"), to its invisibility in heteronormative culture and to its visibility through sign vehicles which denote homosexual identity (for example, gender insubordination), is a central metaphor for the description of the sets of issues that come into existence through same-sex desire and the embodiment of these desires in a homosexual identity. As Eve Sedgwick writes in her seminal text, *Epistemology of the Closet* about homosexuality in the West:

> Our culture still sees to its [homosexuality] being dangerous enough
> that women and men who find or fear they are homosexual, or are
> perceived by others to be so, are physically and mentally terror-

ized through the institutions of law, religion, psychotherapy, mass culture, medicine, the military, commerce and bureaucracy and brute violence. (58)

Since society in the post-Stonewall moment still finds homosexuality "dangerous", the closet—either willingly or unwillingly—becomes a part of homosexual experience. Sedgwick points out: "[F]or many gay people it [the closet] is still the fundamental feature of social life; and there can be few gay people, however courageous and forthright by habit, however fortunate in the support of their immediate communities, in whose lives the closet is not still a shaping presence" (68). The supposed invisibility the closet offers gives the "closeted" individual a zone of safety. To be in the closet, as Siobhan Somerville writes, "is to be palpably invisible in a structure of visibility, proximity, and knowledge" (93). This "palpable invisibility" also allows the "closeted" homosexual to exist and participate in the structures and systems that reproduce heteronormative culture.

West African fiction that encounters homosexual desire and homosexual embodiments in Europe does so from the position of former European colonization. The participation and existence of "closeted" homosexuals in reproducing heteropatriarchal practices takes on a different meaning when exchanges occur between Europeans and formerly colonized peoples. Moreover, the metaphor of the "gay" closet in the West can become a metaphor for other forms of embodiment that are related to heteropatriarchy as it is practiced in West African cultures. An important difference between the existence of the "gay" closet in West Africa and in Western society is that the shaping presence of the closet is an articulated position in the West. And, it is through the articulated position of the "gay" closet in the West that Ghanaian writer Amma Darko exposes the sexual exploitation of African women in Europe as well as Africa.

As Benita Parry shows in her reading of Gayatri Spivak, women in formerly colonized places are "doubly-oppressed" because they are "caught between the dominations of a native patriarchy and [a] foreign masculinist-imperialist ideology" (36). In the case of West African fiction, women's subject positions as "doubly-oppressed" did not initially figure into post-colonial engagements with literature and writing. More often than not, women were presented within a masculinist economy that positioned them as agents in the de-colonization project, and that did not critically interrogate indigenous patriarchal institutions. Areas such as domestic abuse, the trafficking in women as capital between men, domestic rape, and the exploitation of women's bodies were not central issues in post-colonial writing, which was performed primarily by men, during this moment. Kirsten Holst Peterson describes this moment in the follow terms:

An important impetus behind the wave of African writing which started in the '60s was the desire to show both the outside world and African youth that the African past was orderly, dignified and complex and altogether a worthy heritage. This was obviously opting for fighting cultural imperialism, and in the course of that the women's issue was not only ignored [. . .] it was conscripted in the service of dignifying the past [. . .] The African past was not made the object of scrutiny [. . .] it was made the object of a quest, and the picture of women's place and role in these societies had to support this quest and was consequently lent more dignity and described in more positive terms than reality warranted. (253)

It was not until women writers, such as Buchi Emecheta started to articulate the experiences of women in West African contexts that both the "picture" of the pre-colonial African past and the contemporary hybrid moment became a subject of scrutiny from the perspective of gender. Through the work of such writers, gender became a central category of analysis in the West African woman's experience of West African culture and European imperialism. The addition of the workings of sexual difference in post-colonial contexts problematizes masculinist representations of the past as well as the present. Sexual difference also demonstrates the ways in which women and their bodies are often "re-colonized" by European imperialism and indigenous patriarchal institutions. It is this "re-colonization" of women and their bodies that Darko exposes through her articulation of the sexual exploitation of African women by both Africa and the West as "closetedness." That is to say, the sexual exploitation of African women is a "closeted" subject, and its "closetedness" allows for as well as reproduces its existence.

The "closetedness" surrounding the sexual exploitation of African women renders their oppression invisible. Their exploitation is in the "closet" in order to not only conceal its existence, but to also conceal the societal practices that make it possible. The concealment of African women's sexual exploitation and those practices that make it possible allow for its continuation because they place it in a field of ignorance, which I will address later, and in zones of privacy, which dislocate it from the public, institutionalized, societal pressures that position women, especially "Third World" and post-colonial women as the objects of sexual exploitation. The sexual exploitation of African women is the "skeleton in the closet" of West Africa and Europe, and Darko, in her first novel, *Beyond the Horizon* puts that "skeleton" in full view. In fact, she does not only "out" the sexual exploitation of African women, she also demonstrates the ways in which the "gay" closet in the West shares circumstances with this exploitation and how Western culture's closeting of homosexuals participates in this exploitation. As Douglas Crimp writes: "[M]ost of us [queer people] have the experience [. . .] of oppressing other queers in order to elude that oppression [through pretending to be homosexual and/or homophobic]" (305). Darko shows that the performance of heterosexuality by queers can also oppress West African women. She also demonstrates that the invisibility of the closet for homosexuals and sexually exploited African women is what Crimp calls the "open secret" (307). He states: "Outing [from the closet] is not [. . .] the revelation of that secret, but the revelation that the secret was no secret at all" (307). The revelation that West African women are exploited (sexually and otherwise) by European and African heteropatriarchy is the open secret that Darko names, which is no secret at all.

Beyond the Horizon tells Mara's story in stark clarity and unreserved detail in the first person. It reveals the ways in which African women are exploited in Africa and Europe through custom, gender oppression, and the sexualization of their bodies, and it presents African women's sexualization in Europe through the complicity and willful ignorance of Africa and Europe concerning the details of these women's lives. In other words, Darko writes the unwritten, and speaks the unspoken. Darko reveals the condition and cultural mechanisms concerning the sexual exploitation of African women in Europe. She demonstrates that this condition is "closeted" in both Africa and Europe—and it is its closeted nature that helps to perpetuate its existence and continuation.

Sedgwick notes that "[t]he gay closet is not a feature only of the lives of gay people" (68). Darko exemplifies this claim in *Beyond the Horizon*. She shows not only that the sexual oppression of African women in Europe and in Africa is a "closeted" category, but she also demonstrates the ways that the closeting of homosexuals—especially gay men—in the West participates in the "closeting" of African women's exploitation. The silence and the willed acts of ignorance surrounding homosexuality and sexual oppression of African women come together in this novel. As Sedgwick argues "'[c]losetedness' itself is a performance initiated as such by the speech act of a silence—not a particular silence, but a silence that accrues particularity by fits and starts, in relation to the discourse that surrounds and differentially constitutes it" (3). The discourse that surrounds and differentially constitutes homosexuality and the sexual exploitation of African women is one and the same: its rule is to keep these identities in the background concealed in the closet to allow for their exploitation for the benefit of others.

Beyond the Horizon, which was originally written in English, but first published in German as *Der Verkaufte Traum* (The Sold Dream) in 1991, recounts the story of Mara, a village woman who is married off to one of the leading sons of her village who has elected to live a life in the city—rather than following in the footsteps of his father as the village undertaker or living his life as a village farmer. Her husband, Akobi has "other plans" (5). These plans include having a village wife in order to help him realize his life in the city, and his dreams of wealth and prestige. The novel does not, however, limit itself to the issues that come into existence in a marriage between a "city" (or a would-be "city") man and a "village" woman where the man marries the woman in order to acquire her mostly unpaid and undervalued domestic labor. It shows that this kind of unequal pairing helps to produce the later sexual exploitation of this woman in other contexts. As Mara's friend Mama Kiosk tells her: "Your husband is one of those men who have no respect for village people [. . .]. Tradition demands that the wife respect, obey and worship her husband but it demands, in return, care, good care of the wife. Your husband neglects you and yet demands respect and complete worship from you. This is not normal" (13). The "abnormal" treatment of Mara by Akobi highlights the use of village women or women in general to benefit men and to help realize their plans and goals. The depiction of Mara as a woman from the village who is steeped in the ways of a traditional society shows how this system does not benefit women, and how it works to produce their exploitation by interpellating them to perform in or be complicit with their own exploitation.

Throughout the novel, Mara is often presented as a "greenhorn" or as someone who is naive in regard to the ways of the city and the ways people use and exploit others for their own benefit (10). Throughout the initial process of her experience as an exploited woman, Mara often says "I understood the world no more" (11) or "I understood the world no longer" (110) with each successive challenge to her village upbringing, but when she discovers her exploitation, she states: "I have just understood the world a bit better" (127). Mara's situation as a person from the village and as a woman locates her within several cultural and gendered systems that benefit from her interpretations of marriage and sexual difference as a "village woman." However, from Mara's point of view, all of this would change when Akobi goes to Europe to make his fortune, and when he later sends for her to aid him in this endeavor.

Mara is brought to Europe by Akobi "to keep house" for him while he supposedly works two jobs to amass wealth (51). In the economically devastated post-colonial context, Europe is a "promised land" or a "land of promise" where only a few West Africans can go, and from where even fewer return as a "been-to" with wealth, education (in the form of professional degrees), and high amounts of prestige that is heaped upon them by their culture.[1] As Mara notes, "Europe to me was a place so special and so very, very far away, somewhere unimaginable, maybe even somewhere near Heaven, where not just anybody could go" (33-34). Akobi's invitation and plans to bring her to Europe makes Mara think she figures among a select few, but she soon discovers on her arrival that Akobi's "abnormal" treatment of her does not limit itself to West Africa.

Mara arrives in Germany only to be blackmailed into prostitution by Akobi, who has taken a German wife, and who forces Mara to pretend to be his sister, which suspends her rights as first wife and as the mother of his children. Mara's story begins where it ends, which is in Munich, the place she comes to settle to practice prostitution. She begins her journey that constructs the memory of her life by remarking on her position as a prostitute. She states: "What my poor mother back home in black Africa would say to these hideous traces of bites and scratches all over my neck [from her participation in the sex trade], should she ever have the misfortune of seeing them, I fear to imagine" (2). This fear of discovery, of being revealed and exposed begins Beyond the Horizon's juxtaposition of African women's sexual exploitation in Europe with the "gay" closet. Mara does not want her mother "back home in black Africa" to learn of or to see the truth of her condition as a prostitute. Mara's reference to "black Africa" seems to signal a desire for her condition in "white Europe" to remain concealed, bifurcated from her life in West Africa. Mara separates her identity in West Africa from her identity in Europe. She leads a "double life" where her sexual exploitation as a prostitute is closeted in order to conceal its existence from her family, friends, and home in West Africa.

However, Mara's discourse about the fear of revelation and the importance of bifurcating aspects of one's life deepens when she describes the house in which she practices the sex trade. She states that the brothel where she works is located in "a house I hear [that] once belonged to a prominent wealthy German who had it built for the purpose of his frequent rendezvous with the greatest love of his life who, like him, was a male. This led to his suicide when the truth about his sexuality emerged to the public" (3). Mara practices prostitution in a house that belonged to a gay man who committed suicide once his sexuality was revealed. It is interesting that the house had been built for the purposes of sexual encounters. This fact sets a tone that suggests that the private, hidden life of gay men, like the private, hidden life of African women caught in the European sex trade, is something to be located in spaces other than those marked for heteronormative expression. Homosexuality, like prostitution, is something that needs to be zoned, marked off from the rest of society. Mara's remark on the wealthy German's suicide when the truth of his sexuality emerges to the public brings her fears of her mother's discovery of her life to mind. The conditions of her life are able to continue as long as they remain concealed, but if they are revealed or emerge in "black Africa," Mara will be placed in African cultural space where she will always be tainted, ruined. It is possible that Mara's mentioning of the German's suicide suggests her reaction if the truth of her prostitution is revealed.

Darko links truth and sexuality in this passage. To know about someone's sexuality or sexual practices is to know the "truth" about her or him. She plugs into the positioning of sexuality as a "truth discourse" in the West, which was first identified by Michel Foucault in his important work, the first volume of *The History of Sexuality*. Foucault demonstrates that the nineteenth century is the moment when homosexual identity is "invented" through "expert" discourses in medicine, psychology, and law, but heterosexuality is also invented—as is its non-normative expressions, which characterize the prostitute as an "abnormal" subject category. More often than not, nineteenth and early twentieth century discourses pathologize and medicalize the female prostitute and put her on par with the lesbian (the "invert"). Darko's use of homosexuality to mediate the sexual exploitation of West African women taps into Western traditions that link homosexuality and prostitution. And, her connecting of sexuality and the "truth" demonstrates the problems at stake should Mara reveal her prostitution: she will not be viewed as victim who is forced into prostitution. Her prostitution will become the "truth" about her, and will attribute a hypersexual sexual identity to her in her homeland that will effectively erase her status as a victim.

The idea that a discovery of her prostitution would ruin her and others like her in Africa comes up in her talks with another African woman who is also a part of the sex trade in Europe, Kaye. After a discussion with Kaye, Mara observes: "Once a prostitute, always a prostitute. The stamp would never leave me" (119). No matter how her family in Africa might react to her prostitution,

Mara and other women like her would never be able to erase the stigma prostitution brings to their lives. It is a stamp that cannot be erased once exposed. As Mara notes near the novel's end when she comments on how she sends material goods and money to her family through her friend Mama Kiosk: "She doesn't know the truth about me" (139). Prostitution is Mara's "truth"—not the fact that she was abused and blackmailed by her husband, and she fears that even someone as astute as Mama Kiosk would see it as her "truth" as well.

But, *Beyond the Horizon* also reveals what Sedgewick calls the "epistemological privilege of unknowing" and the "privileges of ignorance" (5). Unknowing and ignorance become forms of privilege because they have the power to construct closets as well as to open them or reveal the contents of closets, but they also work to dislocate those invested with unknowing and ignorance from becoming conscious of their participation in oppression. That these women's families in Africa do not know about their prostitution—or do not want to know—allows for and sets the terms of their exploitation. Mara, like many other women in her position, sends material goods and money back home to her family. If her family were to discover the "truth" about Mara, it is possible that they would either help her in her circumstances or disassociate themselves from her totally. In either case, they would no longer be able to gain materially from her prostitution. The profits that the privileges of ignorance and unknowing provide create the circumstances that pressure others to not seek to discover the "truth" or to name it. This participation allows for exploitation and oppression to not only continue, but it also allows for it to provide a service to the post-colonial context because these women can offer the material goods and money that are either too expensive or too difficult to come by in West Africa.

Connected to unknowing and ignorance is the notion that homosexuality—or in the case of this novel, prostitution—is the open secret, the telling secret. While people, such as the families of these women, perform unknowingly and in ignorance, they also perform their knowledge of these women's practices. In other words, they know, but they want not to conceal their daughters' prostitution, but their knowledge of their daughters' prostitution. Mara's friend, Kaye, comments that her family does not know how she makes "the money to buy them the things [they want], but I don't think that it even interest them very much" (17). Her family gains from unknowing and the open secret—both materially and psychologically. They want to conceal their complicity with the systems that make their daughters' exploitation possible. Kaye continues: "Sometimes, I think that my family suspects I'm in the trade but deliberately refrain from asking me because if they knew the truth and then took no action, not wanting to forfeit the luxuries they enjoy at my expense, they would indirectly become a party to my sins" (118). However, her family is already a party to her sins. The "epistemological privilege of unknowing" allows for her family to gain from her participation in the sex trade and locates them in a position where they do not have to act, but Darko's "outing" of this kind of power dynamic between sexually exploited women in Europe and their families in West Africa does the work of locating or naming this arrangement. She identifies its existence in a move that is similar to her naming of Akobi's sexual domination of Mara in a particular scene as "domestic rape" (84). She, as Crimp notes, "outs" the "enforcers" of closets not to reveal the "secret" of homosexuality, prostitution, or domestic rape, but to reveal the "secret" of homophobia, sexual exploitation, and the accepted practices of Western African heteropatriarchy where domestic rape is not a predetermined category (308). By the novel's end, Mara finds that she, too, is in the same position as Kaye. She states in reference to her family: "Material things are all I can offer them" (140).

Darko does not only "out" the complicity of Western African heteropatriarchy in the sexual exploitation of African women in Europe. She also reveals that Europe and European heteropatriarchy are implicated in concealing the "secret" of their complicity in the sexual oppression of West African women. The privileges of unknowing and ignorance as well as the functioning of the "open secret" also reflect on European heteropatriarchy's ordering of Western culture. Europe is more than the market and the provider of the capital that makes this exploitation possible and lucrative (for the pimps and other "overseers" of the sex industry), which, of course, brings up sets of questions about the positioning of women—especially "Third World" and post-colonial women—in Europe, but it also turns a "blind eye" to the conditions and circumstances of primarily "Third World" and African women in its nations. Mara quickly learns that making a living as a domestic is almost impossible because detectives from the Labour Office enforce labor laws in the areas of domestic service (108), but such an enforcement does not apply to work in the sex trade or the trafficking in women from other countries (mostly non-Western) that is connected to that trade.

As Dorchen A. Leidholdt states: "The fact is that sex trafficking and organized prostitution are inextricably connected and share fundamental characteristics and dynamics. [. . .] The reality is that organized prostitution constitutes the economic and structural foundation of sex trafficking" (419). Osey, an associate of Akobi's, who is also from West Africa, tells Mara: "for an illegal nigger woman like you, there is no other job in Germany [. . .]. [Y]ou are too illegal and too black for any proper job" (114). The ways and means of European immigration laws and its structuring of culture render Mara "too illegal and too black." But, it does not render her body a zone that cannot be sexualized for European sexual pleasure, misuse, and abuse. While European heteropatriarchy regulates and enforces laws concerning the entry of West African women in particular sites of labor, it does not do so in sex trafficking and the sex trade. This refraining from entering into the sex industry operates along the lines of the powers of ignorance and the open secret because the act of refraining reveals European heteropatriarchy's participation and regulating of the sex industry that oppresses West African women.

However, the novel does not limit itself to focusing on the complicity of African and European systems that indirectly coerce West African women into the "prostitution closet". The novel also shows how many African women are coerced into sexual slavery by their male partners. The direct participation of husbands and boyfriends in forcing women into the sex industry in the novel is generally represented through blackmail that concerns sexual secrets, which not only threatens to "out" the women as "improper" and "immoral" to their families, but also provides an initial step in "closeting" the sexualization of these women's bodies. The men threaten to reveal the women's recorded impropriety, but offer to "conceal" it once the women further their sexualization by participating in the sex industry, which benefits their partners. The women become "doubly closeted" in the sense that they must be "in" about their prostitution, and remain "in" or the recorded proof of their sexualization will be passed on to their families. This action is an attempt to conceal the women's prostitution so that it can continue for an indeterminate amount of time. Mara's friend, Kaye was blackmailed by a boyfriend with pictures of her engaging in sex acts with different men. For Mara, a video tape exists that shows her sexual defilement at the hands of a group of men while she is drugged and unaware of the taping. Kaye's boyfriend tells her: "You back out today, tomorrow these pictures will be on their way back to your family at home" (117). As for Mara, even though she sinks deeper in the sex trade and goes on to make pornographic photographs, the fear of the original video containing her defilement as well as the other videos she has made surfacing at home haunts her. She states: "I have decided to stop thinking about ever going home. I just don't belong there any longer. Moreover, I have this fear that haunts me day in and day other, that if I show my face there one day, out of the blue that sex video that Akobi made of me clandestinely will show up there, too" (139).

If European and African systems gain from and indirectly condone the forced sexualization of West African women's bodies, their male partners embody the position of direct force and profit. These men cannot claim ignorance and unknowing, but they do participate in the management of the open secret. Their marriages to European women, which Mara and Kaye's husbands partake in, is an attempt to manage their direct participation in the sexualization of West African women by creating representations of themselves as domestic and public (since marriage in Western countries is public act) subjects of European "bourgeois" culture. This gesture is an attempt to manage their direct roles since it serves to distance them from their participation by ensconcing them in the practices of European "respectability," which also often includes "legitimate" jobs that provide "covers" or "beards" for their illegal affairs.

An interesting aspect of the novel is the fact that it demonstrates that the sexual exploitation of African women in Europe is connected to their exploitation in Africa as wives and daughters. Darko shows the "trafficking" of women early in the novel in the ways that women go from being the property of their fathers to being the property of their husbands. The transaction concerning women's bodies through a bride price and through marriage is likened to their prostitution. It is significant that the word "property" occurs in Mara's marriage to Akobi (7) and in her "transfer" to her first pimp, Peepy (114). She calls her pimp in the brothel in Munich her "Overseer," her "Lord," and her "Master" (3).

These are the languages of capital, ownership, slavery, and marriage. Darko demonstrates that if women were not positioned as the property of men they could not be sexually exploited in the ways that they are in the sex industry, because they would not have *already* been sexually exploited by their fathers, who are interpellated to view them as property that can be "transferred" to other men. Moreover, the power of the women's boyfriends to blackmail them into prostitution, and the power of their families to perform ignorance in regard to their prostitution are connected to notion of women as property because as property women have value assigned to them, and this value is often connected to the management of their sexuality. It is possible to "closet" their sexual exploitation, because it engages the means governing the construction of women as property with value. The prostitution of African women in Europe does not signal a failure in the management of their sexualities by patriarchies in West Africa and Europe. It, on the other hand, is yet another regulating force that benefits heteropatriarchy.[2]

Western gay men are also another regulating force that benefits heteropatriarchy. Closeted gay men participate directly in the sexual oppression of African women. Many of the women, such as Mara and Kaye, marry gay men in order to obtain a five year visa to remain in Germany. The closeting of homosexuality in the West creates the opportunity for these marriages, which are financially beneficial for gay men who engage in them. The power of the "gay" closet operates in the continued sexual oppression of these women, because they obtain these visas in order to prolong their work in the European sex trade. If the closet did not remain a "shaping presence" in Western culture the economic ties between illegal immigrant women from Africa and gay men would not exist on the scale in which it does in the novel. The marriages between homosexual men and African women are such a common practice that it is hardly remarked upon by the women. It is represented almost as procedure or in the course of events.

However, the participation of gay men in the sexual oppression of West African women also works to further closet these women. Marriage allows them to stay in Europe longer to practice their trade, but it also provides a sheltering or concealment function of these women's participation in the sex trade. As Crimp noted about the "gay" closet, these oppressed homosexuals oppress others. But, once again, the marriages between gay men and African women are not a failure of or crisis in European heteropatriarchy to manage homosexuality. These marriages are a part of its management. The only example in the text when such a marriage is positioned as not being helpful is when Akobi's lover, Comfort, who is not a prostitute, but who is also married to a gay man, cannot receive state help because her husband is employed (137). Even though Comfort is a "kept woman" by Akobi throughout most of the novel, the fact that she cannot get state assistance because of her marriage brings to mind talk in the novel about the near impossibility of African women to find a "legitimate" space within

European culture. That is to say, Comfort's non-participation in the sex trade penalizes her, because she does not make enough money to support herself in restaurant work, her profession, or without Akobi's assistance. Her marriage to a gay man only helps her to remain in Germany. It does not, as is the case with the prostitutes, help her to remain in Germany in order to make more money.

The "shaping presence" of the closet in Darko's *Beyond the Horizon* demonstrates the complicity of many different subject positions involved in varying degrees with West African and European heteropatriarchies in the sexual exploitation of African women. These do not only participate in the "closeting" of this sexual oppression, but also set the terms for it. In the larger scheme, West African women's bodies are limited to being the property of their fathers and husbands or their pimps and johns. Their bodies are the property of Africa and the West, and the transaction that transfers their bodies as property of West African heteropatriarchy to the property of Western heteropatriarchy is through their sexual trafficking and their exploitation in the sex industry. The concealment of this transaction—from property of Africa to property of the West—is possibly the largest "closet" that Darko "outs."

Acknowledgment

I am indebted to Laura Ann Williams for help in the preparation of this article.

Notes

1. Ken Bugul (Mariètou M'Baye) describes Europe in the following terms in her autobiography. *The Abandoned Baobab*: "The North of dreams, the North of Illusions, the North of allusions. The frame of reference North, the Promised Land of North" (23). Bugul's autobiography also features the sexual exploitation of African women in Europe, but it does so in a way that is very different from Darko's work. Bugul is an educated person who attends university in Brussels, and who comes to terms with racism and her exploitation during the "swinging sixties." In fact, her pen name (Ken Bugul) came into existence from fear by her publishers that her text would cause scandal.

2. The novel also sets up other important doubles that foreground Mara's experience of Europe in West African traditions concerning women. For example, when Akobi and his associate blackmail Mara into prostitution, it evokes the moment when Akobi blackmails her "mentally" in Africa when he fronts her capital to begin hawking eggs. Mara observes: "And to blackmail me mentally into keeping my word, knowing how superstitious I was, he made me swear to the river god to drown me if I didn't" (18). This demonstrates that marriage and superstition are equipped with mechanism to control women. However, this form of blackmail does not have the power of revelation and "truth" that could govern Mara's life in the way the secret of her prostitution can. Another example is Akobi's forcing of Mara to appear as his sister to his German wife, which is not the first time she plays the role of his hidden wife. She must also play his hidden wife in Africa because he

is ashamed of her appearance and that she is a "village woman". Another important aspect occurs during the instruction Mara receives from Akobi's associate, Osey, when she first enters Germany. He tells her: "In the German people's eyes [...] we niggers all look the same. Black faces, kinky hair, thick lips. We don't fight with them about it. We use it to our benefit" (59). But, Akobi and Osey as well as Mara's father who married her to Akobi for his own needs, use African customs and traditions to their benefit as well.

Works Cited

Bhashkaran, Suparna. "The Politics of Penetration: Section 377 of the Indian Penal Code." *Queering India: Same-Sex Love and Eroticism in Indian Culture and Society.* Ruth Vanita. Ed. New York: Routledge, 2002: 15-29.

Bugul, Ken. *The Abandoned Baobab: The Autobiography of a Senegalese Woman.* Trans., Marjolijin de Jager. Brooklyn: Lawrence Hill, 1991.

Crimp, Douglas. "Right On, Girlfriend!" In: *Fear of a Queer Planet: Queer Politics and Social Theory.* Ed., Michael Warner. 300-321.

Darko, Amma. *Beyond the Horizon.* Oxford: Heinemann, 1995.

Leidholdt, Dorchen A. "The Sexual Exploitation of Women and Girls." *Feminism and Pornography.* Ed. Drusilla Cornell. Oxford: Oxford UP, 2000.

Parry, Benita. "Problems in Current Theories of Colonial Discourse." In: *The Post-Colonial Studies Reader.* Eds., Bill Ashcroft, Gareth Griffiths, and Helen Tiffin. London: Routledge,1995. 36-44.

Peterson, Kirsten Holst. "First Things First: Problems of a Feminist Approach to African Literature." In: *The Post-Colonial Studies Reader.* Eds. Bill Ashcroft, Gareth Griffiths, and Helen Tiffin. London: Routledge,1995. 251-254.

Sedgwick, Eve Kosofsky. *Epistemology of the Closet.* Berkeley: U of California P, 1990.

Sethi, Manisha. "Homegrown Homosexuality." *Biblio.* Online. Available URL: www. biblio-india.com/articles/ND02_ar12.pdf. Date Downloaded: 9.24.2003 17-18.

Somerville, Siobhan, B. *Queering the Color Line: Race and the Invention of Homosexuality in American Culture.* Durham: Duke UP, 2000.

Chapter 12

Dangerous Encounters with the West: Gender, Sexuality, and Power in Ama Ata Aidoo's *Our Sister Killjoy*

Miriam C. Gyimah

Ama Ata Aidoo's *Our Sister Killjoy or Reflections from a Black-Eyed Squint* is a groundbreaking work in African literature. Although first published in 1977, it is still a daring text in that Aidoo broaches therein the subject of homosexuality, a topic from which African texts shy away. Aidoo's text, then, is unique in that not only is it one of the first to introduce this theme, but also, it has a politically conscious educated female, Sissie, as its protagonist. The work is also a travel narrative that presents Sissie's experiences which engage questions of gender, sexuality, and power.

The experiential novel is divided into four episodes: "Into a Bad Dream," "The Plums," "From Our Sister Killjoy," and "A Love Letter." While all its parts clearly contribute to the complexity of the issues raised, for the purposes of this work, only the second episode, its largest, will be the focus. Through the experiences of Sissie, a product of a postcolonial African nation, Aidoo critiques being an African in a world where such people are at one moment regarded as inferior and inhuman brutes and in another, exotic commodities. In so doing, Aidoo addresses European imperialism, the colonized mind and the objectification of Africans and the black female body. As Sissie moves through the four episodes, the reader witnesses the dynamics of power between the West and the rest and even people of the same gender.

Sissie's travels in Europe begin in Germany and in the second episode, "The Plums." It is here that she encounters Marija and is introduced to lesbian desire. At the end of this section, Sissie learns through this experience, the significance of her mother's *akatado* and decides to retrieve it. The akatado, which will be discussed in detail later, is the loose cloth, the third piece of the African woman's *kaba*[1], which is usually tied about the waist and hips over her cloth. Sissie's travels lead her into an uncomfortable compromising encounter, and as the lone black woman, the exotic other, she will be in a position to be exploited. It is here that she will have to recall the akatado and make a connection to her homeland. The act of recalling the akatado itself is a call to consciousness, an African centered ideological consciousness.

Historically, part of the exploitation of black women's bodies is their objectification by others.[2] In her discussion of the eroticization of the black female body, Aidoo presents the sexualized image, which is again connected to capitalism. The image is a rare commodity for many. But what she does, which is unexpected, is that she connects the exotic and objectified body to a lesbian theme. The connection might be unexpected, because European's historical contact with African women is usually read as a heterosexual one where black women's bodies were used and abused by white men, particularly during slavery. Nevertheless, Aidoo reveals with this theme that the sexual objectifying should not always be read as heterosexual. For, it is not always the male who desires the black female body. What she is stressing here is the issue of power – who has it and how it is used. The text submits that all powers tend to subject the black woman in one way or another. If "[b]eing a woman/has not/Is not/cannot/ Never will be a/Child's game," then certainly, being a black woman is almost unspeakable (51).

While the reader, particularly the African reader, might be surprised by the lesbian theme, to incorporate it was a very conscious decision on the part of the author. Asked how the lesbian love fits into the work's total statement about power and oppression, Aidoo responds that "...if you let loose an African girl in Europe, she is bound to come across all sorts of experiences, enriching, demoralizing, —ah—positive, negative, etc. It was one experience that this girl, as a character came across. Not to have written about it would have seemed to me rather dishonest" (James 16). Her portrayal of Sissie's body and Sissie's relationship with Marija is a theorization of female sexuality and the commoditization of black women's bodies. The lesbian theme is controversial as far as African literature is concerned, but Aidoo herself has admitted that she was aware people would be made uncomfortable with the work (James). But for her, the theme cannot be separated from the political issues at hand seeing that Marija, a symbol of white dominance and bourgeois lifestyle, attempts to make Sissie one of the decorative collectibles in her home.

As alluded to earlier, the issue of homosexuality is rarely confronted in African literary studies. Nevertheless, Aidoo's introduction of the lesbian theme in *Killjoy*, discomforting or not, has been raised by Chris Dunton in an essay, "'Wheyting Be Dat?': The Treatment of Homosexuality in African Literature." The essay entertains the thesis that within African literature, homosexuality is treated with a "pejorative judgment" (422). He argues that the subject is always handled as alien to African societies and rather as a phenomenon that is introduced to Africa by European settlers or is a demoralizing phenomenon that Africans encounter in Europe. To Dunton, this "treatment of the homosexual theme in African literature provides a convenient reference point—a closely defined narrative element—which helps reveal the general thematic concerns and the larger narrative strategy of the text" (ibid.). Demonstrating the legitimacy of his argument, Dunton surveys numerous African writers' treatment of the subject. However, in Aidoo's, *Killjoy*, according to Dunton, "...the subject of homosexuality becomes liberated, in the special sense that whether or not it is treated sympathetically, it is granted a greater capacity to disturb, to call questions..." (423). Precisely, Aidoo intended with *Killjoy* to disturb, to call things into question.

The scenario between Sissie and Marija reads like a single's ad. Marija, wife of Big Adolf, mother of little Adolf, seeks to fulfill her lonely days and nights with an exotic African female student. Ranu Samantrai says that "Marija befriends Sissie, because the Ghanaian woman is an exotic rarity in Germany, like Indians or Eskimos. And Sissie, in turn, cannot forget that Marija is 'A daughter of mankind's /Self-appointed most royal line, /The house of Aryan.' The two face each other as representatives of their races, each loaded with the baggage of the historical encounter between Europe and Africa" ("Caught in the Confluence of History" 145). And, because both women are carrying this baggage of their histories and themselves, their contact is full of conflicts. Aidoo pushes this envelop of their histories towards their sexual possibilities. Her approach to the lesbian subject is her metaphoric use of plums, a dark juicy and sweet fruit, which is mouth watering not only to Marija but also to Sissie and her companions. The fruit, daily supplied to Sissie by Marija, becomes a symbol of black female sexuality and the "forbidden" love affair between a young black female student and a young white housewife and mother. Ranu Samantrai does not read the sexual connotation attached to the plums. Instead, she sees it as Aidoo's means of drawing a connection between Sissie and Marija and to suggest that the histories that bring these two women together cannot be viewed in simplistic oppositional terms. She says,

> [a] complex multifaceted symbol, the plums undermine neat bina-
> ries of good, bad, white-black, African-European. By assigning the
> fruit a position between two terms, Aidoo uses the plums to collapse
> binary oppositions, forcing attention to similarities and bridges for
> which binary thinking cannot account. The plums link Sissie and
> Marija; through them Aidoo asks the reader to consider the factors
> which unite and divide her characters. (154)

Certainly, the plums seem to serve as a connecting tool for the two women, but what is the motive behind the connection seeing that it is Marija who provides the fruit? What does the very idea of the plum, and its description, say about the historical connection between Europe and Africa? We cannot properly answer this question, if we do not examine the sexual encounter between Europe and Africa or the meaning of "eating the other."

To analyze the entire significance and purpose of the plum and Sissie and Marija's relationship, we must scrutinize the question of sexuality. Above, Aidoo is looking at female sexuality and the commoditization of the black woman's body. Here, she is presenting ideas that bell hooks later writes about. Aidoo's suggestion that the plums, an object to be sold in the markets, is representative of Sissie's person and sexuality, is not only reminiscent of slavery, but also an early discussion of hooks' argument in her essay, "Eating the Other: Desire and Resis-tance." In the essay, hooks argues that eating the other is the commoditization of black bodies, male and female via the media as well as the desire to transgress racial lines, thereby often resisting white racist culture. Nonetheless, she asserts that the desire to transgress and resist is not devoid of racism as whites always maintain a privilege in their ability to cross racial lines. She says, "[t]he commoditization of Otherness has been so successful because it is offered as a new delight, more intense, more satisfying than normal ways of doing and feeling. Within commodity culture, ethnicity becomes spices, seasoning that can liven up the dull dish that is mainstream white culture" (21). With the plums, Aidoo shows how an attempt to transgress racial lines and possess the black woman's body is necessarily linked to capitalism and exploitation. The plums, therefore, become a symbol for Sissie or black women's sexuality and body. It is an object that is placed in the markets for viewing, touching, and consumption. While this is the idea the text suggests, it is simultaneously obvious that Marija, the young white housewife and mother clearly wants all this for herself. Marija, then, the person pursuing the object is in a position of power, because of her economic level and in this case, because of her whiteness. As hooks points out,

> [t]o make one's self vulnerable to the seduction of difference, to seek an encounter with the Other, does not require that one relinquish forever one's mainstream positionality. When race and ethnicity become commodified as resources for pleasure, the culture of specific groups, as well as the bodies of individuals, can be seen as constituting an alternative playground where members of dominating races, genders, sexual practices affirm their power—over in intimate relations with the Other. (23)

Marija's whiteness and the whiteness of Europe become a threat to the traveling student. As a student, Sissie is positioned to learn more from being in the midst of racial politics with her relationship with one white woman.

The hostel where international students like Sissie are hosted becomes the market place for Marija. It is the space where Marija comes to gaze and hopefully touch the object of desire. The hostel was once a castle. Again, the sexual connotation between Marija's and Sissie's relationship in connection to their meeting place evokes the history of slaves in castles, or rather dungeons, where black bodies were kept and black females raped before their exodus to the New World. Sissie meets Marija in front of her hostel with the latter repeatedly commenting on how fond she was of the Indians who she encountered and knew the previous summer. "Are you an Indian?" are Marija's first words to Sissie. She says, "Zey ver weri nice." "I like zem weri much" (20). Sissie assumed they were male. This fleeting information in retrospect becomes a naive assumption as we witness the development and conclusion of Sissie's and Marija's relationship. But prior to the entire drama of their relationship, Sissie notes later in her first conversation with Marija that: IT CANNOT BE NORMAL/ for a young/ Hausefrau to/ Like/Two Indians/ Who work in/ Supermarkets (23). While "normal" is boldly capitalized and is loaded with assumptions, prejudice, phobias and the like, it becomes apparent that Sissie's concept of normal as a reared African and a heterosexual daughter and sister to many is not that of the housewife she befriends. Again, it can be said that it is not normal for an African female to frequent the home of Big Adolf, who although is often referred to by name within the text, is not made familiar to the audience. Big Adolf, for many people of color can be the epitome of white terror, as the name and the history of Germany recall white supremacy and genocide. But, it becomes possible for Sissie to frequent Marija's home and keep her company despite Marija's neighbors and the town's outrage and jealousy over their relationship. "The arrival of Sissie, the exotic other, seems to be a good opportunity (for Marija) to escape 'the deserted looking chamber or its simple funereal elegance...a love nest in an attic that seems to be only a nest now, with love gone...'" (Odamtten 124). Marija's middle class love nest is what hooks calls the "mainstream imposition of sameness," "a provocation which terrorizes" ("Eating the Other" 22-23). Hence, to escape this terror of sameness, one like Marija opts to eat the Other. Food, a symbol of abundance, becomes the medium for the women.

The plums serve a double meaning. While they are representative of Sissie's sexuality, they also symbolize European plenitude. It is the lure of a supposed good life as symbolized by the plum that keeps others bound to the West. The plums are the tangible connection that Sissie and Marija could have without physically and/or emotionally fulfilling any desires that arose between them, although Marija yearns for more than friendship. First, besides the mentioned commonalties between Sissie and the fruit, there is reason to believe that the plums from Marija's garden are especially rare, because of their size, sheen, and succulence. After picking the fruits from the tree, Marija specially keeps them overnight in a polythene bag, in order to soften the plums and rid them of their tangy taste, thereby preserving a soothing sweetness (40- 41). Marija purposely and willingly gives the plums to Sissie, an object of enticement for Sissie and a metaphor of Sissie's sexuality and exoticism for Marija. The text reads:

> ...Marija immediately produced two brown paper bags filled with apples, pears, tomatoes and plums. But/The plums./What plums./ Such plums.

> Sissie had never seen plums before she came to Germany. No, she had never seen real, living, plums ... the fruit stalls were over flowing...her two loves were going to be pears and plums. And on those two she gorged herself.

> So she had good reason to feel fascinated by the character of Marija's plums. They were of a size, sheen and succulence she had not encountered anywhere else in those foreign lands...What she was...not aware of, though, was that those Bavarian plums owed their glory in her eyes and on her tongue not only to that beautiful and black Bavarian soil, but also to other qualities that she herself possessed at that material time:

> youthfulness
> peace of mind
> feeling free

knowing you are a rare article,
Being
Loved (38, 39-40)

So she sat, Our Sister, her tongue caressing the plump berries with
skin colour almost like her own, while Marija told her how she had
selected them especially for her, off *the single tree in the garden* (40;
emphasis mine).

It is important to cite this long passage to highlight Aidoo's careful depiction of
the two women and the fruit and also lesbian desire. Sissie's love for the plums
and Marija's consistent provision of them are loaded with meaning. It is interesting that the fruit, something new and rare to Sissie, is a perpetual welcome
enjoyment for her. After all, a by-product of European domination, Sissie is
mentally familiar with the fruit, just as she might be with snow; thus, the fact
that she is now having access to something that she has been made to know
and appreciate abstractly adds to her fond recognition and enjoyment. This very
reaction to the fruit speaks of a disturbing colonial connection to which even
our critical sister is victim. Here, we see Sissie taking the bait to enter and accept
a world different and far from her own. What makes her enjoying of the fruit
further disturbing is the parallel drawn between her and it. But while Aidoo
says Sissie was not aware of that, it is suggested that part of the enjoyment was
owed to her similarities with the fruit. But as we see Sissie enjoying the plums,
we cannot forget that Marija cultivates them herself.

The similarity between Sissie and the fruit is not only parallel but also symbolic of Sissie's characteristics as a young black female. It is interestingly used
as a same sex double for her. The plum is used to sexualize Sissie and to discuss
a certain forbidden act and enjoyment for Sissie and particularly Marija. But,
Dunton views the plums differently. He sees them as a point of contact and
sharing between Marija and Sissie. He says, "[f]or Marija, the plums are a way of
reaching Sissie, of touching her sensibility, and in their physical appearance, they
are homage. For Sissie, the gift represents what friendship gives more generally,
validation of female qualities in which she can find comfort and self substantia-
tion" (432). There is a sharing relationship between Sissie and Marija, and the
plums, on the surface, represent that. The sharing of the plum, which brings the
two close to each other, can also be viewed as a metaphoric lovemaking as the
lesbian desire is being fulfilled on a symbolic level. But, if this is the case, the
sharing between them cannot be viewed as reciprocal.

A reference to Audre Lorde's *Zami: A New Spelling of My Name* will argue
why Dunton's position is not altogether accurate. In Lorde's biomythography,
the eating of fruit is an identified lesbian symbol and becomes an important
metaphoric medium for Audre and Afrekete. The two's linkage with fruit offers
a similar, but contrasting, reading to Sissie's and Marija's situation. I present this
example to further link the use of the fruit to sexuality and sex and to illustrate
that Marija and Sissie cannot meet each other intimately on an equal level. In
Zami, after engaging in numerous relationships with Euro American women,

where she is constantly the giver and caretaker, who is always disappointed, Audre eventually yearns for and shares an intimate relationship with the black Afrekete. The mutual connection the two realize in their relationship results in love making where they share the use and eating of fruit. Throughout the book, in her discussion of the relations she has with Euro American women, Audre does not share of a bond such as this. She says:

> I took a ripe avocado and rolled it between my hands until the skin became a green case for the soft mashed fruit inside, hard pit at the core. *I rose from a kiss in your mouth to nibble a hole in the fruit skin near the navel stalk, squeezed the pale yellow-green fruit juice in thin ritual lines back and forth over and around your coconut-brown belly.*
>
> *The oil and sweat from our bodies kept the fruit liquid, and I massaged it over your thighs and between your breasts until your brownness shone like a light through a veil of the palest green avocado, a mantle of goddess pear that I slowly licked from your skin.* (251)

What Audre is describing specifically with the mentioning of the color brown is in fact the realization of a desired sexual liaison that involves a racial and cultural connection. She later says of their relationship that "[w]e had come together like elements erupting into an electric storm, exchanging energy, sharing charge, brief and drenching. Then we parted, passed, reformed, and reshaping ourselves the better for the exchange" (253). Audre's relationship with Afrekete is one of mutual sharing unlike Sissie's and Marija's, where hooks maintains that one privileged like Marija will always be in a position of power.

Despite the example above, we can even refer to *Killjoy* to refute Dunton's claims. With her protagonist, and given what Aidoo writes in the first episode, "Into a Bad Dream," the reader should be aware of Aidoo's views about the position of power between the First and Third Worlds. Moreover, the positions are relevant to their women. First World women experience certain privileges at the expense of Third World women.[3] Furthermore, First World women have been hierarchically placed above their sisters of color. As a result, Marija and Sissie cannot meet at an equal level to share and connect in the way that Dunton might hope and suggest they do. For this to be accomplished, their history and political situations have to be erased. In fact, their racial, ethnic, cultural, and personal identities also cannot be significant to their development. Thus, all things being equal, Sissie, then, cannot be an Other that Marija desires. And Marija cannot yearn to transgress racial lines in hopes of indulging in the exotic fruit in the person of Sissie. Obviously, because the mentioned erasure and distancing cannot be and is not feasible, an equal meeting of the two women, as Dunton suggests, is also not possible.

Secondly, in response to Dunton's statement, I see the plums operating in this sense of connecting, sharing, and friendship only on the surface. Symbolically, the plum is a fruit used to entice Sissie to walk into and partake in Marija's world. Now, partaking in this white, lesbian, "bourgeois" housewife's world is loaded with implications. At what level is Sissie to engage in Marija's life, as a friend, sister, sexual object, and substitute for her husband? Perhaps, it would be helpful to apply here Carole Boyce Davies' visitor theory. Although Sissie is geographically the visitor, Marija's presence in her life at this point makes Marija also a visitor, one visiting Sissie's life by befriending her. Sissie must be careful not to go too far with Marija since she, as a black woman, has reason to be ambivalent about her relationship with Marija. Sissie must determine only to "go a piece of the way" with Marija so that her identity as an African woman and all that is implicated with it should not be compromised. Going "all the way home" with Marija would be "taking a route cluttered with skeletons enslavements, new dominations, unresolved tensions and contradictions." It would possibly result in her having to "function either as maid or exotic, silenced courtesan..." (*Black Women, Writing and Identity* 46). Sissie's acceptance of the plum should be one guided with a careful attention to her position in her relationship with Marija. For Vincent Odamtten, "[u]ltimately, despite their succulent appeal, the plums...are about the nature and abuse of power in a world that seems to prevent and over determine the realization of meaningful human relationships" (125). To him, the plums are the "leftovers of (the) imperial handouts" Aidoo mentions in the work (131). If we follow Odamtten's words, the plums then can be read again as the very object separating Marija and Sissie from having an equal relationship. They can represent the privilege Marija has as a Western woman. So, as she introduces the plums to Sissie, Marija reveals to her what Sissie and other Third World people are without, the benefit gained from European exploitation of their Others.

Another discomfort that Aidoo alludes to wanting to evoke might stem from the biblical reference associated with the plums. That the relationship between Marija and Sissie is forbidden and not perceived as normal is indicated by the biblical connection and connotation of "the single tree in the garden." It is from this tree that the fruit is picked. This reference suggests Marija becomes temptress of Sissie, just as the serpent is of Eve. Marija, then, gives Sissie a symbol of what Marija herself wants, the opening of Sissie's eyes to Marija's affection and intentions. Recall that the serpent's reason why Eve should eat the fruit is that eating it would open her eyes. The opening of Eve's eyes would introduce her into a world of knowing, a world in which she would be as wise as God Himself (Genesis 3). It is largely in Marija's interest that Sissie accept the fruit, for taking the plums is to an extent also a seduction into a world of knowing. The opening of Sissie's eyes is not to sexual gratification alone. It is also an invitation, as mentioned earlier, to enter into Marija's world. In Dangerous Knowledge and the Politics of Survival: A Reading of *Our Sister Killjoy* and *A Question of Power*, Caroline Rooney postulates that Sissie and her colleagues' new lifestyle of eating, sleeping, laughing and especially indulging in the plums suggests that "...they are to comply with a certain mythological representation of Europe as a place of utopian plenitude, where nothing is lacking and all *desires* may be *satiated*...In microcosmic terms, it is possible that the plums partially reflect Sissie's seduction into complicity with the myth of Europe's fulfillment of every desire" (104). Rooney's position in light of what Aidoo says about an African girl loose in Europe carries weight here. The critical African Miss does not only stand to enter or perhaps "crossover" into a private world she is not a part of, but she also risks crossing over and assimilating the very ideals she has been rejecting and squinting at all along.

In addition, the sexual overtones connected with the plums are made even clearer as the narrator says that Sissie sat and used her tongue to caress the plump berries with skin-color almost like her own (40). As the black woman's body is sexualized, Sissie becomes like the ripe plum on the stalls of the supermarket for gazing and desired possession. She becomes a product for consumption for their feasting eyes. But she also seemingly participates only at the level of desire. Aidoo writes:

> Sissie in Lower Bavaria was something of a crowd-getter...As for the African Miss, Ah...h...h... look at her costume. How charming. And they gaped at her, pointing at her smile. Her nose. Her lips. Their own eyes Shining. Not expecting her to feel embarrassed. (43)

Sissie, the visitor and tourist, rather becomes the attraction not only for the men, but the women as well. She becomes the object of the gaze, for the feasting eyes and the subject of desire and fulfillment for the likes of Marija, a lonely housewife with a peculiar attraction for "exotic" dark complexioned women. She becomes like the Hottentot Venus that was paraded through France during the nineteenth century and whose body parts, until recently, were yet on display at a French museum. Sissie's exposition can be to an extent compared to that of the Hottentot in that for her German viewers, she is the exotic Other, whose sexuality (and perhaps sexual organs) is somehow a fascination to them. For according to Sander Gilman in "Black Bodies, White Bodies: Toward an Iconography of Female Sexuality in Late Nineteenth Century Art, Medicine, and Literature," Sarah Bartmann's (The Hottentot Venus) sexual parts, her genitalia and her buttocks, served as the central image of the black female throughout the nineteenth century" (216). Her buttocks particularly were connected to the pathology of prostitution and "deviant sexuality" (209). The exposition of Bartmann's body is not distant in meaning from that of Sissie in Lower Bavaria. While Sissie is not particularly observed for her sexual parts and Aidoo mentions that her nose, her lips, and costume are what are being gaped at, what is unmentioned is the question of sexuality. Since the black woman, given the history of which Gilman speaks, is always connected to sexuality, the crowd in Lower Bavaria may not utter the unspeakable, but Aidoo provides that with Marija's sexual interest in the "African Miss," the question of the Other's sexuality cannot be absent from the minds of the gazing audience. What is left unsaid is most crucial to Sissie's image.

As the previous discussion exposes Marija's intentions and motivations, Sissie's also must be questioned. What is she doing there anyway? While Sissie was occasionally curious about Marija's behavior, her naiveté hindered a careful assessment and evaluation of their relationship. For instance, Sissie noticed that "[t]here was certain strangeness about Marija the first time she came to fetch her in the evening. Her eyes had a gleam in them that the African girl would have found unsettling, if the smile that always seemed to be dancing around her lips had also not been more obviously there. She was flushed and hot. Sissie could feel the heat" (45). As the relationship progresses, it becomes obvious to the town's people that Marija's fascination with Sissie is what they call "perverse" (44). However, it appears that while Sissie is a bit suspicious of her companion's behavior, she innocently or perhaps chooses to remain ignorant and unaware of Marija's intentions. Although she is naïve, as the narrator observes, she is certainly not entirely oblivious to the emerging circumstances within which she is entangling herself. The text reveals at various times Our Sister's imaginations about her relationship with Marija:

> Once or so, at the beginning of their friendship, Sissie had thought, while they walked in the park, of what a delicious love affair she and Marija would have had if one of them had been a man.

> Especially if she, Sissie, had been a man…That was a game. A game in which one day, she became so absorbed, she forgot who she was, and the fact that she was a woman….she shivered, absolutely horrified. (61)

The narrator presents the above to clarify that while Sissie is not completely oblivious to what is happening between her and Marija; she only intends to enjoy it should she be a male. But, is this fantasizing, in fact, a veil to cover her desire? One has to wonder where Sissie is on the lesbian continuum[4] that Adrienne Rich suggests all women exist on at one point or another. It is clear that while in a heterosexual marriage, Marija is yet a lesbian as she has sexual desire for other women, but where is Sissie in all of this, particularly as she fantasizes of being a male and Marija her love interest? One must question if this fantasy is in fact already revised as a displaced[5] dream. What is obvious is that Sissie's parameters are not clear to Marija until the inevitable between the two women occurred.

> Sissie felt Marija's cold fingers on her breast. The fingers of Marija's hand touched the skin of Sissie's breast while her other hand groped round and round Sissie's midriff, searching for something to hold on to.

> It was the left hand that woke her up to the reality of Marija's embrace. The warmth of her tears on her neck. The hotness of her lips against hers.

> As one does from a bad dream, impulsively, Sissie shook herself free with too much effort, unnecessarily, so that she unintentionally hit Marija on the right cheek with the back of her right hand.

> It all happened within a second. Two people staring at one another.
> Two mouths wide open with disbelief. (64)

The word "disbelief" in the above passage reveals quite a bit about both Sissie and Marija's confusion and expectations and desires. It might be easy to say that because Sissie is outraged, her disbelief is entirely about the shock of the embrace and kiss initiated by Marija, and Marija's disbelief was a result of the unexpected slap from Sissie. But, I will suggest that part of Sissie's disbelief is how far she herself has extended.

But, it is Sissie's final realization of how far their relationship had extended that shakes her up from her "bad dream" (64). Rooney says that [t]he bad dream is the dream of forgetfulness. After Marija's attempted seduction and Sissie's awakening from the 'bad dream,' it is asked: [a]nd now where was she? How did she get there? What strings pulled by whom drew her into those pinelands..." Rooney concludes that "[i]t is more than a question of a self that forgets itself; it is also a question of historical and cultural self-forgetfulness and oblivion. It is this history—of Europe, of Africa—that the narrating consciousness cannot forget (104). Sissie cannot forget, thus, as she jerkingly wakes up, her immediate thoughts are of home and her mother's akatado-cloth.

> Sissie thought of *home*. To the time when she was a child in the *village*. Of how she always liked to be sleeping in the bedchamber when it rained, her body *completely-wrapped* up in one of her mother's akatado-cloths while mother herself pounded fufu in the anteroom which also served as a *kitchen* when it rained. Oo, to be wrapped up in mother's cloth while it rained. Every time it rained. (64) (*my emphasis*).

Aidoo's use of the words "home" and "village" refers to a background, a source and it connects Sissie to what life for her largely is outside of Western ideological infiltration. The home in the village speaks of a cultural and traditional space where she is sheltered and raised as an Akan or specifically, a Fante. Sissie is obviously yearning to return to this source completely wrapped up within the cloth. The source is home and all the good things for which it stands. Anindyo Roy in "Postcoloniality and the Politics of Identity in the Diaspora: Figuring 'Home,' Locating Histories," says that "[t]raditionally the home has served as the site of origin, as a source of nostalgic understanding of the continuities of private and public self, and a place for recovering or maintaining the stability of this self" (104). Sissie at this point becomes nostalgic; she is feeling a nostalgia, which seeks stability reinstated in the Roy manner. The stability is connected to a national cuisine, familiar space, and a most important item, the akatado. Sissie recalls her mother pounding fufu in a room, which sometimes serves as a kitchen. The mention of the kitchen space, mother, and the akatado cloth here is significant in that the kitchen space is where the nation is educated and a space in which, according to hooks, resistance to oppression is learned.[6] Sissie's remembering of these crucial elements in her life allows her to resist Marija, for Marija and her plums represent the trappings and exploitation of African peoples. The immediate racing of the mind home is a rush back to the nurturance and security of her culture, training, the developing of her identity and her ideologies. Her mother's akatado, then, is the appropriate shelter for her.

The mother's akatado-cloth is not only referring to her biological mother's nurturance, but also her motherland's embrace and protection.[7] Boyce Davies sees the connection of the akatado as a source linking mother and daughter. Her essay, "Wrapping One's Self in Mother's Akatado-cloth: Mother-Daughter Relationships in the works of African Women Writers" points out that:

> [b]eing wrapped up in mother's cloth represents not only warmth and security but the closest possible identification with mother. In a sense it is an attempt to experience life with her. The child who is wrapped in his/her mother's cloth and carried along on her back is in many ways part of her, yet a distinct entity. The adult woman-child who makes this journey back to mother's cloth is therefore making the most explicit mother-daughter connection possible and simultaneously redefining herself. (14)

Furthermore, to emphasize the importance of the akatado-cloth, Anne Adams Graves' comparison of it to the African woman's text is her relevant. Graves uses the Igbo word for akatado, lappa. Chikwenye Ogunyemi in *Africa Wo/Man Palava* cites Adams who says that the lappa[8] is the most important item in the African woman's wardrobe.

The akatado (lappa) is an essential cultural and communal tool for the African. As this particular tool has been used to cover and protect those within African societies, individuals like Sissie, emerging from those societies are responsible for being careful to carry and cover themselves with the akatado so that they are shielded from foreign ideological infiltration. This is not to say that the African should exist in isolation and not be able to experience and learn from other cultures, for after all, Aidoo says in her interview with James that one can gain positive and enriching experiences in foreign lands. But the idea is for Sissie and all other been-tos not to end up like the Ghanaians Sissie met in England, people who have completely forgotten themselves and assimilated or those like Ato, the main character of Aidoo's play, *The Dilemma of a Ghost,* who are caught between two worlds and do not know which one to choose.

Finally, important to the akatado and assimilation is the kiss between Marija and Sissie. Not resisting the kiss can be read as a betrayal or forgetting who she is and from where she comes. This is why Aidoo mentions her awakening and Rooney specifically refers to Sissie's forgetfulness. Symbolically, the kiss can be the oral transference of ideology. It is transference of ideology via the tongue. In a parallel version, we see the importance of the tongue in Neale Hurston's *Their Eyes Were Watching God* when Janie, after relating her story to her best friend Phoebe, tells her she can regurgitate the testimony, because her tongue is in her friend's mouth (6). Placing the tongue in another's mouth is a symbolic means of passing a story, an ideology. By Marija placing her tongue in Sissie's mouth, Sissie will be able to tell Marija's story or become familiar with her ideals, making it her own. Again, the tongue is not just an instrument in relating a story or ideology, but also a tool for the teaching of language. Marlene Philip talks of the gaining of a mother tongue, a mother language via the female tongue ("She Tries Her *Tongue*"). Sissie's embrace of Marija's kiss will also be one of her language. Note that at the point of the kiss, the two women were only able to communicate on a superficial linguistic level. Sissie is not fluent in German and neither does Marija know Fante. The two are able to reach a medium where Sissie uses English and Marija, a combination of English and German—a broken English of sorts. English becomes a medium for them, a compromise. But their means of communication, although communication is indeed taking place, is artificial because English, the medium, is not a concrete one for them. Because English is not their mother tongue, they both cannot always adequately express their emotions and thoughts through it. There is a gap between the two where they are not able to meet directly, but the embrace and kiss symbolically suggest the possible erasure of the third party, English. If the gap is filled or the erasure of the third party accomplished, the fulfillment of the seduction would be Sissie's embrace and acceptance of Marija's world, which for Sissie will be a direct compromise of her ideals and perhaps, even a rejection of her world. As a result, Odamtten sees language in the text as portraying the part of power and dominance. He says that "...this language of power is presented as the power of language to inflict concrete harm. What is shown is that destructive abstractions are not merely abstractions but a matter of real violence and so a question of survival" (109). Sissie's escape from Marija's arms and Western abduction for survival is her return to the source. "While they may have significant similarities, Aidoo's narrative suggests that there is no neutral ground, no place untainted by history, where women from opposite sides of the colonial divide can meet to develop the bonds that could result from the recognition of shared experience" (Samantrai 145). Because there is not a neutral ground but rather historical baggage and the threat of losing oneself, Sissie goes back to retrieve mother's akatado-cloth, in order to reposition herself with her mother country and her ideologies.

Thus, in *Our Sister Killjoy*, Aidoo provides a critique and theory of dominance and the sexual, capitalistic, and imperialistic exploitation of the Third World, particularly Africa. Her theoretical postulation is that as black women are seen as "other," because of colonial and imperial dominance, they are often not seen as complete beings. Rather, the hegemony established by Western colonial and imperial forces that renders them primitive, allows exploitation of not only their resources, but also of their sexuality. Hence, it is not only within heterosexual encounters that black women's bodies are seen as objects of desire. By providing a critical female protagonist, she shows how dangerous it can be for black women in a Western space. Aidoo suggests with Sissie's awakening that the people of the "Third World" do not only have to resist being objectified and abused, they also have the responsibility of staying grounded in their cultural ideologies and always connected to the akatado-cloth.

Notes

1. The kaba is made out of textile waxed material. A complete kaba has three pieces, a blouse like top, a traditional long skirt called a slit, and a loose cloth, which serves as a third piece usually tied about the waist and hips. Sometimes, the third piece is often used as a duku, a head covering. The traditional outfit is usually worn by Western and Eastern African women. But important here is that the third piece can be used in numerous ways. The third piece is the akatado, which basically means a cover. Also, see Carole Boyce Davies' "Wrapping One's Self in Mother's Akatado Cloth."

2. See Sander Gilman's "Black Bodies, White Bodies: Toward an Iconography of Female Sexuality in the Late Nineteenth-Century Art, Medicine, and Literature." *Cultural Inquiry* 12 (Autumn 1985), bell hooks, "Eating the Other: Desire and Resistance," and "Selling Hot Pussy: Representations of Black Female Sexuality in the Cultural Marketplace." *Black Looks: Race and Representation.* Boston, Ma.: South End Press, 1992).

3. See Filomina Steady's introduction in *The Black Woman Cross Culturally*, Omolara Ogundipe-Leslie's "Not Spinning on the Axis of Maleness" in *Re-creating Ourselves. African Women and Critical Transformations*, Cleonora Hudson-Weems' *Africana Womanism* as well as other texts discussing African women and feminism. These texts always make this point to put forth clearly why there is a different focus between Western and African women's feminist agenda.

4. In "Compulsory Heterosexuality and Lesbian Existence," Adrienne Rich suggests that all women exist on a lesbian continuum because all women have woman-identified experiences. Women identified experiences can include or exclude sexual experiences between women. Women may move in and out of the continuum or stay in it all her life.

5. In *Critical Theory Today*, Lois Tyson explains that psychoanalytic theory suggests that people tend to censor their dreams to protect them from repressed experiences, emotions, etc. This censoring of dreams, where a figure or even is replaced with another, is called displacement (20).

6. bell hooks argues that the home space is a place of learning against resistance in her essay, "Homeplace. A Site of Resistance." *Yearning: Race, Gender and Cultural Politics.*

7. Akatado also means to cover. More specifically, it means that which covers. But, I must also note that technically, the akatado is for married women, mothers, and grandmothers. That is, technically and traditionally, a teenager or one who is a young and unmarried woman is not supposed to have the akatado, since it is also connected to a woman's status as regarding maturity. Hence, Sissie's desire to retrieve mother's akatado is even more significant because it is only from her mother or another maternal figure that she can retrieve the item. By referencing the importance of the akatado in this way, Aidoo highlights the important role of the woman in Ghanaian/African society.

8. The full quote by Graves is: "the lappa is the most important item in the African woman's wardrobe. The simple two or three yards of fabric is versatile: it can be used as a dress, a blanket, a pillow, a curtain or screen, a mattress or a mat, a sheet, a bed cover, a table cloth, an umbrella, a headgear, a baby carrier, a sling, a wall decoration, or an aju to cushion and protect the head from the load it carries... Women use it often, men use it also...women's novels, like the lappa, are intended primarily for women who mostly bear burdens, yet they are indispensable for communal use (4).

Works Cited

Aidoo, Ama Ata. Our *Sister Killjoy. Or Reflections from a Black-Eyed Squint.* England. Longman, 1977.

—. *The Dilemma of a Ghost.* England: The Longman Group, 1965.

Azodo, Ada Uzoamaka. "The Multifaceted Aidoo: Ideologue, Scholar, Writer, and- Woman." *Emerging Perspectives on Ama Ata Aidoo.* Eds. Ada Uzoamaka Azodo and Gay Wilentz. Trenton, New Jersey: Africa World Press, 1999. 399-425.

Boyce Davies, Carole. *Black Women, Writing and Identity. Migrations of the Subject.* London: Routledge, 1994.

—. "Wrapping One's Self in Mother's Akatado-Cloths: Mother-DaughterRelationships in the Works of African Women Writers." *Sage* 4.2. (Fall 1987): 11-19.

Boyce Davies, Carole and Ann Adams Graves, Eds. *Ngambika: Studies of Women in African Literature.* New Jersey: Africa World Press, Inc. 1986.

Dunton, Chris. "Wheyting Be Dat?: The Treatment of Homosexuality in African Lit- erature." *Research in African Literatures.* 20.3 (1989): 422-448.

Gilman, Sander. "Black Bodies, White Bodies: Toward an Iconography of Female Sexu- ality in Late Nineteenth-Century Art, Medicine, and Literature." *Critical Inquiry* 12 (Autumn 1985): 204-41.

Hoeller, Hildegard. "Ama Ata Aidoo." *Postcolonial African Writers: A Bio-Bibliographi- cal Critical Source Book.* Eds. Pushpa Naidu Parekh and Siga Fatima Jagne. West- port, Conn., 1998. 32-39.

hooks, bell. "Eating the Other." *Black Looks. Race and Representation.* Boston, Mass.: South End Press, 1992. 21-39.

—. "Homeplace. A Site of Resistance." *Yearning. Race, Gender and Cultural Politics.* Boston, Mass.: South End Pres, 1990. 41-49.

—. "Selling Hot Pussy." *Black Looks. Race and Representation.* Boston, Mass.: 1992. 61- 77.

Hudson-Weems, Cleonora. *Africana Womanism: Reclaiming Ourselves.* Troy, Michigan: Bedford Publishers, 1995.

Hurston, Zora Neale. *Their Eyes Were Watching God.* New York: Harper and Row, 1990.

James, Adeola. *In Their Own Voices. African Women Writers Talk.* London: James Currey, 1990.

Lorde, Audre. *Zami: A New Spelling of My Name.* Freedom, CA: The Crossing Press, 1984.

Odamtten, Vincent. *The Art of Ama Ata Aidoo. Polylectics and Reading Against Neocolo- nialism.* Florida: University of Florida, 1994.

Ogundipe-Leslie, 'Molara. *Re-creating Ourselves. African Women and Critical Transfor- mations.* New Jersey: Africa World Press Inc., 1989.

Ogunyemi, Chikwenye. *Africa Wo/Man Palava.* Chicago: University of Chicago Press, 1996.

Philip, Marlene Nourbese. *She Tries Her Tongue. Her Silence Softly Breaks.* Edward Island, Canada: Ragweed Press, 1989.

Rooney, Caroline. "Dangerous Knowledge and the Poetics of Survival: A Reading of *Our Sister Killjoy* and *A Question of Power.*" *Motherlands. Black Women's Writing from Africa, The Caribbean and South Asia*. London: The Women's Press, 1991. 99-128.

Rich, Adrienne. "Compulsory Heterosexuality and Lesbian Existence." *Signs* 5.4 (1980): 631-60.

Roy, Anindyo. "Postcoloniality and the Politics of Identity in the Diaspora: Figuring'Home,' Locating Histories." *Postcolonial Discourse and Changing Contexts: Theory and Criticism*. Eds. Gita Rajan and Radhika Mohanram. Westport, CT: Greenwood, 1996. 101-115.

Samantrai, Ranu. "Caught in the Confluence of History: Ama Ata Aidoo's Necessary Nationalism." *Research in African Literature*, 2 (1995):141-157.

Steady, Filomena. *The Black Woman Cross-Culturally*. Massachusetts: Schenkman Publishing Company, Inc., 1981.

Tyson, Lois. *Critical Theory Today*. New York: Garland Publishing, 1999.

AFRICAN FILM

Survey of the Historical and Geographical Scope of Gender and Sexuality in African Film

Where African literature uses story writing as a means of communication to document, educate, and motivate society, African film's mode of communication is visual imagery, although other forms, including music and story telling, may be employed. Africans have been involved in the cinema since its inception, with filmmaking in the Maghreb as early as the 1900s. In 1924, the Tunisian Albert Chemama Chikly became Africa's first film producer with *The Girl from Carthage* [*Ain el Ghezal*]. Today, African cinema is garnering international recognition, although filmmakers continue to struggle with funding and distribution. African cinema has also gone through several phases, which Manthia Diawara (*African Cinema: Politics and Culture,* 1992) has summed up into three: "social realist," "historical confrontation between Africa and Europe," and "return to the sources." Teshome Gabriel in *Third Cinema in the Third World* (1982) posits political phases that include uncritical assimilation of Western (western Hollywood film industry), a combative phase, and a remembrance phase. However, in *Black African Cinema* (1994), N. Frank Ukadike has coalesced Diawara and Gabriel's rubrics into thematic development of African cinema. Perhaps, the difficulty in delineating clearly the development of African cinema stems from the reality that African cinema is still emerging, has not quite fully defined itself. It has nonetheless gone through several phases: the foreign colonial production; the African filmmakers imitative genre of the colonial films often financed by foreign interests (see *Monday's Girls* by Ngozi Onwura), films of the radical genre that shun Western stereotypes as they embrace African realities and experiences and most recently, video-cinema in Nigeria and Ghana. Despite this difficulty in categorizing African films, African filmmakers and their critics agree that African cinema has struggled with its dependency on Western or foreign funding sources, reception and distribution. While these issues are not the focus of our study, we wish to draw attention to those as key areas of tension for African cinema.

To combat the dependency on foreign funding and distribution, many African filmmakers since the 1990s have resorted to self production and other media, manifesting themselves strongly in the emergence of a video film culture in Nigeria and Ghana. Thanks to funding efforts by Festival Pan Africain du Cinéma et Télévision de Ouagadougou (FESPACO), the bi-annual African film festival in Burkina Faso, and other organizations such as Société Nationale de Cinématographie du Burkina Faso (SONACIB), many African filmmakers have benefited from financial help. Some filmmakers have achieved some measure of success in the real sense of the word, and these include Sembène Ousmane in *Le Mandat* [the *Money Order*; 1963], *Borom Sarret* (1966), and *Noire de* (Black Girl; 1966), *Ceddo* (1977), and recent films like *Faat Kiné* (2000), and *Moolade* (2004); Safi Faye in *La Passante* (1972); Haille Gerima in *Sankofa* (1993) *Adwa* (1999); Cheick Oumar Sissoko in *Yaaba* (1989), *La Genèse* [Genesis; 1999], and *Finzan* [Dance for the Heroes; 1989], and Djibril Diop Mambety in *Hyenas* (1992), to mention only these few. This list of African films and filmmakers is by no means exhaustive. As indicated above, African cinema is still undergoing extensive self-redefinition today. The efforts of FESPACO, as well as the emergence of the post-apartheid South Africa as a contending force in African filmmaking, and the explosion of video production in Nigeria and Ghana have contributed to the rapid growth of African filmmaking. Also, the growing cooperation of national and regional producers in filmmaking, such as the partnership between the Cameroonian Jean-Pierre Bekolo and the Malian Souleymane Cissé as well as collaboration between African filmmakers and international partners, such as that between Sembène Ousmane and Dany Glover, augur well for the future of filmmaking in Africa.

African filmmakers are also exploring new areas previously not fully explored, such as environmentalism, sexuality, gender, and human rights. Particularly important, and thanks to its historical experience is South Africa as a pioneer for human rights in Africa. According to the National Film Theatre of the South Bank of London, in 2003, the 9th Out of Africa celebration of African Gay and Lesbian films saw as many as 50 films screened in three South African cities--Cape Town, Johannesburg, and Durban--in the month of March, before the 17th London Lesbian & Gay Film Festival, 2-16 April, 2003. The objectives of Out of Africa are to "expand and promote the talents of Lesbian and Gay Filmmakers all across Africa." Their initiatives include film production and distribution, lesbian film production (presently they are calling for contributions of 15-minute lesbian film scripts), and video suitcases, which make it possible to distribute films free of charge in the forms of short dramas, features, and documentaries from the cities into the rural areas in places like Botswana, Zimbabwe, Namibia, and Mauritius.[1]

Contributions on gender and sexuality from film in this anthology are limited. Those on homosexuality as such are based on the study of three West African films on gay life and love--*Dakan* (Destiny; 1997, 87 minutes) by Guinean director Mohammed Camara in French and Mandikan with English subtitles; *Woubi chéri* (1998, 60 minutes) by co-producers/Directors Philip Brooks and Laurent Bocahut in French with English subtitles, and Senegalese opera *Karmen Geï* (2001, 86 minutes), complete with Senegalese dance and music, by Senegalese Joseph Gaï Ramaka in French and Wolof with English subtitles. *Karmen Geï* is a modern adaptation of Bizet's opera *Carmen*, and so reinvents the free spirit of the Carmen legend. It shows a bisexual heroine and a cross section of Senegalese musicians and dancers working together to pull off a sensual exploitation of minority sexuality on the continent. Observe in passing that Ramaka is a celebrated and controversial Senegalese filmmaker whose formative background is in Filmmaking and Visual Anthropology. Over the course of the past fifteen years, Ramaka has founded production and distribution companies in Senegal and France, and has won wide acclaim for his documentary and feature films. He is also an activist for press freedom in Africa and throughout the whole world. More recently, in 2006, he has made a film essay, *Et si Latif avait raison*! [What if Latif were Right!], in French and Wolof with English subtitles, a blend of fiction and documentary, which is an acerbic criticism of the Abdoulaye Wade regime in power presently in Senegal. Ramaka takes a jab at the former strong opposition leader for four decades, before he won a landslide victory as president in 2000, but who now, in Ramaka's view, increasingly puts restrictions and denies freedom of expression to the media.

Even with the paucity in the number of African films that address gay life or homosexuality in this volume as noted above, homosexuality has been better and more profoundly addressed in film than in literature in Africa. Observe that a one-year period is between the production of *Dakan* and *Woubi chéri*, yet curiously both films claim to be the first of their kind in sub-Saharan Africa to treat homosexuality as a film theme. If we learn nothing from this confusion, it is that there are not nearly enough films on homosexuality in West Africa. Decidedly, *Dakan* precedes *Woubi chéri* in chronological order of publication, but critics distinguish the two films further by saying that *Woubi chéri* is the first to supply a language and vocabulary to describe homosexual practice and the practitioners of homosexuality: a lesbian (*toussou*); a transvestite (*bat*; comes out only at night, because forbidden by the free society to express his erotic desires openly); a gay man who prefers to be penetrated (*woubi*; female or 'passive' male); a gay man who prefers to penetrate his partner (*yossi*; 'active' male); the yossi can be a bisexual, who could actually be married to a woman.

Homosexuality in *Woubi chéri* is all the more interesting, because of its distinction between transvestites and transsexuals. Transvestites, states Corraze, are predominantly men, who like to cross dress, for sexual excitement, which could often lead to spontaneous orgasm, masturbation, or sexual intercourse. Transvestites are mainly heterosexuals, are hardly homosexuals, and no matter what happens, keep whatever notion of gender they reserve for themselves (1996: 47). Murray and Roscoe note that among the Swahili of East Africa sometimes male transvestites are described as "passive homosexuals" (1998: 70). The film *Woubi chéri* manifests a situation where a transsexual, Barbara, deeply identifies with the female sex in diverse forms of behavior or attitude, including sex role, sexual identity, and clothing, maintaining a weak identification with the male Ivorian homosexual community.

Nonetheless, the transsexual seeks secondary characteristics of the female sex, through the taking of hormone pills, which make his breasts, grow large like a woman's, and giving him the skin and looks of a woman. He refrains from going all the way to acquire the primary characteristics of a woman, through a surgical and corrective intervention, as is evident in Barbara in *Woubi chéri*. Hence his (Barbara's) gender inversion appears to happen at the behavioral and self-identification levels only. Unlike most transsexuals, he does not reject the homosexual status, yet affirms that of the female gender, or the identity of a bisexual, according to his fancy. Hence *Woubi chéri* denotes two extremes of homosexuality--transvestites and transsexuals (see Corraze 47-48).

Talking about transsexuals, a controversy surrounds a transsexual such as Barbara in *Woubi chéri*, who would objectively carry on like a homosexual, but who would reject homosexuality for himself and other homosexual partners that he may have, and harboring a particular and stifling disgust for his own sex organ. Such a refusal of homosexuality is made all the more serious, because he is rejected by real homosexuals, who make it difficult for him to integrate fully in their group, hence he seeks out bisexuals (see Corraze 48). Thus, *Woubi chéri* is the filmmaker's exploration of an extreme form of homosexuality in contemporary times in one African cultural space, where transvestites adorn female clothes and dance like women as a means of identification and pleasure. More importantly, a traditional form of transvestite transforms into a nuclear form--the transsexual--that identifies with the opposite sex and makes a homosexual choice, when he wants.

Another very interesting point that *Woubi chéri* raises is the subject of intersexuality, again seen in the major character, Barbara. In a recent scientific claim by John Money, John's Hopkins School of Medicine's world-renowned psychologist and sex researcher and benefactor of The Kinsey Institute, at least 12 million Americans today were born with ambiguous sexuality. He says that the concepts of masculinity and femininity are culturally constructed, adding that the link between sex and gender is somewhat weak. Hypothetically, he adds, a male intersex baby can lead a successful life as a female, if treated surgically and with hormones early enough in life. A counter viewpoint, however, holds that this may not work, due to the influence of pre-natal hormones on the child. In the book, *As Nature Made Him*, which details his exploration of the potentials of social agents on sex and gender, Money focuses on a boy raised as a girl after a failed circumcision (see SEX♂ SEX♀ AND MORE SEX☿, *Indiana Alumni Magazine*, November/December 2004, 43), and the untoward consequences of early sex change for children. Also worthy of note is *Kinsey*, a film on the Kinsey Institute's work, released November 2004 by Fox Searchlight Pictures. According to the director Sanders, "Kinsey was just starting to grapple with how important the social roles of men and women are in shaping their sexual behavior. Today we're paying more and more attention to how gender roles influence sexual behavior" (ibid.). Furthermore, Anne Fausto-Sterling argues for the imperative of including three new, middle sex categories to the already existing male and female categories, namely, hermaphrodites (Herms); fermaphrodites (Ferms), and mermaphrodites (Merms), in "The Five Sexes: Why Male and Female Are Not Enough," published in *Sciences*, a journal of the New York Academy of Sciences, March/April 1993 (see also Fausto-Sterling 2005, "The Five Sexes Revisited"). According to Fausto-Sterling, true herms are rare, but function as male and female, with one ovary and one testis each that work; one part is Hermes, and the other part Aphrodite, both Greek gods. In Ferms, the female parts predominate, despite the presence of some male parts, such as a penis that can be found in the area where a clitoris would normally be in a female. On the other hand, Merms have dominant male features, with some few feminine features, such as a penis that looks like female labia that did not close properly during the early development of the sex organs (2005: 13-18).

Since then, research on intersexuality has come into vogue. A new, more layperson-like term "intersex" has taken over the relay from the more scientific three terms used by Fausto-Sterling--Herms, Ferms, and Merms--to designate all children born neither completely male nor female. According to executive director, Cheryl Chase, of The Intersex Society of North America (ISNA), established in 1993, whose objective is to inform, counsel, and guide intersex children and their parents, the institute has a double mission: "[to] create public awareness and understanding of intersex conditions, to lessen the trauma to parents who have a child with intersex characteristics and to lessen the stigma and trauma thrust upon adolescents and adults who find out they are intersex" (*Indiana Alumni Magazine*, November/December 2004, 41). The ultimate goal is to fight what ISNA perceives as outmoded views of sex and gender. Chase continues: "We are working to move from an entrenched medical system dominated by surgeons and endocrinologists who believe the goal is to make intersex children gender 'normal.' We are moving toward a team approach in which mental health professionals play a leadership role in helping these children grow up into adults with happy, fulfilling lives" (ibid.). According to Janssen, a psychologist who studies sex and gender based on the findings of Fausto-Sterling:

"Intersex helps us look at sex and gender in a way that isn't possible with those who are sexually male or female" (ibid.).

Dakan, the Guinean film on African homosexuality is also innovative in its own way for a number of reasons. California Newsreel states:

> *Dakan* begins with the most sexually explicit opening scene in African cinema. Rather than the usual rural landscape or urban panorama locating the characters in a recognizable social or geographical context, the camera focuses on an isolated couple locked in a clandestine embrace in a sports car at night. The shot becomes even more transgressive when we recognize the couple is two young men. When one of them later tells his mother he's attracted to another man, she replies: "Since time began, it's never happened. Boys don't do that. That's all there is to it." Dakan thus becomes the story of two men who by "coming out" disappear; become invisible to their families and society, because their society has no language which recognized their love.[2]

California Newsreel sees the similar psychological profiles of the two gay lovers, student protagonists Sori and Manga, as rendering *Dakan* peculiar, touching on Sigmund Freud's theory on the origins of homosexuality as an over-bearing father or father figure or an over-protective mother or mother figure as the cause of certain children turning homosexual as they grow up. Sori's father, Bakary, an entrepreneurial and successful businessman, would have liked his unambitious son to be strong and successful in business too. He threatens him at every opportunity. It is at that point in his growth that the homosexuality emerges as essentially a search for the male element that seems to be missing or is obliterated in him. Manga, for his part, has a mother, Fanta, who doted on him since his father disappeared from the family. When signs of homosexuality emerge, all his mother does is take him to the native doctor for healing, again persisting in her doting and spoiling game. Hence, in seeking out same-sex desire, Manga appears to be searching eternally in vain for the male element of his being that eludes him. A psychoanalytic exploration of homosexuality here has nothing to do with biology.

According to another Sigmund Freud's psychoanalytic view on human sexuality, detailed in a letter to an American mother of a homosexual, homosexuality is not a disease, yet is a variation of sexual function, which results from a cessation in sexual development at a certain period of childhood. Furthermore, what is seen as normal sexuality is heterosexual, and aims at the reproduction of the species. For those who would become homosexual, there is a complex development, due to three obstacles: stagnation in development of the individual, two fixations, and the absence of a solution to the Oedipus complex. Jacques Corraze explains:

> Il y a « un certain arrêt sexuel du développement sexuel » (Freud) parce que l'homosexuel, comme le pervers, renonce à la procréation, mais alors que le second n'a pas dépassé le stade de l'objet partiel,

celui de l'autoérotisme, le premier ne s'est pas affranchi d'un stade ultérieur : celui où la libido abandonne le propre corps du sujet comme objet d'amour (narcissisme) pour se porter sur un autre corps qui lui ressemble (choix d'objet homosexuel). La première fixation se situe au niveau du stade anal : la relation anale avec sa dichotomie Activité-Passivité, actualisée par l'expulsion active des féces et leur passage contre la muqueuse anale, se transpose sur un autre plan sexuel par une série d'identifications (bâton fécal = pénis ; perte fécal = castration ; matière fécale = enfant ; anus = vagin). La seconde fixation se trouve au stade phallique : le pénis est présent dans les deux sexes ; chez le garçon apparaît l'angoisse de castration, conduisant au fantasme de la femme phallique ; chez la fille se rencontre le refus de son absence, conduisant au complexe de virilité ou à la revendication masculine. Enfin, au moment complexe d'Oedipe, l'angoisse de castration du garçon peut aboutir à une identification inverse important : identification à la mère et désir d'avoir une enfant du père, renforcée par un attachement génital excessif au père. « L'homosexualité est l'ensemble des conduites qui expriment une relation féminine au père » (Pasche). Chez la fille, la valorisation du clitoris, au détriment du vagin, débouche sur l'identification au père et sur le désir d'avoir un enfant de la mère (1996: 34-35).

[A "certain cessation of sexual development" (Freud) occurs, because the homosexual, like the (sexual) pervert, renounces procreation, but whereas the latter has not grown beyond the autoerotic phase of seeing self as a partial love object, the former has not gone beyond the ulterior stage, that in which the libido abandons its own body as love object (narcissism), rather it seeks another body that resembles itself (homosexual object choice). The first fixation is at the anal phase, that is to say, the anal relationship with the activity-passivity dichotomy, actualized by the active expulsion of feces and their passage against the anal mucosa, transposed on another plane, the sexual plane, by a series of identifications (fecal stick = penis; fecal loss = castration; fecal matter = child; anus = vagina). The second fixation is at the phallic phase in which the penis is present in both sexes. Castration anguish occurs in the boy, leading to fantasy for the phallic woman. The girl, for her part, refuses the absence of the phallus, leading to virility complex or affirmation of masculinity. Finally, at the Oedipus complex phase, the boy's castration anguish can lead to a significant inverse identification, namely, identification with the mother and the desire to have the father's child, reinforced by an excessive genital attachment to the father. "Homosexuality is the outcome of behaviors that express a feminine relationship with the father" (Pasche). For the girl, valorizing the clitoris, to the detriment of the vagina, results in identification with the father and desire to have a child by the mother [*Azodo's translation*].

Thus, the male homosexual would eternally look for the absent father/ maleness in loving other men, and the female homosexual the absent mother/femaleness in loving other women. Accordingly, he or she must necessarily seek affairs with numerous men or women, since it is near impossible for him or her to find what he or she is missing. This seems to be an affirmation that explains the tendency of homosexuals in general to be promiscuous. Dr. Elizabeth Moberly shares Freud's view of the psychology of human sexuality as given above.[3] But, certain other psychologists, like Bieber, have refused these assertions, arguing that accepting them would be tantamount to accepting that all human beings are latently homosexuals. They affirm that in their own practices they had not encountered anything that validated the omnipresence of latent homosexuality in humans (Corraze 1996: 38-40). On the other hand, however, at the pre-human level, there persists the problem of animal homosexuality, where certain animals, like the cock, and rat, have sometimes been observed to take the female pose of submission that invariably encouraged a male animal to mount them (Corraze 41-46).

Thus, bisexuality is another issue worthy of exploration, and implicit in the films *Woubi chéri*, *Dakan* and *Karmen Gei*. According to Freud, "*En chacun de nous, tout au long de la vie, la libido normale oscille entre des objets mâles et femelles.*" [In each one of us, through out all the days of our lives, the normal libido oscillates between male and female objects of love. *Azodo's translation*]. He adds that bisexuality is more frequent with girls, due to the clitoris, where the conflicts that lead to homosexuality are more prevalent, and constitute the source of their inferiority complex. Briefly put, through virility with another boy the boy tries to compensate for his feminine nature, just as the girl in seeking out other girls tries to compensate for her desire of a phallus (Corraze 1996: 36-37).

Finally, Freud's affirmation on bisexuality also raises the question of latent homosexuality in all human beings: « *En plus d'une hétérosexualité manifeste, une quantité très importante d'homosexualité latente ou inconsciente peut être trouvée chez des gens normaux.* » [In addition to overt heterosexuality, a significant amount of latent or unconscious homosexual tendency is possible among straight people. *Azodo's translation*]. Corraze explains further that this type of sublimated latent homosexuality finds expression in relationships of friendship, fraternities, and sororities, as can be seen in clubs, convents, seminaries, armies, and churches. These kinds of covert homosexuality show up in dysfunctional heterosexual relationships and in a multitude of difficulties of relationships with the two sexes (Corraze 37).

Fundamentally, *Dakan* is about human love in many unfamiliar shapes and forms (California Newsreel), often in defiance of the norm, or convention. It is ambiguous, for example, for Manga to confess to his white girlfriend Oumou that his mother is his wife, and to Sori his partner his disappointment that he, Sori, could not be the mother of his children; it is a failure that Manga sees as the injustice that Sori has done to him. Ironically, it is Oumou, Manga's white girlfriend, who takes care of Sori's son with a woman. Manga's mother, despite her objections to the relationship of Sori and her son Manga still asks Manga to give Sori a bracelet with the inscription, "Take care of my child." Clearly,

Dakan is complex and complicated, differing in more than a few ways from *Woubi chéri*.

Dakan is not about the reality of Guinean society in the way that *Woubi chéri* is a mirror of a section of Ivory Coast transvestite homosexual community. That would be limiting the scope of this unprecedented African homosexual film too unnecessarily and unfortunately. On the contrary, the unhappy ending of the story, the lack of integration of a homosexual couple into traditional community (California Newsreel), speaks to the need for the mass media to facilitate communication between sections of African societies, to work towards the integration of all marginal peoples in small African communities into the larger societies.[4]

Notes

1. (www.outuk.com/llgff/features_reviews_03.html).
2. (www.newsreel.org/films/dakan.htm).
3. In *Homosexuality: Opposing Viewpoints*, p. 190, the editor Mary E. Williams cites one school of opinion led by Dr. Elizabeth Moberly on the unconscious behavior of homosexuals in search of their natural identity saying:

> The repressed love-need of the young child may be reactivated in later years. This is the phenomenon which, when it happens to involve a love-source of the same sex, is labeled homosexual. On our data, this condition is essentially the reactivation of a thwarted infantile love-need that has persisted unmet and hence still requires to be met. We are not, however, suggesting on account of this that homosexuality is not truly involved in this condition. What we are suggesting is that this is the so-called homosexual condition in its essence, viz. an unmet need for love from the parent of the same sex (109).

Moberly explains further that homosexuals have ambivalence about their same-sex relationship, because it is more an activity to meet their need for love that has consistently been denied them, and not a rejection of the opposite sex:

> Homosexuality...is fundamentally a problem of gender identity, rather than of sexuality as such.... The homosexual's love for men is but the boy's thwarted love for his father, i.e. it is a masculine and an identificatory love of the boy's gender identity. Hence it is in no way analogous to the love of the female for the male, since this latter kind of love does not aim at fulfilling an incomplete gender identity, but rather presupposes the completion of the identificatory process (ibid).

An opposing viewpoint holds, after exploring Freud's ideas on homosexuality in his "Letter to an American Mother of a Gay Son," as well as the ideas of a German sexologist and homophile theorist, Magnus Hirschfeld, the 1949 Kinsey Report, and Evelyn Hooker's studies of homosexuals and heterosexuals, that "Gayness Is Normal: Myth 2: Gay and lesbian people are psychologically maladjusted." It adds that "individuals with a homosexual orientation were as normal as heterosexuals" (Kinsey Report, 196). Mary E. Williams, Editor of *Homosexuality: Opposing Viewpoints*, further notes that it was in 1973 that the American Psychiatric Association declassified homosexuality as a mental disorder that needs to be treated, starting with a battery of psychological tests. It continues:

> In fact, the American Pediatric Association stated that trying to change gay or lesbian sexual orientation would be unethical and grounds for malpractice. Therefore, the idea that gay and lesbian people are somehow less mentally healthy, well-adjusted, or able to cope compared to their heterosexual brothers and sisters can be put to rest for good. Of course, as with any group, some persons who are gay and lesbian may have psychiatric or psychological disorders, but this occurs no more or less often than in the rest of the population (196).

See also Paul Robinson, "Freud and Homosexuality," in *Homosexuality and Psychoanalysis*. Eds. Tim Dean and Christopher Lane, 91-97. Robinson sees Freud's treatment of homosexuality as not "pathologizing," but rather as "normalizing." He says that in "Three Essays on the Theory of Sexuality" (1905), Freud's view is that "All human beings are capable of making a homosexual object-choice and have in fact made one in their unconscious." He continues:

> In Freud's psychic universe, homosexuality is everywhere, insinuating itself into the psychic lives of the most impeccably "normal" and presentable individuals. Indeed, no one has done more to destabilize the notion of heterosexuality than Freud. In Freud's universe there simply are no heterosexuals, at least not psychologically. Similarly, he insists that manifest heterosexuality, far from being a fact of nature, is a precarious psychic achievement, and one that needs to be accounted for. As he writes, again in "Three Essay," "The exclusive interest felt by men for women is also a problem that needs elucidating and is not a self-evident fact based upon an attraction that is ultimately of a chemical capture" (93).

4. www.newsreel.org/films/dakan.htm.

Chapter 13

Woubi chéri: Negotiating Subjectivity, Gender, and Power

Maureen Ngozi Eke

They are like bats, they live hidden. They move in groups like birds nesting in the trees. They gather bit by bit and you don't see them 'til suddenly, the tree is teeming with them. That's woubis for you.
—*Woubi chéri*, 1998

Addressing his representation of the marginalized life of black gay men in London, who must find secret spaces, such as the parks, to meet in his film, *Young Soul Rebels*, Isaac Julien comments in "States of Desire," his conversation with bell hooks: "I think that a lot of black men . . . who are probably bisexual, who are not gay-identified, go to spaces where they're able to make some sort of acknowledgment of their own desires. I think it's dangerous that people are driven to those spaces" *(Transition* 0.53 (1991) 183-184). Julien's comments while referring specifically to the dilemma of black gay men in London also applies to the dilemma of woubis as suggested by my epithet. In a number of scenes in the film *Woubi chéri* (1998), the characters struggle to find safe place to meet, to host their party, away from the threatening gazes of the public, outside the confines of a society where they are often threatened with physical violence.

Embedded in my opening epithet and in Isaac Julien's description of the life of black gay men in London is a desire to articulate one's subjectivity differently and outside or away from the confining boundaries of society. For like bats, which use sonic sensory to locate one another, woubis "know how to find each other; they always manage to have their own hideouts."

In documenting the life of a group of woubis and yossis in Abidjan, Ivory Coast, directors Phillip Brooks and Laurent Bocahut ask us to question with "open eyes" our cultural construction of gendered identities and the codification of black masculinity. The woubis' representation of their own subjectivities—themselves as speaking subjects of their own narratives—are fraught with tensions, which underscore each individual's struggle to clarify her/his identity, role, and relationship with the community. The film is composed of multiple vignettes of narratives: individual narratives about the woubis and yossis, although the dominant narrative is about Barbara, and a collective narrative about the woubis and yossis who organize to form Ivory Coast Transvestite

Association (ICTA). Each of these narratives attempts to clarify each individual's journey from closeted passivity to "outed" subject position and agency. These narratives, which migrate and dance around each other, eventually coalescing into the party and dancing at the end of the film, organized by the ICTA, give the subjects opportunity to announce their collective identity to the public.

The group's public demonstration of unity through the party is a deliberate and carefully choreographed act of resistance against cultural and traditional definitions of heterosexuality and binary male/female gendered roles as normative. In fact, part of the film's goal is the teasing, exploding, and undermining of cultural constructions or normative definitions of identities, more specifically, gendered identities and notions of masculinity. We are informed, almost belligerently, that woubis belong to "the third millennium," as Barbara puts it, "a different community," and as such, "they act and live differently." They have their own language, their own "lingo, our own dictionary," Barbara asserts. Through this self-narration into emergence, in other words, "outing" on film, they acknowledge the performance of woubi identity as a transgressive act. They explicitly reject traditional boundaries that codify them as men, not women, insisting that such definitions of gender and sexuality have been culturally constructed to prescribe or create ideas about appropriate roles and sexual identities for people and to contain such subjects.

In her book *Gender Trouble*, Judith Butler postulates that gender is culturally constructed. "Originally intended to dispute the biology-is-destiny formulation," she says, "the distinction between sex and gender serves the argument that whatever biological intractability sex appears to have, gender is culturally constructed; hence, gender is neither the causal result of sex nor as seemingly fixed as sex" (6). Then she adds, "[the] unity to the subject is thus already potentially contested by the distinction that permits of gender as a multiple interpretation of sex" (6). Butler's contention would suggest that social or cultural notions and definitions of gender are unstable and can be transgressed. In fact, she contends that "if gender is the cultural meanings that the sexed body assumes, then a gender cannot be said to follow from a sex in anyone way" (6). So, "it does not follow that the construction of 'men' will accrue exclusively to the bodies of males or that 'women' will interpret only female bodies . . . there is no reason to assume that genders ought to also remain as two" (6). Butler's hypothesis creates a space for the possibilities of multiple sexes whose presence transgresses traditional normative definitions of the binary sex/gendered identities. If as Butler postulates gender does not mirror sex, then we cannot easily designate roles as female or male, except for those that are mutable or biological (i.e. reproductive roles). Indeed, as Butler states, "when the constructed status of gender is theorized as radically independent of sex, gender itself becomes a free floating artifice, with the consequence that man *and masculine* might just as easily signify a female body as a male one, and woman *and feminine* a male body as easily as a female one" (6).

Such radical reading of gender lends itself well to my analysis of *Woubi chéri* and calls into question what is perceived as traditional (perhaps African) normative definitions of gendered identities—male/female or masculine/feminine. *Woubi chéri* suggests that such identities are performed, "posed," framed by the performative acts of subjects in search of their identities. Indeed, the making of gender, (maleness/femaleness) according to the film, stems from the agency of subjects whose acts inform the particular subject identities they perform. The film seems to postulate, therefore, that unlike the delineation of gendered identities through culturally prescribed roles and acts or behavioral practices which presuppose that biology invests bodies with gendered attributes, agency, rather, claimed by subjects who transgress the sex-gender binary, invests those subjectivities with gender. Ironically, while the film vogues gendered identities codified in traditional terms as male/female by emphasizing the transgressiveness of the identity acts of the filmed subjects, the subjects signal their difference by appropriating certain attributes, often traditionally associated with the binary male/female gendered identities. Consequently, the film renders problematic sexual/gender identities by underscoring their ambivalence. The camera also helps to make problematic our own desire to invest the bodies with meanings, hence, to fix the identities as gendered. We are seduced by the camera's gaze; we become voyeurs of African male bodies, which offer alternative and multiple meanings.

Whereas we can fix only the blackness of the bodies, we are uncertain about the specific gender of the subjects. As woubis (gays, some of whom are also transvestites), the physical bodies, on camera, presented as female, further destabilize our conceptions of gender and sexuality and any attempts to fix them. Barbara, for instance is biologically a man, but dresses as a woman and presents herself to us as such. In all the screenings of this film that I have attended, a large percentage of the audience has failed to identify Barbara as a man until provided that information. That difficulty is driven home further at the end of the film, when Khorogolais describes Barbara to a group of men as "a double-edged knife." Gesturing to the men with a knife, he adds, "[you] see this knife?" It's sharp here and sharp there." Khorogolais finds it difficult and uncomfortable to define Barbara's sexual and gendered identities to a group of African men without reverting to metaphors. In this instance, it is Barbara who interjects silently to another man, "I am a boy like you," and then tells Khorogolais to inform the men that she is not a woman. Indeed, it is Barbara, not Khorogolais, who actually names her gender. The announcement prompts the men to wonder "who is Barbara really?" as Khorogolais puts it.

Barbara's duality seems to suggest that gender is performative. Barbara is able to migrate through her society as "female," although she is biologically a man. As Butler points out, the performativity of gender does not simply mean waking up one morning and donning a gender. Rather, this performativity is ritualized, requiring repetition. "As in other ritual social dramas," Butler states, [this] repetition is at once a reenactment and a re-experiencing of a set of meanings already socially established; and it is the mundane and ritualized form of their legitimation" (*Gender Trouble* 1990, 140). As a transvestite, Barbara must physically transform herself daily into the female identity that is perceived and received publicly. Like wise, some of the other woubis, Tatiana and Tina, for instance, employ similar self-transformative acts in order to create their public selves. In fact, it is through the (re)evaluation of the various representations of these bodies and consciousness that we come to know their subjects.

As a transvestite, Barbara is able to embrace an alternate gender identity from that by which she is biologically or anatomically inscribed, inverting one identity to foreground the other, and as Butler has suggested, playing "upon the distinction between the anatomy of the performer and the gender that is being performed" (1990: 137). Barbara is not anatomically a woman, but her public identity is female. Indeed, Barbara's performance as would that of several others in the film supports Esther Newton's contention that "drag" is a "double inversion that says my appearance is an illusion" because "my outside appearance is feminine, but my essence 'inside' is masculine" (qtd. Butler 1990: 137).

But such identity as Newton acknowledges is fraught with internal tensions and contradictions. For woubis, the outside is really the inside / "reality" concretized. Hence, it is not illusory. Rather, to them as Newton suggests, what seems to be illusory, the unreal, is the imaginary outside, now submerged under the clothing. For Barbara, the woubi, the perceived public persona or "outside" identity is more real than the submerged maleness. She states: "I am a transvestite. It's special. But I am still called a woubi in so far as I'm a boy who behaves like a woman." Accordingly, Barbara is pre-occupied with performing a female self signified by her various acts of self-creation: dressing, facial make-up, bodily gestures and poses. While for the audience /observer, these acts may "vogue" femininity, they, nevertheless represent ritualized affirmations of the self for Barbara, because they have become daily acts and reminders of her resistance against maleness or the codification of her identity as male.

LIVING LIFE LIKE AN ARTIST

Unlike Barbara, whose "battle" is waged against a rigid society, unseen boundaries and terrains which attempt to contain her, Laurent's resistance is against social strictures represented by his father. Thus, it is against patriarchy, a male-ordered society, that he directs his frustration. In a semi autobiographical segment of the film, he narrates poignantly his anguish at discovering his difference, a difference which alienated him from his family and from other males. Narrating to the camera he states, "One day, I didn't want to go to school anymore and my dad told me his brother, a mechanic, had a garage and that he had a job for me as an apprentice mechanic. I thought I'd get all dirty. It was a man's job; I didn't want to. I bravely told him: 'Dad, I can't.'" Laurent challenges cultural ideas and ideals about maleness and male roles and jobs by becoming a hairdresser instead of an automobile mechanic apprentice as his father had suggested. Although to westerners, hairdressing may not carry the same gender codification as women's domain and effeminate, which it carries for some Africans, Laurent is clearly aware of the implications of his choice and its violation of assumed ideas about men's work. Laurent suggests that he can not live up to the masculine standards which his father embraces; he cannot be the man his father wants. The masculine ruggedness or hardness and dirt associated with automobile mechanics, which both Laurent and his father define as a man's work, are not easily evoked by hairdressing, especially among many African communities, a reality that Laurent acknowledges. In a similar vein, Laurent's self-gendering into femaleness can only be seen as a production or performance based on assumed attributes of femaleness.

According to Gargi Bhattacharyya in *Sexuality and Society*, "[sexuality] holds a special place in the conception of techniques of the self—because it is in this arena that the competing impulses of pleasure and constraint are balanced in the artwork of selfhood" (8). Although Laurent reads sexuality and gender in relation to socially codified roles, Barbara refuses to be contained, opting to employ her own creativity like an artist. As Bhattacharyya adds, "[t]echniques of the self refer to the ways in which we learn to present ourselves as our own special creations, works of art that we make everyday" (8). Indeed, Barbara would agree with Bhattacharyya. Barbara sees herself as an artist engaged in self-creation. "You have to be creative, live life like an artist," she says. "You can't always be down-to-earth," she adds. Clearly, the obvious display of deliberate identity shifts by the woubis suggests that down-to-earthiness does not help them transcend the daily assault of hostility which they experience. But as a transvestite, Barbara is able to mask her "inside" identity as male with clothes and make up that offer the possibility of an "outside" identity as female. In several scenes we observe Barbara and the other woubis work at transforming themselves into women. Tina, for instance, is frequently seen making up her face. In one scene, we notice her observing herself in the mirror. She is wearing facial make-up, white lipstick and a long wig. Another is the market scene where the woubis go to purchase clothing and items in preparation for the ICTA party. We observe some getting their hair braided while Barbara tries out a number of colorful fabrics one of which she will use for her party gown.

As drags, the woubis reject or even mock the categorization and reduction of their identities to a unitary gender. Sostene's outburst, "I refuse categorically to be labeled," is clearly a verbalization of resistance. In fact, their drag is a public act of resistance as well as self affirmation. Barbara, the President of ICTA flaunts her sexual identity, declaring war on her society's rigid categories, and desiring a mixed up collective. "I do battle every day when I am out and about," she declares. Then, she adds, "I spread my magic powder to change controus into yossis, toussous into lesbians. I promote woubia . . . . The good and the bad all mixed up." Like Shakespeare's Puck, performing magic acts or fantastic tricks on individuals who remain inflexible and intolerant, Barbara wishes to transform her society into a genderless entity—making toussous lesbians and yossis controus. For her and the other woubis, gender is irrelevant, only individual subjectivities and acts of self-affirmation matter.

Indeed, the film is transgressive in challenging the often flat, "one-dimensional textured," to borrow bell hooks' term, representation of black male identities. Such transgressive representation as Isaac Julien contends, "becomes an exciting new way of uncovering various taboos in black politics or black cultural representations" (171). While blackness or Africanness is central to the identities of the individuals in *Woubi chéri,* Julien contends that blackness as "a sign is not enough." He asks, "What does the subject do, how does it act, how does it think politically?" In many ways, those are the questions the film and its subjects attempt to answer. Barbara's closing comments address her desire to re-figure herself as subject. "Who is Barbara? What is Barbara?" one of the speakers in the film asks. As if in response to these rhetorical questions, Barbara offers: "the boy who made herself into a woman." That is Barbara's autobiography. It is one anchored to acts of resistance aimed at locating one within alternative oppositional spaces. "You can't always be down-to-earth. Tradition is fine, but you have to be in-between. I think that's what the third millennium will be all about, a mix of modern and traditional, different ways of life and sex," Barbara announces to us. The "third millennium," the in-between space, as Homi Bhabha has suggested, provides the "terrain for elaborate strategies of selfhood—singular or communal—that initiate new signs of identity and innovative sites of collaboration, and contestation..." (*Location of Culture* 1-2). For Barbara, this middle ground—this state of being bi-sexual, in-between genders, belonging to the "third millennium"—is fertile ground for the retranslation of oneself. It is the site for transformative creative acts of identity construction. This for her is where the artistic spirit resides.

In her book *Bisexual Spaces*, Clare Hemmings describes bisexuality in the "current sexual and gendered imaginary" as "always the middle ground between sexes, genders, and sexualities, rather than being a sexuality, or indeed a gender or sex, in itself" (2). She points out that bisexuality, however, as perceived in contemporary queer and feminist theories is not neutral. Indeed, as creative and liberating as Barbara and the woubis may perceive it, this "third millennium" location is a space of contestation, filled with ambivalence.

Certainly, this declaration of one's agency is empowering. In a patriarchal society where power is perceived in terms of gendered roles and sexual politics, the woubis and yossis are ultimately disempowered by their location outside those traditional paradigms. They are all "theories," Barbara says, but she acknowledges that those theories define her as different, even from childhood. Jean Jacques' comment, "Despite my present situation, I'm still respected by my family" (as male) underscores his awareness of the disenfranchising nature of woubia life. Ironically, what he finds threatening is his perceived loss of masculinity, which has been described as rugged, hard, preferred, and therefore, honorable. Hence, he insists on a reaffirmation of his respectable status within traditional society: (I am ok as long as I am still respected as a man by my family).

But, Isaac Julien insists that although black masculinity can be constructed as hard and rugged, it is equally important to "show another kind of representation. . . the kind of construction of black masculinity that is something very fragile and vulnerable" (177).

For Barbara, Tatiana, Tina, Sostene, and Laurent, woubia life renders them vulnerable. Sostene's initial reaction and description of woubia life as "weird" and woubis as "pariahs" who should be rejected underscore the "outsideness" of woubia life. While these subjects struggle to insert themselves into their society by demanding recognition, some of them are tripped by their own language, which reveals their own ambivalence about the life they lead. Even as they claim difference in opposition to dichotomized male/female, masculine/feminine identities, they revert to expected social positions, those culturally associated with women and men or read as masculine and feminine. They expect their men to protect them. Again, Tatiana states: "if you are with an imperfect man, he'll hide, he'll shun his responsibilities. A perfect yossi is someone who asserts himself totally." For Tatiana, "a perfect yossi is a man who lives with his queen, his wife." Indeed, although Tatiana's refusal to be identified as male is transgressive, she is still caught up in the socially delineated roles ascribed to individuals based on gendered identities. She reads herself as female, and consequently dresses up as such—red dress, heavy makeup, white scarf and wig in the bus scene—but expects a "prince" or king or "knight" to rescue her or another woubi from public threat or social ostracization.

A similar tension exists in the relationship between Jean Jacques and Laurent. Jean Jacques sees all woubis and yossis as essentially male first. He states, "no matter what, we're born men. And we have to assert that. Everyone must know that first. I mean we all have our vices." Really, he privileges maleness or a socially ascribed male identity, although he is a yossi—bisexual man. For him, being bisexual, a yossi or a woubi, is a vice, as if it were a temporary falling off of the socially correct, accepted, normative path or state of being. His perception of the yossi or woubi identity is predicated on the social construction of binary gendered identities, maleness/femaleness as normative. But for him, his maleness is primary. "If I take Laurent to a little family gathering in my village, people will look at us both," he says. He is unsettled by Laurent's "use of all kinds of cosmetics on his face." "That doesn't do me no honor," he adds. For Jean Jacques, Laurent's performance of femininity dishonors him as a man, because Laurent, male, although a woubi, should behave like a man not a woman. In other words, Laurent should present himself as any male friend rather than a cross-dressing man wearing make up. Or, perhaps, Laurent should present himself as a woman without makeup that draws attention to him. Still, Jean Jacques reads himself as male, hence his remark, "[despite] my present situation, I'm still respected by my family." Indeed, his double consciousness is acute, for while he accepts Laurent as his woubi on the inside (private space), he continues to read him as male on the outside (public space). Even when Jean Jacques reads Laurent as a woubi, he evokes patriarchal structures of gender relationship and behavior, insisting that his manhood and honor be preserved. Clearly, Jean Jacques' relationship with Laurent like Barbara's personality underscores the inherent tensions in woubi-being.

Unlike Laurent and Barbara, Jean Jacques does not seem comfortable in his sexual identity. He is still pre-occupied with the codification of gendered identities in terms of perceived "normative" attributes for each gender. A man must be and behave accordingly, even if he is a yossi, because he still sees himself as a man; having sex with another man is simply a vice. In fact, Barbara points out, "[Y]ossis are bisexual boys who usually sleep with girls. If they sleep with a boy, they don't think of it as such because for them woubis are like girls." Stephen O. Murray and Will Roscoe in their edited volume, *Boy-Wives and Female Husbands: Studies of African Homosexuality*, note that the practice of "gender-based homosexuality" in "patriarchal cultural contexts" demands that "individuals who are sexually penetrated (male or female), whether they enjoy penetration or are merely performing a sexual duty, are expected to conform to the behavior and social roles of women" (7). Hence, Jean Jacques sees Laurent as a woman and expects him to behave accordingly. Murray and Roscoe further assert that the penetrated men are thought of as "'womanlike' rather than as 'socially women.' Their behavior is often an exaggeration of that of women, and they fulfill some but not all the social roles of women (for example, women's productive work but not their reproductive roles)" (7-8). As if to affirm Murray and Roscoe's assertion about the expected social behavior of the woubi or men-wives, Laurent and Barbara often flaunt themselves in displays of exaggerated gestures that seemingly should signal femininity. In one scene with Jean Jacques, Laurent declares, "I feel like a woman," gesturing with his body. The camera reveals Barbara engaging in a similar display in the scene at the river where she tries to perform "Malaika" and finally as she prepares herself for the celebration at the end of the film.

DISEMPOWERMENT & ALIENATION—
"SOMEWHERE OUT OF THE WAY"

Sexuality, specifically, one's sexual orientation and one's gender (publicly signaled) empower or dis-empower one. As Tatiana suggests, woubis are endangered species, not because they are rare, but because of the public outrage against them. Their identities are unclear to those who do not understand them. Interestingly, the woubis are also acutely aware of this ambivalence in their identities. Clearly, it is their ambivalence, this awareness of their status as "in-between" that is threatening and therefore, potentially disempowering. Their vulnerability as woubis or yossis is echoed in Tatiana's descriptions of the dangers and ostracization associated with woubia life. "It's not easy for us to go out in the daytime. They throw stones at us. It's not easy for us here in Africa..."

While coming out is painful, being closeted is equally alienating. "You feel alone, and you don't dare tell anyone. You've no one like you to turn to. No yossis who might reassure you," Barbara confesses. "You think of the scandal it might cause and all that," she adds. For some woubis, secrecy provides a cloak of safety. Sostene, for instance, refuses to be labeled; he opts for secrecy, believing that it is the key to maintaining control. He indicates that he is a woubi who intends to marry another woubi. But for "the moment," he confesses, "I am going out with a woman." Forced heterosexuality becomes the mask which helps him to navigate through "normal" society. Ironically, while secrecy like a veil might shield him from a rigid and hostile society, it reinforces oppression and disempowerment. The woubis cannot organize as a social or political group if they maintain their closetedness. As Eve Kosofosky Sedgwick has suggested in her book *The Epistemology of the Closet*, "[the] closet is the defining structure of gay oppression . . ." (71). Sedgwick, nevertheless, confirms that "[the] image of coming out regularly interfaces the image of the closet, and its seemingly non ambivalent public sitting can be counter posed as a salvational epistemological certainty against the very equivocal privacy afforded by the closet" (71). While coming out can be liberating, it is not without tensions. Tatiana, Barbara, and their friends acknowledge that coming out ostracizes them just as closetedness is painfully lonely. Commenting on the group's organization into an activist body, Tatiana informs us that they have to plan something outside society, "somewhere out of the way," because they are constantly harassed by people who see them as different. Even as a group, they are still closeted, hidden, locating themselves on the margins of society to organize. Tatiana adds that the attendance at their first public party was low because "people are scared; they don't want to come . . . The woubis don't even come." In addition, she informs us, "people here think that transvestites are gangsters." Consequently, she confesses that she likes "being with my own. I stick to my milieu."

Although these woubis acknowledge their disempowerment, they refuse to be silenced, elided, or removed. They claim power by insisting on being heard and seen. Barbara says, "you find others like you and organize," founding the ICTA, which as a collective becomes their buffer against harassment from the media and which also provides them with an alternative community or family. Laurent, who has rejected his traditional family, recognizes the importance of his woubi family/community, declaring, "It was like a new family. Your real family was the one you created. Nobody had to hide anything." Perhaps, the most affirming and empowering act is the embracing of one's difference. Tatiana and Bibiche who are cross-dressing woubis exploit their identities to attain economic security. "Thank God, for whoring," Tatiana proclaims, noting that as a woubi, whoring or prostitution is an act of economic survival, one which has rescued her from relying on a man or a yossi for sustenance. Barbara, however, embraces herself and her potential as a voice for change for her group, telling us: "I've come to terms with my nature and I'm proud of it. Not just physically, but because it is so different. I need people to know what I'm like, that my fight be known." She says, "Africa is a strange place, like my country," adding, "I need to be here to speak my own language. There are so many controus; there's always work to be done. So many towns in which to spread the word. It's like cleaning a house that's constantly dirty. You just have to keep cleaning."

CONCLUSION

Woubi chéri's power lies in its teasing of the boundaries of representation—saying and showing what has not or cannot be said, going to places where we refuse to visit. Perhaps, it is the boldness with which the film offers us an alternative voice, alternative representations of gender, subjectivity, and power that is affirming. But, perhaps, it is the clearly articulated refusal to be silenced or muzzled by intimidating and rigid patriarchal and cultural structures, as well as the desire to birth themselves, defining their own agency that makes these woubis and yossis such daring and powerful transgressors. Clearly, Barbara's straddling of gendered identities—male and female—and her undressing of herself in the closing scenes of the film force us to look/see in a different way, with eyes wide open.

Works Cited

Ajen, Nii. "West African Homoeroticism: West African Men Who Have Sex with Men." In: *Boy-Wives and Female Husbands: Studies of African Homosexuality*. Eds. Stephen O. Murray and Will Roscoe. New York: St. Martin's Press, 1998. 1-18

Bhabha, Homi. *Location of Culture*. London/New York: Routledge, 1994.

Bhattacharyya, Gargi. *Sexuality and Society: An Introduction*. London: Routledge, 2002.

Butler, Judith. *Bodies That Matter: On the Discursive Limits of "Sex"*. New York/London: Routledge, 1993.

—. *Gender Trouble: Feminism and the Subversion of Identity*. New York: Routledge, 1990.

Hemmings, Clare. *Bisexual Spaces: A Geography of Sexuality and Gender*. New York: Routledge, 2002.

hooks, bell. *Black Looks: race and the representation*. Boston: South End Press, 1992.

—. Interview with Isaac Julien. "States of Desire." Transition 0.53 (1991): 183-184.

Murray, Stephen, O. and Will Roscoe, Eds. *Boy-Wives and Female Husbands: Studies of African Homosexuality*. New York: St. Martin's Press, 1998.

Sedgwick, Eve Kosofsky. *Epistemology of the Closet*. Berkeley: University of California Press, 1990.

Woubi chéri. Director Phillip Brooks and Laurent Bocahut. California Newsreel, 1998.

PART FIVE

SOCIAL CONSTRUCTIONS OF MASCULINE AND FEMININE IDENTITIES

Masculinity, Femininity, and Power; Eroticism and Constructions of Gender

Chapter 14

"Stand up, boy!" Sidney Poitier, "boy," and Filmic Black Masculinity[1]

Keith M. Harris

The main title of this essay, "Stand up, boy!," is taken from *In the Heat of the Night* (Jewison 1967), and it serves as the introduction to the star in a star vehicle.[1] *In the Heat of the Night* is a pivotal film in Sidney Poitier's career, since it is one of the three top grossing films for 1967, and Poitier appears in all three; *To Sir with Love* and *Guess Who's Coming to Dinner* are the other two top gross-ing films of 1967. The use of this dialog clip is deliberate, and signifies the irony of Poitier's career until that date: Poitier was able to command record salaries, have record grossing films, receive an Academy Award, yet in the formal tradi-tion of star vehicles—a tradition which provides a character type and generic setting for the star persona, provides an opportunity for a star to relish in his or her performative persona—Poitier is introduced as a "boy" in the derogatorily racist address of a deputy sheriff. It is the direct address "Stand up, boy!" that informs the audience of the narrative presence of a motivating character and of a performer who has achieved a star status. Granted that Mr. Tibbs, Poitier's Philadelphia police detective, is only a character and not an index of an actual person, the discursive textual address as "boy" and the paratextual discourse of stardom and its ethos of achievement and equality, as well as the metatextual discourse of race, open an ironic space at the site of the signifier *boy*. It is from this ironic space that I wish to interrogate the image of Sidney Poitier and black masculinities in contemporary American cinema.

The purpose of this essay, therefore, is to examine what I posit as a moment of continuity in a seemingly discontinuous and heterogeneous array of repre-sentations of black masculinity in Hollywood film. In order to do this, I briefly provide an understanding of filmic black masculinity, providing a framework for the understanding of the main topic of this essay. Second, I examine the star persona of Sidney Poitier as one point in the array of black filmic masculinity. In order to do this, I have chosen to discuss Poitier's first autobiography, *This Life*. Furthermore, I consider the transition from Poitier to Blaxploitation as an expression of racial performativity and black cinema. By this I mean to consider Poitier as a singular figure in Hollywood, as a monolithic figure of the black masculinity within the framework of racial performativity, as an expression and instance of black cinema, and as an ethical construct of masculinity who, through his engagement with racial discourse of the era, configures a discursive dialog within black masculinity. This requires that I interrogate the monolith of Sidney Poitier, during his peak, social problem film phase, and the fashioning and his self-fashioning of race and cinema during this phase.

I

What do I mean by filmic masculinity? On a simplistic level, I mean the masculinity portrayed in film. However, this presupposes that there is difference between the social and the filmic. Indeed there is, for the filmic form provides a spectacle of gender. Gender in film, as in other media, is a fully discursive form positioned for idealization, critique, and deconstruction. Filmic masculinity, then, is also determined by the use of film, the mode of production, the genre, aesthetics, aesthetic movements, and the historical moment, to name a few. My interest, in particular, is in filmic black masculinity. The category, or the categorization, of filmic masculinity is intended to imply dialog and discursivity. For if one constructs filmic masculinity as a product of society, as produced within the social for the purpose of entertainment, polemic, or document, one must consider social forms, hierarchies, and continuities and discontinuities in masculinity.

In *Toms, Coons, Mulattoes, Mammies, and Bucks*, Donald Bogle (1973) outlines a catalogue of stock character types of black men and women in the Hollywood tradition of "mainstream" film. For Bogle these five types provide the traditional coding of blackness as informed by race and gender. The types are elaborated as follows: 1). *Toms*: Uncle Tom figures, a literary trope, complacent, politically inactive, gendered masculine, but asexual; 2). *Coons* (also known as zip coon): less docile figures than the Toms, ostentatious, descended from the minstrel shows, entertaining black men, playful and silly; 3). *Mulatta/oes*: another literary trope, transcoded and transferred to film, highly sexualized, most often female; 4). *Mammy*: female Tom, of sorts, aggressively maternal, physically unattractive, usually asexual; and 5). *Buck*: overly sexual, and therefore, necessarily, narratively contained, black men.

Bogle argues that this economy of image types governs the representation of African-Americans in film. I emphasize Bogle's work, because it provides a point of reference for filmic black masculinity, a history informing my work here. Bogle's schema has its advantages: it is an exhaustive reference for blacks in film, names and titles. It offers a catalogue of stock figures, archetypes, and tropes of blackness. However, there are disadvantages: Bogle does not interrogate his cataloguing as part of the process of stereotyping that is presented. The list of figures has an essentializing motive, presupposing a racial authenticity in the inauthenticity of the images. *Toms, Coons, Mulattoes, Mammies, and Bucks* is the limit of expressions of blackness, and it, in turn, is limiting of expressions of blackness as *post-, neo-, remade,* or *re-interpretations* of the limit, never allowing the possibility of excess, engagement, dialog, or discontinuity: every black character, in every film, black or not, is a variation of the same thing. It is my contention that *Toms, Coons, Mulattoes, Mammies, and Bucks* are a source book of imagery and types, but the source itself is to be brought into question. One way of doing this is through examining texts around films or film stars. I take on the object of some of Bogle's, and a number of other critics', venom and disparagement, Sidney Poitier, and I do this through Poitier's own efforts at understanding his relationship to film and film history, through the paratext of autobiography.

I use the autobiographical instead of the filmic for several reasons. First, as Dyer (1986) notes, "The star phenomenon consists of everything that is publicly available about stars. A film star's image is not just his or her films, but the promotion of those films and of the star through pin-ups, public appearances, studio hand-outs and so on, as well as interviews, biographies and coverage in the press of the star's doings and 'private' life" (2-3). I have, therefore, chosen the paratext of the autobiography in an effort to understand not only the star phenomenon, but also the ethical construction of the self that emerges in the becoming of a star. Second, in keeping with the public and ethical dimension of the first, there is the autobiography and the autobiographic function of the text as the construction of an exemplary figure, as an ethical construction of the self; and third, there are the specific cultural and textual ramifications of the African-American autobiography.

II

[S]ince the dominant view holds prideful self-respect as the very essence of healthy African-American identity, it also considers such identity to be fundamentally weakened wherever masculinity appears to be compromised. While this fact is rarely articulated, its influence is nonetheless real and pervasive. Its primary effect is that all debates over and claims to 'authentic' African-American identity are largely animated by a profound anxiety about the status specifically of African-American *masculinity* (Harper 1996, ix).

The book's [*The Films of Sidney Poitier*] introductory essay stated that Poitier, though born in Miami, was reared in the Bahamas and arrived in New York in 1943 with nothing but a thick accent and great ambition. [. . .]But Sidney, whose career was built on masquerading as an African-American, successfully avoided our prejudices. The qualities I admired in Sidney were the things that made me resent the West Indians that I knew. The irony is that a lot of the regal bearing he projected could, in another context, have been seen as insufferable superiority (George 1994, 17-18).

The two quotations above serve as guideposts for the following discussion of Sidney Poitier. The first taken alongside the criticisms of Poitier at the height of his career labels the criticisms as indicators of a crisis in the African-American identity and what Harper identifies as the "status of blackness." Nelson Gorge's comments mark yet another debate about blackness that is lost in Poitier's image, in its singularity during the period, but given presence by Poitier in both installments of his autobiography. This "presence," as I call it, is one of ethnicity, of an ethnic blackness which in the monologic racial imagery of his career is silenced as a signifier of difference, but in the self-restoration of himself in the autobiographical form, his cultural difference from the overdetermined blackness of his film characters is significant in understanding his model of gender and race.

This Life (1980), Poitier's first autobiographical installment, is a textual nexus, simultaneity of narratives: it is an immigrant tale, a migration tale, a testimonial, a confessional, a chronicling of the black experience, a conservative "picked myself up by the boot straps tale," as well as a liberal tale of cultural pluralism. However, first and foremost Poitier's autobiography is a star's tale and the story of a public life. As a star's tale, *This Life* implies certain meanings and social functions. For Dyer (1986) stars are particular expressions of individuals in society:

> Stars articulate what it is to be a human being in contemporary society; that is, they express the particular notion we hold of the person, of the 'individual.' They do so complexly, variously—they are not straightforward affirmations of individualism. On the contrary, they articulate both the promise and the difficulty that the notion of individuality presents for all of us who live by it (8).

Furthermore, as Marshall (1997) elaborates, stardom and celebrity are an expression of a democratic ethos within which there is an oscillation between individual and collective expression of possibility in a "democratic age" (6), or as Marshall explains: "The celebrity is centrally involved in the social construction of division between the individual and the collective, and works discursively in this area. . . . Also, expansion of celebrity status in contemporary culture is dependent on its association with both capitalism, where the celebrity is an effective means for the commodification of the self, and democratic sentiments, where the celebrity is the embodiment of the potential of an accessible culture" (25-26). From these notions of the star and celebrity, one gathers that the star functions as a commodity to be consumed; however, the affective consumption of stars is through the discourse of individuality, as a contradictory expression of a collective identity. In addition, and of importance to Poitier's persona, the *telos* of individuality in the discourse of stardom is personhood, as an individual whole, as a unit in a democratic society in which stars signify possibility. Poitier demonstrates this discursive relation to stardom and personhood clearly in a modestly self-congratulatory moment:

> With the release of each of my fifteen films, my name had become increasingly familiar to filmgoers, and by the end of 1962 there was developing in Hollywood a historymaking new attitude countering the long-held conviction that the appearance of blacks in other than menial roles would offend the movie industry's principal constituency. [. . .] (*TL*, 241). [b]

It is clear here that the notion of the individual person as a success has a community relation, at least for Poitier, which is tempered by the notion of race. The discursive personhood of stardom is embedded in the trajectory of personhood which mediates the function and mode of address of the self in African-American autobiographic tradition. Upon closer examination the sense of communal self present in the quote above becomes integral in understanding the ethical and exemplary self put forth by the autobiography.

In the discourse of stardom, personhood is most prominently articulated through the dichotomy of public and private. It is no wonder that as the story of a public life, Poitier's *This Life* is a private story. With stars and celebrities, private *versus* public provides a framework for the negotiation of a set of oppositions, among which is the individual *versus* the collective, but also the sincere *versus* insincere, country *versus* city, racial *versus* ethnic, among them (Dyer 1986, 11).[3] Drawing on the distinction between the private/public dichotomies, Marshall (1997) adds: "This disintegration [between private and public] as represented by celebrities, has taken on a particular form. The private sphere is constructed to be revelatory the ultimate site of truth and meaning for any representation in the public sphere" (247). As a consequence the star biography or autobiography becomes a revelation of a private self.[4]

The star autobiography has, like the autobiographical form in general, truth claims, in this instance, truth claims to the "realness," the somewhat combatively real story of a star's life. The star autobiography is, on the one hand, a constructed, narrative self-representation; and, on the other, it is an answering to criticism of the public image, a projection of another truth claim, a true persona, to counter the film persona, the star type. This answering is mediated across the private/public divide, as confessional of or testimony to a private self, perhaps in opposition to or celebration of the public self that is the star.

In the case of Poitier, considering that the autobiography arrives some ten to fifteen years after the height of his career (as opposed to writing his autobiography in 1967 or the early Seventies), the mediation of the private/public sets of opposition perform a self-restoration of his image in certain capacities. In the chapter entitled "Black Films," Poitier discusses the private shock of the public proclamation against him, the *New York Times Article*, "Why do white folks love Sidney Poitier so?" by Clifford Mason:

> In that article Clifford Mason ripped to shreds everything I had ever done. He ripped up *In the Heat of the Night*, [...].Then he went on to destroy *To Sir With Love* and *Guess Who's Coming to Dinner* [...]. I was an 'Uncle Tom,' 'a lackey,' 'a house Nigger'—current terms for a lot of people, including some highly visible blacks who were perceived as not doing whatever they did in a way to win the applause of all their fellow blacks (*TL,* 335).

This passage is late in the book (Chapter 25: "Black Film"), which approaches a chronological order from childhood to 1980; and it serves to proceed into a calculated invective against Mason and Hollywood. The impact of this invective, in tandem with the strategy of chronological placement, is further buttressed by the fact that in the preceding chapters Poitier fashions himself in such a manner that he inveigles, to some extent, a trust and justification in his argument against Mason, bestowing even an absurdity upon Mason's comments. Poitier's quoting of "Uncle Tom," "lackey," and "house nigger," as Mason's references to him, are rendered, at the point when they are presented in his autobiography, moot and, indeed, mute (as signifiers of complicity, compliance, complacency, race treason, or effeminacy and emasculation) in light of the restoration of race and masculinity that has been performed in the preceding chapter. The restoration of race and masculinity is through a manipulation of the private/public set of oppositions, especially ethnicity (private) and race (public).[5] Poitier's autobiography presents the reader with a narrative/developmental/geographical mapping of departure and return as a movement from community to individual back to community, from ethnic black to racially, monolithically black to racial exemplar. The departure begins in the opening Chapters 1-4 ("Cat Island," "Nassau," "Miami," and "New York," respectively). In Chapter One, Poitier tells of his family name:

> The name 'Poitier' comes from Haiti. Slaves bearing that name, having made successful escapes from the Haitian plantation system, ventured into the Bahamas Island areas, settling in on the first islands they encountered on their escape routes. [...] A generation later, my mother's branch (bearing the name 'Outten') arrived from one of the numerous plantations scattered about these British-owned islands... (*TL*, 6).

This reference to heritage and genealogy serves several functions: first, it positions Poitier, his family and community in the particular Caribbean and American—North and South—African diaspora. This provides an ethnic framework for understanding his early childhood and later young adult experiences as culturally different from the African-Americans of Harlem, Miami, and the Hollywood acting community. Second, the reference to heritage initiates what Boelhower (1991) (*viz.* Sollars [1986]) describes as "the constitutive play between descent and consent" in the construction of the American identity: another dichotomy, a bipolar movement in which issues of race, Old World heritage and tradition, and memory (issues of descent) are brought into a productive dynamic process of becoming self-determined, self-reliant, and independent (issues of consent) (Boelhower 1991, 130-131). The idyllic world of Cat Island is implicitly positioned in opposition to the conflicted, urbanity of Hollywood, America, and particularly the African-American blackness associated with Poitier's black star persona. This world is later portrayed in more economic and communal terms, which implies a sense of loss in the language of the narrative recounting of it:

> There was no welfare on Cat Island. [...] Older people were an integral part of the family structure... assured of their continued—and revered—place in the family unit. [...] Respect for the old ones was

> everywhere in evidence in this patriarchal society. Young people were required to be honest, live up to their responsibilities, and respect their elders (*TL*, 12).

There is an implicit other in these descriptions of life and family on Cat Island. The description of landscape and geography performs a critique of the urbanity of Poitier's Harlem and Hollywood self. The descriptions of family, with "no welfare," directly refer to welfare, social programs and dissolution of family that Poitier must encounter in his immigration to the United States. The dynamic of descent and consent early in the narrative initiates a critical hermeneutic device from which the present star figure is presented as a figure of transformation.

The figural movement of the private self (the island self) to the public self (black star persona) is doubly signified as a figure of transformation when one considers notions of gender that are presented and critiqued in these opening chapters. The most critical commentaries on Sidney Poitier's star image were that he was asexual and his characters often isolated from the black community and, therefore, non-threatening to the established cultural imagery of whiteness. The image was not a threat to masculinity or the social barriers of race, which his characters seemingly challenged (see Bogle 1988; Boyd 1997; George 1994; Guerrero 1993; and Reid 1993). Indeed, Poitier's screen image was saintly, overly dignified, and within the confines of the social problem film[6], Poitier's image was overdetermined by the narrative and generic use of race (the "problem") and the overcoming of race as a coming to consciousness of whiteness: Poitier's image was the consciousness of the nation. However, the movement between ethnic and racial (which parallels the movement between descent and consent) mediates a dialog between the public image of Poitier's masculinity—the critical commentary on it—and the private man. This dialog on gender is more confessional than not, establishing the first chapter as a recounting of a passage into manhood and loss of innocence. Episodic vignettes provide a frank discussion of his childhood sexuality (the fluidity and aggressiveness of which counters his asexual, docile screen image), recounting his adventures in the wilds of the island, culminating in his father sending him away (to Miami and to the control of an older brother) because of his quickly burgeoning manhood (*TL*, 9-16).

Later in Chapters Two and Three ("Nassau" and "Miami," respectively), the critical, confessional engagement with the acquisition of masculinity, via adventure, sexuality and rites of passage into manhood are allegorically re-configured in the motions of migration and immigration. In the early discussions of his family's migration from Cat Island to the urban island of Nassau, at the young age of ten, Poitier is full of awe and wonder:

> We sailed all that evening and into the next day, until someone called out, 'There's Nassau.' [...] Suddenly I could make out objects in motion, scurrying about at great speed. I asked my mother what they were and she said they were cars. I had never seen a car before, and as we drew nearer to the island these beetlelike fellows absorbed my complete attention. With eyes wide and mouth dropped open,

> I stepped ashore into this fascinating new place, this big city with
> people—cars—electricity—and other strange things I had never
> seen before (*TL*, 18-19).

From this moment of movement and wonder, Poitier narrates his loss of virgin-
ity, the development of his "hustling" skills, and his burgeoning criminal skills.
Consequently, four years later, with the street name of Sidney "P," Poitier had
become a young urban denizen, complete with the hazards and potential long-
term problems of urban youth and his father's admittance to his loss of control
over his son. After stealing corn and having to see a judge about the possible
legal consequences, Poitier recounts his father's decision to send him to Miami
and his own fear of himself and his situation:

> On the way home, [my father] said to me, 'You know, boy, I can't
> run after you anymore. I'm getting on in years and you seem deter-
> mined to get into trouble... you were born in the United States and
> we want you to go back there. You will have a chance to go to school
> and try to make something of yourself...'. [...] I had a devil-may-care
> attitude, while at the same time I was scared of what the devil might
> decide to lay on me. I knew if I got caught at some of my devil-may-
> care stunts, I was gone—four years gone (*TL*, 29).

I have gone through these rather lengthy excerpts from the first two chapters in
order to demonstrate that, first, Poitier places an emphasis on the acquisition
of masculinity as movement, as a passage, but also as a certain loss of innocence
and as a threat of loss (for the "four years gone" is a reference to the potential
for reform school and to the actual loss of a friend to the reform school system
[*TL*, 28-29]); second, the emphasis on acquisition, ambiguity and loss directs
the reader to the instability, and learned management of that instability, in masculinity.

Furthermore, the double signification of movement as migration and
acquisition is seen in the performative attainment of African-American blackness. Though in his move to Miami Poitier does not legally immigrate (because
of his status as an American citizen), his upbringing on Cat Island and in Nassau
allows for a distinctly different understanding and confrontation to race. Once
in Miami with his older brother, sister-in-law, and family, Poitier experiences
cultural differences which are first linked to lifestyle, country/city distinction
and then to notions of race and cultural blackness; there is an estrangement, a
defamiliarization of blackness in language and cultural value:

> Instantly upon meeting my sister-in-law and my nieces and nephews,
> I realized I was in an entirely new set of social and cultural circum-
> stances. I didn't understand these people—and they didn't under-
> stand me. [...] I spoke with a different accent from theirs. I know
> nothing of the kind of life they lived, and because their values were
> quite foreign to me, naturally communication was difficult. [...] In
> fact, it was so traumatic, that whole experience, that I was never able
> to adjust to Miami (*TL*, 41).

And there is also the confrontation with the "fact of blackness" in the American context. In his recounting of his experience as a pharmacy delivery boy being asked to use the backdoor, Poitier records a sense of astonishment at this treatment:

> [When asked to go around to the backdoor] I wasn't accustomed to such behavior on the part of ladies, white or black, and having been reared in an area where I never ran into that kind of thing, I was definitely not about to accommodate myself to it in this strange new place. Furthermore, while admittedly I was not completely naïve about racial matters, I was certainly not afraid of white people (*TL*, 42).

The outcome of this experience, and the later encounter with the Klan, leads Poitier to view blackness critically in respect to whiteness, allowing for distancing of self from external images. In a moment of observation at his own behavior, Poitier considers his predicament as one of cultural self-image: "Possibly because I didn't know any better at that time, which was due in part to my spending the first fifteen years of my life free of the crushing negative self-image hammered into black children by this system, in this Miami, in this America" (*TL*, 42-43).

Poitier's cultural position, his relation to American blackness as outsider, as immigrant, as ethnic black in relation to his family and the Miami (and by extension American) community initiates a narrative of cultural assimilation and integration into American society, a narrative of racial consciousness, a consciousness of the self which is at odds with societal notions of race. Poitier recounts meticulously and frankly the loss of his Caribbean accent, his self-education, his individual success and failure as a restaurant owner, and his overall achievement of the "American dream" with his success as an actor. Yet, throughout his narrative self-presentation, Poitier maintains a critical insight into the question of race and blackness, an insight which is linked to an internal dialog between the struggles of black manhood and masculinity in America and the honor and responsibility of manhood instilled in him by his father and in his Caribbean upbringing.

The Americanization of the self is tempered by a particular formation of blackness, one which is directed at the struggles—social and political, as well as representational—of the black man as blackness and black men as they are constructed in American society: monolithic, emasculated, pathological and in constant battle against these constructions. What emerges in the private narrative development of masculinity and blackness is what Hazel Carby (1999) has called the Race Man, a public figure of both gender and race. For the Race Man there is an imagined black community whose future (social, political, and intellectual) is determined by gender and a "struggle among men over the bodies of women" (Carby 25). The figure of the Race Man is also informed by DuBois, Carby's paramount figure of the Race Man, and his notion of the Talented Tenth (". . . Leaders of thought and missionaries of culture among their people. . ."), a model of exceptionalism and uplift. The aforementioned development of Poitier's racial consciousness is simultaneously a development of a gender consciousness.

There are two specific sites in the development of the gender/race conscious Race Man in *This Life*. First, gender (the anxiety and the failure of gender responsibility) and race responsibility figure in Poitier's discussion of "tensions" in his first marriage. In Chapter 13 ("Tensions"), Poitier is an exemplar and a figure of patriarchal masculinity, the breadwinner, the father figure, the husband; it is an image quite to the contrary of popular notions of black masculinity. Furthermore, it is an image in conflict, in turmoil, in crisis, brought about by the burden of responsibility during his first comments about his marriage and in opposition to the "kind of woman" his wife, Juanita, had become during their marriage:

> Tensions in the marriage were surfacing more frequently by the middle of 1957. I was more likely to roam around than not. I began to grow resentful that I was growing in one direction and Juanita in another (*TL*, 197).

And still further:

> My wife just didn't understand enough of what was going on inside me to help—perhaps I hadn't been able to open myself up to her. I believe the only person who might have understood the kind of pressure that could build up in a young man locked into rat-racing in New York, who twelve or thirteen years before was walking around the sandy beaches of the Caribbean with not a thought in his head (*TL*, 198).

Masculinity, indeed, becomes a mysterious, indecipherable "thing." "Tensions" becomes a pivotal chapter in that it chronicles not only the crisis of masculinity, as loss of freedom and as a burden of responsibility, but also links the resolution of this crisis to the development of a responsibility to race and black manhood:

> I was somehow being pushed to save the world [,...]being pushed to change the world as it related to me and mine [,...]being pushed to do the impossible. I figured that black people just wouldn't survive without me saving them through dealing with the pressures on myself. I didn't think the *world* would survive if I didn't live and develop in a certain way (*TL*, 198).

The projection of the crisis of race and masculinity is further elaborated in the commitment to responsibility to his family and the threat to his family caused by his affair with Diahann Carroll. In Chapter 16 ("Diahann"), Poitier recounts the beginning of his affair with Carroll and raises ethical questions as gender questions and questions of responsibility to the family and to the wife. There is a re-articulation of exemplary behavior through his re-statement of his father's words about family and fatherhood as his own motivating dilemma:

> Those words [the words of advice from his father][7] began to waken in me on that morning when I told my wife I was involved with another woman, and they came surging up with a vengeance that evening to jam my thoughts whenever the possibility of leaving my children was verbalized, creating what was to become in time a conflict of such proportions that I can hardly describe it (*TL*, 231).

Through the use of autobiography, Poitier is an exemplar with the ethical dilemma of fidelity in the marriage. However, this problem is gendered, is a "man's take," so to speak, because of the way in which the wife, her incompleteness, becomes the problem; and she becomes a problem because she is *only* a wife, which is not enough for the man, to the exemplary figure of race and masculinity that he has become. His wife, Juanita, therefore, falls short, is to blame. The construction of himself as a victim, here and in the next chapter, serves to vilify femininity:

> I was still living by trail and error—by instinct. I was living by a body of reactive mechanisms I had accumulated in my strange, overcrowded existence. There I was in my thirties and had been through several lifetimes already. And I was in a mess—a real mess. On the one hand I had found a woman who was in tune with my needs, a woman who I believed would satisfy both my mind and my body [Diahann Carrol]. On the other hand, I was married and had children who my father said I must protect and never leave (*TL*, 232).

Coming to consciousness of gender and race, consequently, is an overcoming and transcending of a prior self. This is an almost typical story.

However, it is in the next chapter (Chapter 17: "A Raisin in the Sun") where we find the second site of the simultaneity of gender and race consciousness. Here Poitier works to raise questions about the construct of black masculinity. He does so by constructing the "black masculine problem" as the problem of a victim, which is in and of itself the nature of the construction of a problem:

> I believed from the first day I went into rehearsal that the play should not unfold from the mother's point of view. I still believe that. I think for maximum effect, *A Raisin in the Sun* should unfold from the point of view of the son . . . (*TL*, 234).

His explanation is that to have the play emphasize the mother would detract from the problems of the black man, but before that:

> They accused me of 'star' behavior. Of wanting to be the top dog on stage. The simple truth of the matter was that if the play is told from the point of view of the mother, and you don't have an actor playing the part of Walter Lee strongly, then the end result may very well be a negative comment on the black male. . . . They professed to be at a loss as to the underlying reason for my feeling about the image of the black male. But I was in the dark every bit as much as they were . . . (*TL*, 235).

The image of the "black man" becomes paramount in the portrayal of the black family: the battle over the character of "Walter Lee," the need to relocate the signification of race and the critique of race relations in the play is now re-thematized by Poitier within the notion of black manhood as the responsible expression of race and family/community. It is no wonder that when Poitier recounts the reception of the Academy Award for Best Actor in *Lilies the Field* that there is the pronominal shift from "I" to "we" and the autobiographical movement of voice from the individual to the community: Poitier has fully confirmed his status as a Race Man by speaking for the race: "We black people had done it. We were capable. We forget sometimes, having to persevere against unspeakable odds, that we are capable of infinitely more than the culture is yet willing to credit to our account" (*TL*, 255).

It is through these processes of racialization and gendering, of becoming an African-American man, a model and spokesman, both exceptional and ordinary, that Poitier is charged with the responsibility of racial representation and uplift. Furthermore, through his expressed privacy (as a public figure), performance style and characters performed, and through his presentation of the self, Poitier embodies a solidly middle class model of black manhood. His styling of race and class offer his viewing and reading public a process of masculine attainment, which incorporates class moral and ethical values as racial and gender values.

Let me summarize the discussion thus far: By following the developmental narrative of Poitier's autobiography, I have tried to demonstrate, first, that as a star text Poitier articulates personhood through a discourse of individuality, signifying possibility, the possibility of the average individual to succeed. Second, Poitier's personhood is also a negotiation of the ethnic *versus* racial self as the ethnic black confronts African-American cultural blackness. In this instance, Poitier maps, through migration and immigration, his assimilation into African-American blackness. Moreover, the consent to this blackness is demonstrated through the rescue and acquisition of the trope of black manhood from the loss of family and masculine responsibility. On the one hand, Poitier's autobiography itself as a star text posits these developments as exemplary, as a model of race and gender. On the other hand, the ascent to Race Man posits an ethico-political incompleteness which in the gesture of self-presentation in the autobiographical form is a process of authentication. *This Life* provides a catalog of Poitier's coming to gender and racial consciousness and provides the space for him to offer authenticating "facts" and gestures of his commitment to the black community.

To return to the opening comments about "Black Films" and Poitier: the gathered racial, ethnic, and masculine self that Poitier presents through the developmental narrative strategy allows for the textual confrontation between Mason's critique and Poitier's star persona to be configured as a confrontation about commitment, authenticity and cultural authority. For as a Race Man, Poitier's status as spokesman is predicated upon his "proof" of blackness, his commitment to community, the authenticity of his "black experience" and his black masculinity--all of which he has demonstrated through the telling of his story and all of which serve to strengthen and authorize his critique of Hollywood and his own self-critique of his function in Hollywood as counter-critique to his critics:

> What I resented most about Clifford Mason by the time of our second encounter was his laying of all the film industry's transgressions at my feet. [...] Hollywood had not kept it a secret that it wasn't interested in supplying blacks with a variety of positive images. In fact, in only a few isolated corners of the industry could one find committed souls who could be classified as interested in supplying blacks with a different image from what they had been accustomed to. Thanks to that handful of committed souls, the image of the black man just scratching his head was changing. . . . Where was that kind of representation [of an honest, everyday, community based, working black man] on the motion picture screen for blacks? It didn't exist. The closest Hollywood came over a twelve-year period was the one-dimensional, middle-class imagery I embodied most of the time. . . .[I]t was not a step that could in any way alleviate all the frustrations of the past decades. I understood the value system of a make-believe town that was at its heart a racist place (*TL*, 337-338).

Though these comments mark a strong critique of Hollywood, they also signal, even within his own autobiography, the end of the star persona, Sidney Poitier. At this juncture Poitier becomes the cultural critic, focusing his comments on film, the function of film, and the responsibility of the artist. Within the trajectory of his public image and career, the shift is marked by an increased presence behind the camera in production and directing.

His fall from grace, as it were, was a sign of the times. Poitier, as a film star, cultural producer, and Race Man, was suspended in a web of representation which extended in debate across the two domains of simulacra realism and mimetic realism. Drawing on Baudrillard, Harper (1996) describes television programming and televisual aesthetics, where they portrayed African-Americans, as simulacra realism, as "propounding scenarios that might subsequently (or consequently) be realized through out the larger social field, regardless of whether they actually pre-exist there," against the demands for mimetic realism, which would properly "'reflect' the social reality on which it was implicitly modeled" (160).[8] Though Harper makes this aesthetic difference in reference to television shows of the late 60's and early 70's (shows like *Julia*, *I Spy*, *The Leslie Uggams Show*), the same distinction can be made in reference to Poitier's social problem films and the ensuing criticisms against them. In films like those of his 1967 reign (*Guess Who's Coming to Dinner*, *In the Heat of the Night*, *To Sir with Love*), the germane issues of racism, integration, and interracial marriage raise the question of realism as one of Poitier's characters' failure to re-present everyday African-Americans, thereby, in that failure, representing an inauthentic black experience and unrealistic societal race relations. The films re-present progressive, integrationist scenarios as representations of already existing realities, realities which, criticism argued, were unrealized in the social world outside of the films.

Poitier's characters were, indeed, visions of black men and blackness not realized, or not yet realized on the scale imagined in the films at that time: his characters were ironic figures of integration: singular, high-ranking doctor/administrator, marrying a white woman; a northern, black detective in the South, waiting for a train; and a black school teacher bringing order to white hoodlums: figures of an outsider integrated into or integrating white communities, while simultaneously removed and isolated from the filmic black community. Furthermore, his performances were linguistically isolated from the vernacular performances of the few black characters in his films, and particularly, in *Guess* and *In the Heat*, Poitier's characters are an economic class removed from the few members of the black filmic black community.[9]

The ironic moment of the integrated black man, on the one hand, can be understood within the notion of entertainment, offering utopian fantasies of integration. However, on the other hand, as the core divergence of the aesthetics of simulacra and mimetic realism suggest, and as the then contemporary criticism of Poitier and television further suggests, the debate about Poitier is about authentic versus inauthentic blackness. This core debate has overlapping discursive oppositional sets, such as vernacular *versus* middle class; black arts *versus* American pop cultural forms of blackness; and separation *versus* integration, roughly corresponding to the authentic versus inauthentic.[10] In further examination of these debates and the rise of the black athlete as actor and Blaxploitation, the oppositions in the authentic/inauthentic debate are also debates about masculine difference.

III

Prior to Poitier, the catalog of imagery for black men in film, as outlined by Bogle (1973), was that of toms, coon, and bucks. These images were in the service of the perpetuation of the myth of whiteness, as one of humanity, civility and superiority. Though hasty in his categorization, Bogle's schema does have the advantage of tracing this image history from *Birth of a Nation* to the Blaxploitation era of the '70's, an image history which is fairly accurate except where it concerns Poitier. As Cripps (1977 and 1993) notes, Poitier's image emerged out of turmoil in the film industry. Cripps notes the change in the industry and in the image to the post-World War II national consciousness was in part due to the political actions of the National Association for the Advancement of Colored People (NAACP) across the national front and specifically in Hollywood, where the organization called for a change in the kind of imagery produced. The social problem film soon emerged as the genre of film which most allowed for the re-configuration of race and its associates, gender and class. Films like *Home of the Brave* (dealing with the black veteran), *Pinky* and *Lost Boundaries* (dealing with passing) and *Intruder in the Dust* (the screen adaptation of Faulkner's novel by the same name, dealing with Southern racism and lynch mob mentalities) appear in 1949, marking a dramatically different discourse of race than preceding generations. Race in these films was a sign of human consciousness, though quite problematically: as the narrator comments about Lucas Beauchamp (Juano Hernandez) in the end of *Intruder in the Dust*, Beauchamp, his dignity and suffering through the false accusation of race, of being black, is the "conscience of us all."

Indeed, by the 1950s, race in American film had become the site of redemption for whiteness. It is from this conflicted site of noble savagery, redemption and race-serving humanism that Poitier emerges to become the most significant black star of post-WW II American film.[11] Poitier's characters were noble figures of masculine dignity, but again, not without problems. Poitier's characters were often counter to the toms and coons tradition in that they were doctors, teachers, ordinary workers, or rebellious youth or race conscious clergymen or the black detective. However, Poitier's character were always "saint like" in that their constructions as characters isolated them from the filmic black community or their inordinate amount of human sacrifice rendered them a series of long suffering nobles in the service of the salvation of the white characters. His characters were once removed from the privilege of whiteness, only serving, in the long run, to buttress whiteness, and especially white masculinity, as a signifier of humanity. In other words, Poitier's characters had indeed achieved a status, an ethical and categorical status, above the shuffling and jiving of Tom-dom residing black men; however, Poitier's black men were merely a stage, of sorts, in the attainment of ethical and just masculinity of white characters. Yet, Poitier and his characters are not without achievement in their historical context and certainly worthy of re-evaluation in light of the overall project here.

For Cripps (1993), Poitier's integrationist image had been an instrument, along with the social problem film genre, promoting the film industry's liberal ideals; and his usefulness promoting these ideals, as the public response to him suggested, had exhausted itself (284-294). Guerrero (1993) similarly notes that the social problem film formula offered little relevance to the changing cultural climate; and, therefore, neither did Poitier. Guerrero further links Poitier's downfall to the rise in consciousness as seen in the Black Arts Movement and the release of *Sweet Sweet Back's BassdassssSong* (Melvin Van Peebles 1971).

However, as I have tried to suggest, the Poitier project was part of a larger plan. To return to Poitier's self-restoration and the autobiography: through the use of autobiography as a technique of the self and self-fashioning, Poitier posits himself as an exemplar and as ethically incomplete. In doing so, Poitier establishes himself as a Race Man, an ascent to a racialized "boy," a re-articulation of the "boy" in this essay's title. In racializing the category of boy, Poitier foregrounds the construction of race and gender in class, ethnicity and social and civil ideals of democracy.

Acknowledgment

"'Stand up, boy!' Sidney Poitier, Boy, and Filmic Black Masculinity," appeared originally in a slightly different form in *Boys, Boyz, Bois: An Ethics of Black Masculinity in Film and Popular Media*. Copyright © 2006 from *Boys, Boyz, Bois* by Keith M. Harris. Reproduced by permission of Routledge/Taylor & Francis Group, LLC.

Notes

1. This essay is part of a larger work on race, masculinity and ethics entitled *Boys, Boyz, Bois: The Ethics of Masculinity in Popular Film and Television*.

2. Discussions of stars, celebrity, stardom, star phenomenon and star vehicles are informed by Britton (1991); Dyer (1979 and 1986); and Marshall (1997). Specifically for the notion of star vehicle, I rely on Dyer's (1979) definition of star vehicle: "[Star vehicles] were often built around star images. Stories might be expressly written to feature a given star, or books might be bought for production with a star in mind. . . . The vehicle might provide a) a character of the type associated with the star. . ., b) a situation, setting or generic context associated with the star. . ., c) the opportunity for the star to do her/his thing [as in singing or dancing]. . . . As with genres proper, one can discern across a star's vehicle continuities of iconography . . ., visual style . . ., and structure. . ." (70-71).

3. All references to *This Life* (Poitier, 1980) are hereafter cited as *TL*.

4. Dyer (1986) presents a useful private/public dichotomous set of oppositions as follows: individual/society; sincere/insincere; country/city; physical/mental; body/brain; naturalness/artifice; sexual intercourse/social intercourse; racial/ethnic; and *viz.* Romanticism and Lacanian psychoanalysis: subconscious/conscious; Id/Ego; Imaginary/Symbolic (11).

5. Dyer (1986) notes of the star biography, which is equally true about the star autobiography, though through the different means of self-presentation: "Star biographies are devoted to the notion of showing us the star as he or she really is. Blurbs, introduction, every page assures us that we are being taken 'behind the scenes,' 'beneath the surface,' 'beyond the image,' there where the truth resides. Or again there is the rhetoric of sincerity or authenticity . . ." (11).

6. Again, the use of private *versus* public oppositions as a framing discourse of stardom is informed by Dyer (1986). However, in Dyer's discussion of stardom, and especially that of Paul Robeson, the ethnicity-race set is the opposite. For Dyer, race is private and ethnicity is public, a set and order applicable to notions of whiteness which are determined by European ancestry and ethnic stereotyping/marketing in the Hollywood publicity machine. But, where race concerns blackness, I have necessarily reversed this oppositional set. The publicness of blackness as race and the singularity of "black" as a signifier of racial difference (from whiteness) and ethnic erasure (of Africans from the diaspora as culturally and ethnically different from each other) necessitates that there be a re-orientation of ethnic black as private and racial black as public. The distinction, and reversal, becomes important when considering Poitier's upbringing and confluence of immigration and migration and subsequent assimilation into African-American black culture.

7. For more on Poitier, and the social problem film, see Cripps (1993), 215-294.

8. His father's words were as follows: " '. . . Never beat on a woman. If you ever find that you must beat on a woman then you must leave her. Because if you have to beat on her once, you will have to beat on her again. There is no life for a man who has to reason with his woman through fists. [. . .]And another thing you must learn—always take care of your children. Under no circumstance, ever in your life, must you allow yourself to neglect your children. Take care of your children before you do anything else. That is a law of life'" (*TL*, 230).

9. Harper continues to elaborate the differences: "Insofar as they diverge, these differing demands for simulacra and mimetic realism might be taken to indicate distinct concerns with the soundness of society generally, in the case of the former, and the psychological well-being of blacks specifically, in the case of the latter" (160).

10. And this is most apparent in *In the Heat of the Night*. Specifically there is the scene which parodies this aspect of Poitier's typecasting by having the white, southern sheriff jokingly say, "There'll be none of that for you, huh, Tibbs," as they drive by a field of black workers picking cotton.

11. For a specific discussion of the origins of this debate as the question of the designation of African-American *versus* black, a debate encompassing the authentic/inauthentic debate, see Harper (1996), especially 55-77.

12. To note, I say most significant black star of post-WW II, American film. There were other stars before and during Poitier's career (which went roughly from *No way out* [1950] to *Guess Who's Coming to Dinner* [1967], after which his career as an actor began to wane). These other figures would include the following: pre-dating Poitier were Paul Robeson, Nina Mai McKinney, Lena Horne, Louis Armstrong, Nat King Cole, Ethel Waters, Hattie MacDaniels, and to a lesser extent Juano Hernandez and Canada Lee; contemporary to Poitier were Harry Belafonte, Sammy Davis, Jr., Diahann Carrol and Dorothy Dandridge. Again, however, Poitier is singular because of the longevity of his career; the confinement of that career as an actor, producer, and director (as opposed to the dispersal of his stardom across forms as the ubiquitous "black entertainer"); the marketable success of it and the esteem garnered around him as a black star.

Works Cited

Adell, Sandra. *Double Consciousness/Double Bind: Theoretical Issues in Twentieth-Century Black Literature*. Chicago and Urbana: University of Illinois Press, 1994.

Andrews, William. "Introduction." In *African-American Autobiography: A Collection of Critical Essays*, edited by William L. Andrews, 1-8. Englewood, New Jersey: Prentice Hall, 1993a.

—. Ed. *African-American Autobiography: A Collection of Critical Essays*. Englewood, New Jersey: Prentice Hall, 1993.

—. "African-American Autobiography Criticism: Retrospect and Prospect." In: *American Autobiography*, edited by Paul John Eakin, 195-215. Madison: University of Wisconsin Press, 1991.

Barton, Rebecca Chalmers. *Witnesses for Freedom: Negro Americans in Autobiography*. London and New York: Harper & Brothers Publishers, 1948.

Benson, Kimberly. *Performing Blackness: Enactments of African-American Modernism*. London and New York: Routledge, 2000.

Bercovitch, Sacvan. "The Ritual of American Autobiography: Edwards, Franklin, Thoreau.*Revue française d'études américaines*, 14: 139-150, 1982.

Boelhower, William. "The Making of Ethnic Autobiography in the United States." In *American Autobiography: Retrospect and Prospect*, edited by Paul John Eakin, 123-141. London and Madison: The University of Wisconsin Press, 1991.

Bogle, Donald. *Blacks in American film and Television: An Encyclopedia*. London and New York: Garland Publishing, Inc., 1988.

—. *Toms, Coons, Mulattoes, Mammies & Bucks: An Interpretive History of Blacks in American Films*. New York: Continuum, 1973, reprinted in 1994.

Britton, Andrew. "Stars and Genre." In *Stardom: Industry of Desire*, edited by Christine Gledhill, 198-206. London and New York: Routledge, 1991.

Buell, Lawrence. "Autobiography in the American Renaissance." In *American Autobiography: Retrospect and Prospect*, 47-69. Madison, Wisconsin: The University of Wisconsin Press, 1991.

—. *Literary Transcendentalism: Style and Vision in American Renaissance*. Ithaca and London: Cornell University Press, 1973.

Butler-Evans, Elliot. *Race, Gender and Desire: Narrative Strategies in Fiction of Toni Cade Bambara, Toni Morrison, and Alice Walker*. Philadelphia: Temple University Press, 1989.

Carby, Hazel. *Race Men*. Cambridge, MA and London: Harvard University Press, 1998.

Cripps, Thomas. *Making Movies Black: The Hollywood Message Movies from World War II to the Civil Rights Era*. New York: Oxford University Press, 1993.

Dyer, Richard. *Heavenly Bodies: Film Stars and Society*. London: The Macmillan Press Ltd., 1986.

—. *Stars*. London: British Film Institute, 1979.

Gates, Henry Louis, Jr. *The Signifying Monkey*. New York: Oxford University Press, 1988.

George, Nelson. *Blackface: Reflections on African-Americans and the Movies*. New York: HarperCollins Publishers, 1994.

Gordon, Lewis R. *Existential African: Understanding Africana Existential Thought*. London and New York: Routledge, 2000.

Guerrero, Ed. *Framing Blackness: The African American Image in Film*. Philadelphia: Temple University Press, 1993.

Harper, Phillip. *Framing the Margins: The Social Logic of Postmodern Culture*. New York and Oxford: Oxford University, 1994.

Kester, Gunilla Theander. *Writing the Subject: Bildung and the African American Text*. New York: Peter Lang, 1995.

Lejeune, Philippe. *On Autobiography*. Minneapolis: University of Minnesota Press, 1989.

Marshall, P. David. *Celebrity and Power*. Minneapolis and London: University of Minnesota Press, 1997.

Olney, James. "The Value of Autobiography for Comparative Studies: African vs. Western." In: *African-American Autobiography*, Ed. William Andrews, 212-334. Englewood, New Jersey: Prentice Hall, 1993.

Paquet, Sandra Pouchet. "West Indian Autobiography." In *African-American Autobiography: A Collection of Critical Essays*, edited by William Andrews, 196-211. Englewood Cliffs, New Jersey: Prentice Hall, 1993.

Poitier, Sidney. *The Measure of a Man*. San Francisco: HarperCollins, 2000.

—. *This Life*. New York: Alfred A. Knopf, 1980.

Reid, Mark. *Redefining Black Cinema*. Berkeley, CA: University California, 1993.

Russell, Catherine. *Experimental Ethnography: The Work of Film in the Age of Video*. Durham and London: Duke University Press, 1999.

Sartwell, Crispin. *Act Like You Know: African-American Autobiography and White Identity*. Chicago: University of Chicago Press, 1998.

Sollars, Werner. *Beyond Ethnicity*. New York: Oxford University Press, 1986.

Spengemann, William and L.R. Lundquist. "Autobiography and the American Myth." *American Quarterly*, 17: 501-19, 1965.

Steptoe, Robert B. *From Behind the Veil: A Study of Afro-American Narrative* (Second Edition). Chicago and Urbana: University of Illinois Press, 1979 (1991).

Stone, Albert E. "After *Black Boy* and *Dusk of Dawn*: Patterns in Recent Black Autobiography." In *African-American Autobiography: A Collection of Critical Essays*, edited by William Andrews, 171-195. Englewood, New Jersey: Prentice Hall, 1993.

—. "Collaboration in Contemporary American Autobiography." *Revue française d'études américaines*, 14: 151-65, 1982.

Chapter 15

Does *The Season of Men* Require the Harvest of Women?
A Tunisian Filmmaker's Vision

Anastasia Valassopoulos

In 1991, the African Women Professionals of Cinema, Television and Video produced this significant statement:

> A half-century after the birth of cinema, a quarter of a century after that of television, about fifty women from various states of the continent, fifty women of different political, religious and philosophical backgrounds united for the sake of their professional requirements to express their will to struggle unflinchingly:
>
> - to put forward their female vision of the world;
>
> - to have a controlling position on their pictures (Bakari 36).

The two requirements put forward in Burkina Faso in 1991 offer a significant guide with which we can navigate African women's filmmaking. Certainly, it is impossible to decide which takes priority over the other, presenting a 'female vision of the world' or overcoming the obstacles that a women filmmaker may encounter, due to her position as a woman. Then, even if the subject matter of the product is not 'female,' who the director is will remains significant. Comedian Nassifatou Latoundjidi from French-speaking Benin has made remarks on the present position of African women directors: "It seems to me that African cinema still suffers from a masculine malaise. There is now a need [...] for the African woman's imaginary to be expressed [...] women have much to say about the technique involved in the making of image and sound" (Brahimi 70).

This study will deal in particular with the Tunisian filmmaker Moufida Tlatli's second feature film *The Season of Men* (1999), and how she imbues her work with a particular female vision that is both complex and subtle. Tlatli's position within a feminist discourse operating in a North African country shall be considered, as shall be examined the topics she chooses to 'control' within this wider discourse.[1] Ultimately, we shall trace the components of the film that in fusing together form an involved and intricate picture of the shifting position of women vis-à-vis tradition, interaction with modernity, and, most significantly, encounter with their self-image.

In her work *Women's Cinema: The Contested Screen*, Alison Butler positions Tlalti's subject matter:

Tlatli belongs to the first generation of women in Tunisia to experience relative freedom. After independence was achieved in 1956, the secular regime outlawed polygamy and the veil, allowed women to enter professions [...] (101).

This relative freedom, however, manifests itself in Tlalti's production of two films dealing with issues of gender and sexuality, two topics that have *not* been resolved through the achievement of political independence. In his work, *Cinémas d'Afrique Francophone et du Maghreb*, Denise Brahimi reflects on the particular position of Tunisia in African film production, and concludes on a point that is integral to our speculation on Tlatli's vision, namely, that whereas Tunisian film's preoccupation in general is to "reveal the suffering of individuals" through the depiction of social/traditional and political scenes, what Tunisian filmmakers attempt to realize in particular is how these scenes often function as *barriers to self-analysis*:

> une excuse pour ne pas analyser le détail des situations
> (Brahimi 101).
> [An excuse for refusing to analyze situations in detail]
> (*my translation*).

In other words, filmmakers denounce the potency of the socio-political as legitimate justification for non self-reflection and personal responsibility. A culture of blame is not accommodated; in its place is the depiction of persons who enter into self-reflection through the medium of self-account, in Tlatli's case the intense use of flashbacks, scenes of solitude, and the depiction of vast spaces, among other techniques to which we shall return. Meanwhile, injurious moments are depicted, yet balanced with the portrayal of moments of thought and introspection. Paramount to Tlatli's subjects is a *working out* of ideas and preconceptions surrounding sexuality and gender roles, and her particular use of location. These will be discussed in detail, in order that we can appreciate Tlatli's 'control' over her story, as well as the 'female vision' portrayed within the boundaries of the film.

THE SEASON OF MEN

Tlatli's film is set in the present, in Tunis the capital of Tunisia, as well as in the past, in the protagonist Aicha's memory of the island of Djerba of the 1970s. Unable to find a cure for her child's autism, Aicha decides to leave Tunis and return to the island of Djerba, the home of her husband and the place she has tried to escape from all her married life. Her grown-up daughters, Miriam and Emna, accompany her. They temporarily remain with her on the island where the past unfolds for Aicha and the reader. Throughout the film, Tlatli presents this exciting technique in relation to her underlying themes. By slowly revealing the past, we learn what suffering and experience have fed into the present of the film, thus simultaneously offering a background and, in many ways, an explanation of the present. As Tlatli has remarked in a recent interview:

> For me it's important to understand why people behave as they do, and this structure is my way of showing a whole life. I think everything you do is related to your past (Said 24).

This approach specifically allows us to view the way in which ideas surrounding the expression of sexuality, relationships between men and women, as well as the suffering and loneliness that arise from unresolved sexual and gender issues are embedded in a traditional past that weighs heavily on the women in the present. All the memories of the past are of life on the island. This, in many ways, comes to represent the traditional aspects of North African norms surrounding femininity and female behavior. As SF Said has noted in the article 'Island of Silences':

> [...] uniting past and present is the *simmering frustration* of the female characters and the *silence* that surrounds their sexuality (Said 23; *my emphasis*).

While this is, undoubtedly, an important issue to be borne in mind, it is also insightful to view the past as that which *informs* and *offers* the present with the possibilities of elucidation and optimism. Whereas modern day Tunis is represented as technologically advanced, the psychic spaces the women inhabit with regards to their sexuality reflect their unchanged condition. 'Silence' and 'simmering frustration' do find outlets and solutions. In this way, Tlatli simultaneously engages both with the *trappings* of the past and the possible *benefits* of this past. Thus, cultural history is not denied its influential position. Characters do not simply take on 'modernity'; instead, they endure what ties them to tradition and understand it anew, ultimately refashioning it for survival in the present. Tlatli confirms this point in her insightful comment concerning this dilemma:

> After independence in 1956 the government passed laws which *in theory* brought Tunisian women a lot of liberation—we had the right to vote before French women [...] we were proud to be the freest women in the Arab Muslim world, but it wasn't so easy in practice to wipe out 14 centuries of taboos. Even now girls can't really do what boys do (Said 22; *my emphasis*).

Political independence means little to Tlatli in terms of actual change in the treatment of women and their sexuality. Coupled with this is the expected submissiveness of women to a behavioural code that does not take into account personal choice and individual will. Tlatli recognizes this unstable and psychically confusing position and seeks to address this in ways that we shall elucidate below. However, her persistent use of flashbacks forbids us to see the past as simply that which produces the consequences that are the future. On the contrary, Tlatli's manipulation of time forces us to re-read the past as a site of a complicated and elaborate *life* that has the potential to reveal more than a *frustration* or indeed a *silence*, but can instead expose *tension* and *critical reflection* even if from within the boundaries dictated by tradition. The past does not simply function as an *explanation of the present*, but rather as an open-ended process. Tlatli's 'editing,' Said notes, "continually juxtapo[ses] different moments in [the women's] lives—captures their relationship with time" (24).

ISLANDS

The greater part of the action in the film takes place on the island of Djerba, in eastern Tunisia. What characterizes life on this island for the particular family we encounter is the fact that there is no employment for the men, who are then forced to leave their wives to escape to the city in search of work. They are only able, due to financial constraints, to visit the island once a year; this time is nicknamed 'the season of men.' The film, according to Alison Butler:

> Shows a version of traditional family life in which patriarchal social rules are enforced tyrannically on behalf of the absent husbands by their mothers. Despite the centrality of mother-daughter relationships to Tlatli's work, femininity is represented as a shifting construct defined in relation to family, nation, tradition and modernity, never a timeless essence to be sentimentalized (Butler 104).

Though the understanding of femininity is undeniably defined in its 'relation' to circumstances, there *is* the space for the questioning of what it might mean to be a woman outside of all these influences, namely a 'timeless essence.' In this way, Tlatli succeeds in exercising control over her subject matter; she is aware of and takes great pains to reveal the extent to which 'family, nation, tradition and modernity' are embedded in the construction of femininity. However, what gives the film a particular ethereal quality is the imagining of a space where these influences are elusive and benign and where there is the time and the space to imagine another feminine existence divorced from the limiting factors of this same family, nation, tradition, and modernity. The island comes to function on two levels: as a symbol of the restricting factors outlined above, and as a mirror of the potential of the women that inhabit the island of Djerba to realize an alternative utopian existence. In the time and space of the film, however, Djerba is initially revealed as a foreclosing fate over which the women have no control. It is only later, when Aicha's memories become more and more detailed, that we begin to form a wider picture of life on the island. Aicha herself moves from viewing her past as the place of blame to understanding it as the beginning of the process of experience. Initially described as the place from which she wants to escape at all costs, Djerba is, however, the place to which Aicha decides to return. This double use of the island compels us to revisit the importance of the past and view the movement from past to present and back again as Tlatli's evocation of a 'structure' or control over her subject matter.

Small families that work the land and the few men that still inhabit the island mostly populate the Djerba of the past that is initially described. Life is confined to the domestic space ruled by Aicha's mother-in-law Ommi. What overshadows and propels daily activity in this narrow environment is interaction with the remainder of the family and the collective waiting for the arrival of the men for their one-month visit. The time referred to as the 'season' of men is the moment that epitomizes the presence of the women in Djerba, be they mother, sister, daughter or wife. It is impossible to view the notion of a 'season' without conceiving of ripe fruit, harvest, as well as the more direct suggestion of *change*. Within the parameters of the film, the 'season of men' does imply that their return may bring with it the possibility of a real conception, the planting of a seed in the loving wives. Indeed, this is the only opportunity for sexual union between the married couples, and the necessity of 'ripeness' is ever present.

The men from Tunis arrive at Djerba in time for the 'harvest' of their women, and the difficulty of resuming a relationship that has been dormant for eleven months is evident in the complications that arise when Aicha and her husband Said attempt to resume where they left off. Added to this is the sense of urgency with respect to consummation. The consequences of eleven months of separation are then crammed into one month of reparation.

It is rather simplistic to base the complications of marital relations that arise purely on this separation. For a better understanding of the issues involved, their difficulties and implications with regard to male-female relations, it is necessary to take a moment to elaborate on the trope of islands and seasons.

IBN TUFAYAL AND WOMEN HANGING OFF TREES

The notion of islands is riddled, characteristically, with the attributes of isolation, loneliness, and separation. All of these, however, can feed into more regenerative experiences associated with alienation, such as self preservation and the time allocated to observation. A slight diversion at this point may provide us with a framework within which to discuss islands and women in the same breath.

Twelfth century Arab philosopher and physician Ibn Tufayal in his much discussed 'philosophical fable' *Hayy ibn Yaqzan* tells the story of a boy:

> abandoned at birth and cast ashore on an uninhabited desert island [...] suckled and looked after by a doe. In Ibn Tufayal's fable, Hayy, since he has no contact with human beings, has to teach himself about the world through observation, experiment and reason (Irwin 291).

Hayy also develops a strong sense of the divine and upon completing his "intellectual and spiritual self-education" meets another man on the island. Together, they set out to try and convert a more 'civilized' island to their perceptions on truth and the divine (Irwin 291). They soon decide that it is impossible to convert unenlightened minds, and Hayy returns to his island. In her work *Woman's Body, Woman's Word: Gender and Discourse in Arabo-Islamic Writing*, Fedwa Malti-Douglas makes the observation that Ibn Tufayal does away with the need for women by supplying Hayy with a surrogate mother in the form of a doe. Set on the imaginary island of Al-Waqwâq, an island that is impossible to pin down geographically in medieval Islamic texts,[2] Malti-Douglas focuses on the fact that this was concurrently "the island whose trees bore women as fruit (85)." Malti-Douglas tells us that Al- Waqwâq,

> tickled the fancy of almost every medieval author whose work touched on the geographical or on that area of fantasy and marvel [and] receives one of its fullest treatments in the book of wonders by Ibn al Wardî (86-87).

Ibn al-Wardî describes the island as though it were a sexual haven, a locus for the realization of male sexual fantasies. The shifting use of this 'fantasy island,' from the site of male utopia to female abundance and plenitude will be very useful in our further discussion of Tlatli's narrative. As Malti-Douglas emphasizes:

> Ibn al-Wardî's narrative continues with a description of the women-bearing trees. On this island, he says, there are trees that bear 'fruit like women, with shapes, bodies, eyes, hands, feet, hair, breasts, and vulvas like the vulvas of women. They are the most beautiful of faces and hang by the hair. They come out of cases like big swords and when they feel the wind and sun, they yell, 'Wâq Wâq' until their hair tears apart.' When their hair tears, they die. The people of this island understand this sound and see it as an ill omen. The reader is told that he who goes beyond these women-trees will fall on women that also come out of trees but are greater than the earlier women in build [...] when one of these women's hair gets torn, she falls from the tree and lives a day or part of a day. He who has cut her or has attended her cutting can have sexual intercourse with her. He will find a great pleasure in her, not to be found in normal women... [on this island] there are no [other] inhabitants... (Malti-Douglas 88).[3]

The use of the same island(s) for these varying purposes is an exciting and abundant trope. The island or islands of Al-WâqWâq function as imaginary spaces that allow for a proliferation of experiences, be it a male utopia or a fantasy of female plenitude. Where Malti-Douglas rightly and insightfully discusses the role of these islands in the perpetuation of myths of women as available sexual objects, on the one hand, and the supremacy of male utopias on the other, it is in fact both of these two disparate motifs that we find resurrected in Tlatli's island tale, though presented with a twist.

In a more complicated approach, Tlatli evokes multiple *female* utopias that, however, collide with each other. Simultaneously, the island, for the men who return on their visit, takes on the attributes of a woman-bearing land of plenty that produces female pods awaiting their season of harvest. Tlatli's women experience both a self-education (to reuse Irwin's phrase of *Hayy*) as a result of life in isolation, *as well* as an understanding of their role as sexual beings. The time spent living the utopian possibility is where the women's role as sexual beings is reconsidered, and that is precisely where they seek to move away from the image of ripe fruit. Ibn Wardî's images of women hanging from trees by their hair reflects the suspended state of the women of Djerba who, though they may not die one day after they have been picked, certainly suffer a metaphorical death once their husbands have returned to Tunis. On the other hand, Ibn Tufayal's narrative of *Hayy ibn Yaqzan* presents us with an isolated man, who learns self-reflection as a result of his separateness. Observation and experiment allow him to develop a theory of the world that ultimately feeds into his realization of a divine image. Although the realizations and observations attributed to Aicha, her sister-in-law Zeinab, and her two daughters are not divine in nature, they do affect their present lives profoundly and distinctly. The island functions both in the past and the present as the scene of hardship and experience, and a scene that can be drawn on to offer solutions for the present. In the same way that Hayy has to learn to live on his own and be self-sufficient, so Aïcha learns to draw on her own resources in order to shape an image of the world.

Tlatli fuses these two images of islands as male utopias and loci of erotic fantasy, in order to complicate the function of the island setting. The next short section will relate these two possibilities to Tlatli's narrative, in order to unlock some of the key strands in the film.

FEMALE UTOPIA

What is distinct and yet goes against the notion of an all-encompassing utopia is that not all can realize their utopian existence in an interdependent community, like the one described in *The Season of Men*. In the medieval text discussed above, Hayy can live out his utopian dream, because he is alone. In *The Season of Men*, however, Tlatli challenges this idealism by presenting several women whose visions of perfection clash. An added difficulty is the possibility of a female utopia, continually tainted or challenged through the intervention of the absent male. There are several examples that reveal this. One glaring example is Ommi, Aicha's mother-in-law, who attempts to construct her own version of a perfect household. Here, her strict authority rules all her daughters, daughters-in-law, grandchildren, and dependants, an authority granted to her by her absent sons. In this way, the sons' authority is transmitted and maintained through their mother, and, in turn, she gains power that is then used to control others. It is possible to view this as Ommi's utopia; a position that grants her respect, control and influence. Through this figure of the mother-in-law, Tlatli hesitatingly reveals the potential power for a woman, albeit a second-hand power, only attainable by mothers of sons. Ommi retains strong traditional ideas over the occupation of women in her household. She strongly upholds the notion that they should not work for profit (as this demeans their position as cared-for women). It is here that Ommi and Aicha clash, precisely at the juncture where Aicha decides to take up weaving, in order to aid her husband's carpet-selling business. Coupled with this, Zeinab, Ommi's daughter, who has been abandoned by her husband, learns to weave with Aicha. Aicha and Zeinab, together with Aicha's two daughters, form a utopia that collides with that of Ommi. Determined to make herself useful, and realize her creative potential,

Aicha continues to weave and, against her mother's wishes, Zeinab continues to help Aicha with her work, as well as form an intimate bond with her.

What emerges is a most perfect version of a 'family,' one that is sustained throughout the story. Aicha and Zeinab constantly challenge Ommi's alternative to a traditional family that conceives of and maintains a clear authoritative figure. When Ommi tells Zeinab to stay away from the loom, Zeinab bitterly reminds her mother of her disastrous marriage, how she has not seen her husband since her wedding day, adding that she can no longer wait, but must fulfil her days somehow. Interestingly, these two parallel experiences of female utopia form the strain that define the action during the absence of the men. When the men arrive to spend their month in Djerba, primarily, they meet a group of women who have created an existence based on their absence. Their arrival momentarily functions to correct the supposed imbalance. For example, on two occasions, Said reminds Aicha that she must obey his mother, yet the women return to their lives once again after the men have departed. This schizophrenic existence ultimately leads to Aicha finally convincing her husband that she must go to live in Tunis with him. The relationship between Aicha and Zeinab reveals both the consequences of tradition as well as those of modernization. Whereas tradition dictates that Aicha must remain with her mother-in-law, modernization insists that Said earn his living in Tunis as a salesman. Aicha is restrained by a tradition that does not allow her to be independent and a modernity that has no place for her. To add to this confusion, though she attempts to challenge her restrictions head on, Aicha is nevertheless lured into the romantic atmosphere created around the time of the arrival of the men.

This is masterfully conceived by Tlatli, who, on the one hand, reveals a subjugated Aicha in revolt against her mother- in-law, thereby achieving an independent status within her dependency, yet, on the other hand, gives in to the feminine preparations involved in the few days coming up to the visit. Each of the men's visits symbolizes the possibility of change, and allows for an encapsulated vision of renewed romance to blossom.

The creation of a 'fantasy island' for the husbands cannot but be tempting for the women, who view this time as an escape into romance and love. What remains interesting is that these visits carry with them an inevitable disappointment, and a realization of the fleeting nature of hope and romanticism.

FANTASY ISLANDS

To the husbands who arrive once a year, Djerba seems a 'fantasy island,' one where wives and children, mother and home, await them with feverish sentiments, and bequeath them immense attention. The preparation that precedes the arrival of the men is such that, in many ways, it feeds into the illusion of an island where beautiful women fall from trees. In what is one of the most colorful and memorable scenes of the film, all the women of the household (except significantly, Ommi) come together for a group 'make-over.'

Said arrives for one of his yearly visits. He embraces his two daughters while his wife Aicha looks on from the doorway.

The women prepare for the 'season of men.'

Applying facemasks, plucking eyebrows, and removing unwanted hair, the women prepare and beautify themselves for the arrival of their men. Even Zeinab, who never hopes to see her husband again, and though she initially refuses, eventually succumbs to these rituals. The height of preparation comes in the application of the henna that has to be rinsed off in the sea, momentarily staining the water black. These scenes highlight the preparation that the women make for their romantic encounters. In this way, though Aicha takes an independent stand against her mother-in-law, she still partakes of traditional female tools of seduction. Furthermore, though the isolated state of the island allows Aicha to become resourceful in terms of her own fulfilment, it also reinforces the fact that she cannot leave it. By pleasing her husband, Aicha may be able to persuade him to take her back to Tunis, and this is a route she is prepared to take. Still hoping for an amorous reunion, Aicha prepares for her husband's arrival year after year. The encounters after long months of separation are, however, strenuous, given that the aesthetic preparation does not prepare Aicha for her husband, who returns to the island and assumes the authority that she has learned to live without in his absence. The island and its women, for Said, exist in a limbo that awaits his command, mediated through his mother in his absence. Aicha desperately attempts to pick up where they left off, but this proves difficult, as Said cannot accommodate the life that Aicha leads without him. His notion of a fantasy island that he can return to, and that awaits his command, is shattered as he realizes the closeness that has appeared between Zeinab and his wife, a closeness that all too obviously has replaced the possible intimacy that should have been reserved for himself. Here, Tlatli reinforces this point by ensuring that Zeinab and Aicha are shown to be physically close to each other in opposition to Said.

Their determination and love for each other overcomes his authoritative stance. The fantasy island image is destroyed as it becomes obvious that the women are able to construct new ways of living.

DAUGHTERS

Ultimately, Aicha does make her way to Tunis after giving birth to a son, Aziz. We also learn that Zeinab accompanies her and becomes intimately involved in the family. However, Aziz is autistic and, Said, not able to cope with this condition, leaves his family following Aicha's refusal to send their son to an institute for the mentally disabled. Unable to find a solution to his condition, Aicha, Zeinab, and her daughters take Aziz to Djerba in the final hope of finding a cure. Whereas Aicha remembers her past and what brought her back to Djerba, it is Tlatli who tells us about her (Aicha's) daughters Miriam and Emna, two women who are troubled by their sexuality. Miriam is unable to receive any pleasure from her sexual life with her husband, whereas Emna has embarked on an affair with a married man and has given herself to him with no guarantees. Miriam and Emna's experiences of their sexuality form yet another picture of the difficulties that arise with reconciling modernity to tra-

Zeinab and Aicha present a united front after Said has again refused to take Aicha back to Tunis.

ditional views on sexuality. Though Miriam has an understanding husband, she is unable to envision her sexuality as something that deserves attention. Emna takes advantage of her relative freedom and continues a dangerous affair. "The Arab woman's body suffers so much," confirms Tlatli. "After I married I had so many difficulties with sex: I was in love with my husband but I was ashamed. Slowly I changed, but it took many years (Said, 23)." Tlatli articulates Miriam's pain through emphasizing shame. The notion of sexuality as something that is shameful presents itself all too clearly as a problem that persists in its intensity. Emna, on the other hand, challenges this perception strongly. Whereas Miriam struggles with her sexual experience, Emna moves ahead to meet the challenge.

TLATLI'S VISION

In many ways, Tlatli offers us a range of possibilities for women from varying local contexts. Her vision is a complex, but captivating one, as she attempts to sustain a certain erotic dimension to sexual experience while upholding a certain vision of feminism that demands equality in sexual rights and needs. In a recent interview, Tlatli discusses this sensitive position vis-à-vis her audiences' expectations:

> I've had to defend *The Season of Men* a lot to the community in France. Most of them just want to see a movie about Tunisia and when they discover it's not what they expect, they claim what I'm showing isn't true. But I've also screened the film for hundreds of Muslim women in France and I was very moved when they said it wasn't just about Djerba but about their own situation (Said 24).

In her discussion of Tlatli's first feature film *The Silences of the Palace*, Viola Shafik claims that "Moufida Tlatli disconnects national liberation from women's liberation, showing that the one does not necessarily result in the other"(206). Tlatli moves from this position in *The Season of Men* and inhabits a more subtle stance as a director negotiating women's liberation *from ideas they have of themselves*. As Said has pointed out, Tlatli "eschew[s] grand national narratives in favour of the micro-politics of daily life, identity, and sexuality" (22). Yet, these micro-politics affect entire lives and futures. In placing herself at this difficult juncture, Tlatli allows us to experience contradictory images that nonetheless highlight the process by which her heroines understand their position vis-à-vis traditional ideas on men, sexuality, and marriage.

The scenes of the past in Djerba emphasize the impossibility for the women of choosing between the female utopia and the imaginary locus of the fantasy island. Whereas Aicha and Zeinab use their time creatively, grow to love each other as sisters, and defy the strong presence of Ommi, the arrival of the men throws their convictions into disarray as they submit to the expectations surrounding their social position as wives. Clearly, it is difficult for Tlatli to choose between these two positions, both of which are important to all the women. Independence, strength, and decisiveness are attributes sought after, which, nonetheless, collide with the actions of the women once faced with eroticism and passion. The pain suffered at the lack of love is ingeniously exposed through Zeinab. Though active in her role as Aicha's companion in work and life, a position from which she gains immense satisfaction, yet, her pain is revealed through the aching song she sings to herself about loneliness: "Go little bird, bring me back my man, take a message to him, tell him I miss him." Zeinab tells Aicha of the pain she feels as a result of her untouched skin that has never housed anything but fat, no life, no love, no child.

The impossibility of achieving contentment and peace without fulfilling her desire is emphasized by Tlatli as Zeinab has a secret sexual encounter with a friend, who has not left the island. Towards the close of the film, Zeinab and Aicha decide to remain on Djerba as Aziz learns to weave, an unexpected cure in the shape of a loom. What is intensely revealed by Tlatli, however, is the strong community of women that are able to experience, discuss, and empathize with one another's position regarding their sexualities and identities.

Tlatli brings difficult issues to the fore, and does so in a way that is not overtly political, but instead is subtly polemical. In choosing to go back and revisit a scene where traditional ideas on the role of women is upheld, Tlatli takes us on a journey of possibilities where femininity is expressed and experienced in many different ways. Modernity is represented neither as the solution nor the restriction, but, in fact, as a change that brings with it inevitable choices and dilemmas.

Tlatli's use of the island remains significant overall. The island placed in opposition to the mainland functions to imply Aïcha's determination to achieve liberation from her suffocating mother-in-law, within the physically stifling island life. This, too, is turned on its head when Zeinab and Aisha are allowed to visit Aïcha's mother on another part of the island. From a cinematic point of view, Djerba is conceived through wide-open spaces surrounded by the infinite blue sea. Yet, while out on this day of liberty, Aïcha's daughter Miriam is almost raped. Ommi punishes Aicha for this as she arrives late from her sojourn. The island here does not function as a safe haven for the women; instead they are shown to be even more vulnerable. Tlatli here infuses one liberating experience with a constricting one. Both consequences arise from the position that women inhabit within this North African community that Tlatli represents.

It is timely that Tlatli chooses to question the ways in which women negotiate their position vis-à-vis an image of themselves for which they may not be responsible. Miriam and Emna both seem to suffer versions of the traumas suffered by the women of Djerba. Zeinab's fear of losing the ability to be passionate is recreated in Miriam's uncertainty and shame over her sexual intimacy. Emna's boldness can also be conceived as a reaction to the unhappy marriage of her parents. However, it is through the visit to the past and to Djerba, where Aicha and Zeinab are shown to survive and love *in spite* of the constrictions of tradition, that the present is perceived as one riddled with as yet unknown possibilities. Though the image of Aziz weaving is a significant one (here tradition more concretely offers solace) Tlatli's ability to reconcile the past and the present is indeed significant to our understanding of constructive feminisms and films that allow for the "flexibility of cinematic identification" (Butler 16) across time and space. As regards sexuality and personal relationship, Tlatli constructs a complicated situation for her characters when confronted with modernity. Here, she shows that it is difficult, if not impossible, to understand the current position of the North African woman's awareness of her sexual rights without pressing further into the past.

Notes

1. Today there are approximately six female directors in Tunisia.
2. The Island of al-Waqw could be located in places as distinct as Japan or South Africa.
3. Malti-Douglas informs us that *Hayy ibn Yaqzan* is 'alive and well in the modern Arabic consciousness. Not only has it been reprinted on numerous occasions, but its hero and his adventures have become the subject of films, television specials, and even children comic strips [a connection has also been made between this text] and Daniel Defoe's *Robinson Crusoe* (68).

Works Cited

Bakari, Imruh, and Mbye Cham. Eds. *African Experiences of Cinema*. London: British Film Institute, 1997.

Brahimi, Denise. *Cinémas D'Afrique Francophone et du Maghreb*. Paris: Éditions Nathan, 1997.

Butler, Alison. *Women's Cinema: The Contested Screen*. London: Wallflower, 2002.

Malti-Douglas, Fedwa. *Woman's Body, Woman's Word: Gender and Discourse in Arabo-Islamic Writing*. New Jersey: Princeton University Press, 1991.

Halberstadt, Ilona. "The Homecoming." In: *Sight and Sound*. Vol. 11, No. 6. 38-39.

Irwin, Robert. *Night and Horses and the Desert: The Penguin Anthology of Classical Arabic Literature*. London: Penguin, 1999.

Said, SF. "Island of Silences." In: *Sight and Sound*. Vol. 11, No. 6: 22-24.

Shafik, Viola. *Arab Cinema: History and Cultural Identity*. Cairo: American University in Cairo Press, 1998.

Tlatli, Moufida. Ed. *The Season of Men*. Carthage: Maghrebfilms, 1999.

Chapter 16
The Sex-Appeal of Idrissa Ouedraogo's Films: *Yaaba* (1989), *Tilaï* (1990), *Samba Traoré* (1993), *Le cri du coeur* (1994), and *La colère des dieux* (2002)

Christiane P. Makward

Idrissa Ouedraogo's films have been recognized with various awards. *Le cri du coeur* was nominated in competition, and won La Navicella Venezia Cinema award at the Venice Film Festival in 1994. *Tilai* won the Special Grand Jury Prizes at the Cannes Film festival in 1990, and *Yaaba* also won the International Critics Prize, Fipresci for Best Film Outside Competition at the Cannes Film Festival in 1989. The artist is now firmly established as a major African figure in the seventh art. Ouedraogo belongs to the third generation of post-colonial film makers whose work, occasionally boosted by special foreign support, battles perennially with lack of resources. In 1997, Ouedraogo gained special visibility in Paris: he was invited to direct Aimé Césaire's *Christophe* at the most prestigious French national theatre, La Comédie Française. Wrought with a primarily white, unmasked cast, the result was a controversial but historical consecration of his engagement with the Arts. More recently, he chaired the feature film jury at the FESPACO 2003 in Ouagadougou, where his film *La colère des dieux* premiered off competition.[1] Although he started with shorts, including silent films (*Les écuelles, Tisserands),* Ouedraogo's long feature films soon achieved a more plastic, esthetically arresting style than those of most African directors who focus on social satire and use more intricate plots. Inevitably, his work has been acclaimed and criticized, appreciated and misrepresented, especially in rushed press releases and film reviews. Melissa Thackway recalled how the movie-director was expected by some to remain tied to his successful original setting of Northern Burkina Faso (although he was born in the southwest, his cultural roots are from the Sahel region). Olivier Barlet also substantiates this point on the basis of several interviews with Ouedraogo (Barlet 1996, 223). Critics were indifferent to the refreshing perspectives of *Le cri du coeur* on Africans in big French cities (Lyon in this case) as "strangers" rather than the usual destitute immigrants (55, note 9). Ironically, Ouedraogo's home audiences seem to appreciate his "exotic" films, shot abroad, over the rural stories in the genre of "bush films" acclaimed by Western audiences.

As my title lightly suggests, a "gynocentric" approach is a gendered assessment rather than a systematic film analysis. I was originally intrigued by the strong positive impact Ouedraogo's films had on such unintended viewers as mature, white, academic women. The debate on an artist's targeted and actual audiences is a rich one where there prevails a consensus that great works show the universal—which can be shared—through the specific or the particular. A work of art in today's diversity-friendly world may be appreciated primarily on its own creative terms, but it cannot avoid the expectations and judgments of culturally different and gendered audiences. Like real life, no film can function untouched by gender consciousness even when the feminine seems excluded. An exemplary war-time drama, such as Ousmane Sembène's all-male *Camp de Thiaroye* draws its strength from history: the betrayal of African soldiers by the French colonial military can hardly leave feminists indifferent, precisely as an illustration of male (white) domination.

Approaching "Francophone" African cinema with gendered goggles is a rather uncommon sport, possibly considered suspect if not irrelevant. A recent article provides a notable exception by discussing the modesty of African cameras in representing sex, and the enduring uneasiness in dealing with eroticism, and even more so, male homosexuality. Alexie Tcheuyap concludes a brief exploration of this issue of "sex off screen" in the following terms: "It can be said that the vast majority of African films establish a hierarchy between the discourse on sex and the visual representation of it, including those very works that attempt to work out African forms of eroticism" (40, my translation). In 1989, Ouedraogo thought he might venture towards unveiled nudity (Jousse 9), and he did—for a lively ten seconds or so, without frontal exposures—in *Le cri du coeur,* which is set largely in Lyon. But the boldest he gets in his 2003 film, set in Burkina Faso, is a screen filled with a male shoulder (in order to show a birth-mark) and a blissful "after the act" female face (Ina Cissé's). So, despite expectations for sexually explicit materials and the circulation of Western video pornography in Africa, nobody as yet has taken up the challenge of following Désiré Ecaré's explicit eroticism in *Visages de femmes* (1984); "To do so, one would have to overcome certain tenacious traditions, unwritten laws, and primarily a stern sense of the sacred" (Tcheuyap 40). Most likely, this particular "sense of the sacred" can be related to gender and such is my modest proposal in accounting for the charisma of Ouedraogo's own vision. Olivier Barlet has considered the status of women in African cinema. He accounts for several characters resisting patriarchal concepts of polygyny and gender roles through adultery in particular, but he does not treat Ouedraogo in that respect (Barlet 1996:116-118).[2]

In the beginning, there was silence: Mooré, Ouedraogo's native tongue, is one of Burkina's forty-two languages. So it was only logical to signify as much as possible through images rather than dialogue at a time when providing subtitles was a forbidding financial burden. *Poko* (1981) won the short film award of FESPACO: "I tried to speak through images," confides Ouedraogo to Tam Fiofori (821), but for *Yam Daabo* (1987), his first feature film, he was able to rely on dialogue and music, including the gracious participation of Cameroonian singer-poet Francis Bebey. According to Clément Tapsoba, in a recent, masterful overview of Burkina film of the past two decades, this film appears to be Ouedraogo's most politically committed movie, dealing with the economic situation in the Sahel region and showing the difficult, "purer" choice of emigration to the south rather than dependence on international aid. Tapsoba explains: "The commitment to a type of film with political content is rooted, of course, in the dominant political discourse of the period, particularly within the college and high school students' associations to which Idrissa Ouedraogo belonged in the late seventies and early eighties" (126). He would eventually move on to the more symbolic narratives "focusing on themes of exclusion, tolerance, and identity quest" that brought him fame (127).

Now turning to the films under consideration, I propose to outline the dynamics of gender in the plots—this constitutes the director's androgynous gaze—and then I relate them to larger esthetic considerations. It will then be possible to account for Ouedraogo's refreshing "reserve" behind the camera, and his special "sex-appeal" to "the feminine" in his audiences.

Yaaba (1989) remains for some this director's masterpiece to date. The title means "grandma." The genre is that of the unlikely "love-story" of an old woman and a young boy, a genre heralded by Romain Gary's novel The *Life before Us* (1975), adapted as *Madame Rosa* (1977). Within African film, it also falls into the category of the country or "bush" films richly illustrated by other African film makers. Yaaba (or Sana) is extremely old, toothless, and shriveled but regally tall, and straight as an arrow. This primeval beauty and enviable posture are enjoyed by several of the leading characters, primarily the two children: Bila and his girl companion Nopoko. Ouedraogo's actors are mostly untrained, non-professional actors who play themselves along a rough narrative plot line. In his later films, especially city films, he has used more trained actors. Briefly summarized, the story focuses on the old woman, who lives at a distance from the village because she is considered a witch. Her own joyfulness brings on complicity between her and the boy who brings her little presents and tries to defend her even before her shack is burnt by angry villagers. Narrative tension sets in when the girl falls ill from a wound incurred in fighting along with the boy, indirectly to protect Yaaba. A traditional healer proves greedy and useless, so the girl is only saved, because Yaaba undertakes a journey across the desert and a mighty river. She returns with a good herbalist's remedy, administered in secret by the girl's aunt (Bila's father and other villagers have chased away the good medicine-man with his medicine, and the old woman).

Character distribution is uneven between the tolerant women and the shrews who denounce Bila for keeping company with the "witch" (their sons attack him and wound Nopoko). One prettier, younger woman has been married off for family reasons to an impotent drunk who turns out—like his young adulterous wife—on the "good" side of Yaaba's friends. Among the personable women (who clearly outnumber the "bad" ones), rank Bila's mother as well as Nopoko's aunt who, like Yaaba, looks on the pre-adolescent couple with true delight.

Nopoko's mother is dead but Bila's father has forbidden him, for no apparent reason, to go out to the graveyard, too close perhaps to Yaaba's territory (or is the grouchy father afraid of the dead?). Both the opening and closing scenes of the film are burial sites (associated with cleansing or life-giving waters), and they are ultimately "framed" by the same shot of the two children running after each other. There are several other deep shots with the children running into the distance, a motif that will be dramatically resumed in *La colère des dieux*. In such playful races, the leader is alternately the girl or the boy. Although Nopoko, like Bila, displays traditional behaviors in terms of gender (he taunts her for her fearfulness, she mocks him for carrying a water-pot to the pond, teasing "all you need is earrings to be a woman"), Nopoko is also a brave companion, and she can defy authority. The camera actually shows her stepping in front of Bila to ward off the trio of no-good-doers who attack him on the way from the pond. Only Yaaba's arrival on the scene saves Bila from a serious beating since the children are outnumbered. Clearly, Nopoko is equally brave, and she takes part in the fight, getting jabbed in the process. In the film's closing scene, the girl is the one who initiates a chasing game: she will give back the bracelet he just presented her with—it was Yaaba's gift to the boy—if he catches up with her. Since they disappear in the distance of space and time, we will never know who wins. The suggestion is of course that they will jointly "own" Yaaba's bracelet, symbolic of the gift of love, caring and tolerance. In this closing episode, the viewer also learns why Yaaba had been marginalized from the village: she was presumed "bad luck," because her mother had died in childbirth, soon followed by the father. In other words, a family never developed, and the child grew into an outcast through the classic scapegoat process.

Among the more fully developed female characters in this film, Bila's mother is shown powerful, productive and gentle. In a monogamous marriage, she is endowed with all the required qualities for a perfect role-model for Nopoko. She knows to observe and bear with, or to resist or trick, to order or indulge appropriately her rather ridiculous husband (the diminutive husband will take on a fully clownish development in *Samba Traoré*, 1993). On Bila's mother (probably the real-life person) Idrissa Ouedraogo comments: "[Bila] is lucky to have a marvelous mother, contrary to the other three children. When Bila's father says 'such mother, such son', it's because the fundamentals of an education come from the mother. The boy is someone who learns [...]. He is an ideal: he is not absolute purity, but he brings about tomorrow's world" (Jousse 9, *my translation*). One must add: the boy only heralds a positive future, because he is the focus of love for three generations of women: Yaaba, his mother, and his girlfriend Nopoko. Yaaba is, of course, a wonderful character who breathes goodness, serenity, and endurance. Her steady, slow trek through the desert with only a calabash and a loin-cloth in the blazing sun ranks as the high point of the film in terms of a philosophical statement through image, admirably served by the gentle musical score (Francis Bebey's) of discreet percussion and low-key modern brass melody. It is quite arresting to hear how, during the shooting,

Fatima Sanga (Yaaba or Sana) grumbled about being moved around by car, which made her lose her natural, inner sense of time (Barlet 1996: 191).

Various critics have invoked classical tragedy to assess the somber appeal of *Tilaï* (1990), commonly referring to the myth of Oedipus. Here, the father's law—which is the weight of tradition and the price of social cohesion—is indeed rooted in the clash of desires for the same woman. Nogma, once engaged to the son, and then taken as second wife by the father, is subject to the taboo, but, she is still enamored with the son. A similar scheme: a young couple's love violated by the power figure, and the same actress, Ina Cissé will provide the tragic romance of *La colère des dieux* (2003). Nogma's love is requited by Saha (Rasmane Oue-draogo), who is sentenced to death at the hand of his gentle, confused brother, as fate would have it. The plot is also reminiscent of the myth of Phaedra in that the (forgivable) "incest" takes place between the younger wife and the older wife's son, who has been betrayed by his father. Ouedraogo, facetiously or not, has cast the father as a light-weight, frail, vaguely molieresque character with an authentic, tyrannical "acting" style. As in *Yaaba*, Ouedraogo presents adultery as understandable, and the punishment as a tragic, unjust necessity. If the younger wife has borne a child to the father, the film does not show it: there is no visible evidence of the father's appropriation of the son's sweetheart. The older co-wife, Saha's mother, shares Nogma's resentment of the old man's abuse. She actually mocks him as they both refuse to open their door to him one night. The old wife displays motherly tenderness and physical closeness to her son during a secret visit. Later, she extends this nurturing sympathy to Nogma. She actually spoon-feeds her adulterous co-wife, who is tied to a tree. In other words, the film demonstrates, albeit tragically, the paramount value of true love over old men's exercise of power. Ouedraogo says of love, it is "the first sentiment of life" (Fiofori 820). The brother in charge of Saha's execution by stabbing also betrays the father, because he shares the prevailing feeling of sympathy for the lovers. When Nogma leaves the village, banned by her mother (after her own father's suicide), she undertakes a prolonged trek away from the village, in search of Saha. The lovers eventually are rejoined and blessed by a charming old aunt, and we find out that Nogma is pregnant. But fate gives a final twist to the resolution of the plot. It is through his irrational—but admirable—determination to see his dying mother that Saha is finally shot by his brother, falling dead upon his mother's dead body. So, the father's name is cleansed at the terrible cost of one son's death and the other son's departure from the village. This tragedy pitches the rule of the father against the love of the mother. Such is "The law," that is "Tilaï" in Mooré.

Nogma's primary ally and observer is a young girl, eager to understand the world of adults and passion. Kuilga is played by Roukieto Barry, the lovely Nopoko of *Yaaba*, and she also appears as an adolescent, Sana in *Karim and Sana*. Kuilga seems to have a special friendship with Kouri, the hapless young brother who spares his brother's life once, but angrily shoots him on his return to the village. In an early dialog, Kuilga asks Kouri why everybody is so unfair to the lovers. The young man, speechless at first, vaguely refers to "destiny." This triggers Kuilga's dart: "You are as stupid as all the others." In *Tilaï* as in *Yaaba*, most of the individualized female characters (as opposed to the anonymous women in the village) sympathize with the lovers, except Nogma's mother but including her co-wife.

Ouedraogo's gaze undoubtedly questions traditional patriarchal authority both through caricature, pitching unimpressive father figures against noble, even beautiful female resisters, and through bloodshed. His modest means may well be the foundation of his style; the budget for *Tilaï* was lower than *Yaaba*'s, just over one third the budgets for *Le cri du cœur* of 1994, and thirty-five times less expensive than *Le Hussard sur le toit* (Barlet 1996: 247). This paucity and the decision to use real life characters playing largely themselves result in poetic charisma, a mysterious attraction akin to that afforded by Duras' or Kieslowski's films where a quasi-biological sense of time is achieved. According to Sabouraud, *Tilaï* has the strength, the nostalgic appeal of emerging cinema, staying clear of "wanton psychologizing, which is the unresolved plight of speaking movies." This, he adds, is "a strange, unique power which recalls the origins of cinema, where myths still conjugate with life" (70). Indeed, punctuated by the celebrated African "tchp!," which is often featured, sparing dialogs, respectful silences and secrets with devastating consequences are common features of Ouedraogo's early as well as recent movies.

A secret (for the village, while the viewer knows) is the narrative cornerstone of *Samba Traoré* (1993), a story of crime and punishment that falls short of tragedy, because jail rather than death resolves the situation in the end: the crime was only armed robbery. The focus is on Samba's change of heart about living away from family and his inability to be integrated back into the village because he has become mysteriously rich. Even though his childhood friend Salif and his newfound love Saratou constitute keys of acceptance by the villagers, his money sets him apart, if not above the village folks, despite the generous ways in which he spends it in the community, building a business (a controversial bar) and owning a bicycle he lends willingly. When his pregnant wife's time arrives, it turns out life-threatening. An extremely sensitive sequence takes place: on their way to town Samba suddenly runs away while his friends arrange for his endangered wife to be driven by truck. But she delivers en route with the help of the women while the men respectfully keep their distance. Then Saratou and her two children are kept away from Samba, in a different village. Thanks to her older son, however, a son she had by Samba's arch-enemy from town, they are reconciled. Indeed, Samba has endeared himself to the boy as well as the mother. Eventually, Samba's money cache is discovered and his house burnt by his own father. An unhappy suitor, Ishmael tips the police and Samba is taken away to pay his debt to social order, with the understanding that his wife will await him.

This film was awarded the Carthage Silver Tanit 1992 and the Berlin Silver Bear 1993, possibly to acknowledge Ouedraogo's work as a whole rather than the single film. It has considerably less "gender-appeal" and no such archetypal qualities. The rural space is put in balance with the city (at least thematically, if not visually), and money rules over the narrative, although friendship, comedy, and true love, as well as true feminine heroism (in the magnificent but not graphic childbirth scene), amply illustrate Ouedraogo's humanistic vision and modern male sensitivity. The protagonist's psychology, shown through gestures, plans and situations rather than words, overshadows the love-story which was paramount in *Yaaba* and *Tilaï*. While it represents a new direction in Oue-draogo's range of concerns, including a rapprochement with modern realism, it offers less inspiring images of women. Skinny Salif and his enormous wife Binta (who can carry him on her back) belongs to classic comedy. Older women do not play prominent roles and the major female role, Saratou's, lacks character except in her stoical delivery scene. I am not suggesting that the film deserves less attention but certainly that it does not engage a feminist viewer in pleasurable nuances regarding gender roles. Critics have suggested a debt to Hollywood (Lequeret 51) and a coherent approach to the fleeing syndrome, the intrusion of guilt and despair, presumably akin to Far-Western and "film noir" genres. The protagonist belongs to the type of "magnificent losers," as an ambivalent character he is "carried by the combined energies of despair and faith" (ibid.). Denise Brahimi pays tribute to Saratou's courage in painfully revealing to Samba the shady nature of her own experiences in the city, while Samba tries to bury his secrets, thus breeding misunderstanding and suffering. Brahimi astutely proposes that *Samba Traoré* is "less interesting as potential tragedy than as tragedy circumvented and rejected, that is as the will to signify that where love rules, tragedy will not prevail" (Brahimi 98, my translation). This is the closest we can get to a gynocentric appraisal of *Samba Traoré*.

About *Le cri du coeur* (*Cry from the Heart*, 1994)—which was disappointingly underrated by critics—Ouedraogo declared: "With this, my sixth feature film, I chose to shoot in Europe, at the very heart of her cultural values [...] Feelings are essential for me: feelings that can unite beings above and beyond nations and continents [...]" [3] To take a superficial look at the cast and role distribution, we find only secondary female characters: a fine mother whose love is never tried beyond normal limits (here too, tragedy is warded off), a fiery artist named Deborah as jealous mistress who, at first, does not accept her lover's infatuation with the African boy. The focus is the boy Mokhtar, first shown in a strong bond to his (very handsome) grandfather while in Africa. Once in France, he develops anxiety with visions and dreams of a hyena. Concurrently, he establishes a friendship with Paulo, a marginal person who dabbles in magic tricks and has enough of the child left in him to lend Mokhtar an ear. Thus, Paulo provides a helpful alternative to the Cartesian fantasy denial, and professional psychiatric treatment for «culture shock.» Mokhtar's father is absorbed in his successful business, though a loving father and husband. The immigrants' usual woes are not an issue in this film, nor are marital complications, nor ordinary racism, although there is no idealization of France.

The use of the hyena (named Blondie in real life) has not drawn much positive commentary. I propose that it is Ouedraogo's key, like Cocteau's mirror in *Orphée,* to the "reality" of the yonder world. The hyena appears both in the child's dreams and in his "real" life, mostly at night. Mokhtar fails to convince his parents and the psychologists that the hyena is real, but Paulo gives him a chance to set up a trap, a circle of fire, and to destroy the beautiful beast (at least in his own mind). Against tradition, which associates the hyena with scavenging for dead bodies and represents it as ugly, this hyena is a "real actress" (it is not a virtual, special effect) and a very handsome specimen. It is, appropriately, a frightful symbol of death and a fascinating creature of beauty, totally out of place in Lyon, like death in a child's consciousness. One might say that it embodies the ambivalence of death in ancient mythologies. When trapped by Mokhtar in "real" life, it metamorphoses into a flash appearance of the child's good (and divinely good-looking) grandfather. As the scenario has already alerted us, the hyena is linked to the grandfather's life-force. If the latter appears briefly, serene, smiling, and waving to Mokhtar, it is because his spirit has just been released: he has passed away, as we learn in the next sequence; thus we (should) understand that Mokhtar's hallucinations were signs of the old man's struggle with death. In other words, *Le cri du coeur* (*Cry from the Heart*) is a tale of belonging *also* or *at heart* to the African roots. To put it more theoretically, it is a visual metaphor. It carries meaning over from the old country; it signifies that "the Dead are not dead": Birago Diop's famous poem is quoted by the boy to Paulo when the latter tries to comfort him on his grandfather's demise. Paulo tells him exactly the same thing in his own modern, pop-mystical words. This tale of a film should be read as a poetic statement that leaving the motherland does not destroy spiritual identity. Whether Ouedraogo himself is perfectly Cartesian (and an atheist) or has retained some "premier" beliefs, as Maryse Condé claims to have when she discusses *Histoire de la femme cannibale,*[4] is of no consequence for those in his audiences who see poetic freedom where it is at play.

In *Africultures* online, Olivier Barlet provides crucial information about the genesis of *La colère des dieux (The Gods' Wrath,* 2002*).* Ouedraogo struggled for ten years to gather financial support for an epic on Boukari Koutou (aka Ouobgbo), who resisted French colonial invasion in the late nineteenth century. The new film is the result of a down-sized dream. Indeed, the French appearance is limited to a few effective shots of a single officer's face ordering "Fire!" five times, resulting in a panoramic tableau of dead bodies that evoke romantic painters' war scenes. Barlet warns it would be a mistake to see in *La colère des dieux* a return to the rural, intimate dramas of the early nineties:

> Idrissa Ouedraogo is convinced that the divisions and internal strifes for power have undermined Africans' power of resistance, and that this problem continues today. In a culture where, at the time [of colonial invasion] but also in today's people's unconscious, the gods are supposed to rule over the destiny of men who implore their protection, and ritualize it through countless charms and magic

devices, this rapport with the divinities determines the understanding of phenomena. Suicidal strifes could only unleash the gods' wrath. Thus, supernatural phenomena punctuate a film where legend is woven into a warp of power struggles and very human love stories.[...] Ouedraogo succeeds through his radical manipulation of ellipsis, too obvious on occasion—as when Salam runs across time—but generally endowing the film with a rhythm that had not been achieved earlier on (Barlet 2003).

The critic brings his tribute to a vibrant climax as follows: "Idrissa Ouedraogo, obsessed with his quest for truly African images in the face of a deluge of external [foreign] images, tries to ground his vision in a tradition he knows to be rich in unexploited resources confronting globalization. He draws close to human bodies to inscribe his search within the human" (Barlet 2003, film review online).

In this film, in part a study on male power, the female characters are icons of traditional femininity: lovers, victims, companions, objects of desire, and child-bearers. The fundamental reason for this is that the purpose of the projected, un-achieved film was not characterization, or highlighting a ferocious family drama; instead, it was to give a historical event an epic dimension. It aimed to retrieve from oblivion a case of resistance to colonial invasion, and its failure; primarily to recall such an episode a century later, at a time when oral transmission of history may appear doomed. The film maker could in a manner substitute himself for the bard. Needless to say, a lesson for the present disasters of the African continent is embedded therein, as well as an identifying myth. The time of the action is the late nineteenth century, the span of two generations of kings. It starts with the demise of the old king, who tells his mature son of his concern about proper transmission of power (it should befall the king's younger brother). The son, Tanga, significantly tall and massive, vows to reign without delay. The film ends, nearly twenty years later, with a most "un-African" solution to a very ancient problem: the young, new king, Salam, who has magically overpowered the illegitimate king, shoots himself. With Ouedraogo's characteristic reserve and economy of means, all we see is a spectacular close-up on the trigger of a period rifle. The gods are angry, because he has been unable to prevent the massacre of his people by the French, because he has betrayed his "spirit" and killed the human form of the eagle, the king surrenders his life.

The leading female character in the first part (lengthwise uneven parts, divided by the ellipsis Barlet questions (it enchanted me)[5], Awa first appears as near victim of rape during an attack on her village by war-mongering Tanga. She is saved by a benevolent peace-lover (the old king's brother, who should have been the ruler, but yielded to his nephew to avoid internal strife). The next evening at a dance, Tanga the conqueror takes a fancy to Awa's beauty and she is forcibly taken away her while her lover Rasmanè implores the spirits' mercy. Nine months later, (now) Queen Awa gives birth to a son and discovers to her dismay (because of specific birthmarks) that he is not the king's child. She is advised to keep it secret, but eventually a diviner challenges the king to face the truth. A link is made with the various problems afflicting the land: Salam, now twelve, is not his son. Several signs (an ugly front tooth, birthmarks, fits of mischief or rage) set the child apart, and the king's benevolent uncle (who has surrendered his rights in the name of peace) reveals to Salam that the white eagle is his allied spirit.[6] The eagle in this film, like the hyena in *Le cri du coeur*, serves as point of contact with or key to the marvelous, the mythical. The eagle in flight recurs in the final scene, after the massacre by the French, and the king's suicide. Ouedraogo actually freezes it in flight as a terminal punctuation mark to the movie.

The young queen, Salam's love, has a reduced role since the two reigns (Tanga's and Salam's) occupy uneven film time. Her "Madonna and Child" portrait closes the film with beauty, dignity, and understated grief: the baby seems to nod and assent to her words, recalling the archetypal resemblance or connivance of Mother and Child in countless paintings. She wipes a tear, as she hears the king's suicide gunshot in the distance and explains the eagle to the baby. Her love is lost, but its fruit, the child, may again be protected by the spirit, a striking, fundamental statement of life's law to go on. Thus, in this film, women are essentially the feminine face of iconic pairs. Rasmanè's father, a peasant, is put to death by Tanga and buried by his wife. Rasmanè and Awa die together—she chooses to die with him after they hide their child, Salam, underground, in a hole. Salam re-emerges only to watch their execution (but we don't see it or hear it) by Tanga.

As quoted above (Barlet's review online), the "radical use of ellipsis" is a major feature of Ouedraogo's style. Clearly, in his 2002 film, Ouedraogo's female characters are no inspiration for Western (or any) feminists except as embodiments of "the way it was." But a male film maker's vision of the destructiveness of African tyrants is bound to seduce peace-loving souls. This is revisitation of *Le devoir de violence* by Yambo Ouloguem, an ill-fated and unduly maligned novel of the sixties. Ouedraogo's vision, limited as it is, fortunately, thanks to the poverty of his means, nonetheless appeals to our sensitivity. His camera is classical or prudish by Hollywood standards, far less so by French *auteur* film standards. It understates the violence of the narrative, substituting magic for blood on screen. In Tanga's and Salam's power struggle, Salam outdoes Tanga by using heavy rain against fire: the power of life quenches the power of death (and in traditional mythologies, the feminine overwhelms the masculine principle). Ouedraogo's elliptical style combines well with the use of surrealistic ("animistic") motifs: it rests on his determination to appeal to his own people first, to respect their modesty in representing violence by masquerade, magic, and ellipsis. Music and sound never assault the viewer's eardrums. Violent death scenes are understated: we do not even *hear* the fatal shots in Awa and Rasmanè's deaths, or the shot in Salam's suicide. In other words, instead of a convergent multitude of signs, Ouedraogo selects a few, and spares our senses usually overwhelmed, if not de-sensitized, by high-speed, high-volume, high-tech commercial cinema, from the brutality gentle people abhor. Thematically, children and the couple (monogamous love) are major foci. Mavericks, power-thirsty figures fail or meet justice. Esthetically, Ouedraogo's films tie time to open spaces, alternately using up precious time for splendid leisurely close-ups. This results in a tempo that can be reminiscent of Duras' esthetics. Naturally, knowledgeable critics[7] will place him in the wake of Souleyman Cissé's *Yeelen* (1987), more recently illustrated by Abderrahmnane Cissako's luminous *Heremakhonon* (2002).

It is not clear how far Mooré's syntax distinguishes gender,[8] but to a romance language user, the masculine and feminine are delightfully close, linguistically, symbolically, and «actually» in pairs such as Bila, the boy, and Nopoko, the girl. It can be said in a capsule that Tanga, the violent, illegitimate king of *The Gods' Wrath* (a film dedicated to the director's young daughter Nora), fails to listen to love. But Samba, the accidental accomplice to murder, or Saha (the oedipal lover of *Tilaï*) do open up to their own inner other, "anima," or femininity. Understating graphic violence, keeping erotica off screen, creating images of beauty for renewed spiritual identity, African and universal, Ouedraogo's films "thrive" on poverty and a-commercialism. They inscribe him on the hearts of simple viewers, and academic consumers of poetic cinema. He seems to wish more femininity, less tyranny on the African continent, therefore on the planet. In the memory of past and present massacres and epidemics, Ouedraogo serves on the side of the Mandelas, against the Amin Dadas of the world.

Notes

1. According to Aïssatou Bah Diallo, "The plot revolves around the thirst and quest for power and the internal strife it generates, while love remains a major source of contention along with the question of an out-of-wedlock child. Tanga, son of the dying king, wants to usurp the throne and eliminate the queen's adulterine son. Informed opportunely, the latter engages in a fatal struggle that spares no one." See *Amina* 398 (2003): 23.

    I am very thankful to Mme Ouedraogo who graciously allowed me to view an unmixed working copy of the film, and equally indebted to Karim Ouedraogo for helping me understand crucial points in the Mooré dialog in Paris, prior to the Fall 2003 release of the film in France.

2. The same remark applies to Barlet's 2001 article: «Femmes et hommes dans les cinémas d'Afrique noire,» *Africultures/Masculin Féminin* 35 (February 2001): 49-56.

3. Quotation on the cover of the video published by Médiathèque des Trois Mondes.

4. Maryse Condé, entretien avec.

5. The sequence shows the twelve year-old Salam and his girlfriend running away into the distance (an intertextual reference to *Yaaba*) while the music starts a rhythmic beat in step with the children's feet. The camera soon shows only their legs and eventually, when it travels back to the upper bodies, we understand that ten years have passed: an archetypal human pair is running along their life-path. This is a welcome variation to a caption on screen informing the viewer that "nine months" or "twelve years" have passed, a technique also used in the film. One advantage will

be that joggers and sports lovers will definitely delight in these two pairs of legs running in "timeless" synchrony with the music, for a couple of minutes.

6.   The same motif was used in Noyce's *Rabbit-Proof Fence* (2001, about an Aboriginal girl), but the white eagle, being rare, is indeed an omen in Mooré culture according to my informant.

7.   Among them, Denise Brahimi has been my much appreciated mentor in the field.

8.   My thanks to Africanist linguist Simon Battestini for answering my query in the following terms: "As I remember, Mooré (or 'gur') is 'Niger-Kordofanian'. As such, it ignores gender, but it has many borrowals (sic!) from Peul, which marks gender, so there is room for the kind of question you ask."

Filmography

1981. *Poko* (20 min., 16 mm, color).

1983. *Les écuelles* (11 min. 16 mm, color).

1983. *Les funérailles du Larlé Naba* (30 min. 16 mm, color).

1985. *Ouagadougou, Ouaga Deux Roues* (16 min. 16 mm, color).

1985. *Issa le Tisserand* (20 min. 16 mm, color).

1986. *Tenga* (35 min., 16 mm, color).

1986. *Yam Daabo (The Choice)* (80 min., 16 mm, color).

1989. *Yaaba* (90 min., 16 mm, color).

1990. *Tilaï* (81 min., 16 mm, color).

1991. *Karim et Sala* (90 min., 35 mm, color).

1992. *Samba Traoré* (85 min., 35 mm, color).

1993. *Gorki* (52 min., 16 mm, color).

1993. *Obi* (23 min., 35 mm, color) [for TV Canal +].

1994. *Afrique, mon Afrique* (52 min. color)

1994. *Le Cri du coeur* (86 min. 35 mm. color).

1997. *Kini et Adams* (set in Zimbabwe).

1999. *Kadi jolie* (TV serial).

2003. *La colère des dieux (The Gods' Wrath)* (90 min. 16 mm, color).

Works Cited

Barlet, Olivier. *La colère des dieux* (film-review). Accessed May 6, 2003:http://www.africultures.com/revue_africultures/articles/affiche_article.asp?no=2809.

—-. "Les nouveaux films d'Afrique sont-ils africains?" («How African Are New Films out of Africa?»). *CinémAction* 106 (2003): 43-49.

—-. *Les cinémas d'Afrique noire*. Paris: L'Harmattan, 1996.

Brahimi, Denise. *Cinémas d'Afrique francophone et du Maghreb*. Paris: Nathan, 1997.

Fiofori, Tam. Interview. «Film Realities.» *West Africa* (April 27, 1987): 820-21.

Jousse, Thierry, and Nicolas Saada. "Pourquoi juge-t-on les gens?" ("Why Judge people?"), (Interview). *Cahiers du Cinéma* 421 (1989).

Lequeret, Elisabeth. *Le cinéma africain*. Paris: Cahiers du Cinéma/Les Petits Cahiers, 2003.

Pfaff, Françoise. Interview. «Africa through African Eyes.» *Black Film Review* IV, 1 (Winter 1987-88).

Sabouraud, Frédéric. "La soustraction" ("The Negative Bill"). *Cahiers du Cinéma* 438 (December 1990): 69-70.

Tapsoba, Clément. "1980-2000: Les très riches heures du cinéma burkinab" ("1980-2000: The Very Rich Hours of Burkina Cinema"). *CinémAction* 106 (2003): 124-137.

Thackway, Melissa. «Images d'immigrés» ("Images of Immigration"). *CinémAction* 106 (2003): 50-55.

Chapter 17

Representations of Gender in Three West African Films: *Finzan* (1989), *Touki Bouki* (1973) and *Hyenas* (1992)

Victoria Pasley

The position of women in African society has received significant attention from African filmmakers, particularly those directors who have their roots in Third Cinema. Yet, there has been little analysis of gender itself and few alternative role models have been put forward. This paper explores issues of gender in three West African films, *Finzan*, (Cheikh Oumar Sissoko 1989), *Touki Bouki* (Djibril Diop Mambety 1973) and *Hyenas* (Djibril Diop Mambety, 1992).[1] Each of these films has a strong female protagonist whom the male directors depict quite differently. All three women are marginalized in their non-conformity and present challenges to the patriarchal power structures. These women raise issues of gender and changing gender relations and their relationship to tradition.

Cheikh Oumar Sissoko and Djibril Diop Mambety are very distinctive filmmakers. Sissoko was educated in France and attended the French national film school and is currently the Minister of Culture in Mali,[2] and is actively involved in Malian society. Mambety on the other hand was not educated in France and did not study film. He studied theater in Senegal and taught himself filmmaking. His films are much less didactic than Sissoko's *Finzan* but at the same time Mambety's films clearly, if subtly, are politically charged with social messages. *Touki Bouki* denounces a post-colonial culture of alienated youth who dream of escaping the poverty of Senegal for France while *Hyenas* attacks the World Bank and International Monetary Fund (IMF) to which Africans are selling their souls. Both directors are concerned with marginalized people and see their role of filmmaker as a continuation of the story telling of the traditional griot.

Although much has been written on these films, very little has been written on how they represent gender. Furthermore, most critics seem to take patriarchal power for granted without analyzing its portrayal.[3] Thus this chapter will closely examine how women are represented in these films and also look at what they tell us about patriarchal power and masculinity. As Mambety so clearly shows in *Hyenas*, international bodies such as the World Bank and IMF pose far greater threat to African societies than changes in gender relations, the relinquishment of a patriarchal power, or the ending of oppressive practices against women.

Manthia Diawara calls Cheikh Oumar Sissoko's *Finzan* (1989) "an impassioned cry for the emancipation of African women" ("Some Notes"). Other critics have been less generous. Most of the reviews in the United States on *Finzan* have tended to pay too much attention to the portrayal of female circumcision in the film, missing the film's focus on broader women's issues and male power. Responses to the film show the dilemma for filmmakers in advocating women's rights and social change without being interpreted as imposing Western values or attacking cultural heritage. Furthermore, the West's reaction to the highly inflammatory and controversial issue of excision, which Sissoko dared to address, has skewed discussion of the film.[4] Indeed the question of excision is not raised until the second half of the film. Although he posits it as an oppressive practice, Sissoko himself has said that he did not want the film to be one about excision (Aufderheide 5). The focus on excision ignores other pressing issues the film raises including women's lack of power in village affairs, and their right to refuse an unwanted marriage. Furthermore, Finzan is a critique of patriarchal power structures that affect men as well as women.

As Mbye Cham has pointed out, African filmmakers tend to be much more actively involved in their societies than are their Western counterparts. Before becoming Minister of Culture Sissoko had headed a Malian government agency, producing documentaries and newsreels and started a small filmmakers co-operative ("Film Text;" Aufderheide, 5). It is therefore necessary to view *Finzan* in its socio-political and historical context. *Finzan* is indeed a didactic film, clearly rooted in the tradition of Third Cinema and in the spirit of the second Fédération Panafricaine des Cinéastes (FESPACI) congress in Algiers in 1975 which, among other issues, advocated that films should be educational (Diawara "African Cinema," 43, 140; Cham and Bakari 25). As Diawara points out, social realist narratives, exploring issues of tradition and modernity, have continued to be an important category in African filmmaking. The plight of women and other marginalized groups is a major focus in these films. *Finzan* shows a move toward a new cultural identity which questions repressive practices that are preventing social and economic development leading to a more just society (Petty 72-78). According to Francoise Pfaff, a number of filmmakers, including Sissoko, have studied the status and role of African women and use film as a means to promote awareness of their oppression and so gain support for women's rights. Sissoko himself asserts that the 1970s women's movement in France had left a lasting impression on him and that he sees women's right as an issue that belongs to the world (Ellerson Interview Pfaff "Sisters" 251-266; Aufderheide 5).

Yet the fact that an African man is trying to give voice to African women clearly illustrates the stark reality that few African women have access to filmmaking on this scale or a voice in social and political affairs. The need for a voice in village affairs that arises in *Finzan* is just one instance of women's lack of access to power and on a broader level to the means of creative expression. Furthermore, that Sissoko dedicates this film to African women as if they were one homogenous group is both patronizing and problematic. It implies that all issues addressed in the film concern African women regardless of class, race and ethnicity, thereby essentializing African women and ignoring their differences.[5]

The issues addressed in the film are similar to the ones being addressed in the international development arena by such bodies as the World Bank and United Nations.[6] Indeed, some of the funding for the film came from UNIFEM. It is unclear if this influenced the issues Sissoko chose to address. Regardless, some women's groups in Africa, with or without the aid of these international organizations, have long struggled to broaden their participation and recognition in society as well as fight against unjust traditions.[7]

It is interesting to note that Sissoko edited the film with an African editor in Burkina Faso, taking with him three Malian assistants to train (Aufderheide, 30). (One can only hope that women were among them.) This, perhaps, shows the influence of the younger filmmakers in le Collectif L'Oeil Vert (1981) who advocated that filmmakers rely less on French technical assistance. Furthermore, most of the credits show Malian crew and technicians. Although very much a Malian film, the opening text suggests Sissoko, like Mambety, is trying to appeal to a pan-African audience in keeping with the goals of the Niamey Manifesto (1982) which promoted regional rather than national cinemas (Diawara "African Cinema" 34-45).

Finzan opens with the birthing scene of a donkey, quickly moving on to goats playing and leading us into a Malian village. Text runs down the screen in French showing the gloomy statistics of women's oppression in Africa, thus placing the film in a wider context than Mali. Yet Sissoko's depiction is more than a Manichean depiction of modernity and education versus tradition. He shows the issues to be much more complex as a careful reading of the film reveals.

There are three main intertwining stories in the film. The first is Nanyuma's rebellion against being inherited by her foolish brother-in-law and forced into marrying him after the death of her husband. The second story is of the rebellion of the village against the District Commissioner and businessmen who try and force the village to sell their millet below market price. (According to Manthia Diawara, it is common in Africa for speculators to stockpile grain so they can re-sell it at exorbitant prices in times of drought and famine (Diawara "Some Notes"). This story also raises the question of women not being allowed a voice in village affairs despite supplying the brunt of the labor. The third story is of Fili, a young woman who has not been excised. Film critics who focus on this third story, however, distort the messages of the film. Within all three of these stories is an inherent critique of the restrictions imposed by patriarchal power.

The lines spoken by Nanyuma at the end of the film eloquently sum up the film's message. As she is leaving the village with her youngest son she states:

> This world comes from our wombs but it mistreats us. We give life
> but we're not allowed to live. We produce the food crops and others
> eat without us, we create wealth and it is used against us. We women

are like birds with no branch to perch. All that is left is we must stand up and tie our belts. The progress of our society is linked to our emancipation. (*Finzan*)

These words clearly put forth Sissoko's viewpoint. Stylistically he uses a mix of social realism and Koteba Theater to tell his story, thus introducing an element of humor to these otherwise serious issues. Besides humor the film also incorporates a very beautiful soundtrack of Malian music. Koteba is an important form of theatrical expression in Mali and some actors trained in Koteba then go on to work in film. Maimouna Helene Diarra, one of the actors in *Finzan*, began her acting career in a Koteba theater group and now focuses on acting in feature films. Oumar Namory Keita, who plays Bala, and Diarah Sango, who plays Nanyuma, are both Koteba actors (Diawara "African Cinema" 145; Aufderheide, 5, 30; Ellerson "Sisters" 75-78).

In shooting the film Sissoko states in an interview that he deliberately chose to use few close-ups in order to avoid idealizing the individual. Instead he chose mostly wide shots and medium shots focusing on small groups. In his editing technique, he wanted to preserve the spirit of oral tradition that is slower paced and less slick than in Western films and shows the body language of the speakers. He also consciously shows women at work in the background in many of the frames to stress the tremendous amount of labor they contribute. Sissoko's adherence to the concept of oral tradition means that we do not grow very intimate with any of the characters as the story is being told through the griot—in this case the filmmaker (Aufderheide, 30; Diawara "African Cinema" 164). Even Nanyuma's character is not fully developed and we learn little of her hopes or dreams apart from her abhorrence of Bala. The film at times is overtly didactic and there are few, if any, moments of joy among the women.

One significant scene, yet one which western critics rarely mention, is the one in which the women intervene in the struggle against the French-speaking officials. When the women arrive at the scene, the chief first tells them that their place is in the kitchen. A woman asks what they would be doing there without grain, so he allows them to stay. A spokeswoman for the women then tells the chief they have something to say. In an eloquent address she tells the District Commissioner and his entourage that:

> Many of these women have slaved in the city as maids for men such as yourselves who think they own the world. Your friend is dressed in a gown worth $600 earned at the expense of poor people—we don't make that much in 5 years. We're tired of killing ourselves for your likes. (*Finzan*)

This speech shows the women's awareness of the issues despite the chief's clear disdain of their knowledge at various moments in the film. It also suggests the rural urban dynamic of women leaving the village to work in town for short periods, showing that village life is far from hermetically sealed. In a later scene, a group of women, gaining strength from their participation in the freeing of the chief who is briefly taken prisoner by the authorities, approaches him to discuss two issues. The first one is regarding their desire to be involved in the dispute with the District Commissioner over grain, and the second one is about Nanyuma's plight. They begin by saying that they know he never asks for the women's opinion. The chief responds angrily, exclaiming that "the dogs have grown horns" and asking the women if they are insane or if they want to teach him his duties. He is very dismissive of them and remarks to his griot that the world has changed. With regard to Nanyuma, when the chief refuses to intervene, the women say they will not sleep with their husbands until it is resolved. They also say that the women are divided over the case of Fili. The chief is adamant that excision is the very basis of their tradition, and he will not allow an un-excised girl in the village.

The chief's views on women's rights are made known early on in the film through a revealing exchange—also overlooked by critics—between the chief and his griot, Wali. Wali remarks to the chief "women give birth to the world but they haven't ruled it . . . that obsesses me." The chief responds that secrecy and knowledge, neither of which women have, govern all powers and asks if Wali knows any women with these qualities. Wali pursues the issue further, saying that he believes that a long time ago there were great women rulers. The chief answers that "either they were legends or the world was upside down. Our history doesn't mention it" (*Finzan*). This exchange shows Wali to be concerned about women's issues, thus proving that not all village men have fixed views, and that progressive views on women are not necessarily espoused only by those influenced by western culture. Perhaps more importantly, as there are ample examples of powerful women rulers in Africa, this distortion of history throws a shadow on the accuracy of oral tradition.[8] And it is precisely a call to tradition that will be used by the chief to allow Bala to inherit Nanyuma and to insist that Fili be excised. So here Sissoko points a subtle finger at the permutations and manipulations of tradition.

Nanyuma had wanted to marry another man before she was married to her first husband. They still want to marry each other, yet the family of Nanyuma and the chief again refuse the man permission. Furthermore, the man is given a whipping under the chief's orders, thus showing that the hierarchical, patriarchal power held by the village leader also subjugates men. It is not clear in the film why the man is not allowed to marry Nanyuma.

Two leading authorities on African film, Manthia Diawara and Frank Ukadike, express opposing views about the film; they show two distinct interpretations. Frank Ukadike states that films like *Finzan* with their details of village life run the danger of reinforcing "the fascination with the exotic African images in Western ethnographic films" (Ukadike "Black African Cinema" 254). That is, they are little different from the ethnographic films made in the past. On the other hand, he argues that the images and reality presented in African films show an African view of ethnography, which, in showing the way that African people actually live, as well as their histories and cultures, explore value systems that differ from the West and evaluate them without a comparison to Western ideals. In other words African societies are being re-evaluated by Africans. Some traditions and customs that once were seen as primitive are instead revered (Ukadike "Black African Cinema" 254).

As Ukadike states *Finzan* examines traditional cultural systems and strongly denounces the contradictions within them. He also concedes that the film deals with a number of issues, but that the main focus is on women's emancipation. Yet Ukadike focuses his critique on Sissoko's depiction of excision. Acknowledging Sissoko's sincerity, and saying that he presents "a critique of indigenous culture in a manner recalling the liberationist injunction to fight for freedom, a call for rebellion," Ukadike argues the following:

> While the filmmaker presents this issue with utmost concern, his camera fails to present a detailed representation of the culture from a logical perspective enabling us to understand how the ritual evolved. Rather what we see is a farcical analysis which treats the subject of excision, in the words of Francoise Lionnet, "peremptorily, in an impassioned, reductionist, and/or ethnographic mode which represents the peoples who practice it as backward, misogynistic, and generally lacking in humane and compassionate inclinations. (Ukadike "Black African Cinema" 254)

Ukadike's argument is somewhat unfair. What he calls "farcical" is Sisokko's use of stock characters from Mali's Koteba Theater. As Diawara points out, African filmmakers often use comedy to portray serious matters such as the excesses of polygamy, (Diawara "African Cinema" 144) and the use of Koteba humor in *Finzan* gives it a distinctive Malian style. But this humor is not used in the excision scene, which is very short. One also wonders how excision can be shown as anything other than misogynistic as its only purpose seems to have been to curb women's sexual desire and pleasure. As film theorist Keyan Tomasilli very eloquently states, "African nationalist ideologies blind some scholars and ideologues to the fact that female circumcision was always an unacceptable form of oppression of women" (165-174). While traditions such as polygamy can be shown to have their roots in an economic reality, this is not true of excision. Nor are its origins very clear. Diawara, a Malian, claims that tradition states that clitorodectomy discourages women from extra-marital sex by lessening women's sex drives (Diawara "Some notes").[9] In a later essay Ukadike gives a more thoughtful and charitable critique of the film and further explores the issue of circumcision and whether the practice meets its original intent. He still criticizes the manner in which Sissoko portrays the practice but acknowledges that *Finzan* is a daring film for questioning the practice (Ukadike "African films," 43-60).

It is beyond the scope of this discussion to fully examine the arguments around female circumcision, but it is important to note that Sisokko's portrayal shows villagers to be divided on the issue and that it is not simply a question of tradition versus modernity but more a decision about the selection of traditions deemed essential for cultural integrity. Fili's boyfriend, for example, who has been living in France and dresses in the latest French fashion, says that he could not marry an un-excised woman (although as she points out he was happy to have sex with her—and with un-excised white women). He is concerned he would be the laughing stock of the Malian population in France. Nanyuma, the rebel woman, is not opposed to the practice saying that the clitoris is dirty, although she does support Fili's decision not to have it done. Fili's father is against her being excised as he fears that she might bleed to death like her mother had. He is a traditional man, but is also able to break with tradition.[10]

Laura De Luca and Kamenya Shadrack offer a more balanced and insightful critique of *Finzan*, than Ukadike's first critique, but argue that having Fili nearly die of a hemorrhage makes the excision scene too extreme. They state that, while some African women choose excision, this is not shown in the film. But in the village in Mali where *Finzan* takes place, excision is done to children, so they do not have choice. And it had to be an extreme case because, if not, Fili would have been circumcised as a child. Furthermore, in the campaign to stop circumcision, health workers in Africa warn of the dangers of fatal infection, hemorrhaging and infertility, (Diawara "Some notes on Finzan") all too common side effects of the practice (not to mention the numerous gynecological complications).

Ukadike also accuses Sissoko of sensationalism by showing a hand brandishing a razor. But it is a razor that is now used for circumcision, rather than a sharp knife or stone. Moreover the scene shows how tradition can utilize modern instruments and is therefore not impervious to change. Ukadike further argues that this is the most talked about part of the film because of the way it was shot. It is unclear what he means by this other than it was of short duration. I argue that it is the most talked about part of the film because it is an issue that attracts Western condemnation, thus ignoring other more pressing concerns such as questions of patriarchal power.

Finally Ukadike asserts that "*Finzan* is a film that no African will watch or feel proud of, nor want to purchase for subsequent viewing," adding that "Finzan is extremely popular with western audiences and widely distributed for class room showing" (Ukadike "Black African Cinema" 275). (Perhaps the reason for its popularity as a teaching tool is that it is one of the few films that so overtly addresses women's issues.) An important question to ask here is what audience is the film aimed at? The probability that Western audiences are more likely to see it does not necessarily mean that the film has to be or was directed at them. Indeed by using Koteba Theater in *Finzan*, Sissoko is directly talking to a Malian audience, and is in fact alienating Western audiences who are unfamiliar with it and this sort of humor. According to Sissoko, the film had been shown in Mali in mainly large towns. It was released in Mali in 1989, and, by Ramadan that year, 84,000 spectators had seen it. He claimed a positive response that more women than men came to see it and that women had congratulated him on the film. Unfortunately these claims are very hard to verify (qtd. in Aufderheide 30).

Diawara presents a more convincing interpretation of *Finzan*. He sees *Finzan* as a social realist film in the tradition of the didactic but at the same time entertaining. Yet, he says, "on the serious side the film thematizes the problems of excision and polygamy, and it posits women's emancipation as the condition of progress." This comes from an African feminist discourse that sees women's rights as a vital part of social and economic progress (Diawara "African Cinema" 151-152). It is now hackneyed to argue that feminism is simply a product of Western influence. Women in developing countries from Latin America and Asia to Africa have successfully argued for indigenous forms of feminisms coming from a history of struggle from women both within and outside indigenous cultures. Diawara quotes Fatou Sow, who argues that "The marginalization of women has contributed to the failure of many development projects." And as Diawara points out, *Finzan* positions the viewer to identify with the women in the film and to accept women as equal players in the development of Africa (Diawara "African Cinema" 152).[11]

Diawara also points out that in the film the children see more clearly than the adults. They immediately see Bala for the fool he is and proceed to trick and terrify him by dressing up in Koteba ghost costumes (Diawara "Some notes on Finzan"). They strongly support Nanyuma in her rebellion. At one point, a child comments that "our fathers are mixed up" (*Finzan*). One child also uses herbs to give Bala diarrhea and gas, a trick the boy learned from his father who used the plants on French officials. Thus Sissoko draws some parallel between the oppression of women by men like Bala and colonization. More importantly the children are seen as agents of change who will be more sensitive to women's rights. The pain we see in Nanyuma's youngest son and the close relationship he has with his mother will undoubtedly lead him to support women in their struggle for change.

Ultimately the fight for women's rights in different African countries will be won by African women themselves, many of whom have more agency than Sissoko allows for in *Finzan*. Two Burkinabe women directors, Fanta Régine Nacro and Aminata Ouedraogo, argue that there are no specifically women's issues but human issues which both men and women can address through film. However, Ouedraogo adds that how they treat these issues might be different. Women's names appear among the students being trained at the film school in Burkina Faso, and a recent collection of interviews with African woman in cinema and television attests to their small but increasing numbers.[12] As more women gain access to the means of cultural production through film and television, they will offer more diverse interpretations. The support, however, of African men like Sissoko is of great importance if change is to come about precisely because men hold power and have to relinquish some of that power. Even though decision making is a complex process and women of course have input and influence, it is often men like the chief in *Finzan* who make many of the decisions about women's lives from circumcision to their right to speak.

As De Luca and Shadrack argue, one of the values of the film is that it shows that traditions are not stagnant, but rather that they "constantly adapt, change and absorb new ideas." (De Luca and Shadrack 86). Ukadike points out that some traditionalists of African culture argue that "if one continues to infringe upon aspects of traditional culture, [as in *Finzan*] the time will come when a pattern of life disappears," (Ukadike "African Films" 43-60) but this view fails to take into account culture's inherent adaptability. Ending oppressive practices is not a rejection of that culture and all its traditions, but rather a revaluation that can strengthen the positive aspects by eliminating the negative ones. *Finzan* is a positive step towards airing some of these concerns.

While Mambety does not directly make films that address women's issues in the manner of *Finzan*, the two protagonists in *Hyenas* and *Touki Bouki* offer unique portrayals of "rebel women," and, in *Touki Bouki*, Mambety subtly critiques a masculinity that subordinates women.

Djibril Diop Mambety made *Touki Bouki* approximately sixteen years before Sissoko's film. The radical movements and mood, which inspired Sissoko to make *Finzan*, have their roots in the era of *Touki Bouki*. Ukadike points out that Mambety explores the principal themes of ". . . love, alienation, fear, justice and urban stress" (Ukadike "Black African Cinema," 173). Although the focus of the film is not specifically about women's rights, Anta represents the dilemmas young women in changing societies face as they strive for a life different from their mothers' lives. *Touki Bouki* is the first avant-garde film in the history of African cinema. As Diawara notes, the film uses " a mode of narrations, repetitions of scenes, dream sequences, association of contrasting spaces and sounds, and digressions" (Diawara "Iconography," 85). It interrupts conventional narrative structure. At one point, for example, we see Anta undressing, before the scene in which this incident actually takes place. Mambety's rendering of the sex scene in *Touki Bouki* is also quite remarkable in that it powerfully evokes the eroticism of the love making without showing the couple having sex at all; as Francoise Pfaff so well describes it:

> *Touki Bouki*'s love scene . . . is thematically and stylistically erotic because it discontinues and defers (through cuts and repeated action) the viewer's vicarious sexual and voyeuristic desire: Anta undresses on the beach, revealing only the upper part of her body, but the scene is unexpectedly interrupted as she prepares to lie down (Mory's body is never shown in the entire sequence). This scene is followed by images of a sheep being slaughtered, perhaps metaphorically sacrificial (sexual violence, rupture of the hymen?), and a full shot of foaming waves hitting black and shiny rocks—here the surge indicates the couples youthful and passionate rapport. A subsequent close-up of Anta's fingers clenching a Dogon cross (a Malian symbol of fertility) on the rear of Mory's motorbike, accompanied by off-screen orgasmic sounds, finally confirms that Anta has actually lain with Mory and the viewer has indeed witnessed a love scene . . . .
> ("Eroticism" 257)

In this sequence Anta takes the initiative, yet there is a feeling of equality in the scene and it is devoid of the power struggles so evident in sex scenes in many western movies in which the woman is eroticized and objectified. Mambety and Sisokko's filmmaking, as well as African Cinema in general, is quite remarkable for its lack of the male gaze in depicting women. The camera does not leer at the female characters, yet Anta's shirt is frequently unbuttoned in casually erotic suggestion. Even when she undresses from the waist down it appears quite natural. The western style male gaze does not fetishize her body.

Touki Bouki opens with a young boy herding cattle then cuts abruptly to a graphic slaughterhouse scene with the throat of a cow being cut in a stark gray concrete interior, thus contrasting the modern with the traditional from the beginning. Then the roar of a motorbike precedes the image of Mory riding his bike. The bike is a symbol of modernity, yet it is decked with bull horns and fetish items, suggesting the blending of tradition and modernity. Diawara sees it as confusing the boundaries of the two. In a later scene, Mory rides his bike among cows and uses a lasso to tie up his bike. We assume that Mory was the young cattle herder we saw at the beginning whose life was transformed with the introduction of "modern'" slaughterhouses. Mory is dislocated from his traditional environment and power structures in the village; no longer able to be a herdsman, he looks for alternative means to power. He finds few avenues open to him in Dakar, and focuses his hopes and dreams on France. But at the end of the film it is the sound of the ship's horn reminding him of the bellowing bulls which seem to call him back to his roots, with little thought for Anta's fate as she waits on board ship (Diawara "Iconography" 86). As Mory runs from the boat, the film cuts to the scene of an accident. The wild young white man, who lived curiously in the Baobab tree, had come to grief on Mory's motorcycle. An onlooker states, "From the Baobab tree to the motorcycle that could really kill you," a fine comment on the pitfalls of rapid urbanization.

Diawara points out that the ending of *Touki Bouki*, resembles a "traditional griot narrative" based on a West African folktale about the adventures of the hare and hyena ("Iconography," 86). Touki Bouki in Wolof means the Journey of the Hyenas, and Mambety himself states that he is a modern day griot (qtd. in Givanni "African Conversations"). The film ends with Mory running back to the safety of tradition, while Anta drifts off into modernity and alienation and into the unknown reality of Paris. Indeed the Josephine Baker song repeatedly played in the final sequences, "love's pleasure lasts but a day, but heartbreak lasts all life" becomes a chilling reality when Mambety has Anta return 50 years later as Ramatou in *Hyenas*.

We are first introduced to Anta in the Medina, the slum area on the edge of Dakar. She sits outside at a table covered in books. Bottled mineral water in hand, she is studying. A jet zooms overhead while a baby cries, symbolic of the modern and the traditional that the film continuously juggles. The next shot shows her mother, in traditional dress with head tie, sitting behind a low table spread with tomatoes and other colorful vegetables. Her dress and the brightly colored vegetables contrast sharply to the previous images of Anta who wears a shirt and trousers in earth tones. Anta is slim, her short, trimmed hair uncovered. She is distinctive in the representation of women in African Cinema in that she assumes and androgynous look. As Betti Ellerson has noted, *Touki Bouki* repeatedly shows contrasting images of femininity throughout the film and embodies them in Anta's appearance contrasting with women in more traditional African dress. She notes the low stools on which women sit, which is in contrast to the higher chair where Anta studies. Anta enters the scene in which her mother is selling vegetables on credit to another woman who is wearing a head wrap and a flowing gown. Anta appears rude and defiant as she grabs the goods from the woman, saying that they too need a TV, and rejects the custom of giving credit. She insists that the woman should pay for them in full. Anta is a student and thus allowed to be different but clearly shows the contrasts between the "New African Woman" and the traditional. Yet, as Ellerson astutely points out, "one of the paradoxes of placing Africa within the Euro-defined continuum of tradition and modernity is that African cultures function simultaneously in both" ("The Female Body" 32). African cultures easily assimilate aspects of modernity. Thus rather than see the choice as between modernity and tradition, more important questions for African societies are what modernisms should they absorb and what traditions should they retain or end? In *Finzan*, the call to tradition was made only when gender roles, particularly patriarchal power, were threatened. In *Touki Bouki* Anta and Mory appear to embrace the modern yet their relationship with Mory as "the boss" and the decision-maker remains traditional. Mambety, however, seems to be subtly questioning this relationship by showing Anta to be more astute than Mory and depicting his actions and attitude as ill-considered.

After the confrontation with her mother, Anta then walks through the local washing area where, as in *Finzan*, everywhere women are at work. Again Anta's appearance is a striking contrast to the woman around her. Young women stooped or carrying water on their heads, dressed more casually than the women in the previous scene, but still in contrast to Anta's boyish shirt and pants. Anta moves quickly and deftly unrestrained by the heavy workloads that slow down the other young women, which *Finzan* repeatedly depicts.

In town she is greeted by a car load of revolutionaries, her fellow students, dressed in flares, the latest European fashions. Anta appears to be a member of the group, suggesting her political awareness, an issue that Mambety never really explores. In a very brief exchange (Anta, at this point, is more interested in finding her boyfriend than attending the meeting) one of the young men comments that "all the chicks talk about is screwing." This short comment powerfully evokes the sexism present in many revolutionary movements of the period.[13]

Anta clearly rejects traditional values including traditional ideas of femininity. Yet she embodies a beauty of her own; she is both erotic and feminine if not in a traditional sense. As a college student she has the opportunity of being educated and having a different life from her mother. She is intelligent, independent, and self-reliant, despite her acquiescence to Mory's desire to be the decision-maker and boss. She is clearly more intelligent than he but gives in to his need to assert domination as a part of the make-up of his masculinity. She yields to him even when she is right such as in choosing which box to steal from the stadium. It is in fact Anta who steals the money that allows them to buy the tickets. From the moment we meet Anta we cannot see her allowing herself to be married against her will or accepting a polygamous marriage. Yet she defers to Mory and follows his whim and dreams to go to Paris (apparently willing to give up her studies). Yet in Mambety's depiction of Anta and Mory, he clearly shows Mory's assertion of masculinity to be outmoded and futile. Despite her deference to Mory, Anta is cool and clearly in control. It is also unusual to see women in African cinema running fast and free as Anta does when she searches for Mory by the cliff. Again she is unburdened by heavy work, and her clothes give her the freedom to run.

In her androgynous dress, it seems that Anta is clearly defying the destiny of femininity and tradition, unlike Nanyuma, who only wishes to end practices that directly oppress her. But can Anta be androgynous yet not reject Africa and her African identity? From where does Anta's androgyny come? We do not know whether western feminism has affected her, but her challenge to women's roles is much more likely to have come from within Senegal, from similar circumstances which had pushed western women to question the position of women—circumstances that are not unique to Europe or North America. As modernity and change come to Dakar, along with independence and revolutionary rhetoric, what is the position of women? Her revolutionary comrades remark disparagingly of her as a "chick" who only thinks about sex. She is attracted to Mory's non-conforming outsider image, yet in the end, it is Anta who is less held back by tradition. Despite his rebellious attitude, Mory's bike is adorned with horns and other traditional items which show his roots and respect for tradition. At the same time, Anta and Mory feel marginalized. Mory sees power in accumulating wealth, not in learning, and Paris is where he believes he will get wealth and acquire the accoutrements to be a man—what's in it for Anta is less clear.

Touki Bouki is told from Mory's point of view, depicting his dreams and fantasies as well as his frustration. In one scene the young revolutionary university students rope and humiliate Mory stringing him up like a piece of meat, paralleling Mory's own roping of his cattle. These youths talk of revolution, yet show their elitism in their disdain for Mory, an unemployed former cow herder. It is not surprising therefore that Mory feels alienated from his society. What part does he have if these youths are to be the future leaders? Moreover, this scene is damaging to his masculine pride, rendering him powerless. In Senegal as elsewhere, masculinity and power are constructed as inherently linked, when they can clearly be separate. Mory later mumbles that if he goes to France he will come back as "Mister Mory," so that those youths will have to respect him. On another occasion, after the scene when he loses the gamble, he reflects "these assholes think I am a bum. They haven't seen anything yet—just you wait." His view of an escape to an idealized France and the opportunities open to him there seem to offer the only hope against his powerlessness and of recovering that power. Even in his fantasies, he imagines Aunt Oumy singing praise songs to him, showing that, despite his rebel without a cause image, he cares deeply how people perceive him. Anta appears far less concerned with what people think of her or her femininity. Mory, on the other hand, constantly needs to assert his view of his masculinity and desires people's respect. When he asks her which box to rob from the stadium, she points to what will turn out to be the correct one, but Mory chooses the other one, saying, "don't contradict me, I'm the boss man," and picks the wrong one. Mambety again seems to be subtly critiquing this jaded yet pervasive view of masculinity that Mory espouses.

In another scene Anta and Mory are on the beach, and Mory suggests they pay a visit to Charles, a homosexual who had previously made passes at him. Most critics say that the couple planned to rob him, but a more careful scrutiny of the dialogue between them suggests that Mory intends to prostitute himself. He says to Anta, "There's a fat fag over there—I've never let him make me, but if I close my eyes...I'll take a crap first." In response Anta says ironically, "You're the man, whatever you say." It seems therefore that the idea of robbery occurs as the chance arises. And it is not Charlie's clothes and car that will give them the money for Paris, but the money Anta steals from the wallet of a guest while waiting for Mory.

At Charlie's place Anta does not fit in with the bourgeois women lying around the pool whom Charlie tells her to join. These urbanized westernized women look bored as they languidly sit in chairs around the pool. As she waits for Mory, Anta remains an outsider from this world too. She is neither the industrious rural woman nor the urban bourgeois wife. She thus presents an image of an African woman seldom seen in African cinema.

The depiction of Charles is worth noting as homosexuality, as this collection of essays stresses, has been rarely addressed in African films with the exception of Mohammed Camara's *Dakan* (1997), which sensitively portrays a homosexual relationship. It is disappointing that an independent thinker such as Mambety, who is concerned with marginalized peoples, does not extend his concern to homosexuals. *Touki Bouki* portrays a stereotypical image of a rich gay man preying on young men. Charles is also shown to have links with the police and is well connected further reinforcing the stereotype of homosexuality being linked with corruption. Perhaps he is depicted in such a way so that we have little sympathy when Mory steals his clothes.

Mambety's mixing of reality and fantasy together with his innovative camera and editing techniques have caused some critics to see *Touki Bouki* as bringing the French New Wave to African cinema. Anny Wynchank argues that *Touki Bouki* is an "African illustration of the French New Wave," and that Mambety "heartily adopt[ed] the New Wave techniques,"[n] even though Mambety himself asserts that he was not influenced by European cinema, but by the events of the time. Like Mory and Anta, Mambety wanted to leave Senegal for Europe, believing that is where his dreams would be fulfilled. In an interview with June Givanni, Mambety states that: "The impulse for what I do came at that moment of liberation back in the '60s, and is inspired more by my understanding of the limits of possibility than by any development in European film at that time." Mambety mentions no indebtedness to the French New Wave; rather he denies its influence. His style is the result of his own circumstances and innovation ("African Conversations").

Instead of seeing the stimulus for Mambety's filmmaking as coming from outside of Africa, we should look at the internal global processes that have been producing change within Africa as elsewhere. The experiences of World War II brought about tremendous changes in Senegal: the struggle for and gaining of independence, the subsequent disillusionment following the euphoria of independence, as well as continuing urbanization and unemployment. This is the mood that Mory and Anta represent in *Touki Bouki*. As Clyde Taylor points out, Mambety captures the restlessness of urban youth (Taylor 136-245).

At the same time, the Negritude movement which flourished in the 1960s also inspired Mambety's work. In Senegal, the Senegalese President Leopold Senghor, one of the movement's major proponents, launched *the Festival Mondial des Arts Nègres* in Dakar in 1966. Mambety attended the festival with his short film *Badou Boy*, which, although not officially presented, was reviewed. Of the importance of the festival Mambety states that ". . . for me the festival was sublime! I realized the confidence that Senghor had in black people and that he was right to celebrate black culture. I experienced this as the first significant stage in my life." The turn away from the culture of the colonizers to a focus on the production of African culture also helped Mambety gain funding for *Touki Bouki* which was funded in part by the Senegalese government (qtd. in Givanni "African Conversations"; Shiri, 7).

Interestingly, when Ukadike asked Mambety the inspiration for the gyrating camera movements, the jump cuts and colliding and parallel montages, Mambety responded with "it is the way I dream." We should take him at his word (qtd. in "Hyenas"). *Touki Bouki* is thus an innovative contribution to African Cinema, its inspiration coming from within the African continent. Even the magical-realism sequences in both *Touki Bouki* and *Hyenas* are likely more the work of Mambety's imagination than the surrealist movement in Europe, or even the magical realism that Latin American artists and writers employed as an expressive tool.[15]

Although *Touki Bouki* is not a social realist film and is far less didactic than *Finzan*, Mambety clearly has politically charged and social messages he wants the film to portray, bringing the film far closer to the tradition of African cinema than the French New Wave. As Frank Ukadike points out:

> While non-Africanist critics have read the film as an avant-gardist manipulation of reality, an African analysis [or perhaps more

appropriately a non-Western centered analysis] would attempt a reconfigurative reading that synthesizes the narrative components and reads the images as representing an indictment of contemporary African life-styles and socio-political situations in disarray. Mouri and his girlfriend, Anta, feel the urge to leave Senegal. But the film ironizes the dreamworld, France, where they hope to go. ("Black African Cinema," 173)

Indeed the repetitious playing of Josephine Baker's "Paris" throughout the movie stresses this irony. Furthermore, as Diawara notes, the naked Mory waving from the limousine resembling a politician in the fantasy sequence on the way to the port "parodies political campaigns in Africa in which the leaders hide the 'naked' truth from the people" (Diawara "Iconography" 86). Not only does *Touki Bouki* offer a critique of post-colonial Africa; it also makes important statements about gender roles in Senegal.

Anta is an unusual and welcome character to the world of African cinema, an African woman who is neither the modern bourgeois wife nor the hard-working, traditional, rural woman. Instead she tries to pave her own path by breaking the paradigms of roles for African women. Mambety gently shows the irony of her deference to Mory who, at the end of the film, abandons her at the last minute, forcing her to continue the journey alone. One hopes that perhaps Anta's fate is better than that of Ramatou in *Hyenas*, whom Mambety found when he returned to look for Anta.

Mambety states that when he went back to find Anta, he found her both in a very rich prostitute he had known in his youth, a "beautiful and fascinating prostitute who offered champagne to the sailors at the port of Dakar," and in the play "The Visit" by Swiss-German Friedrich Durrenmatt from which he adapted *Hyenas*. Mambety states he made the story his own, even though the story line and dialogue remain close to the original play. He uses a narrative style closer to realism in *Hyenas*, the second part of what was to be a trilogy on madness and power of which *Touki Bouki* was the first (qtd. in Ellerson "Video"; qtd. in Givanni "African Conversations).

The film *Hyenas* is visually a hauntingly beautiful film. Mambety uses the ochre colors of the Sahel to paint his film. Many frames seem to have been carefully constructed in a color scheme of ochre: from terra cotta and amber, yellows and brick reds seen in a piece of cloth, or the sack cloth of the court that will try Draman, to the richness of the clothes of Ramatou's entourage. The dust and even the car in the ending scene are a reddish brown. These earth tones are at times contrasted with rich blues, reds, and yellows. Mambety spoke of the beauty African landscapes offer filmmakers—the richness of images—which he evokes so strongly in this film. In one interview he talks of creating an African film language "that would exclude chattering and focus more on how to make use of visuals and sounds" (qtd. in Ukadike "Hyenas"). Mambety accomplishes this with this film. As in *Touki Bouki*, he uses a wide range of sounds and music and stresses the importance of sound in his work. The evocative and sometimes melancholy musical score of Wassis Diop (Mambety's brother) contributes to the beauty of the visuals. Mambety also believed that African cinema should be universal rather than national, and with this aim in *Hyenas* he incorporates elephants from Kenya, African dress from no specific region, and Ramatou's Asian aide (Givanni "African Conversations"; Ukadike "Hyenas"; Fiombo; Mermin 216).

Anta becomes Ramatou, and yet the two are not the same literally. Ramatou left Senegal shamed by her lover who refused to admit to their affair. She left outcast and pregnant, unlike Anta. (Although Anta may well have been pregnant, but would she seek the kind of revenge that Ramatou sought?) Ramatou's only means of survival was prostitution, and she amassed a fortune as rich as the World Bank as the film frequently proclaims. In that way then she did achieve the dream of untold wealth in France, but she found little respite from her pain and humiliation.

If indeed Anta ended up as a prostitute in France, then Mambety has allowed women no room for an independent existence outside that of a bourgeois housewife or traditional rural wife. Furthermore, it is very rare for prostitutes to become wealthy. In *Finzan*, Fili's uncle feared she would turn into a "whore" if she stayed in the city, thus narrowing the choice between submission or prostitution. Sissoko gives us more hope at the end of *Finzan* when Nanyuma leaves the village, but will she have to resort to a similar occupation? Although the directors clearly support the liberation of women, they do not show us alternative strategies for survival for women who challenge gender roles.

Like *Finzan* and *Touki Bouki*, *Hyenas* opens with scenes of animals. The use of animals perhaps shows their closer integration in African societies, and both directors seem to make allegorical references to them. The film *Hyenas* opens with the majestic striding of African elephants which Mambety believes follow the wind and represent the passing of time. He sees hope for humanity in elephants, whereas hyenas represent our basest tendencies. Hyenas are more like the World Bank, waiting quietly to devour their prey. They have patience because they know eventually they will feed on their prey. At various times Mambety uses a cutaway of a monkey tied to a wheel who seems to imitate the mood of the villagers, and he also shows shots of an owl and vultures. The villagers of Colobane are juxtaposed with a pack of hungry Hyenas as the material goods flood into the village (Rawlins).

After the elephants the film cuts to close-ups of the elephants' feet to shots of the villagers' bare feet as they walk towards Draman's grocery store. Later they will buy yellow leather shoes from Burkina Faso (the latest fashion) and there is another shot of their feet. Apart from Ramatou, women do not feature strongly in the film and as in *Finzan* the decisions are made by men in an unquestioned assumption of masculinity equaling power. In the final scene of Draman's judgment none of the village women is present. The clientele who drink in the bar are all men, although we see women coming in to buy groceries. The village counselors are all men, and it is they who meet to discuss the arrival of Ramatou, and their hopes that she will be able to save Colobane from its poverty and decay. Yet these very same men would condemn her as a whore, were it not for her extreme wealth.

Hyenas is set in a small town in the Sahel, Colobane, which is Mambety's birthplace. As Mamadou Diouf points out, the film is set in the period of

> . . . structural adjustment and conditions laid down by the World Bank and the International Monetary Fund . . . [The film is] the fiercest critique against the theatre of power the insanity of political and economic discourses for reform and good government. One must finally ask if the World Bank is not a high class prostitute, with identical conditions to those of Lingère Ramatou, calling for blood, sweat—as the mayor and deputy mayor abundantly prove—tears and death. (Diouf 239-250)

Critics like Diouf have unquestionably accepted this view that the World Bank is the equivalent of a prostitute. A much more accurate description of the institution, however, is that of a pimp. It is, after all, dominated by men— and it is the African people who are forced to prostitute themselves to the bank for survival. Furthermore, it is the people of Colobane who are willing to kill their friend Draman, one of the most popular men in the village, for material goods, who have sold out to prostitute themselves for wealth. Despite Mambety's attack on the World Bank and the International Monetary Fund, he was able to finance the film from a consortium of European media and cultural institutions, including Thelma films of Switzerland. In an interview with Ukadike he asserted that it did not matter where the money came from and it is unlikely that Mambety's independent spirit would have been compromised by fund providers (qtd. in "Hyenas").

In order for Ramatou's wealth to give her access to patriarchal power, Mambety renders her masculine to some extent by giving her hard steel body parts. Her artificial parts thus de-feminize her. In addition she is long past her childbearing years. Her sexuality is no longer important; what matters now is that she has extreme wealth. Draman, who like Mory was a cow herder in his youth, is very ingratiating toward her. He feels guilty for his betrayal but also defers to her wealth—wealth he wants her to give to the town. Ramatou's entourage consists of two witnesses who testified against her. She sought them out and sold them into slavery, where they were castrated. The witnesses say, "They castrated us—made women of us." They appear to be wearing women's dresses. So, in this instant, in a Freudian take, to be female means to be castrated, or lacking, and suggests that manliness and masculinity rest in the genitalia. Yet none of these films represent fertility and virility as definitions of masculinity even though they are part of the masculine construct. In all three films, manliness is associated with wealth and power transcending genitalia in the construction of masculinity.

Ramatou brings consumer goods such as refrigerators, TVs, air-conditioners and fans to the impoverished town along with a Ferris wheel and fireworks. The scene turns into a surreal sequence with a carnivalesque quality. She will give the people all the material goods they desire if they will kill her former lover Draman. At first villagers strongly protest, but we see their gradual acquiescence to greed. As the villages gravitate toward the material goods we see cutaway close-ups of Ramatou's face watching and waiting. Even she seems a little surprised at their eagerness to embrace materialism over Draman's life. She remarks to her valet (played by Mambety) that "The reign of the Hyenas has come." Mambety is not only indicting the World Bank, but also humanity. When at the end of the film the village men meet to determine Draman's fate, they appear strangely attired in wigs and sackcloth. Mambety states in an interview that they are dressed this way to disguise themselves and thus distance themselves from the responsibility of their decision (qtd. in Ukadike "Hyenas"). Although women are excluded from this scene and unequal in the town's decision making, Mambety depicts them as equal in their greed and demand for luxury goods. Like the men they demand luxury items on credit from the store and eagerly embrace the refrigerators, fans, and air-conditioner—knowing full well the conditions of acceptance. In Mambety's view equality in material greed and consumerism predominate over inequalities of class and gender.

Unlike *Finzan* and *Touki Bouki*, which rarely showed close-ups, *Hyenas* uses the more conventional sequence of close-ups and medium shots enabling us to get to know Draman and watch his gradual transformation. At the beginning of the film there are moments of tenderness as he puts his arm around the shoulder of his wife but they seem to drift apart as he gravitates toward Ramatou and her sentence on his life. His wife is at first an observer. Close-ups show her calmly watching various scenes. We do not know how she feels about Ramatou's return. At one point a group of women come to the store to await the arrival of a woman healer/spiritualist with special powers who gives Draman's wife a formula to protect herself. When the death sentence is pronounced, she at first announces that Ramatou will have to kill her first. Then gradually she too begins to acquire luxury goods and accepts the refrigerator, air-conditioner and TV. The women (all of whom appear to be "wives") seem to act more independently than the "wives" in *Finzan*, and there are no scenes in which we see them working.

The close-ups of Ramatou toward the end of the film reveal that she still has some humanity, beauty, and feelings, not much evident in the earlier scenes where she seems rigid, distant, and uncaring. Yet when she is alone with Draman shortly after her arrival, we see both bitterness and love in her face. She scorns the people she can buy so easily but clearly still loves Draman. It is only by having him killed that she believes she will finally possess him forever. The final scene between them is poignantly depicted on top of a cliff overlooking the sea. Draman has accepted his fate. He tells her that he is going to die. He sits down beside her and lights her pipe. He asks about their daughter who died and she asks him to tell her how she was at seventeen years of age when he loved her. For the first time a close-up shows her face moved close to tears. She regains her composure as Draman states that he is coming to the end of an empty existence.

He has been contemplating his past and seems to perhaps regret his betrayal of Ramatou. She replies:

> I will have you carried to my island [which we can see in the distance] It is under the protection of the Gods and the sea is blue. You'll be mine forever. You belong to me, you'll stay with me forever. (*Hyenas*)

As Draman leaves to meet his fate, she tells him to die in peace and come and join her. This scene is poignant for the sadness and memory of love she has carried around all these years, which has turned her so bitter and revengeful. We see in her face the harshness of her life, the loss of her lover and of her child, and the love she still has for Draman. The scene recalls the words of the song playing in *Touki Bouki* as Anta left for France alone: "love's pleasure lasts but a day, but heartbreak lasts all life." Yet it is a love that has become so chillingly twisted that she wants her lover dead to enable her to make him her own.

As Dennis Essar notes, *Hyenas* pits tradition against modernization. Modernization in the form of greed ousts traditional values of caring, integrity and humanity as represented by Draman. Draman is the hero whereas Ramatou is revengeful, callous, and bitter—willing to kill to possess her former lover. She states at one point in the film that everybody can be bought. The villagers seem to prove her right. Ramatou has some of the characteristics of the Central West African water spirit "Mami Wata" such as her association with wealth and consumerism, her earlier life as a beautiful prostitute, and finally in her desire to take Draman's soul to her tiny island surrounded by water (Bastion). But her depiction is more universal embodying stereotypical images of the vengeful woman—a medieval witch. As Essar points out, Draman is the model citizen; the holder of traditional values (78-80). Ramatou is an aberration. She is not a role model for women—on the contrary she embraces modernization in the form of money, power, and greed. She represents the values of modernism as materialism. The traditional values as espoused by Draman are, however, very different from the values espoused by the Chief in *Finzan*. Draman's values have a sense of the universal, whereas in *Finzan* the village leader's calls to "tradition" were made to control women and enhance the caller's own power. Draman's values are distinct from this. Neither is there evidence of the dominating and abrasive masculinity asserted by Mory in *Touki Bouki*. Instead, Draman's values have the same appeal to humanity and integrity as Sissoko's. Mambety does not focus on women's emancipation in *Hyenas,* but Draman's moral principles suggest that human equality is innate. Perhaps Draman has the beginnings of a new African masculinity based more on humility, integrity, and compassion rather than wealth, power, and patriarchy, that is, if, of course, we can forgive his betrayal of Ramatou in his youth.

My project has been to examine what these films reveal about the construction of masculinity and femininity and the representation of gender, and to unravel the wider concept of the connection between gender and power. It has shown how gendered messages both overt and covert can be found in a close reading of the film text. Nanyuma, Anta, and Ramatou present diverse portraits of women who rebel against tradition. Yet neither filmmaker presents us with an alternative model for women who wish to pursue a different life from currently prescribed roles—a necessary choice in the struggle for equal rights.

As discussed earlier, African Cinema, rooted in the founding philosophy of FESPACI, provides African perspectives on the ways that African peoples live as well as their cultures and histories. Through the medium of film African filmmakers are depicting and helping to re-evaluate issues in African societies. These films then, overtly or covertly, inherently show constructions and representations of gender and gender relations. Analyzing the way African filmmakers present the elements that make-up gender and the way they affect relationships between men and women is a useful step toward understanding how gender is constructed and linked to power. Challenging ideals of masculinity and its connection to power and wealth may ultimately enable its redirection in a manner that allows for women to share in the higher echelons of decision-making.

Notes

1. *Touki Bouki* was funded in part by the Senegalese government, *Finzan* was funded from a variety of sources including the German TV channel, ZDF, the Malian government, private investors and UNIFEM and *Hyenas* is a co-production with Thelma Films, in Switzerland. Both directors utilize a wide range of sources both at home and in Europe. In an interview with Ukadike, Mambety argues that "Where the money comes from to make a film doesn't matter to me" ("Hyenas"). It seems unlikely that either director would allow himself to be compromised by fund givers. For example, the Malian government censors wanted Sissoko to cut out the part of Finzan showing corrupt government ministers but he stood firm (Aufderheide 5). Nevertheless, acquiring the funding from diverse sources is obviously a difficult, sometimes slow, process.

2. Cheikh Oumar Sissoko was appointed Minister of Culture in October 2002. "Interview with Cheikh Oumar Sissoko" 9 February 2003. *Africultures* No. 53, http://www.africultures.com.

3. See, for example, Imrah Bakari and Mbye B. Cham. Eds. *African Experiences of Cinema*. British Film Institute, 1996. Manthia Diawara. *African Cinema: Politics and Culture*, Bloomington: Indiana University Press, 1992; Frank Ukadike. *Black African Cinema*, University of California Press, 1994; Frank Ukadike, "The Hyenas Last Laugh: A Conversation with Djibril Diop Mambety" California Newsreel, Library of African Cinema, website (reprinted from *Transition* 78 vol.8. no 2 1999. 136-153).

4. See, for example, reviews in the local San Francisco papers when the film was shown there in 1991 and *Variety* review, May 9, 1990. The *Variety* review twice uses the loaded and, to many, offensive word "tribal" to describe the women. It does not even mention the village fight over grain. It is important to note that African women's organizations, together with some West African governments, have been fighting to eradicate circumcision. African Women's Organizations met in Dakar in 1984 to put it firmly on the agenda creating the Inter African Committee Against Harmful Traditional Practices (IAC). IAC has been an important agent

in bringing circumcision to the attention of governments. See Frances A. Althaus, "Special Report: Female Circumcision: Rite of Passage or Violation of Rights?" *Family Planning Perspectives* Vol. 23, No. 3, September. 1997. More recently some governments have banned it. Senegal, for example, banned it in 1999. Sissoko was aware of the conferences and discussions on women's rights. (Aufderheide).

5. See Laura De Luca and Shadrack Kamenya, "Representation of Female Circumcision in Finzan, a Dance for the Heroes" in *Research in African Literatures*. 26 (3): 83-87. Fall 1995.

6. See, for example, The World Bank website on gender issues, which contains extensive information and research reports. http://www.worldbank.org/afr/gender/kdocs.htm. Some of the issues have evolved through conversations with grassroots African women as researchers have in recent years taken a much more grassroots approach to international development. Yet the upper echelons of the bank seem to take little notice of this research in the implementation of its policies.

7. See, for example, Chislaine Lydon, "Women in Francophone West Africa in the 1930s. Unraveling a Neglected Report" in *Democracy and Development in Mali*, edited by R. James Bingen, David Robinson and John M. Statz. (East Lansing: Michigan State University Press, 2000) 61-86. Lydon shows how women used the French colonial judicial system to file for divorce.

8. Med Hondo's portrait of Sarraounia is but one example of a woman leader. Sembène Ousmane's *Ceddo* also includes a woman ruler.

9. Ukadike concurs with this purpose, yet seems to be demanding a more laudable explanation, "Black African Cinema" 271.

10. See Aufderheide, 30. *Variety* Review, May 9, 1990. The reviewer notes that Nanyuma is at first surprised by Fili's stand.

11. See also Sheila J. Petty "'How an African Woman Can Be': African Women Filmmakers Construct Women," for a discussion of African feminisms in film and literature.

12. See Betti Ellerson. "Sisters of the Screen." See in particular the interviews with Fanta Régine Nacro, 211-220 and Aminata Ouedraogo, 239-250.

13. See, for example, Elaine Brown, *A Taste of Power*, on the Black Panther movement in the United States.

14. See for example Anny Wynchank "Touki Bouki: The New Wave on the Cinematic Shores of Africa" *South African Theatre Journal* 12 (1-2): 53-72, 1998. Wynchank does not consider that Mambety modifies his own style in *Touki Bouki*.

15. Filmmakers from Africa and Latin America as well as North Africa met at the Third World Film-makers Meeting, Algiers, Algeria, in 1973. Although I have not been able to find a full list of participants to determine if Mambety was involved, other African filmmakers attended so that influences are likely to have permuted both continents. See "Resolutions of Third World Film-Maker's Meeting Algiers, Algeria, 1973" reproduced in Cham, 17-24.

Works Cited

Aufderheide, Pat. Interview with Cheick Oumar Sissoko in *Black Film Review*, No. 6 (Winter 1991).

Bakari, Imrah and Mbye B. Cham, Eds. *African Experiences of Cinema.* British Film Institute, 1996.

Bastion, Misty. http://www.fandm.edu/departments/Anthropology/mami.html.

Bingen, R. James, David Robinson and John M. Statz. *Democracy and Development in Mali.* East Lansing: Michigan State UP, 2000.

Brown, Elaine. *A Taste of Power.* New York: Anchor Books, 1994.

Cham. Mbye. "Film Text and Context: Reweaving Africa's Social Fabric Through its Contemporary Cinema." California Newsreel website http://www.newsreel.org/articles/context.htm.

De Luca, Laura, and Shadrack Kamenya. "Representation of Female Circumcision in *Finzan, a Dance for the Heroes*" in *Research in African Literatures.* 26 (3): 83-87. Fall 1995.

Diawara, Manthia. *African Cinema: Politics and Culture.* Bloomington: Indiana University, 1992.

—-. "Some notes on *Finzan.*" Courtesy of California Newsreel. No date.

—-. "The Iconography of West African Cinema" Givanni 81-89.

Diouf, Mamadou. "History and Actuality in Ousmane Sembène's *Ceddo* and Djibril Diop Mambety's *Hyenas,*" Cham and Bakari 239-250.

Ellerson, Betti. "The Female Body as Symbol of Change and Dichotomy: Conflicting Paradigms in the Representation of Women in African Film" *Matatu,* No. 19, Special Edition, "Women with Open Eyes: Women and African Cinema" Ed. Kenneth W. Harrow, Amsterdam-Atlanta 1997. 31-44. .

—-. *Sisters of the Screen: Women of Africa on Film. Video and Television.* Trenton, NJ: Africa World Press, 2000.

—-. "Video Interview with Mambety" Reels of Color Series. Washington DC .

Essar, Dennis F. "Hyenas, Djibril Diop Mambety," *African Arts,* Vol. 29, Issue 4, Autumn 1966: 78-80.

Fiombo, Angelo. "African Up for Auction," *Ecrans de Afrique,* No 2, Third Quarter 1992.

Givanni, June. "African Conversations" and interview with Mambety, *Sight and Sound,* September 1995.

—-. Ed. *Symbolic Narratives/African Cinema: Audiences Theory and the Moving Image.* London, British Film Institute, 2000.

Mermin. Elizabeth "A Window on Whose Reality? The Emerging Industry of Senegalese Cinema," In: *African Cinema: Post-Colonial and Feminist Readings.* Ed. Kenneth W. Harrow. Trenton, New Jersey: Africa World Press, 1999. 201-224.

Petty, Sheila J, "'How an African Woman Can Be': African Women Filmmakers Construct Women," *Discourse.* 18(3): 72-88. Spring 1996.

Pfaff, Françoise. "New African Cinema," *Cineaste* 22, No. 4.

—-. "Eroticism and Sub-Saharan Films," Cham and Bakari 257.

—-. *Twenty-five Black African Filmmakers: A Critical Study, with Filmography and Bio-Bibliography.* New York: Greenwood Press, 1988.

Rawlinsm Rachel. "Interview with Djibril Diop Mambety," Southern African Film Festival-1993, *Africa Film and TV Magazine.* Nd.

Shiri, Keith. "Djibril Diop Mambety," *Black Film Bulletin* V. 6 No. 4, Winter 1999, 7.

Sklar, Robert. "Anarchic Visions," *Film Comment,* V. 36. No. 3. May/June 2001.

Tomaselli, Keyan G. "'African' Cinema: Theoretical Perspectives on Some Unresolved Questions," Cham and Bakari 165-174.

Taylor, Clyde. "Searching for Postmodernism in African Cinema." Givanni 136-145,.

Ukadike, Frank Nwachukwu. *Black African Cinema*. Berkeley: University of California Press, 1994.

—-. "Djibril and Aesthetics: Touki Bouki, a film of Rupture," Tribute/Djibril Diop Mambety in *Ecrans d'Afrique No* 24, Second Semester 1998.

—-. The Hyenas Last Laugh: A Conversation with Djibril Diop Mambety" California Newsreel, Library of African Cinema, website (reprinted from Transition 78 vol.8. no 2, 1999: 136-153).

—-."African films: a retrospective and a Vision for the Future", *Critical Arts*, 7 (1), 1993: 43-60.

Wynchank, Anny. "*Touki Bouki*: The New Wave on the Cinematic Shores of Africa," *South African Theatre Journal* 12 (1-2): 53-72, 1998.

Other Works Consulted.

Fanon, Frantz. *Wretched of the Earth*. New York: Grove Press, c1968.

MacRae, Susan. "The Mature and Older Women of African Film." In: *African Cinema: Post-Colonial and Feminist Readings*. Ed. Kenneth W. Harrow. Trenton, New Jersey: Africa World Press, 1999. 241-254.

Variety Review of *Hyenas* by Ron Holloway, *Hollywood Reporter*, Friday May 15, 1992.

Editors and Contributors

EDITORS

Dr. Ada Uzoamaka Azodo obtained her Diplôme d'Études Supérieures de Français (DES) from the Université de Dakar, her B. A. (Honors, French) from the University of Ife, her M. A. and Ph. D. (African Francophone Literature) from the University of Lagos. Azodo has taught in various capacities at the University of Lagos, St John Fisher College, Rochester, New York, State University of New York at Geneseo, Valparaiso University, and is currently affiliated with Indiana University Northwest campus at Gary. In addition to her academic appointments, Azodo has provided service to professional bodies she is affiliated with as member, and in the case of the African Literature Committee (ALD) of the Modern Language Association (MLA) of America rising to the position of president. Azodo has been a member of the African Literature Association (ALA) since 1990, is currently vice-president of the Women's Caucus of the African Literature Association (WOCALA), and will become President for 2007-2009 academic years. Azodo's teaching and research interests include African Literature, African Studies, Women's Studies, Gender Studies, Postcolonial Studies, French, Development Studies, Diaspora Studies, and Cultural Studies. Publications include: *L'imaginaire dans les romans de Camara Laye.* New York, San Francisco, Berlin, Paris: Peter Lang, 1993; *Emerging Perspectives on Ama Ata Aidoo.* Co-ed. Trenton: Africa World Press, 1999; *Emerging Perspectives on Mariama Bâ: Postcolonialism, Feminism and Postmodernism.* Ed. Trenton: Africa World Press, 2003; *Gender and Sexuality in African Literature and Film.* Co-ed. Trenton: Africa World Press, 2006; *Critical Essays on Aminata Sow Fall: The Real and the Imaginary in Her Novels.* Ed. Trenton: Africa World Press, (forthcoming 2007), and *Emerging Perspectives on Ken Bugul: From Alternative Voices to Oppositional Practices.* Co-ed. Trenton: Africa World Press (in progress). Six scholarly articles are in refereed journals: *Journal of Religion in Africa*; *Mots Pluriels*; *Palabres*; Africa World Press *Annual Selected Papers of the ALA*; The Feminist Press of New York *Women's Studies Quarterly*; *African Literature Today.* Upwards of fifteen chapters are in critical and scholarly anthologies on Flora Nwapa, Buchi Emecheta, and Chinua Achebe and their writings, a book review and a review essay respectively in academic journals, *Research in*

African Literatures and *Palabres*, and two entries in international *Who's Who in Contemporary Women's Writing*.

Dr. Maureen Ngozi Eke obtained her B. A. (Special Honors, English) from Ahmadu Bello University, Nigeria, her M. A. and Ph. D. (Comparative Literature) from Indiana University. Eke has taught African Literature, African Cinema, Postcolonial Theory and Literature, African American Literature, Women's Writing, Comparative/World Literature, and Literature and Film at Central Michigan University. In addition to her faculty position as professor of English, Eke was associate vice-president for Diversity and International education. Eke has received several Central Michigan University Faculty Research awards, College of Humanities, Social and Behavioral Sciences Summer Faculty Research award, US Department of Education Title VI FLAS Fellowship, AAUW Fellowship, and International Peace Organization Scholarship. She has participated in National Education for the Humanities (NEH) Summer Institutes at Harvard University and the University of London, and directed several NEH and US Department of Education summer seminars and institutes. She has provided services to professional bodies she is affiliated with as chair of the MLA African Literature Division (ALD), secretary of the African Literature Association (ALA), board member of the Michigan Humanities Council, founding member and secretary of the Women's Caucus of the African Literature Association (WOCALA), member of the African Studies Association (ASA), National Association of Multicultural Education (NAME), editor of H-Afrlitcine discussion list. She is on the editorial board of *Critical Arts: A journal of Media and Cultural Studies; Pedagogy;* and *Screening the Past*. Her publications include: *Cross Rhythms 3: Papers in African Folklore*. Co-ed. Bloomington (IN). Trickster Press, 1989; *African Images: Recent Studies in Cinema and Text*. Co-ed. Trenton (N.J.): Africa World Press, 2000. Her articles have appeared in *African Cinema: Post-Colonial and Feminist Readings*. Ed. Kenneth Harrow. Trenton: Africa World Press, 1999. Seventeen scholarly articles and six book reviews are in refereed encyclopedias and journals, including *Research in African Literatures* and *Callaloo*; two book chapters are in scholarly anthologies, three non-academic works and publications in magazines, and three videos and CDs scripted and/or produced also exist. She is currently editing a volume of interviews with African women writers.

CONTRIBUTORS

Ada Uzoamaka Azodo is associate faculty in African Diaspora and African American Studies in the Department of Minority Studies and the Women's Studies Program at Indiana University Northwest at Gary.

Jill Eagling holds a Ph. D. from the Department of European Studies of the University of Western Australia, and is currently teaching French at Schools of Isolated and Distance Education (SIDE), in Perth, Western Australia. She contributed to *The Companion to African Literatures*. Ed. Douglas Killam and Ruth Rowe. Oxford: James Currey, 2000.

Maureen Ngozi Eke is professor of English and former associate vice-president of Diversity and International Education at Central Michigan University.

Stacy E. Fifer earned her Ph. D. in French from the University of Illinois, Urbana, Champagne, and is presently a freelance scholar, while taking care of her infant baby.

Miriam C. Gyimah is assistant professor of English and African Studies at the University of Maryland Eastern Shore. Her teaching and research interests include African literature, African-American literature, American literature, Black Women Writers, Cross-cultural Feminist Theories, Caribbean literature, and World literature. Gyimah has published in *West African Review* and in *Emerging Perspectives on Ama Ata Aidoo* by Africa World Press, Inc.

Keith M. Harris, assistant professor in the School of Interdisciplinary Arts at Ohio University, graduated in Cinema Studies from New York University. His areas of specialization include film, African-American and African cinema, gender studies and queer theory. However, his recent research and writing interests primarily concern masculinity, performance, and gender(s) as ethical constructs within performance and cultural production. He recently published *Boys, Boyz, Bois: An Ethics of Masculinity in Popular Film, Television* with Routledge Publishers. He is also editing the proceedings from *The Commemorative Symposium: Black Cinema Aesthetics: Issues in Black* Film for a special edition of *Black Praxis*.

Erica Hoagland is a doctoral candidate in Theory and Cultural Studies at Purdue University. Her research interests include postcolonial literature and theory, particularly literature of First Nations and West Africa, contemporary British fiction, and cultural studies. She is currently at work on her dissertation, which explores postcolonial appropriations of the bildungsroman genre.

M. Catherine Jonet is completing her Ph. D. in the department of English at Purdue University. She specializes in Women's Studies, Post-Colonial Studies, and Queer Theory.

Bernadette Kassi teaches at Université Laval, Quebec, Department of Languages. She received her Ph. D. in Quebec literature from Université Laval in 2002, and an M. A. in Education in 1994, from the Université nationale of Ivory Coast, specializing in Francophone literature.

Amy Lee is assistant professor in the Humanities Program and Department of English Language and literature, Hong Kong Baptist University. Her research interest includes gender and fiction, contemporary women's fiction, the Chinese Diaspora, mother-daughter relationships in contemporary Chinese women's writing, representation of marginal experiences, and fiction of detection. She is a contributor to various reference collections, including the *Encyclopedia of the Novel*, an *Ann Petry Encyclopedia*, *Encyclopedia of the Harlem Renaissance*, *The Literary Encyclopedia and Literary Dictionary* (online reference), and *Black Diaspora Drama* (Electronic Database).

Christiane P. Makward is a retired professor of French and Women's Studies at Pennsylvania State University. The author of at least five books and some forty-three scholarly articles, mostly on well-known and lesser known women writers, she has published in major academic journals, including *Revue des Sciences Humaines*, *Yale French Studies*, *Women in French Studies*, and *Callalo*. Professor Makward has taught in Nigeria, Senegal, Quebec, and the United States of America.

Pinkie Mekgwe is a lecturer in English at the University of Botswana.

Chukwuma Okoye is a lecturer in the Department of Theatre Arts, University of Ibadan, Nigeria.

Victoria Pasley is assistant professor of History at Lane College in Jackson, Tennessee. She has a Ph. D. in History, and an M. A. in Film and Video. Her research interests focus on African and African Diaspora history and film, with a particular interest in gender.

Najat Rahman, is assistant professor, Département de littérature comparée (Department of Comparative Literature), Université de Montréal, Québec, Canada.

Egodi N. Uchendu holds a Ph.D. in History from the University of Nigeria where she is currently a lecturer. She spent a session at the University of Kansas,

Lawrence, as a Fulbright visitor in 2001- 2002. She is currently a Leventis Research Scholar at the Centre of African and Oriental Studies, University of London. She has written a number of articles that have appeared in journals and as book chapters.

Anastasia Valassopoulos has a special interest in music, film, and literature, teaches in the School of Comparative Literature, University of Kent, Canterbury, and has published on film in *Movie Music, the Film Reader*. Ed. Kay Dickinson, London: Routledge, 2002, on the influences of Edward Saïd's *Orientalism* in contemporary feminist writing in *After Orientalism*. Eds. Inge Boer and Caryl Smith. Amsterdam: Rodopi, 2003. Born in Beirut, her research interest is in the cultural production of Arab women, both in the Middle East and North Africa. She has also written on the relationship between medicine and gender in North African writing by Egyptian Nawal EL-Saadawi and Ethiopian Fatima Conteh in an article submitted to *Feminist Studies*. Valassopoulos is planning a book-length work on contemporary postcolonial Arab women writers.

Index